ST. PAUL'S OPPONENTS
AND THEIR BACKGROUND

SUPPLEMENTS
NOVUM TESTAMENTUM

VOLUME XXXV

LEIDEN
E. J. BRILL
1973

ST. PAUL'S OPPONENTS
AND
THEIR BACKGROUND

A STUDY OF APOCALYPTIC
AND JEWISH SECTARIAN TEACHINGS

BY

JOHN J. GUNTHER

LEIDEN
E. J. BRILL
1973

ISBN 90 04 03738 1

PRINTED IN THE NETHERLANDS

CONTENTS

FOREWORD

The abundance of literature of the past twenty years on the Dead Sea Scrolls, Jewish apocrypha and Hebrew Christianity has enhanced our appreciation of the complexity of the wellsprings of the latter. Although resemblances of Qumran documents to all New Testament writings continue to be pointed out, surprisingly there has been no systematic study of Paul's various opponents in light of what is known of Jewish sectarianism and heterodoxy. One barrier to progress in this area is the prevailing assumption that the background of the Apostle's antagonists (apart from those in Galatia) was in official Judaism, the mystery religions, Hellenistic philosophy, Gnosticism and/or syncretism. Even when they are (rightly) labelled as Judaizers, a search is commonly made for some contemporary pagan influence.

This monograph is meant to present data from non-conformist Judaism and apocalypses to illumine what may deduced concerning the doctrine and life of Paul's opponents. They did use Hellenistic terminology (e.g. eusebeia, gnosis, musterion, pleroma, stoicheia), and Iranian religion probably left a deep imprint on their spiritual ancestors. Nevertheless, in this study we report evidence for viewing the substance of their beliefs and practices as being akin to contemporary esoteric Palestinian Judaism, qualified by the teachings of Jesus. As spiritual descendants of the anti-Seleucid Hasidim they resisted religious Hellenization, and where use of the Greek language and their desire to win proselytes colored their presentation of the gospel, it is still possible to interpret their teaching in light of the Dead Sea Scrolls, apocalypses and Essenism. Hellenism and Palestinian sectarian Judaism had more in common than was once recognized; the Therapeutae and Gospel and Letters of John, for example, drew heavily from both worlds.

Recognizing the profuse variety of thought in first century esoteric Judaism, we have selected those elements which resemble those echoed by the Apostle's adversaries in one or more of his letters. The reader is invited to judge for himself which variety of sectarianism bears greatest or least resemblance to the opponents in each Pauline epistle which is under consideration.

Our purpose in setting forth parallels is more to delineate the type of Judaism in the opponents' background, than to exclude the possiblity of contemporary syncretism (in Colossians for example). We do not intend to imply that nearly all converts from esoteric Judaism scorned and resisted Paul, or that they alone did.

ABBREVIATIONS

BJRL   Bulletin of the John Rylands Library
CBQ   Catholic Biblical Quarterly
DCB   Dictionary of Christian Biography, ed. William Smith & Henry Wace
DTC   Dictionnaire de Théologie Catholique, ed. A. Vacant & E. Mangenot
HTR   Harvard Theological Review
IB   The Interpreter's Bible
IDB   The Interpreter's Dictionary of the Bible
JBL   Journal of Biblical Literature
JQR   Jewish Quarterly Review
JTS   Journal of Theological Studies
NT   Novum Testamentum
NTS   New Testament Studies
PEQ   Palestine Exploration Quarterly
PO   Patrologia Orientalis (ed. F. Graffin)
RB   Revue Biblique
RGG   Die Religion in Geschichte u. Gegenwart, 3rd edition
RQ   Revue de Qumran
TLZ   Theologische Literaturzeitung
TU   Texte und Untersuchungen zur Geschichte der altchristlichen Literatur, ed.
        O. von Gebhardt & A. Harnack
ZNTW   Zeitschrift für die Neutestamentliche Wissenschaft
ET   English translation

Wherever possible, or unless otherwise specified, translations of texts are drawn from:

Revised Standard Version (Bible)
Works of R. H. Charles (Old Testament apocrypha)
Hennecke-Schneemelcher-Wilson (New Testament apocrypha)
Qumran literature and ancient accounts of Essenes (Dupont-Sommer—Vermes)
Ignatius-Ante-Nicene Library

CHAPTER ONE

SOURCES

Scholarly opinion in the 19th and 20th centuries has been very diverse concerning the identification of the opponents whose teachings were warned against in letters of the Pauline corpus.

On Galatians we find the following views:[1]

Local Jews (K. Lake)
Judean pneumatic, syncretistic Jews (Crownfield)
Judaizers (vast majority of commentators)
Local Judaizing Gentiles (Munck)
Syncretistic Jewish Christians (Fitzmyer)
Gnostic Jewish Christians (Schlier, Stahlin, Wegenast, H. Koester)
Libertine Gnostic Jewish Christians (Schmithals)
Judaizers AND libertine pneumatics (Lütgert, Ropes, Knox, Enslin, McNeile
    Williams, Richardson, Stamm, Jewett)

II Corinthians has evoked a richer variety of opinions:[2]

Wandering Jewish preachers taking over Gnostic pneumatic opposition of 1
    Cor. (Windisch). Same Jewish Christian Gnostics opposed in 1
    Cor.(Bultmann, Schmithals, Dinkler, Wilckens, Güttgemanns)
Pneumatic-libertine Gnostics (Lütgert, Schlatter)
Gnostics (Bousset, Reitzenstein, Schniewind)
Alexandrian syncretistic, antinomian pneumatics (K. Lake)
Jewish-pagan-Christian gnostics (Allo)
Hellenistic Jewish Christians (Menzies, Bornkamm, Georgi, H. D. Betz)
Non-Judaizing Jewish Christians (McGiffert)
Palestinian Jewish Christian Gnostics (Kümmel, Gilmour)
Jewish Christian syncretists with Gnostic elements (Marxsen)
Jerusalem Judaizers (F.C. Baur, Klöpper, H. J. Holtzmann, Hausrath,
    Holsten, Schmiedel, Hort, T. W. Manson, Käsemann, Schoeps, Barrett)
Palestinian Jews-not Judaizers in the Galatian sense (F. F. Bruce)
Judaizers (Jervell, Prumm, Oostendorp, Bandstra)
Judaizers AND pneumatic Gnostics (Lietzmann, Wikenhauser)

---

[1] Donald Guthrie, *New Testament Introduction: The Pauline Epistles*, London (Tyndale, 1961), 88; Paul Feine-Johannes Behm-Werner G. Kümmel, *Einleitung in das Neue Testament*, Heidelberg (Quelle & Meyer, 1963), 193-95; Roy B. Ward, "The Opponents of Paul," *Restoration Quarterly* 10 (1967), 186-89.

[2] Feine-Behm-Kümmel, *op. cit.*, 210-11; Dieter Georgi, *Die Gegner des Paulus im II Korintherbrief*, Neukirchen (1964), 7-16; Walther Schmithals, *Die Gnosis in Korinth*, Göttingen (Vandenhoeck & Ruprecht, 1965), 110-17; Derk W. Oostendorp, *Another Jesus*, Kampen (J. H. Kok, 1967), 1-4.

Assessments of the opponents in Phillippians 3 are more diverse:[3]

Jews (Lipsius, Rilliet, B. Weiss, Schmidt, Goguel, Meinertz, Scott, Kümmel,
    Munck, Klijn, George Johnston)
Jewish Gnostics (Bornkamm)
Jewish Christian Gnostics (R. B. Ward, Marxsen)
Jews OR Jewish Christians (Moffatt, Duncan, Bonnard)
Proselytes to Judaism (Jülicher)
Judaizers (F. C. Baur, Ewald, Hausrath, Hort, Pfleiderer, Feine-Behm, T. W.
    Manson, Müller, Bonnard, Cerfaux, Cullmann, Reicke, D. W. B.
    Robinson, Fitzmyer)
Jewish Gnostics perfectionists with "radicalized spiritualistic eschatology" (H.
    Koester, C. R. Holladay)
gnostics (Goguel)
Jewish Gnostic libertine pneumatics (Schmithals)
Judaizing Gnostic libertine pneumatics (J. Müller-Bardorff)
Jews AND pneumatic Christians (Heinzelmann)
Jews AND immoral Christians (Michel, Dibelius)
Jews AND nominal Christians (Hockstra, Holsten)
Jews AND *lapsi* Christians (Lohmeyer)
Judaizers AND Gentile Christians (Haupt, Zahn, Lueken)
Judaizers AND libertines (Appel, Friedrich, Michaelis, J. B. Lightfoot, J. H.
    Michael, McNeile-Williams, H. C. G. Moule, Martin, Delling, Beare)
Judaizers AND Gnostic pneumatics (Lütgert, R. Jewett)
Jews AND pneumatics AND libertines (Albertz)

Similar difficulties in interpreting Romans 16 have led to
somewhat different assessments:[4]

Judaizers (Meyer, Hort, Kühl, Sanday-Headlam, Kirk, Murray, Lietzmann,
    Müller, Althaus, H. W. Schmidt, H.-M. Schenke, Fitzmyer)
Judaizing Gnostics (Baur, Reicke)
Gnosticizing heretics (H. J. Holtzmann)
Gnostics (Michel)
Jewish Christian libertine Gnostics (Schmithals) [5]
Second century Gnostics (Pfleiderer, J. Knox)
Libertine quasi-gnostics (Best, Dodd)
Libertines (Hofmann, J. B. Lightfoot, Appel, H. C. G. Moule, McNeile-
    Williams, Guthrie)

---

[3] H. J. Holtzmann, *Lehrbuch der Historisch-kritischen Einleitung in das Neue
Testament*, Freiburg im Br. (J. C. B. Mohr-Paul Siebeck, 1892), 268-69; Feine-Behm-
Kümmel, *op. cit.*, 235-36; Schmithals, *Paulus und die Gnostiker*, Hamburg (H. Reich,
1965), 297-99, 309-11; A. F. J. Klijn, "Paul's Opponents in Philippians iii," *NT* 7
(1965), 278, n. 2: Carl R. Holladay, "Paul's Opponents in Philippians 3," *Restoration
Quarterly* 12(1969), 77ff.
[4] Schmithals, "Die Irrlehrer von Rom. 16, 17-20," *Studia Theologica* 13 (1959), 51-
52, 67; Schenke, "Aporien im Römerbrief," *TLZ* 92 (1967), 882, n. 1.
[5] He argues cogently that οἱ τοιοῦτοι (16:18) constitute a definite people and that
only Christians could divide the community internally (*ibid.*, 53); moreover, "not
serving Christ" would be superfluous if they did not wish to be Christians.

The greatest disparity of opinion is found when Colossians has been examined:[6]

Essentially pagans (E. F. Scott)
Chaldeans or Magians (Hug)
Platonic & Stoic philosophers (Heumann)
Pythagorean philosophers influenced by Judaism (Grotius)
Speculative, ascetic Judaeo-pagan syncretists (Leclercq)
Pharisees (Eichhorn, Schoettgen)
Syncretistic, universalist Jews (Schneckenburger)
Non-gnostic, esoteric, apocalyptic, cultic-ritual, militant Jews(N. Kehl)
Heterodox Jews (Nock)
Cabbalists (Herder, Kleuker)
Alexandrians (Juncker, Schenkel, Koster, von Soden, Erbes)
Ascetic, non-legalistic, syncretistic Jews influenced by Alexandrian
    speculation (Huby)
Semi-Gnostic, syncretistic, esoteric Jews (J. B. Lightfoot, Moffatt, Kümmel,
    Meinertz)
Hellenistic Judaic incipient Gnostics (T. H. Olbricht)
Incipient Gnostics (von Dobschütz, J. Knox, Bruce)
Heretical pre-gnostic Jews (H. Hegermann)
Gnostics (Renan, Pfleiderer)
Gnostic Ebionites (Baur, Lipsius, Hoekstra, Sabatier, Davidson, Blom,
    Schmiedel)
Ascetic Judaizers (Foerster)
Judaizing syncretists (Lyonnet)
Judaizing syncretistic gnostics (Goppelt)
Judaizing gnostics (S. L. Johnson, Marxsen)
Jewish Christian Gnostics (H.-M. Schenke)
Jewish gnostics (Bornkamm, Goppelt, E. W. Sauders)
Cerinthian Gnostics (Neander, Mayerhoff, Nitzsch, R. Scott)
Non-Jewish oriental gnostics (Reitzenstein, Bultmann)
Non-Jewish oriental-Hellenistic mystery cult, pre-gnostic syncretists
    (Dibelius-Greeven)
Pagan and Jewish mystery cult syncretists (Radford, G. H. P. Thompson, G.
    Johnston, Beare)
Syncretistic, pre-gnostic, dualistic, mystery cult ascetics (E. Lohse)
Syncretistic ascetics influenced by philosophy, myths and the mysteries (J.
    Lähnemann)
Pharisaic-legalistic, theosophic ascetics (Bleek, Reuss, Oltramare)
Jewish Christian mystic ascetics (Francis)
Jewish Christians appealing to Moses and natural philosophy (Hofmann)

---

[6] Heinrich A. Meyer, *Critical and Exegetical Handbook to the Epistles to the Philippians and Colossians*, Edinburgh (T.& T. Clark, 1875), 238-41; Holtzmann, *op. cit.*, 250; J. B. Lightfoot, *St. Paul's Epistles to the Colossians and to Philemon*, London (Macmillan, 1875), 74; James Moffatt, *Introduction to the Literature of the New Testament*, New York (Charles Scribner's Sons, 1918, 3rd ed.), 153; Guthrie, *op. cit.*, 162-66.

A link between heterodox Jews and the Gnostics of Chenoboskion (E.
    Yamauchi)
Syncretistic Jewish Christians influenced by non-Gnostic Hellenistic
    philosophy and asceticism (Percy)
Judaeo-Hellenistic ascetic gnostics influenced by the mysteries (N. Hugedé)
Hellenistic Jewish Christians influenced by non-speculative, esoteric
    asceticism (Hort)
Esoteric Jewish Christians (Danielou)
Syncretistic Jewish-Greek gnostics worshipping Christ (Meyer, Goguel,
    Humphries, Guthrie, J. Stewart)
Jewish Christians combining Greek philosophical speculations and oriental
    mystical theosophy (McNeile-Williams)
Syncretists combining pre-Gnostic paganism and Jewish Christianity
    (Cerfaux)
Disciples of Apollos (J. Michaelis)
Judaizing disciples of Apollos and John (Heinrichs)
Pure Gnostics AND pure Judaizers (Hilgenfeld)

It is not surprising that the obscure references of the Pastorals have
led to so many diagnoses:[7]

Jews (Otto)
Jews influenced by oriental philosophy (Hug, Heydenreich, Kling, Maier)
Gnosticizing Jews (Grotius, Herder, Schneckenburg, Olhausen, Baumgarten,
    Kittel)
Jewish-syncretistic Gnostics (Mack, Reuss, Guericke, Böttger, Matthias,
    Huther, Bultmann, G. Holtz)
Judaizing incipient Gnostics (Hort, Moffatt, Kümmel, Lietzmann, E. F. Scott,
    Jeremias, Dibelius-Conzelmann, Humphries)
Proto-Montanists (J. M. Ford)
Cerinthians (Neander, Mayerhoff)
Incipient Gnostics (von Dobschütz, Klöpper, Beker)
Gnosticizing enthusiasts despising the natural order of creation (Foerster)
Early Valentinian Ophites (Lipsius, Schenkel, Pfleiderer)
Naassenes (Lighfoot)
Marcionites influenced by Valentinianism (Schwegler)
Marcion (Baur, Volkmar, Weizsäcker, Jülicher, Goodspeed, Bauer, Riddle-
    Hutson, Knox, Barnett, Gealy, Rist)
Antinomian Jewish Christian Gnostic pneumatics (Lütgert)
Jewish Christians influenced by Hellenistic speculations (Meyer,
    Wohlenberg, Goppelt, Spicq)
Various unidentifiable gnosticizing types (Harnack, Brückner, Goguel, Lock,
    W. Michaelis)
Jewish Christian antinomians AND oriental ascetics (McNeile-Williams)

---

[7] Holtzmann, op. cit., 287-88; Bernard Weiss, Die Briefe Pauli an Timotheus und
Titus (Meyers Kommentar), Göttingen (Vandenhoeck & Ruprecht, 1902), 21-27;
Moffatt, op. cit., 408-09; C. Spicq, Les Épîtres Pastorales, Paris (J. Gabalda, 1947), 1xx-
xx-, n. 6; Feine-Behm-Kummel, op. cit., 274-77.

Gentile Gnostic Docetists AND Judaizers (Hilgenfeld, Davidson)
Pharisaic Judaizers AND Gnostic spiritualists (Thiersch)

Perhaps partially because the letters of Ignatius have been less studied than the Pauline corpus, there is less of a spread of opinion concerning the Martyr's opponents:[8]

Docetists (Goodspeed, Molland)
Jewish Christian Docetists (Zahn, Lightfoot, von der Goltz, Monachesi)
Judaizing Docetists or Judaeo-gnostics (Huther, Batiffol, Bareille)
Judaizing Gnostics (Bauer)
Cerinthians (Bull, Lightfoot-?)
Saturninus (Pfleiderer, Zahn-?)
Valentinian Gnostic Docetists (Merx)
Judaizers AND Docetists (Hilgenfeld, Schmidt, Bruston, Schlier, Richardson,
    Bartsch, Corwin, Rathke)
Docetic ultra-Pauline forerunners of Marcionism AND Hellenistic Gnostic
    Judaizers (Goguel)
Ebionites AND Docetists (Pearson, Denzinger)

While there is unanimity of opinion that the above-mentioned letters were directed by their authors against the teachings of definite opponents, only a minority of scholars has detected controversy and definite heretics in the Epistles to the Ephesians and Hebrews. The resemblances of Ephesians to Colossians as well as the admonitions found in Eph. 4:14-15 and 5:6 have led to the detection of the following opponents:[9]

The Colossian heretics (J. Michaelis, Haenlein, Flatt, Schott, Neudecker,
    Vosté, Schlier, Percy, Bruce and most proponents of the Ephesians
    encyclical hypothesis)
More advanced Gnostics than in Colossians (Goguel)
Gnostics (Hilgenfeld)
Libertine Gnostics (E. F. Scott)
gnosticizing and antinomian Gentiles (R. P. Martin)
Antinomians (Olshausen)
Montanists (Schwegler)
Various sectarian tendencies (Mitton)

Over thirty scholars, mostly of the 19th century, have been of the opinion that the Hebrews addressed in the epistle of that name were

---

[8] Lightfoot, *Apostolic Fathers*, New York & London (Macmillan, 1885), II-I, 363, n. 2; Virginia Corwin, *St. Ignatius and Christianity in Antioch*, New Haven (Yale Univ., 1960), 52, n. 1.; Joachim Rohde, "Häresie und Schisma im ersten Clemensbrief und in den Ignatius-Briefen," *NT* 10 (1968), 230.

[9] Heinrich A. Meyer, *Critical and Exegetical Handbook to the Epistle to the Ephesians*, New York (Funk & Wagnalls, 1884), 307.

converted Jerusalem priests; generally they have been considered potential *lapsi* into Judaism, and the whole Epistle has been deemed as directed toward dissuading them. However, two verses (6:1 and 13:9) have led other scholars [10] to detect views and practices stranger than those of Jerusalem priests:

Ascetic abstainers from foods (Estius, Tholuck, Delitzsch, Keil, Hoffmann, Menegoz, Zahn, Strathmann, Behm)
Incipient Gnostics (Perdelwitz)
Syncretistic Gnostics (Pfleiderer, Bruce)
Judaizers (Frost, Wickham)
Judaizing Gnostics (Weinel)
Jewish Gnostics (Narborough)

Relatively few investigators think these two verses are to be understood in relation to the rest of Hebrews.

The bewildering variety of conclusions concerning the nature of the opponents in all of the above-mentioned epistles as a whole stems from two chief sources: disagreement in exegesis and disagreement in defining the boundaries and relations between (1) incipient and developped Gnosticism, (2) Hellenistic, Jewish and Iranian Gnosticism, (3) Gnosticism and Judaizing, (4) Gnosticism and asceticism, (5) Gnosticism and pneumaticism, (6) pneumaticism and Judaizing, (7) Judaizing and Judaism, and (8) Palestinian and Hellenistic Judaism. Implicit in describing these boundaries and relations is the problem of syncretism. How did it proceed? How diverse could its roots be? Could and did syncretism draw together mystery cults, philosophy and any or all of these eight pairs? Was Christianity an added root or "tail on the kite" of a pre-existent Gnosticism or syncretism, or did Christianity degenerate into a new Gnosticism or syncretism? What one scholar calls "gnosticism" another might call "syncretism".[11] Accordingly, the various labels attached to Paul's opponents must be understood in light of each investigator's definitions of the terms. Conceivably, if an ascetic, pneumatic, Judaizing, gnosticising, syncretistic group or movement or tendency could be found in pre-Christian times, there might be a convergence of opinion concerning the identity of Paul's opponents.

---

[10] Holtzmann, *op. cit.*, 305, 308; Spicq, *L' Épître aux Hébreux*, Paris (1952), i, 227, n. 5; Erich Grässer, "Der Hebräerbrief 1938-63," *Theologische Rundschau* 30 (1964), 179-80.

[11] Johannes Munck, "The New Testament and Gnosticism," in *Current Issues in New Testament Interpretation (Essays in honor of Otto Piper)*, ed. W. Klassen & G. Snyder, N. Y. (Harper & Bros., 1962), 236.

At first sight it may seem folly to postulate a similarity or some degree of identity of opponents who are detected in the Pauline corpus, Hebrews and in Ignatian Epistles. Partial identities, or at least kinships, have not infrequently been observed:

Galatians and 2 Corinthians (Lütgert, J.N. Sanders; most who have found opposition to Judaizers in 2 Cor.)
Galatians and Philippians 3 (Jewett)
Galatians and 2 Corinthians and Philippians 3 (Jülicher, T. W. Manson)
Galatians and Colossians (Lyonnet, Fitzmyer)
Galatians and Colossians and Philippians 3 (Marxsen)
Galatians and Hebrews (A. M. Dubarle)
Galatians and Hebrews and Colossians (Bornkamm)
Galatians and Colossians and Pastoral Epistles (Schlier)
2 Corinthians and Colossians (Gilmour)
2 Corinthians and Hebrews (Montefiore)
Philippians 3 and Romans 16 (Meyer)
Philippians 3 and Pastoral Epistles (C. R. Holladay)
Romans 16 and Colossians (Dodd)
Colossians and Hebrews (Hort, Pfleiderer, Narborough, J. H. Davies, W. Bousset- H. Gressman, T. W. Manson, Francis)
Colossians and Pastoral Epistles (Humphries, E. F. Scott, Jeremias, Behm-Kümmel, Kelly, Holtz)
Colossians and Ephesians and Pastoral Epistles (Lightfoot)
Colossians and Ignatius (Goguel)
Colossians and Titus and Ignatius (Richardson)
Pastoral Epistles and Ignatius (Hilgenfeld, Davidson, Dibelius-Conzelmann)

The most comprehensive modern view of Paul's opponents has been taken by Walter Schmithals,[12] who finds the same heretics in Galatians, Romans 16, Philippians 3, 1 and 2 Corinthians and 1 and 2 Thessalonians. Baur had identified them everywhere with emissaries from the Jerusalem apostles.

Before the hypothesis of an identity or kinship of opposition can be seriously examined, reasons must be suggested for the differences in the teachings of opponents which may legitimately be deduced from the various epistles. The picture of the opponents that may be drawn from 2 Corinthians, for example, does not match well whatever may be drawn from the Epistle to the Hebrews. Why? Moods, backgrounds and spiritual gifts of each author and missionary varied. Writers differed in their ways of reacting to, and dealing with, opponents and their boasts. Readers or listeners differed. Galatians

---

[12] "Zur Abfassung und ältesten Sammlung der Paulinischen Hauptbriefe," *ZNTW* 51 (1960), 225-36.

and Phrygians especially were receptive to circumcision and honoring
cosmic angels and their calendar, perhaps because of earlier
"ecumenical relations" between local Jews and Gentiles. Situations
differed. Tactics of opponents differed. To the extent that the
"circumcizers" had inadequate success, for example, they might
postpone or put on a supererogatory basis their Gentile followers'
circumcision. The intruders at Corinth first sought holiness and
gained a following by apostolic and pneumatic credentials. The
opponents' teaching had different levels of depth; neither their
converts nor Paul gained immediate knowledge of the γνῶσις.
Teaching within sectarian and apocalyptic Judaism was not uniform,
and Christian missioners represented various tendencies within this
framework. It is possible, moreover, that their teachings developped,
as did Paul's, and that their teachers had individual differences as did,
say, Paul and Barnabas of Antioch (Acts 15:35-41; Gal. 2:13). It
would be natural for initial contact with opponents in Galatia to lead
Paul to look for resemblances in their teachings to those of the
Jerusalem Pharisee circumcision party,[13] which had earlier troubled
him. Likewise, Ignatius, after many battles with Docetists at Antioch,
would be extra-sensitive to any points of resemblance of their
teaching to his new opponents in Asia. Paul's counterattack in Rom.
16 and Phil. 3 includes the use of epithets appropriate only after a
lengthy period of controversy; old enemies were involved. Romans
16:18 and Phil. 3:18-19 would have been as puzzling to the recently
exposed Galatians as they are to modern exegetes. The stereotyped
diatribe and distortion of the opponents' position as found in the
Pastoral 'Epistles were a product of further controversy with non-
Palestinian locally established professional teachers of *gnosis*. As time
passed, new issues were found to dispute and new polemics were
learned on both sides. This point is illustrated by the first ten years of
the Protestant Reformation. Some old issues were laid to rest. New
literature was written and read. Finally, it would be misleading to
argue *ex silencio* that there were no common opponents because
many features of the anti-Pauline teaching detectable in Galatians are
not detectable in 2 Corinthians, and vice versa, for example. Whether
the features detectable in different letters are incompatible is more
significant. Paul often learned of adversaries through different
messengers, whose reports differed in their emphases. The allusions

---

[13] See pp. 86-87.

in Rom. 16 and Phil. 3 are few and brief. Paul's failure to use many of his opponents' slogans in Galatians, as he did in Colossians, indicates either a lesser acquaintance or lesser time to think of compelling responses. The Corinthians, Philippians and recipients of Romans 16 (i.e. the Ephesians) already had heard Paul's oral warnings; but the Galatians and Colossians had not and therefore needed a fuller rebuttal. For these reasons Colossians should contain a fuller and more knowledgeable account of the opponents, if they were common. Hebrews is generally non-controversial and contains a relatively comprehensive theology. Accordingly, if it were directed against a theology which was seductive to the readers, its lack of polemical distortions and its attempt to utilize the opponents' thought patterns would make it an especially valuable source of their assumptions. The late date of the Ignatian letters and uncertainty concerning the unity and location of the heresies attacked, make them less reliable sources of information.

The hypothesis of common or similar Judaizing, ascetic, pneumatic, gnosticizing, syncretistic opponents gains some support and clarification from the detection by many scholars of Essene or Qumran influences upon the opponents in:

Galatians (Davies, Gaster)
Colossians (Mangold, Klöpper, Credner, Ewald, Thiersch, Lightfoot, Flatt, Hort, Ritsch, Storr, Meyer, Rheinwald, Salmon, B. Weiss, Wittichen, David Smith, Narborough, Williams, Godet, Brownlee, Cross, Yamauchi, Foerster, Benoit, Davies, Bruce(?), Lyonnet, Coppens, A. R. C. Leaney, S. Zedda, G. Johnston, Kehl, Saunders),
Ignatius (Corwin) and
the Pastoral Epistles (J. D. Michaelis, Mangold, Grau, Credner, Immer, Oosterzee, Platt, Zöckler, Ritschl ("Therapeutae"), Wegscheider, Heinrichs, J. H. Bernard, Humphries).

Essene or Qumran influence has also been found in the thought and language of the less controversial:

Hebrews (Friedländer, H. Braun, Michel, Yadin, Spicq, Flusser, Danielou, Schubert, Kosmala, Schnackenburg, Betz, Schelke, Bruce, Bowman, Brownlee, G. R. Driver, Albright, Carmignac) and
Ephesians (Kuhn, Mussner, Flusser, Rabin-Yadin, Murphy-O'Connor, Coppens, Driver)

The most abundant parallels to Essene and Qumran teachings are found in the two letters which could be the most fruitful sources of information about the hypothetical opponents. Constantin Daniel [14]

---

[14] "Une mention paulinienne des Esséniens de Qumran," *RQ* 5(1966), 553-67.

believes that Essene doctrine and Christianized Essenes are resisted in
Rom. 8:38-39; 1 Cor. 6:3; 7:2 Cor. 2:17; Col. (e.g. 2:18); 1 Tim. 4:3;
Hebr. 1-2, and are alluded to in Rom. 14:1-2.

In order to use any of these sources for reconstructing the
opponents' teachings, it is necessary to decide whether there be one
or more groups being argued against in each source. More
specifically, what is the relation of Judaizers to pneumatics, libertines
and Docetists? Where such features are opposed in one letter, should
the existence of different groups be deduced? Considerable caution is
necessary when speaking of heretical pneumatics, since the gift of the
Spirit and other χαρίσματα was general in apostolic times (e.g. Acts
2:4, 17-18; 8:17; 10:44-47; 15:8; 1 Cor. 1:7) and was mark of divine
approval. The claim of being "spiritual" was not distinctive mark of a
heretic (1 Cor. 2:15; 3:1; 14:37; Gal. 6:1). Therefore, the dichotomy
of "Judaizer" and "pneumatic" is not illuminating. That between
"Judaizers" and "libertines" is more significant; a legalist cannot be an
antinomian, though both can (claim to) be "spiritual."

Accordingly, whether or not Paul's warnings in Gal. 5:13-24 were
directed against potential or actual libertines, and whether or not they
defended their "freedom", there is no need to relate them to the
Judaizers. Rather, the latter asserted that liberty from the law leads to
antinomianism. It is with the legalists that our interests for this study
lie. Libertinism has also been detected in the references to "belly-
service" in Rom. 16:18 and Phil. 3:19. But as will be clarified below
(see pp. 98-99), this sort of appetite does not belong in the .same
category as a libertine's lust, and there is no need to segregate these
or other references in these two chapters as applicable to an
antinomian group. The ostensible anti-libertine reference of Eph.
5:3-18 need have no more historical significance than that of Col.
3:5-9; converts from paganism had to be warned. If there was a
theoretical defense of filthy talk and behavior, it was not by a group
elsewhere alluded to in Ephesians.

At Corinth, C. K. Barrett points out [15], "Paul had to walk the
tightrope between the legalism of Jewish Christianity and the false
liberalism of gnostic rationalism." The mention of the weak brother
and conscience (1 Cor. 8:7-13; 10:29-32) witnesses to the existence of

---

[15] "Things Sacrificed to Idols," *NTS* 11(1965), 152. "Waging his war on two fronts,
with the libertines and ascetics, ... he goes along with each party as far as he can, ...
but adding something which neutralizes its position" (F. F. Bruce, *I and II Corinthians*
[New Century], London [Oliphants, 1971]), 62.

both scrupulous and liberated groups.[16] T. W. Manson[17] judged that
the party advocating freedom and immortality constituted for Paul "a
more deadly peril than the threat to his own status involved in the
attacks of the (Palestinian) Cephas party. He is forced to fight on two
fronts ... Wherever Paul finds himself forced to endorse the
criticisms of the Cephas party, he is careful to find his own grounds
for agreeing with them." Henry Chadwick[18] observes that chapter 7
"oscillates between statements which surrender virtually everything to
the ascetics, and qualifications which Paul subtly insinuates, which
tell for the opposite standpoint. The consequence is ... a masterpiece
of ingenuity." Elsewhere[19] we present evidence for the following
views and practices of the antinomian wing of the Paul and Apollos
"parties". They went beyond Scripture (4:6) in their sophistry in
defence of their liberty to eat food offered to idols (chh. 8 & 10), to
commit πορνεία, even with a prostitute (ch. 5; 6:12-20), and to
become drunk, even at the Lord's Supper (5:11; 6:10; 11:21). Having
been already resurrected to reign in the Kingdom, they lost interest
in cosmic eschatological fulfillment and denied the resurrection (4:8;
6:14; ch. 15). However, both the Judaic and the "liberal" wings of the
Corinthian church considered themselves πνευματικοί (2:11-16; 3:1-3;
6:19; 14:37-39) endowed with spiritual gifts (1:7; 4:7-8; 7:40; chh. 12-
14), including wisdom and γνῶσις (chh. 1-2; 4:6; 10:15; 13:2; 15:34). I
Corinthians can be divided into the sections aimed at the Judaic
wing (chh. 7, 9, 13-14 plus 3:10-15; 12:28-31) and against the
anomian wing (chh. 1 to 6, 8, 10, 15, plus 11:1, 19-30; 16:12-14, less
3:10-15). A few passages (1:10-13; 3:21-23; 10:29-32; 11:18-19; 12:1-
27; 13:2b-7, 13) are relevant to the existence and views of the
church's various personal loyalties and theological-moral divisions.

Though there were many Hebrews in the Corinthian church (Acts
18:5-6, 8; 1 Cor. 10:1), the majority of the readers of 1 Cor. were
Gentiles (6:10-11; 8:7; 12:2). As the Greeks were more prone than the
Hebrews to the primary danger of antinomianism, and because the
Judaic Cephas party (see pp. 300-302)[20] at first appealed to the
minority, Paul did not in 1 Cor. address himself so vigorously or

---

[16] Bibliography in John C. Hurd, *The Origin of 1 Corinthians*, London (SPCK, 1965), 116, n. 4.

[17] "The Corinthian Correspondence," in *Studies in the Gospels and Epistles*, Manchester (University, 1962), 207.

[18] "'All Things to All Men' (I Cor. ix. 22," *NTS* 1(1954-55), 264-65.

[19] In a forthcoming monograph on the development of antinomianism.

[20] Bibliography in Hurd, *op. cit.*, 101, n. 1.

exclusively to the Judaizing problem, as he did in his later correspondence with Corinth. The situation changed, however; the antinomian problem was more readily controlled than the Judaizing because in the former case Paul was dealing with excesses among his own local converts and some of his co-worker Apollos, whereas his missionary opponents in the Cephas party undermined his apostolic authority (see below, pp. 300-302). F. F. Bruce writes [21] "If there is a connection between the troubles of 2 Cor. x-xiii and those of 1 Cor., it is to be found . . . in the group of Cephas; though indeed there has been much development between the two epistles." By a balanced treatment in 1 Cor. of excesses of opposing groups, he was able to disgrace the antinomians, but the Cephas party stepped up its campaign against Paul. Maurice Goguel [22] reckoned that the Judaizers' "tactics were not the same in each case. While they worked by gradually worming themselves in secretly in Greece, in Galatia they attacked directly." Even in Corinth, nevertheless, their assault on the Apostle grew in ferocity once they had established a secure foothold in the Cephas party.

The Pastoral Epistles, however, evidence an organized antinomian group. It was led by Hymenaeus and Philetus, who rejected their conscience, blasphemed God through their actions (cf. 1 Tim. 6:1; 2 Tim. 3:2ff.; Tit. 2:5; Rom. 2:2:23-24; Jas. 2:6-7; 2 Pet. 2:2), and who, by their upsetting of some people's faith, promoted impiety (ἀσέβεια) and iniquity (ἀδικία) (1 Tim. 1:19-20; 2 Tim. 2:16-19). Those with corrupted minds who have opposed the truth were guilty of a folly which would be very clear to *all* (πᾶσιν) men (2 Tim. 3:8-9), i.e. including pagans. Their success (cf. 2:16, 18; 3:6) will proceed (προκόψουσιν) no furthur (3:9). the evil men (πονηροί) and imposters, deceivers and deceived, "will go on (προκόψουσὶν) from bad to worse" (3:13). While they may have claimed that their teachings made men "advance," the arrival of the last days will be evidenced by all sorts of evil doers having the form of piety but denying its power (3:1-5). Their practice of magic is implicit in the epithet γόητες (3:13) and the comparison to Jannes and Jambres (3:8). These corrupt errorists "make their way into households and capture weak women, burdened with sins and swayed by various impulses (ἐπιθυμίαις), who will listen to anybody and can never arrive at a knowledge of the truth" (3:6-7).

---

[21] "Galatian Problems. 2. North or South Galatians?", *BJRL* 52 (1970), 297.
[22] *The Birth of Christianity*, transl. ed. H. C. Snape, New York (Macmillan, 1954), 307.

"People will not endure sound teaching, but having itching ears they will accumulate for themselves teachers to suit their own ἐπιθυμίαις, and will turn away from listening to the truth" (4:3-4). Accordingly, Timothy is instructed to flee ἐπιθυμίαις and to pursue righteousness and to "correct his opponents with gentleness. God may perhaps grant that they will repent and come to know the truth, and they may escape from the snare of the devil, after being captured by him to do his will" (2:22-26). Morality was undermined by their denial of such truths as the eschatological resurrection and judgment; allegedly they had already been raised and were reigning (2:12, 18; 3:1; 4:1-8). That they rejected part of the Torah as irrelevant to their new righteousness may be deduced from 2 Tim. 3:16 ("All Scripture is inspired by God and profitable for teaching, for reproof, for correction, and for training in righteousness. . .").

Such antinomianism belonged neither to isolated converts merely still attached to their pagan ways, nor to the Judaizers elsewhere attacked in the Pastoral Epistles. Both antinomians and Judaizers could, like all believers, claim the Spirit, piety and γνῶσις, and both could be ridiculed by the Pastor for their "myths", their corrupt minds and consciences, profane (βέβηλος) talk, questionings (ζήτησις), shipwrecked faith, opposition (ἀντίθεσις) to sound doctrine, βλασφημία, swerving aside and missing the mark, deception and love of money: for such was the nature of the Pastor's general polemics.

The references to the antinomians are found only in 1 Tim. 1:19-20 and 2 Tim. 2:11-4:8. Alexander was an anti-Pauline (1 Tim. 1:19-20; Tim. 4:14-15; Acts 19:33-34; see below, pp. 304-305) "founding father" of the Judaizing sect. Hymenaeus and Philetus were "ultra-Pauline" teachers (2 Tim. 2:17-18) who had overestimated the spiritual gifts of their "resurrected" followers (cf. Eph. 2:1-7; Col. 2:10-15). Eventually their pagan libertine tendencies found a home in a new sect.

The existence of incompatible teachings is likewise evidence of two different heresies in the Letters of Ignatius. True Docetism is a high Christology and Soteriology carried to unbalanced excess; the deity of the Savior is emphasized at the expense of his ("illusory") humanity. But the Judaizers could not be convinced from the Old Testament, and therefore would not believe, that the one God manifested Himself only through His Word who had existed with Him before the ages (ad Philad. 8:2; ad Magn. 7:2; 6:1; 8:1-2). The Docetists called themselves Christians (ad Eph. 7:1; cf. ad Trall. 6:1), but the Judaizers did not (*ad Magn.* 10:1; cf. Rev. 3:9). The Docetists were to be altogether avoided (*ad. Eph.* 7:1; 9:1; *ad Smyrn.* 4:1; 7:2), but Ignatius himself was willing to associate with the Judaizers (*ad Philad.* 8:2); believers, though, were not to listen to their doctrine (*ad Philad.* 6:1-2). Ignatius gave no indication that he had found Docetists in Asia Minor (cf. *ad Trall.* 8:1) and chose not to write their names (*ad Smyrn.* 5:3), which, presumably, he knew from experience at Antioch. The Judaizers celebrated their own Eucharist (*ad Philad.* 4:1), but the Docetists had none (*ad Smyrn.* 7:1). Possibly because both Judaizers and Docetists saw Jesus as a γνῶσις-bringer and found no significance in his suffering in the flesh, Ignatius emphasized against both groups the birth, crucifixion and resurrection of Jesus.[23] For, the Martyr saw in all heresy a faulty view of Christ and the Cross, i.e. of the Gospel.[24] Because Ignatius found the denial of the true Incarnation and of the salvation coming from the Crucifixion and Resurrection to be common to both Judaizers and Docetists, he issues warnings in *ad Magn.* 9:1; 11:1; *ad Philad.* 5:1 against any deviations from the Gospel. But in writing to the Smyrnaeans, Trallians and Ephesians Ignatius attacked Docetism explicitly and exclusively; there is not the slightest hint of Judaizing in the anti-Docetic sections (*ad Smyrn.* 1-7; *ad Trall.* 6-11; *ad Ephes.* 7-8, 17-20). He did not know of any Judaizing among the Magnesians (11:1), but he did know of a division from the bishop and church unity which some had caused at Philadelphia (3:1-3; 7:2; 8:1). Ignatius did not say where he argued with the Judaizers (*ad Philad.* 8:2), but before reaching Philadelphia he would have passed through Colossae and Laodicea if he took the chief highway. The Martyr does not indicate as thorough a knowledge of the Judaizers as of the Docetists. Only against the latter did he urge: Jesus was of David's lineage, the begotten (γεννητός) son of Mary, carried in her womb (*ad Eph.* 7:2; 18:2; *ad Trall.* 9:1; *ad Smyrn.* 1:1).

The detection of opposing viewpoints is admittedly a hazardous undertaking, as Paul did not intend to present them clearly or plausibly, much less perpetuate memory of them. But there are several types of reaction in Biblical writings which indicate that the writer is resisting a misinterpretation of the Gospel. Sometimes the signs are negative and the intention more obvious:

---

[23] Lightfoot, *Apostolic Fathers* II-I, 375.

[24] The history of Christian polemics reveals many attempts to trace all heresies to common denominators.

(a)   a direct statement of objectionable observances and practices (1 Cor. 7:5; Gal. 4:10, 14, 17, 21; 5:1; Col. 2:16, 18, 21-22; Tim. 1:4; 4:1-4, 7; 6:20; Tit. 3:9; Hebr. 6:1-2; 10:25-29);

(b)   an insult or caricature (Rom. 16:17-18; 2 Cor. 4:2; 11:13-15; Gal. 1:6-7; 3:2, 10; 4:9, 11; 5:4; 6:12-13; Eph. 4:14; Phil. 3:2, 18-19; Col. 2:4, 8; 1; Tim. 1:7; 6:3-5; Tit. 1:10-11, 13:10-11; Hebr. 5:11-13);

(c)   rhetorical questions (1 Cor. 9:1; Gal. 3:2, 5; Col. 2:20; Hebr. 1:5-6, 13; 7:11);

(d)   reduction of opposing view to an absurdity (Gal. 5:3-4);

(e)   making distinctions and denying a part (2 Cor. 3:6-16; Gal. 2:14-16; 3:16; 5:6; Eph. 2:8-9; Phil. 3:6-10);

(f)   repetition of opponents' charges and arguments in order to refute them (2 Cor. 10:2-5, 10; Gal. 1:10-12, 16-17; 2:17-18, 21; 3:11-12, 18-21, 27-4: 10; 5:2; Phil. 3:3-10; Col. 2:23; 1 Tim. 4:8; 5:23; Hebr. 1:13-2:9; 7:26-28; 8:6-7; 9:11-15; 13:9) or to qualify them (1 Cor. 7: 1, 34)

Sometimes the Biblical writer makes affirmations which seem counter to beliefs or practices elsewhere attacked:

(g)   contrary statements (1 Cor. 7:19, 28, 36, 39b; Gal. 3:23-26; 4:21-31; 5:24; Eph. 1:14; Col. 1:15-20, 28; 2:9-10; 1 Tim. 2:4-6; 3:16; 5:14; 2 Tim. 2:11-13; Hebr. 1:2-4; 2:5, 9-18; 5:7-9; 7:11-19; 9:9-10; 10:1; 1 Pet. 1:10-12);

(h)   definition of the Gospel (Rom. 16:25-27; 2 Cor. 4:2-6; 11:4; Gal. 1:6ff.; 2:2-5; Eph. 3:2-12 [cf. 1:3-14]; Col. 1:22-28);

(i)   definition of Christ's unique and complete work (Gal. 3:13-14, 24-29; 4:4-7; 5:1; Eph. 1:9-10, 20-23; 2:13-16; 4:8-10; Phil. 3:7-11; Col. 1:12-14, 20-22; 2:10-17; Tit. 3:5-6; Hebr. 7:22; 9:9-14, 24-28; 10:10-12, 19ff.)

On other occasions the enemies' "thunder is stolen":

(j)   terms and concepts are used *ad hominem* or in a different sense or reinterpreted (Rom. 16:19, 25; 2 Cor. 11:14; Gal. 1:8; Eph. 1:17-18; 2:19; Phil. 3:15; Col. 1:9, 12, 16, 19, 26, 28; 2:2-3, 18, 23; Tit. 2:14; Hebr. 8:5; 9:23, 26; 12:22; 13:15-16; 1 Pet. 2:5, 9; Rev. 7:1; 8:3; 19:11-15; 20:6);

(k)   repetition with approval of opponents' warnings against antinomianism (Gal. 5:16-17, 19-21; Col. 3:5ff.);

(l)   Paul's application to himself of his opponents' claims (1 Cor. 7:40; 14:18, 37; 2 Cor. 2:14-16; 3:1-3; 6:4-7; 10:7-12; 11:5-6, 12-12:12; 13:9; Gal. 1:10, 14; Phil. 3:4-6, 12).

In order to carry out the explicit purpose of this study, primary attention must naturally be focused on analyzing all of these signs of controversy in Paul's controversial writings. We have sought elsewhere[25] to establish the following settings of each:

---

[25] *Paul, Messenger and Exile. A Study in the Chronology of His Life and Letters,* Valley Forge, Pa. (Judson, 1972), 66ff.

Galatians: written shortly after his return to Ephesus from Antioch (Acts 18; 22-23; 19:1) following a trip through his older churches in southern Galatia.

2 Corinthians: chapters 10-13 written after the short, painful visit (2:1) to Corinth; chapters 1-9 written a few months later in Macedonia, where he met Titus, who was returning from Corinth (2:12-13; 7:5ff.). Nearly all scholars assume a unity of opponents throughout 2 Cor., [26] except for 6:14-7:1.

Philippians 3:1b-19: written as a summary of his oral warnings while at Philippi restlessly awaiting Titus' arrival (2 Cor. 2:13; 7:5-6) from Corinth.

Romans 16:1-27; written from Corinth to the Ephesians as a letter of introduction for Phoebe (16:1).

Colossians: written during his Caesarean imprisonment.

If these are accepted as Paul's writings, it is to them that we must look for clues to his opponents' teaching. The circumstances of writing and the division of labor between Paul and his secretaries in the writing, are not significant in this search for clues. It is worth noting, however, that because of circumstances Paul was in a different mood and humor when each letter was written; events had led to different types of relationships between Paul and his various readers.

In the same study we sought to show that Ephesians was written by Timothy under Paul's supervision during the Caesarean imprisonment; at least, Timothy wrote Ephesians to serve as the letter from Laodicea which was to be read by the Colossians (Col. 4:16). Accordingly, in conformity to Paul's intention, Timothy sought to make the letter relevant to the similar problems of Lycus Valley churches. "Its purpose is wholly positive", as F. J. A. Hort once commented.[27] Yet it has been widely recognized as "a general safeguard against the spread of the Colossian heresy." [28] A precautionary purpose and a positive method are not incompatible.

The Epistle to the Hebrews is one of the New Testament's most puzzling documents. Though its Pauline authorship is seldom defended these days, some relationship with the churches and/or theology of the Apostle is generally assumed. We have presented evidence [29] for its authorship by Apollos ca. 62-63 while he was at

---

[26] For reasons against identifying the opponents in 1 Cor. and 2 Cor. 10-13, see C. K. Barrett, "Christianity at Corinth," *BJRL* 46 (1963-64), 286-87; cf. Georgi, *op. cit.*, 10-16.

[27] *Judaistic Christianity*, London & New York (Macmillan, 1904), 115.

[28] Guthrie, *op. cit.*, 134.

[29] *Op. cit.*, ii, 151-60.

Corinth; its addressess were the Ephesians, who were threatened by the "heresy" which split believers in Asia and Galatia. Nevertheless, even if the common opinion be preferred that the Epistle has Italian connections(13:24) in the ninth decade of the century, there would be no resultant barrier to the hypothesis of its relevance to the "Asian heresy." By such a late date knowledge of strange teachings (13:9) could have spread to Rome from any part of the Empire.

The editorial portions of the Pastoral Epistles are far more controversial in tone than Hebrews and Ephesians, and their bonds with Paul's churches (1 Tim. 1:3; 2 Tim. 1:15; 2:16; Tit. 1:5, 12) are more specific. Though we would prefer a date from 75 to 95, a later date would not destroy the historical connection between the Judaizing of Paul's day and that of the Pastor's day; for such a bond was affirmed by the writer himself.

The persistence, though also the diminution, of the Judaizing threat in Asia is confirmed by Ignatius' letters to the Magnesians and Philadelphians.[30] Eusebius in his *Chronicon* dates the martydom of the bishop of Antioch in 108, but an equally plausible date would be one following the earthquake in 115 when Trajan was in Antioch on his second Parthian expedition.

Ca. 90-95 A.D. 1 Peter and the Revelation of John were addressed to God's elect" in Pontus, Galatia, Cappadocia, Asia and Bithynia" (1 Pet. 1:1) and "to the seven churches that are in Asia" (Rev. 1:4), respectively. The prophet "was on the island called Patmos" when called to write to the seven churches (1:9-11). The instruction and exhoration contained in these two books were deemed by their authors to be relevant to the situation and needs of the addressees in Asia Minor. Though neither has scarcely a mention of false teaching and controversy, one should not be surprised. The inhabitants of Asia Minor had been subject to a generation of polemics, and the crisis had receded. The time had come for Christological and ecclesiological adaptations of the opponents' terminology and for finding positive counterparts to their theological distortions. This process had begun with the authors of Ephesians and Hebrews and (to a lesser extent) of Colossians, and had been continued in the liturgy; at least this development is detectable in New Testament liturgical fragments.

Among older scholars, John the Baptist was occasionally judged an

---

[30] His other letters were directed against "Syrian Christian Dualism" (my article in *VC* 25 (1971), 81-93.

Essene (H. Graetz, I. Abrahams) or a   Pharisee with Nazirite and Essene tendencies (Klausner). Surprisingly his nomadic, "uncivilized", wine-less manner of life has not evoked comparison with Rechabite ideals. More substantive parallels to the Dead Sea Scrolls are generally acknowledged, though the relation of Qumranic washings and the Johannine baptism, asceticism, Messianology, etc. is much disputed [31] John's training by the Essenes or Qumran community seems sure to A. S. Geyser and E. Stauffer, probable to W. H. Brownlee, O. Betz, J. Danielou, W. Allbright and J. A. T. Robinson, and possible for F. F. Bruce, E. Wilson, J. Allegro, D. Howlett and K. Schubert; a negative reaction to this hypothesis has come from F. Nötscher, H. H. Rowley, H. Braun [32] and G. Richter. A realistic and balanced historical assessment has been put forward by Jean Steinmann, Robinson, Bruce and John Scobie:[33] "John's attitude to orthodox Judaism and to the Jerusalem authorities marks him out as a sectarian and a non-conformist." Though adopted by some baptizing or Essene sect, he received a prophetic call and revealed an individual and original message. He became a dissident preacher from a dissident community and school of apocalyptic exegesis [34]. That this sect was at least akin to that located at Qumran seems to be confirmed by stylistic similarities of the Benedictus of Zechariah (Lk. 1:68-79) to the Qumran hymns and Rule (11.15-28) (F. M. Braun, Danielou, Bruce, Schubert, R. E. Brown)[35]. The parallelism of the nativity and childhood stories of John and Jesus in Lk. 1-2[36] has led many scholars to postulate an underlying Baptist document. This hypothesis requires proof of an unique theology in these two chapters. Otherwise we can only assume that these traditions took shape among converted followers of John simultaneously and in

---

[31] Herbert Braun, *Qumran und das Neue Testament*, Tübingen (J. C. B. Mohr [Paul Siebeck]), ii(1966), 2ff.

[32] *Ibid.*, 20-21.

[33] *John the Baptist*, Philadelphia (Fortress, 1964), 39.

[34] *Ibid.*, 59, 209-11; Jean Steinmann, *St. Jean-Baptiste et la spiritualité du désert*, Paris, 1956, 60; John A. T. Robinson, "The Baptism of John and the Qumran Community," in *Twelve New Testament Studies*, London (SCM, 1962), 12-13.

[35] Douglas Jones ("The Background and Character of the Lukan Psalms," *JTS* 19 [1968], 43) concludes: "These psalms showed acquaintance with the thought-world, sometimes the vocabulary of the Testaments of the XII Patriarchs" (pp. 24, 38, 39, 41) and Qumran writings (pp. 28, 33, 38, 39). They were produced in "sophisticated, even learned" circles (p. 44) by "professionals in the art of psalmody" (p. 46).

[36] Walter Wink, *John the Baptist in the Gospel Tradition*, Cambridge (University, 1968), 60.

conjunction with each other.[37] In the present state of research it is impossible to determine whether the information about John was believed before that concerning Jesus, or vice versa, or whether pre-Christian Messianic expectations (about one or two figures-?) promoted parallel developments. Any credible explanation must account for the differences[38] as well as the similarities in the two accounts and if must recognize that most Baptists became Christians, including members of the Twelve (Mk. 1:14-20: Jn. 1:37ff.; 10: 40-42; Acts 1:22; 19:1-7). Indeed, "the Christian church was a direct outgrowth of the Baptist movement." [39] Kraeling [40] proposed "by far the simplest solution" to the rapid growth of the Judean churches (Acts 4:4; Gal. 1:22):

> large numbers of Baptist disciples entered into or were counted as members of Christian fellowship, and if, as the Infancy Narrative suggests, the Baptist cause was well represented among the rural priests, a subsequent enumeration of a 'great company' of priests among the Christian believers would be entirely logical. [Acts 6:7].

The mysterious group of twelve disciples whom Paul found at Ephesus (19: 1-7) apparently had some bonds with each other by virtue of their common belief and baptism. A synagogue is the most likely place where they were found (Acts 18:19, 26, 28; 19:8); perhaps they had been speaking there about the fulfillment of prophecy. Yet as Ernst Käsemann observes,[41] "They know neither Apollos, who would at least have been able to enlighten them about the gift of the Spirit, nor the Christian community at Ephesus, which was ... sufficiently influential (according to 18:27) to send letters of commendation to Corinth." How could they have come under the influence of Baptists and Christians? How should we account for their isolated existence and the primitive form of their religion? Had Diaspora pilgrims visited Jerusalem (cf. Lk. 23:26; Acts 21:27; 24:18) and been baptized there? Or, less plausibly, had a semi-Baptist, semi-Christian group in Palestine sent out "apostles" without an apostolic baptism (Acts 8:13, 38)?

The chief Judaizing heretics opposed by Irenaeus, Tertullian,

---

[37] *Ibid.*, 81.

[38] René Laurentin, *Structure et théologie de Luc I-II*, Paris (Libr. Lecoffre, 1957), 35-38.

[39] Wink, *op. cit.*, 81, 83, n. 2.

[40] *John the Baptist*, New York & London (Charles Scribner's Sons, 1951), 172-73.

[41] "The Disciples of John the Baptist in Ephesus," in *Essays on New Testament Themes*, London (SCM Press, 1964), 138.

Hippolytus and Origen were known as Ebionites or followers of "Ebion." A large body of literature [42] has appeared which compares their teachings and writings to the Dead Sea Scrolls. While the two groups shared certain features of Jewish sectarianism, the Ebionite rejection of animal sacrifices, the Temple and many of the Old Testament books and prophets is akin to the negations of the Nasaraean sect (Epiphanius, *Haer.* 18), rather than to teachings of the Essenes or Qumran. These same rejections and opposition to virginity, as well as Christology, set the Ebionites apart from Paul's opponents, as we hope to show below, though again they were both Judaizing sectarians. According to Epiphanius, the Ebionites and the Elkesaites influenced each other (30.3 & 17); the Ossenes coalesced with the Sampsaeans and Elkesaites (20.3; 19.2); the Book of Elkesai was used by the Ebionites, Sampsaeans and Ossenes (19.5; 53.1; cf. 19.1 on the relation of Elkesai and the Ossenes). Lietzmann equated the Sampsaeans and Ossenes; Harnack viewed the Sampsaeans and Elkesaites as identical; Joseph Thomas identified the Ossenes as Essenes, while Matthew Black thinks Ὀσσαῖοι is a variation of Ἐσσαῖοι. A. Schmidtke made a sharp distinction between the Ebionites and Elkesaites, while Carl Schmidt and H. J. Schoeps have accused Epiphanius of confusing the two groups. Thomas[43] thought Ebionites were influenced first by Essenes and then by Elchesaites. Hence there was "un conglomerat de communautés" or Ebionisms.

Early Christian apocalypse coming from prophets and visionaries may be of some assistance in understanding the Jewish traditional categories and material used by Paul's opponents. The Revelation of John, the Apocalypse of Peter, the Ascension of Isaiah and the Book of Elkesai are generally dated not far from the turn of the century (100 A.D.); all have a strong Semitic flavor. The Ascension of Isaiah[44] and Revelation of John [45] have numerous connections with the Qumran literture. The Shepherd of Hermas, emanating from Rome about half a century later by most estimates, has relics of the

---

[42] Braun, *op. cit.*, ii, 211-28.

[43] "Les Ébionites Baptistes," *Revue d'Histoire Ecclesiastique* 30 (1934), 296.

[44] David Flusser, "The Apocryphal Book of Ascensio Isaiae and the Dead Sea Sect," *Israel Exploration Society* 3 (1953), 30-47; Marc Philonenko, "Le Martyre d'Ésaie et l'histoire de la secte de Qoumrán," in *Pseudépigraphes de l'ancien Testament et Manuscrits de la Mer Morte*, Paris (Presses Universitaires de France, 1967), 1-10. Their evidence pertains to the (Jewish) sections of chapters 1-3, 5 known as the Martyrdom of Isaiah.

[45] Herbert Braun, "Qumran und das Neue Testament. Eine Bericht über 10 Jahre Forschung (1950-59)," *TR* 30(1964), 118-36.

same mentality and imagery.[46] Visionary apocalyptic was the area of strongest Hebrew Christian influence on the largely Gentile church in the sub-apostolic age; therefore one is entitled to find analogies and similarities in this literature to what may be deduced of the teachings of Paul's opponents.

In his definitive study of the Ascension of Isaiah, Eugene Tisserant [47] considered "comme acquis definitivement" the agreement of C. F. A. Dillmann and Charles that the work consisted of three parts: the Jewish *Martyrdom* (2:1-3:12; 5:1-14) and the Christian *Vision* (6:1-11:1, 23-40) and *Testament of Hezekiah* (3:13-4:19).[48] F. C. Burkitt [49] and Vacher Burch [50] argued for its unity. Otto Eissfeldt,[51] supposing a Hebrew text for the *Martyrdom*, and Martin Rist,[52] finding Gnostic (Ophite-?) influence on the *Vision*, and Marc Philonenko,[53] uncovering Jewish sources within the *Testament* and *Vision*, continue the tri-partite division. Justin Martyr [54] probably knew both the *Martyrdom* (5:11; *Dialogue* 120.14-15) and *Vision* (9:33ff.; *Dialogue* 36.5). J. Armitage Robinson [55] found evidence suggesting that the *Vision* was known to Irenaeus when writing *Demonstration of Apostolic Preaching*. There is a relation between the resurrection accounts of the *Testament of Hezekiah* (3:14, 16,18) and the Gospel of Matthew (26:31; 27:57-61; 28:2, 4, 19-20); the Virgin Birth narrative in the *Vision* (11:2ff.) has points in common with both Gospel narratives. The deterioration of church life as portrayed in 3:22-31 is worse than that described in the apocalyptic chapters of Mt. (24:10-12) and the Didache (16:3-4). The scarcity of prophets and the rivalry among elder-shepherds (3:24, 27, 29)

---

[46] Jean-Paul Audet, "Affinités littéraires et doctrinales du Manuel de Discipline,"· *RB* 60 (1953), 41-82; J. Massingberd Ford, "A Possible Liturgical Background to the Shepherd of Hermas," *RQ* 6 (1969), 546-49, 551.

[47] *Ascension d'Isaie*, Paris (Letouzey & Ané, 1909), 59.

[48] On the preservation of the Testament of Hezekiah, see M. R. James, *The Lost Apocrypha of the Old Testament*, London (SPCK, 1920), 81-86.

[49] *Jewish and Christian Apocalypse*, London (Oxford University, 1914), 45.

[50] "The Literary Unity of the Ascensio Isaiae," *JTS* 20 (1919), 17-23.

[51] *The Old Testament. An Introduction*, transl. P. R. Ackroyd, New York (Harper & Row, 1965), 609-10.

[52] "Isaiah, Ascension of," *IDB* 3, 745.

[53] "Le Martyre d'Ésaïe et l'histoire de la secte de Qoumrân," in *Pseudépigraphes de l'ancien Testament et Manuscrits de la Mer Morte*, Paris (Presses Universitaires de France, 1967), 1-2.

[54] Burch, *art. cit.*, *JTS* 20 (1919), 22; Erik Peterson, "Die Spititualität des Griechischen Physiologus," *Byzantinische Zeitschrift* 47 (1959), 70-71.

[55] *St. Irenaeus. The Demonstration of the Apostolic Preaching*, London (SPCK, 1920), 41-43, 78, 118, 123, 126, 139; chh. 9, 10, 36, 54, 59, 63, 84; cf. 92.

represent a somewhat later stage than those of the Didache (chh. 11, 13, 15) and Matthew [56] in the evolution of leadership. On the other hand, in the Beliar-Nero apocalypse (Asc. Isa. 4:1-18; Rev. 13; cf. 11:2-3; 16:14; 17:6-11; 19:19-21; 20:3, 10) the *Testament of Hezekiah* seems to preserve an early form of the legend, dating from about 68 A.D.[57] Charles[58] perceived that our writing dates from a period when the belief was dying that Nero was still alive in the East. The παρουσία is still eagerly awaited (3:15, 21-22, 26; 4:1, 14, 18; 11:37-38), and when it occurs some who had seen Jesus would still be left as his servants (4:13). It is prudent to concur in general with the following estimates of date of both Christian sections: 88-100 (Charles[59], Tisserant[60], G. H. Box[61], A. L. Davies[62]), ca. 100 (Johannes Quasten[63], Eissfeldt[64]) or 80-90 (Danielou[65]). The latter's suggestion of a Syrian origin has merit. In apostolic times prophets moved between Jerusalem, Caesarea and Antioch (Acts 11:27-28; 13:1-2; 15:32; 21:10-11; cf. Did. 11-13). Ignatius (*ad Eph.* 18:2-19:1) knew some of the *Vision*'s (11:2, 16; cf. 9:15) Virgin Birth traditions. The semi-Docetic Gospel of Peter known to Bishop Serapion of Antioch (*ap.* Eusebius, *H. E.* vi, 12.2-6) has many resemblances to both Christian sections of the Ascension.[66] Finally, "this dry place" is

---

[56] G. D. Kilpatrick, *The Origins of the Gospel according to St. Matthew*, Oxford (Clarendon, 1950, 2nd ed.), 126.

[57] C. Clemen, "Die Himmelfahrt des Jesaja, ein ältestes Zeugnis für das römische Martyrium des Petrus," *Zeitschrift für Wissenschaftliche Theologie* 39 (1896), 404; James Vernon Bartlett, *The Apostolic Age*, Edinburgh (T. & T. Clark, 1900), 521-24; Ethelbert Stauffer, "Problem der Priestertradition," *TLZ* 81(1956), 148, n. 70.

[58] *The Ascension of Isaiah*, London (Adam & Charles Black, 1900), lxix. The Nero Redivivus legend was especially associated with Asia Minor "beyond the Euphrates" (Naomi G. Cohen, "Rabbi Meier, a descendant of Anatolian Proselytes", *Journal of Jewish Studies*, 23 (1972), 54-59.

[59] *Ibid.*, li-lxxii.

[60] *Op. cit.*, 59-60.

[61] *Ascension of Isaiah*, London (SPCK, 1918), xxiii-xxv.

[62] "Ascension of Isaiah," *Dictionary of the Apostolic Church*, ed. James Hastings, New York (Scribner's), i (1916), 99-100.

[63] *Patrology*, Utrecht & Antwerp (Spectrum), i (1950), 110.

[64] *Op. cit.*, 825-26; he dates the *Testament* (3:13-4:18) ca. 100, and the *Vision* in the 2nd century.

[65] *Histoire des Doctrines Chrétiennes avant Nicée. Théologie du Judeo-Christianisme*, Tournai (Desclée, 1958), 22; translated by John A. Baker, *The Theology of Jewish Christianity*, Chicago (Henry Regnery, 1964), 13-14.

[66] H. Stocks, "Quellen zur Rekonstruction des Petrusevangeliums," *Zeitschrift für Kirchengeschichte* 34 (1913), 13-23; cf. Léon Vaganay, *L'Évangile de Pierre*, Paris (Libr. Lecoffre, 1930), 183-84. We hope in a forthcoming article to reconstruct the Virgin Birth narrative in the Gospel of Peter, wherein Joseph's sons were by a previous

topographically composed of mountains, cities, hills, forests and the desert (4:13, 18; cf. 2:11-13). The *Martyrdom* is Palestinian and datable earlier in the first century A.D.[67]

The Apocalypse of Peter has been dated by Danielou [68] at the end of the first century on the basis of its archaic theology. Its connections with the Gospel of Peter evidence for him a Syrian origin. We would find support for this position in the similar traditions found in the Ascension of Isaiah, the Epistle of the Apostles and 3 Corinthians,[69] as well as from "Peter's" use of only Matthew and possibly Mark. Erik Peterson[70] dates it at the beginning of the second century. An origin later than 130 A.D. is excluded by the inappropriateness of the parable of the fig tree (Ethiopic 2) as a reference to Bar Cochba (in spite of A. Loisy, H. Weinel, E. Amann and W. Michaelis) and by the early widespread popularity of this Apocalypse, as witnessed by Theophilus of Antioch, the Acts of Thomas, Sibylline Oracle 2, Celsus, 2 Peter [71], Clement, Clement of Alexandria, the Carthaginian Martyrdom of Perpetua and Felicitas, the Epistle of the Churches of Lyons and Vienne, the Shepherd of Hermas (unless there were common apocalyptic traditions) and the Muratorian Canon. If ch. 3 (Ethiopic) presupposes literary knowledge of 4 Esdras 5:33, then a date earlier than the end of the first century would be untenable.

The Ethiopic Testament of our Lord Jesus in Galilee is an apocalypse which has been largely ignored or dismissed by scholars. Louis Guerrier [72] believed there are Ebionite and Essene influences on the Testament, and that it was written in Egypt, or possibly

---

marriage and Mary's perpetual viginity was upheld, as in the case of the Book of James (Origen, *Comm. in Matth.* x. 17). The Ascension of Isaiah (ch. 11) preserves an earlier version; later sources include the Book of James, the Epistle of the Apostles, Justin, the Acts of Peter, the two Gospels of Thomas, the Odes of Solomon, the Hereford and Arundel Mss. of the Latin Infancy Gospel, and possibly Tatian.

[67] Albert-Marie Denis, *Introduction aux Pseudépigraphes Grecs d'Ancien Testament*, Leiden (E. J. Brill, 1970, 175-76. Leonhard Rost (*Einleitung in die Alttestamentliche Apokryphen und Pseudepigraphen*, Heidelberg [Quelle & Meyer, 1971], 113-14) thinks its author was a 2nd c. B.C. Palestinian with Essene tendencies.

[68] *Op. cit.*, 35.

[69] On their Syrian origin see my article, "Syrian Christian Dualism," *VC* 25 (1971), 81-83.

[70] "Das Martyrium des Hl. Petrus nach der Petrus-Apokalypse," in *Miscellanea Giulio Belvederi*, Citta del Vatticano, 1954, 184.

[71] F. H. Chase, "Peter, Second Epistle of," *Dictionary of the Bible*, ed. Jas. Hastings, New York & Edinburgh, iii (1900), 814-15.

[72] "Le Testament en Galilée de Notre-Seigneur Jesus Christ," *Patrologia Orientalis* IX, 3), Paris, 1913, 161; cf. 153.

Palestine, ca. 200 A.D. He also believed a common source underlay the Ethiopic Testament and the Syrian Testament of the Lord (a collection of ecclesiastical canons edited by I.E. Rahmani in 1899). Carl Schmidt,[73] who accepts a late date for the Syrian Testament and considers the Ethiopian recension to be an independent branch of the Testament tradition, assigns an unspecified late date to the Ethiopian. Moreover, he believed that the Epistle of the Apostles, which is appended to the Ethiopian manuscripts of the Testament, influenced the compiler of the latter. Kirsopp Lake [74] wrote: "Schmidt has shown beyond all doubt that the little 'Testament of the Lord' was taken from the ordinary book of that name, which was accidentally associated with the other document (Epistle of the Apostles) in the Ethiopic copy. The opening chapters contain merely an apocalypse, important mainly for its delineation of Antichrist." M. R. James, who didn't bother to translate it, observed [75] that parts of "a prophecy of our Lord concerning the signs of the end, ... recur in the Syriac *Testament of the Lord* and part is repeated in the Epistle (of the Apostles) itself. It is noteworthy this prophecy ends with a passage which is identical with one quoted by Clement of Alexandria" (*Protrept.* ciii). E. Amann [76] thought that a 5th centtury Syrian Monophysite joined a small apocalypse (specially edited for use in Syria or Asia Minor) to church ordinances in order to confer authority on them. B. Altaner [77] thought the introduction to the 5th century Syrian book was taken from an otherwise unknown apocalypse (Epistle of the Apostles?).

We suggest that a date after 90 for this apocalypse is indicated by dependence on a Matthew Gospel and Mark.[78] The destruction of Jerusalem and its sacrificial cultus had occurred long enough in the past to ignore; it no longer could be treated as part of the eschatological signs. The Testaments of the Twelve Patriarchs were in the process of being Christianized, or the Christian editing was already complete, or the writing of Jesus' Testament inspired work on

---

[73] *Gespräche Jesu mit seinen Jungern nach der Auferstehung* (TU 43), Leipzig, 1919, 160ff., 357-62, 372.

[74] "The Epistola Apostolorum," *HTR* 14 (1921), 17.

[75] *The Apocryphal New Testament*, Oxford (Clarendon, 1960), 485.

[76] "Testament de Notre-Seigneur Jesus Christ," *DTC* 15 (1946), 199.

[77] *Patrologia*, Freiburg, Basel & Vienna (Herder, 1966, 7th ed. by A. Stuiber), 257.

[78] For Matthew: 28:16-20 (ch. 2); 3:7; 10:21; 24:3-31 (ch. 4); 24:5 (i.e. Simon Magus, Dositheus, Menander) (ch. 6); 5:11; 7:21; 12:50 (ch. 7); 12:36; 16:27; 21:32; 24:29 (ch. 11); for Mark: 4:29 (ch. 6); 9:47-48 (ch. 11).

it; for, knowledge of patriarchal testaments suggested that Christ, too, made a "will". On the other hand, for three reasons it would not be plausible to date the Testament of our Lord far along in the second half of the second century. The second century was the age of post-resurrection revelation apocrypha. Among them, the Epistle of the Apostles and Apocalypse of Peter (to which our Testament is akin) [79] were earlier and further removed from Gnosticism than the present form of the Apocryphon of John, [80] the Apocryphon of James and the Gospel of Mary. The 545 days for which Jesus remained (Asc. Isa. 9:16; cf. 11:21) provided ample opportunity to teach. The grim prophecies of Epistle of the Apostles 34-36 are somewhat lengthier and more elaborately framed with dialogue than very similar ones in Testament of the Lord, ch. 4. Although dependence on one side or one a common source at this point is elusive of proof, it is noteworthy that this mood of eschatological terror pervades the Testament, but not the Epistle of the Apostles. [81] Moreover, when the Testament was written, the sect's apocalyptical expectations were still keen. "Hell has opened its jaws ... fewness of days" (2). "Flee the approaching wrath and flame" (4). "Prepare your throne for your king. Prepare yourself for the day of destruction ... Your woe is coming" (5). The Antichrist's "time has come; his harvest is near" (6). "The time draws near when (the world) will end and the (last) days approach" (11). Jesus said, "I will teach what will happen, not to you, but to those whom you will teach and who will believe on me ... It is not you who (will see) what will happen" (4). The apostolic generation had passed on, but not all of the next generation of converts. Would a late writing leave unaltered an unfulfilled prophecy of the Lord? The church was still ruled by bishops and pastors (παστοφόροι) (9). A date during the last few years of the first century would befit the references to persecution of the God-fearing and righteous (11) and to opposition to corrupt church leaders (9) in language similar to that of the Ascension of Isaiah (3:23-31).

As to place of origin, the Testament author knew the Septuagint. The Syriac Testament of the Lord (chh. 10-12) is closely related to chh. 5-6 of the Ethiopian Testamant. Christian apocalyptic and hope

---

[79] See James, *The Apocryphal New Testament*, 485, 490, n. 1.

[80] See M. Hornschuh, "The Apostles as Bearers of the Tradition," in Edgar Hennecke-Wilhelm Schneemelcher, *New Testament Apocrypha*, transl. ed. by R. Mcl. Wilson, Philadelphia (Westminster), ii (1965), 80-82.

[81] On the differences between the two documents see Guerrier, *Patrologia Orientalis* IX, 3), 159-62.

for a millenial kingdom (germinally expressed in ch. 7) survived into the second century in Asia Minor (John, Papias, Justin, Irenaeus, Montanus). The geographical references in Ch. 6 extend from Judea to Phoenicia, Syria and Armenia; but most and specific attention is given to Asia Minor (Cilicia, Cappadocia, Phrygia, Bithynia, the walls of Pontus, the bloody rivers of Lycaonia, proud Pisidia trusting in its riches, the coastline and ships of Pamphylia). Pastors are mentioned in the New Testament only in Ephesians 4:11 (To the Laodiceans).[82] The descendants of Jonadab, who were called Ἰεσσαῖοι and abstained from wine, are briefly described by abbot Nilus of Ancyra ca. 400 (de monastica exerc. 3; de volunt, paupert, ad Magnam, 39; Migne, P.G. 39, 721 & 1017).[83] Jonadab and his descendents are praised in the Testament (9), which abounds in examples of Essene-like use of Scripture and such phrases as "children of light" (2, 4) and "children of perdition" (5).[84] Voluntary poverty is praised (7). Central Asia Minor is the most likely place of writing.

The Paralipomena of Jeremiah (4 Baruch) has been almost universally recognized as a Jewish writing subjected to slight Christian editing, at least in ch. 9. Only Rendel Harris considered its origin to be Christian. J. Licht and Gerhard Delling[85] deduce a Semitic original text. It has been dated ca. 150 A.D. by Frey and A. Penna; ca. 136 by Harris and Licht; 100-140 (R. Meyer); first third of 2nd c. (G. Beer, Delling); beginning of 2nd c. (F. Nötscher); 70-130 (G. D. Kilpatrick, A. -M. Denis,[86]). Kilpatrick writes:[87] "After A. D. 135 we have only diminishing traces of Messianic beliefs in Judaism and no certain examples of Jewish books passing into Christianity." Kohler dated its Christian editing after Hadrian's reign. Its dependence at 9:13-19 on the Ascension of Isaiah (3:13ff.) is generally recognized. A date of the Christian additions, we suggest, in the early second century is supported by its reference to "the faith" (9:14), Christ's choice of twelve apostles to evangelize the Gentiles

---

[82] Gunther, op. cit., 126-30.

[83] Joachim Schoeps, Theologie und Geschichte des Judenchristentums, Tübingen (J. C. B. Mohr [Paul Siebeck], 1949), 250-51; cf. Kaufmann Kohler, "The Essenes and the Apocalyptic Literature," JQR N.S. 11 (1920), 160-62.

[84] For additional evidence of Essene themes see Jean-Marc Rosenstiehl, "Le portrait de l'Antichrist," in Pseudepigraphes de l'Ancien Testament et Manuscrits de la Mer Morte, 59-60.

[85] Jüdische Lehre und Frömmigkeit in den Paralipomena Jeremiae, Berlin (A. Toepelmann, 1967), 3, n. 11.

[86] Op. cit., 74-75.

[87] "Acts vii. 52 Eleusis," JTS 46 (1945), 140; cf. 141.

(9:18; cf. Mt. 28:19; Preaching of Peter, *ap*. Clement of Alexandria, *Strom*. vi, 5. 43; 6.48) and Jewish stoning of preachers (9:19).[88] Eschatological hope was still strong. That it was edited on Cyprus or Crete is indicated by the prophecy that Jesus Christ "shall bless the islands [89] and make them fruitful ἐν the word ... of Christ himself" (9:19) and by the references to snow and salty water (9:16). The summits of both islands are snow-covered throughout the year and "exalted in the clouds" (9:14: Armenian). Gortyna, capital of the Roman province of Crete and Cyrenaica, was located six miles from the foot of Mt. Ida. Christ's coming into the world on the Mount of Olives (9:18) is reminiscent of Greek myths of the activities of the gods on Mt.Ida (e.g. the rearing of Zeus in one of its caves). Gortyna was in a fruit-growing region (cf. 9:14-16) and was well-provided with fresh water (9:16) by a good aqueduct and springs and fountains (Theophrastus, *Hist. Plants* i, 15; iii, 5). Gortyna had a significant Jewish population (1 Macc. 15:23; cf. 10:67), and its bishop, Philip", wrote a most elaborate work against Marcion," according to Dionysius of Corinth (ca. 167-75 (Eusebius, *H. E.* iv, 24). The editing of the Epistle to Titus for the benefit of errant Cretans, indicates a local church problem not long before 4 Baruch was Christianized.

A lost Jewish apocalypse apparently told of a blessed people living in remote exile since days of Jeremiah.[90] Perhaps, as James suggested,[91] it is to be identified with the Book of Eldad and Medad [92] (prophets of the wilderness camp), which is mentioned by Hermas (*Vis.* ii, 3.3-4) for its teaching how those who turn to the Lord should disown tribulation (θλῖψις); i.e. how those living in ἁπλότες, ἐγκρατεια and ἀκακία prevail against (κατισχύσουσιν) all evils (πονηρίας). Some such work was the ultimate source of the Christian tales of a holy, lost people as found in the poet Commodian (of Gaza, 3rd century-?), the Narrative (Apocalypse) of Zosimus (condemned by the 9th c. Canon of Nicephorus and the Slavonic Index),[93] the Ethiopic

[88] J. L. Martyn, *History and Theology in the Fourth Gospel*, New York (Harper & Row, 1968), 65-68.

[89] W. I. Reed, "Island, Isle," *IDB* 2, 750.

[90] James, *Lost Apocrypha of the Old Testament*, 103-06.

[91] "The Story of Zosimus," *Apocrypha Anecdota (Texts and Studies* ii-3), Cambridge (University Press, 1893), 93-94, n. 1. On the teachings of Eldad and Medad see below (pp. 127, 246).

[92] Francis Schmidt ("Une source essenienne chez Commodien," in *Pseudepigraphes de l'Ancien Testament et Manuscrits de la Mer Morte*, 11-25) finds evidence that he knew books of Essene origin.

[93] *Apocrypha Anecdota (Texts and Studies* ii-3), 87, 94. Louis Ginzberg (*The*

Contendings (Conflicts) of the Holy Apostles,[94] and an Ethiopian "History of the Holy Men in the days of Jeremiah the Prophet." [95]

In Jn. 1:51 Jesus promises Nathanael: "You will see heaven opened, and angels of God ascending and descending upon the Son of man." In the Questions of Bartholomew (1, 6) the Apostle relates to the risen Lord that he "saw how you were hanged on the cross and how the angels descended from heaven and worshipped you." An apocryphal writer in search of a priveleged apostolic visionary, selected Nathaniel, whom he identified with Bartholomew (Bar Talmai), to be the transmitter of esoteric teachings concerning the angels, Hades, etc. Various dates have been assigned: 2nd century (J. Kroll), 3rd c. (A. Romeo, F. Scheidweiler), 4th c. (A. Wilmaert-E. Tisserant, A. de Santos Otero), a late compilation with much earlier sources (E. Amann, M. S. Enslin). The most valuable recension is the unfortunately abbreviated Greek H (Hierosl. sav. 13).[96] Some of the more primitive elements are worthy of selection as parallels. Pantaenus found in "India" (eastern Parthia-?) users of a Hebrew Gospel of Matthew who claimed Bartholomew as their apostle (Eusebius, *H. E.* v, 10.3)

Heterodox Hebrew influences reappeared in later Christianity, both in pseudepigrapha and in exotic practices in isolated communities of Asia Minor. The enigmatic Testament of Solomon has been studied carefully only by F. C. Conybeare [97] and Chester C. McCown.[98] The former thought that in its original form it may have been the Jewish collection of incantations which Josephus (*Antiquities* viii, 2.5.44-49) attributed to Solomon;[99] to this Christian

---

Legends of the Jews, Philadelphia, Jewish Publ. Soc. of America, vi, 1928, 409) held that it is "a Jewish legend with very slight Christian addition"; mention of the sons of Rechab is a Jewish, rather than Christian, variant.

[94] Transl. by S. C. Malan and quoted by James in *Texts and Studies* ii-3, 92-93; the standard edition now is E.A. Wallis Budge, *The Contendings of the Apostles*, London & New York (H. Frowde, 1899-1901).

[95] James, *Texts and Studies*, ii-3, 87-90. Text in Budge, *The Life and Exploits of Alexander the Great*, London, 1896, i, 355-76; ii, 555-84(ET). God orders Jeremiah to hide in a mountain holy objects from the Ark of the Covenant, as in the Lives of the Prophets. Jean-Claude Picard ("L'Histoire des Bienhereux du temps de Jérémie et la Narration de Zosime: arrière-plan historique et mythique," in *Pseudepigraphes de l'ancien Testament et Manuscrits de la Mer Morte*, 27-37) presents strong indications that both writings were based on a common Essene source concerning the history of the Qumran sect.

[96] F. Scheidweiler in Hennecke-Schneemelcher, *op. cit.*, ii, 486-87 (ET).

[97] "The Testament of Solomon," *JQR* 11(1898), 1-45.

[98] *The Testament of Solomon*, Leipzig (J. C. Hinrichs, 1922).

[99] Palestinian amulets show Solomon fighting demons (Bellarmino Bagatti, *l'Église*

elements were added ca. 100 A.D., believed Conybeare. McCown [100] thought the Jewish prototype "may be as early as the first century" and that the paganized Gentile Christian Recension B may have emanated from Asia in the Fourth century, though the astrology and magic are oriental, Hellenistic, Jewish and Egyptian. In the *Jewish Encyclopedia* K. Kohler [101] followed the conclusions of Conybeare, while C. H. Toy [102] though the author was "a Greek-speaking Jewish Christian" of 300 A.D. The article in *The Universal Jewish Encyclopedia*[103] states that it was written in Greek by a first century Jewish Christian. Emil Schürer thought it purely Christian, but M. R. James [104] considered it "mainly Jewish with Christian touches." J. B. Frey [105] thought that it contains an extremely ancient Jewish kernel and that it was revised by a Christian. Angelo Penna [106] and P. Estelrich [107] think that it was written in Greek by a third century Christian using Jewish documents. Bruce Metzger's [108] opinion largely follows that of C. C. McCown.

Just as mysterious is the story of Melchizedek found in several manuscripts of the Slavonic Book of the Secrets of Enoch. It was translated by W. R. Morfill with comments by Charles, who believed it to be "the work of an early Christian heretic." [109] They and G. N. Bonwetsch [110] treated it as an appendix. Harald Sahlin,[111] tentatively, and J. Danielou [112] detect imitation of the Lucan birth narrative. James [113] thought it a Jewish work which is "Christian in its present

---

de la circoncision, transl. Albert Storme, Jerusalem (Impr. des P. P. Franciscains, 1965), 113)

[100] *Op. cit.*, 108; 2, 75, 82-83, 108-110.

[101] Ed. Isidore Singer, New York and London (Funk & Wagnalls), 11 (1905), 448-49.

[102] "Demonology," *Jewish Encyclopedia*, 4(1903), 518.

[103] Ed. Isaac Landman, New York, 9 (1943), 637.

[104] "Apocrypha," *Encyclopaedia Biblica*, ed. T. K. Cheyne & J. S. Black, London (Adam & Charles Black, 1899), i, 254.

[105] "Apocryphes de l'ancient Testament," *Dictionnaire de la Bible*, Paris (Letouzey et Ané), Supplément, I (1928), 455.

[106] *Enciclopedia Cattolica*, Città del Vaticano, 10 (1953), 1695.

[107] *Enciclopedia de la Biblia*, Barcelona (Ediciones Garriga), 6 (1965), 981.

[108] *Dictionary of the Bible*, ed. by J. Hastings, F. C. Grant and H. H. Rowley (2nd ed.), Edinburgh (T. & T. Clark, 1963), 823.

[109] *The Book of the Secrets of Enoch*, Oxford (Clarendon, 1896), 85.

[110] *Die Bücher der Geheimnisse Henochs*, Leipzig (J. C. Heinrichs, 1922), TU 44-2, xviii-xix.

[111] *Der Messias und das Gottesvolk*, Uppsala (Almquist & Wiksells, 1954), 370-72.

[112] *Histoire des Doctrines. . .*, 238 (ET 215-16).

[113] *Lost Apocrypha of the Old Testament*, 18.

form" A. Vaillant [114] considers it an integral part of 2 Enoch; it was written by a Jewish Christian and underwent medieval revisions.

In his thorough articles, "Melchisédech dans la tradition Patristique," Gustav Bardy [115] examines the treatise against the Melchizedekians by Mark the Hermit, abbot at Ancyra ca. 400 A.D. Concerning their insidious character we read:

> Having been expelled and anathematized by the holy bishops and driven where they are not known, they come together secretly... If ever through their feigned piety (εὐλαβεια) they are able to be received by the holy bishops or the visitors (περιοδευταῖς), they secretly vilify the true orthodox believers as men of evil mind (κακόφρονας) (Migne, *P.G.* 65, 1137A).

Jerome saw a strange variety of schismatics in Ancyra (*Comm. in Gal.*, lib. II, cap. II; Migne., *P.L.* 26, 382B-C) ca. 373 A.D. The city had earlier been a Montanist stronghold (Eusebius, *H.E. v, 16.4; cf. Epiphanius, Haer. 48.14,2*). The honoring of Melchizedek was known to Timothy of Constantinople ca. 500. In his Περὶ τῶν πρσσερχομένων τη ἀγία Ἐκκλησία (*De Receptione Haereticorum*) (Migne, *P.G.* 86, 33 B-C) he described a Phrygian sect called the Ἀθίγγανοι which glorified the Priest-King of Salem. Timothy reported that members of this sect had to be baptized when they returned to the holy Church. Bardy [116] thought it possible that the Athinganes of the sixth century were "les légitimes héritiers" of the group described by Mark. He noted that "these errors had little repercussion outside their country of origin, since the fifth century preachers (Nestorius, Eutherius of Tyana, Proclus of Constantinople and Theodoret) spoke often of Melchizedek as the image of Christ without indignation." [117] Further information on the sect is given by manuscripts of the Bibliothèque Nationale de Paris, Paris graec. 364(14th-15th century) fo. 43 and Coislin 39 (17th century) fo. 270.

In the middle of the fourth century (not before 344) a council was held at Laodicea in southwestern Phrygia. Among its sixty canons are several which deal with Judaizing Christianity. Theodoret, F. A. Henle,[118] J. B. Lightfoot [119] and A. Lukyn Williams [120] believed that

---

[114] *Le Livre des Secrets d'Hénoch*, Paris (Institut d'Études Slaves, 1952), xi-xii, xxiv.

[115] *RB* 35 (1926), 496-509; 36 (1927), 25-45.

[116] *Ibid.*, 36.

[117] *Ibid.*, 36-37.

[118] *Kolossä und der Brief des heiligen Apostels Paulus an die Kolosser*, Munich, 1887.

[119] *St. Paul's Epistles to the Colossians and to Philemon*, 67-69, 71.

[120] "The Cult of the Angels at Colossae," *JTS* 10 (1908-09), 435.

these were directed against relics of the Colossian heresy opposed by
St. Paul. However, Theodor Zahn [121] held that such canons
pertained, not to a heretical tendency from apostolic times, but to a
local cult and concessions to Jewish customs. There may be an
element of truth in each viewpoint. Such practices as invoking angels
do not arise spontaneously, whereas the laity was perhaps more ready
for "ecumenical" relations with local Jews than was the fourth century
episcopate.

All of the above-mentioned sources are capable of shedding various
degrees of light upon the teaching and practices of Paul's opponents.
In principle, the closer the source to Paul's churches and letters, the
more relevant it is apt to be; the more remote in time, distance and
person, the less likely it is to be pertinent. Moreover, the more weight
one gives to the Judaic, Palestinian background of Paul's opponents,
the more justified is the search for such parallels in Palestinian
literature. Isolated references may also be made to the writings of
Marcion, Justin, Irenaeus, Tertullian, Cyprian, Theodoret and
Cappadocian Fathers and to the Book (Protevangelium) of James for
interesting illustrations of recurrent themes ostensibly detectable in
the thought of Paul's opponents.

Nevertheless, neither the identity nor the kinship of teachings and
practices detectable in any different sources should be assumed at the
outset. How should points of comparison be sought? Each source
must be examined as an entity and interpreted in terms of itself and
the Old Testament; ideas contained therein may be conjoined and
correlated. Only then may one compare the findings from different
sources. However, occasionally a passage does not "speak for itself"
and neither passages from the same source nor from the Old
Testament adequately clarify the passage or require a preference
among possible alternative explanations. In such a case the exegete is
tempted to look for clarification in other documents: Christian,
Jewish or pagan, according to his impression of the background of
the document's writer or readers. This represents a leap into step
number two; generally it is justifiable only where there is a
compelling likeness of terminology. Accordingly, our quest for
identifying the beliefs and customs of Paul's opponents begins with
the isolation of as many features as possible in Paul's individual
letters. Where similar features are observable in other early Christian

---

[121] *Introduction to the New Testament*, transl. ed. by M. W. Jacobus, New York
(Charles Scribner's Sons, 1917, 2nd ed.), I, 476-77.

documents as enumerated above (e.g. Hebrews, Ignatius' letters, the Shepherd of Hermas), they are noted and analyzed, not in the context of a discussion of a Pauline letter (which would prejudice the comparison), but rather in a paragraph concerning that feature within each document. The reader is thus free to accept or minimize the relevance, for example, of Ebionite food laws for an understanding of the dietary practices of certain Colossian Christians.

In so far as Judaic or sectarian Jewish features are detectable in Paul's opponents from some of his letters, it is fitting to quote, topic by topic, strikingly similar passages from Jewish literature, -but only after all Christian sources have been cited. Hebrew apocryphal and pseudepigraphal writings are potentially bountiful sources of analagous teachings. A rigid separation of Jewish and Christian documents is admittedly arbitrary; for, Jewish sources in the Apocalypses of Peter or of John and in the Ascension of Isaiah and Testament of Solomon are postulated by many scholars. Moreover, most of the Jewish epigrapha which we shall cite have been revised or added to both by Jewish and by Christian authors or scribes. In such a document it is often so difficult to distinguish original from added Jewish passages and both of these types from Christian glosses or revisions, that scholarly opinion is in disarray. What are the interpolations and who made them?

This conflict and confusion of investigators is most obvious with respect to the Testaments of the Twelve Patriarchs, which we find more occasion to cite than any other basically Hebrew work for the clarification of Pauline allusions to opposing doctrine. Reviews of the history of its interpretation are given by R. H. Charles,[122] M. De Jonge,[123] P. Grelot,[124] Morton Smith [125] and Jürgen Becker.[126] An original Jewish writing has been dated as follows:

pre-Maccabean (ca. 200-175 B.C.) (Eduard Meyer, R. Appel, Elias Bickerman, W. F. Albright, J. Thomas)

---

[122] *The Testaments of the Twelve Patriarchs Translated from the Editor's Greek Text*, London (1908), xxxviii-xli.

[123] *The Testaments of the Twelve Patriarchs*, Assen (van Gorcum, 1953), 9-12; "Christian Influence in the Testaments of the Twelve Patriarchs," *NT* 4 (1960), 182-83.

[124] "Le Messie dans les apocryphes de l'ancien Testament," in *La Venu du Messie* (Recherches Bibliques vi), ed. É. Massaux et alia, Brussels (Desclée de Brouwer, 1962), 34-40.

[125] "Testaments of the Twelve Patriarchs, The," *IDB* 4, 576-578.

[126] *Untersuchungen zur Entstehungsgeschichte der Testamente der Zwölf Patriarchen*, Leiden (E. J. Brill, 1970), 129-58.

late Hasmonean (Charles, K. Kohler, W. Bousset, Joseph Klausner, Robert
Pfeiffer, Lods, A. J. B. Higgins, D. Haupt)
first century B. C. (Emil Schürer)
early first century A.D. (C. C. Torrey)

Several scholars have argued for the origin of at least some of the
Testaments in the Essene sect producing the Dead Sea Scrolls (B.
Otzen, O. Eissfeldt, A. Dupont-Sommer, J. T Milik, P. Grelot, A. S.
van der Woude, Marc Philonenko, L. Rost, F. M. Braun). Internal
resemblances are supported by the discovery in the Caves of
fragments of an Aramaic Testament of Levi (4QT Levi) and a Hebrew
Testament of Naphtali. In 1896-97 fragments of an Aramaic T. of
Levi and a complete Hebrew T. of Naphtali were found in genizah of
the Karaite synagogue of Old Cairo, where the Damascus Document
was also uncovered. The affinities of Karaite and Qumran teachings
suggests a common origin of the sects and the writings.[127] These
Semitic manuscripts, in any case, have led nearly all scholars since
Charles to follow the suggestion of J. E. Grabe (the editor of the
Greek Testaments in 1698) that their original language was Hebrew,
and that Palestine was their "birthplace." However, an inaccurate
knowledge of Palestinian geography is manifest,[128] while the absence
of other Semitic texts has led some (J. T. Milik, J. Carmignac, F. M.
Cross, M. A. Chevalier, M. De Jonge, J. Danielou, M. Smith) to see
the Greek Testaments as a Christian work drawing upon the two

---

[127] Bibliography in Helmer Ringgren, *The Faith of Qumran*, transl. Emilie T.
Sander, Philadelphia (Fortress, 1963), 253-54, n. 28. Simon Szyszman, "Das Karäertum
in seinen Beziehungen zum Essänertum in der Sicht einiger Autoren des 17. und 18.
Jahrhunderts," in *Bibel und Qumran*, ed. Siegfried Wagner, Berlin, 1969, 226-31;
Athanase Negoïtsa, "Did the Essenes Survive the 66-71 War?", *RQ* 6 (1969), 523-24.
The two monographs are Naphtali Wider, *The Judean Scrolls and Karaism*, London
(East & West Library, 1962) and André Paul, *Écrits de Qumrân et sectes juives aux
premiers siècles de l'Islam. Recherches sur l'origine de Qaraisme*, Paris, Letouzey et
Ané, 1970.
[128] De Jonge, *op. cit.*, 64-65. However, if many of the place names are of
Maccabean battle scenes whose names changed or were forgotten and corrupted during
a long period of oral transmission, confusion would be expected even among
Palestinians. Apocalyptic veiling of names is possible. T. W. Manson (*Miscellanea
Apocalyptica* III [Test. XII Patr.: Levi viii], *JTS* 48 [1957], 59), supported by De Jonge
(*op. cit.*, 45, 128) and Danielou (*op. cit.*, 15) argued for a Syrian origin on the basis of
unction's preceding baptism (cf. T. Levi 8:3-10). The only ancient reference to the
work is by Origen writing from Caesarea (*In librum Iesu nave, Homily* xv, 6.24).
Johannes Thomas, "Aktuelles im Zeugnis der zwölf Väter," in C. Burchard, Jervell &
Thomas, *Studien zu den Testament der Zwölf Patriarchen*, ed. W. Eltester, Berlin
(Alfred Töpelmann, 1969), 111-14, 131) thinks it was addressed by Palestinian to
Alexandrian Jews.

known Semitic texts (or their ancestor) and Jewish traditions. Until
De Jonge published his study in 1953, the only modern scholar
upholding the theory of a Christian composition was N. Messel in
1918. The most widely held solution since the study of F. Schnapp in
1884 has been to view the Testaments as a Jewish work which has
been interpolated by Christians (Conybeare, W. Bousset, Schürer,
Charles, Lagrange, Baljon, De Faye, Appel, Klausner, H. H. Rowley,
Bickerman, G. R. Beasley-Murray, van der Woude, Leivestad, A.
Lods, Braun, Grelot, J. Jervell). There has long been disagreement
concerning the extent and specification of Christian interpolation,
the existence of earlier Jewish revisions or interpolations (as asserted
by Schnapp, Charles, Bousset, Bickerman, Pfeiffer, Philonenko) and
the identity of the most reliable text(s). Philonenko, van der Woude
and De Jonge [129] agree that a Hebrew Testament of Levi was the
starting point of the present collection of Greek Testaments.
Disagreements among current investigators lie essentially in the area
of deciding "whether a passage is more likely to be Christian or
Jewish" [130] and whether the Greek Testaments are largely or
originally Christian (De Jonge) or Essene [131] (Dupont-Sommer,
Philonenko). It seems to the present writer that it is futile to argue
whether the ten Testaments not found at the Old Cairo synagogue
and Qumran were in oral or written form before the original
Christianized Greek Test appeared. A favorable referece to the
Apostle was eventually interpolated in the Greek recension β of Test.
Benj. 11:3-5.[132] But for purposes of quotation and analysis in
subsequent chapters, it usually matters little what the origin of a
passage has been; its similarity, and therefore relevance, to polemical
passages in the Pauline corpus is our primary consideration.

   The less-studied Testament of Abraham has evoked a variety of
evaluations.[133] Harnack saw it as a Jewish work probably known to
Origen (*Hom. in Luc.* xxxv). K. Kohler specified its origin as Essene
or 1st century Alexandrian. L. Ginzberg thought it to be of "definitely
Jewish origin," possibly Essene or Pharisee; it was of "very early date",
though a few manuscripts contained some late Christian additions. G.

---

[129] *Art. cit., NT* 4 (1960), 188.

[130] *Ibid.*, cf. 187.

[131] Charles and Robert Pfeiffer considered the author to be a Pharisee.

[132] De Jonge (*art. cit.*, 227) thinks 11:2-5 is a late interpolation.

[133] Bibliographies in Box, *The Testament of Abraham*, London (SPCK, 1927), vii-xxix; Frey, *art. cit., Dict. de la Bible*, Suppl. I, 36-38; Peterson, *Encicl. Cattolica* I, 122-23; B. J. Bamberger, "Abraham, Testament of," *IDB* 1, 21; Denis, *op. cit.*, 35-37.

H. Box considered it "essentially Jewish" and "entirely free of Christian influence". He dated the original Hebrew and the revised Greek Alexandrian versions in the first century. B. J. Bamberger holds that it was composed in Hebrew or Aramaic by a Jew; he notes that "this apocryphon is generally dated in the first century of the Christian era", though "the Greek texts contain some Hellenistic additions." Charles Fishburne [134] considers it a thoroughly Jewish work of the first half of the 1st century A.D. J.-B. Frey judged: written in Hebrew or Aramaic in the 1st or 2nd century; as a whole the spirit and conceptions are Jewish, though some passages (especially in recension A) coincide verbatim with the N.T. J.E.H. Thomson considered it pre-Christian Jewish midrash translated from Aramaic by a 2nd century Christian. Denis thinks an Egyptian Jewish Christian of the 1st or 2nd century built upon a Hebrew work. For Nigel Turner [135] it is a 1st century B.C. Egyptian Jewish work tinged with mystical occultism and Christianized by medieval scribes. James presented considerable evidence for its authorship by a second century Egyptian Jewish Christian using earlier Jewish legends, though the work didn't receive its final from until the 9th or 10th century. Erik Peterson believes that the material is partly of Jewish and Christian origin and that some was borrowed from the Apocalypse of Paul. The latter opinion was set forth by R. P. Casey, T. Silverstein and in a qualified form by James. Schürer thought it a product of Christian legend-making.

The Apostolic Constitutions (vi, 16) mention among the Old Testament pseudepigrapha the books "of three patriarchs." "No one but Abraham, Isaac and Jacob can be meant by the three patriarchs" (cf. Act. Andr. et Matth. 16), as James pointed out.[136] Frey [137] believed that the Testaments of Isaac and Jacob were composed on the model of that of Abraham. Apart from a few Christian features, he observed, the veneration of the patriarchs and the promises made to those who honor them shows that the origin of the writings was

---

[134] "I Corinthians III. 10-15 and the Testament of Abraham," *NTS* 17 (1970), 112-15.

[135] "The 'Testament of Abraham': Problems in Biblical Greek," *NTS* 1 (1955), 219-23.

[136] *Art. cit., Texts and Studies* ii 2, 11, 155; Box (*The Apocalypse of Abraham*, London [SPCK, 1918], xviii) concurs. Arabic extracts translated by W. E. Barnes appear in *Texts and Studies* ii-2, Appendix; pp. 140-51 for the T. Isaac and pp. 152-54 for T. Jacob (hereafter quoted as "Arabic").

[137] *Art. cit., Dictionnaire de la Bible*, Supplement, I, 38.

Jewish. The Testament of Isaac, which has survived in Coptic, Arabic and Ethiopic translations, is a 2nd or 3rd century Jewish work with Christian traces, opines Gaetano Stano.[138] P. Estelrich [139] concurs: a 2nd or 3rd century Jewish work with allusions to N.T. passages. James found in the Arabic version of the Testament of Isaac evidence of Essene influence and of the Alexandrian Liturgy. He thought the conclusion inevitable that "the writer, whether identical or not with the author of the Testament of Abraham, was acquainted with that book." [140] He held, further, that the Testaments of Isaac and Jacob "have been to some extent Christianized." [141] Specific references to "Jesus Christ" in both Testaments' texts, we would add, are better evidence of Christian transmission than of origin. S. Gaselee [142] wrote "the violent treatment to which the *Testaments* (more especially the *Testament of Jacob*) have been subjected, lies a long way behind their present Coptic form." James [143] thought that the texts of the T. of Jacob were abridged from a longer original. Genesis 49 was the point of departure for the author. The prophecy in the Testament of Isaac that God shall abide on Jesus "until 100 years be fulfilled" is ancient.[144] Denis,[145] however, dismisses the two Testaments as late Christian legends.

The Testament of Job, according to Kohler, was a midrash which "originated in pre-Christian circles of Hellenistic Jews belonging to the Essene brotherhood"; more specifically, among Therapeutae, "in the outskirts of Palestine in the land of Hauran." [146] Nigel Turner [147] affirms its Jewish, but non-Essene, origin in Hebrew in the 2nd c.B.C. Mathias Delcor [148] concurs on its Jewish origin, but dates it 40

---

[138] *Encicl. Cattolica* 7, 231.

[139] *Encicl. de la Biblia* 4 (1964), 220.

[140] Apocryph., Anecdota, *Texts and Studies* 5 (1897), 155-61.

[141] *Ibid.*, lxxxiii.

[142] Box, *The Testament of Abraham*, 56. The Coptic translations appear in this book (pp. 57-75, "I. The Testament of Isaac"; pp. 76-89, "II. The Testament of Jacob"); hereafter references shall be given as, "Coptic, p. 00."

[143] *Lost Apocrypha of the Old Testament*, 18.

[144] P. 143 (Arabic); see David Flusser, "Salvation Present and Future," *Numen* 16 (1969), 139-55.

[145] *Op. cit.*, 34; with bibliography on this opinion, 34, n. 20.

[146] "The Testament of Job," in *Semitic Studies in Memory of Rev. Dr. Alexander Kohut*, ed. George Alex. Kohut, Berlin (S. Calvary, 1897), 287, 295. Quotations will be drawn from this translation.

[147] "The Testament of Abraham," in *Problems in Biblical Greek in N.T. Studies*, i, 3 (1955), 219-24.

[148] "Le Testament de Job, la prière de Nabonide et les traditions targoumiques," in *Bibel und Qumran* ed. Siegfried Wagner, 72-74.

B.C. and concedes the presence of a few Essene traits; he finds a two-way relationship with the LXX. D. Rahnenführer [149] deems it a 1st century B.C. or A.D. Jewish Hellenistic work with no Christian influence. I. Jacobs [150] agrees it is Hellenistic, but he dates it 1st or 2nd century B.C. Russel P. Spittler [151] judges chh. 1-45 a Greek writing of ca. 40 B.C. by the Therapeutae edited by the Montanists, who added chh. 46-52. Philonenko [152] detects a Therapeutae milieu; he and Danielou [153] concur that it is a 1st c. A. D. Egyptian Jewish writing. F. Spitta [154] argued for its origin in pre-Christian Judaism and its influence on Christianity and the N.T. P. Riessler [155] judged it a 1st c.B.C. Hebrew Essene work. Robert Pfeiffer [156] and C. C. Torrey [157] believed it was written in Aramaic in the 1st c.B.C. and was soon translated into Greek, apparently in Egypt. The religious teaching of the book is characteristic of the Hasidim(Assideans), or strict Jews, living some years after the publication of Daniel," Pfeiffer wrote.[158] Analyzing the Testament's best witness (P), S. P. Brock [159] detects Christian interpolations in an originally Jewish work. Noting its Essene traits, R. Meyer [160] finds it a Christian reworking of a Hebrew work. James deduced that the Christian author was a Jew by birth and that his sources were wholly Jewish. Living in 2nd or 3rd century Egypt, he "put into Greek a Hebrew Midrash on Job" without Christianizing it. Frey essentially agreed: its sentiments are Jewish, with no specifically Christian traces; it was written in Egypt in Greek not later than the 2nd c. if (as James believed) Tertullian (de patientia 13) alluded to it. J.A.G.-Larraya,[161] accepting the Tertullian reference,

---

[149] "Das Testament des Hiob und das Neue Testament," ZNTW 62 (1971), 68-93.

[150] "Literary Motifs in the Testament of Job," Journal of Jewish Studies 21 (1970), 1-10.

[151] In his Harvard 1971 Ph. D. Thesis, The Testament of Job. Introduction, translation and notes, 33, 46-52, 65, 70.

[152] Le Testament de Job (Semitica 18), Paris, 1968, 12, 16, 24.

[153] Art. cit., Recherches de Science Religieuse 58 (1970), 125.

[154] Zur Geschichte und Litteratur des Urchristentums, Göttingen (Vandenhoeck & Ruprecht), III, 2 (1907), 139-206; bibliography, pp. 142-43.

[155] Altjüdisches Schrifttum ausserhalb der Bibel, Darmstadt, 1966 repr., 1333.

[156] History of New Testament Times, New York (Harper & Bros.), 1949), 70.

[157] The Aprocryphal Literature, New Haven (Yale Univ., 1945), 145.

[158] Op. cit., 72.

[159] Testamentum Iobi, Leiden (E. J. Brill, 1967), 8. W. Bousset and P. Volz held likewise.

[160] "Hiobtestament," RGG 3 (1959), 361.

[161] Encicl. de la Biblia 4 (1965), 577.

and Francesco Spadafore [162] think it was written by a 2nd c. Jew.
Schürer, however, held that its origin and author were Christian.
Conybeare [163] observed: "The Testament of Job is composed in the
same sort of Greek as the Testaments of the Patriarchs, and has also
features in common with the Book of Adam as preserved in old
Armenian." Box [164] called attention to its marked affinities with the
Testament of Abraham.

Akin to the Testament of Job is the romance, Joseph and Aseneth.
Its recent investigators (K. G. Kuhn, C. Burchard, M. Philonenko, A.-
M. Denis),[165] judging from the fresh perspective of the Qumran
literature, concur that it is an Egyptian Jewish writing produced in
Greek in the 1st c. A.D. by the Therapeutae or related group. M.
Delcor dissents only in dating it in the previous century and
supposing an underlying Hebrew legend. Earlier Riessler had
identified it as an Essene Hebrew Egyptian work dated between the
Maccabees and 70 A.D. G.D. Kilpatrick and J. Jeremias also prefer a
pre-Christian date, 100- 30 B. C. Denis agrees with Burchard in
making it contemporary with the New Testament.

The Testament of Adam, which is known in somewhat divergent
forms [166] in Syriac, Arabic, Greek and Ethiopic fragments, was
considered to be of Elkesite (Sabian, Mandean) origin by Ernest
Renan. He, Hort and James [167] thought the Testament, Apocalypse
and Penitence of Adam to be identical, or to represent different
recensions, or to contain much common material; Frey disagreed,
and E. Peterson [168] thinks the question obscure. The latter dated the
document in the 5th or 6th century. Hort and Renan, assuming
Epiphanius' knowledge of it, dated it not later than the 4th century.
F. Nau's opinion that the first fragment was originally part of a
talismans book by Apollonius of Tyana, was rejected by James, Frey
and Peterson. James and Frey dated its ideas and sources in the first
or second century. Frey, Denis and J. A. G.-Larraya [169] have found

---

[162] *Encicl. Cattolica* 6, 414.

[163] "The Testament of Job and the Testaments of the Twelve Patriarchs," *JQR* 13
(1900-01), 111. Philonenko (*Le Testament de Job*, 13, 21) finds literary dependence of
the Testaments of the Twelve Patriarchs on the Testament of Job.

[164] *Testament of Abraham*, xxvii-viii.

[165] Bibliography in Denis, *op. cit.*, 44-47. Philonenko suggests 100 A.D. in his
commentary (p. 109).

[166] Frey, *art. cit.*, 118-19; bibliography, pp. 117, 124.

[167] *Lost Apocrypha of the Old Testament*, 1-8.

[168] *Encicl. Cattolica* 1, 278-79.

[169] *Encicl. de la Biblia* 1, 154.

both Christian and Jewish elements. Hort and Frey denied Gnostic
origins, though Hort said that it "appears to lie outside Greek and
Latin Christianity." [170] L. S. A. Wells [171] thought the Apocalypse-
Testament was Christian Gnostic and borrowed from the Apocalypse
of Moses, chh 36-40. There is much scholarly uncertainity as to
whether all fragments should be connected with Adam.

The Greek Apocalypse of Moses and the Latin Life of Adam and
Eve (*Vita Adae*) are closely related. A common source has been
generally assumed, though C. Fuchs and Wells believed that a
condensed form of the Apocalypse of Moses was combined with
other Jewish legends to form the *Vita*. The Armenian, Slavonic,
Syriac, Ethiopic and Arabic versions are in various degrees
Christianized and based on additional sources. That the original,
basic source was a first century Aramaic or Hebrew document
recording Haggada [172] has been the opinion of W. Bousset, L.
Ginzberg, W. Meyer, C. Fuchs, R. Kabisch, Frey, R. Pfeiffer, Torrey
and B. J. Bamberger. [173] O. Eissfeldt [174] considers probable a Hebrew
document written while Herod's temple was standing. Wells thought
parts may be based on Hebrew documents and the Septuagint and
that the pre-Christian Jewish original (of which the Apocalypse of
Moses is a slightly revised version) was written in Greek in
Alexandria. Charles [175] commented: "If the author was an
Alexandrian Jew, he must have drawn on Hebrew or Aramaic
sources." L. Wells and Charles [176] deduced dependence on 2 Enoch,
or at least its school of origin. Wells further held that the Testament
of Abraham derived much material from the Books of Adam and
Eve. Matthew Black [177] finds that universal final judgment by fire
(*Vita Adae* 49:2) is an Essene doctrine. John Scobie [178] thinks
penance in the Jordan by Adam and Eve suggests origin in a Baptist

---

[170] "Adam, Books of," *DCB* 1 (1877), 38b.

[171] "The Books of Adam and Eve," in Charles, *The Apocrypha and Pseudepigrapha
of the Old Testament*, Oxford, 1913, ii, 125-26.

[172] According to Torrey (*op. cit.*, 133), "The haggada closely resembles that which
has so important a part in Jubilees and the Testaments of the Twelve Patriarchs."

[173] Bibliographies in Frey, *art. cit.*, 106; Peterson, *Encicl. Cattolica* 1, 279-80;
Bamberger, "Adam, Books of," *IDB* 1, 45; Denis, *op. cit.*, 6-7.

[174] *Op. cit.*, 636-37.

[175] *The Apocrypha and Pseudepigrapha of the O.T.*, II, 130n.

[176] *The Book of the Secrets of Enoch*, xviii.

[177] "The Dead Sea Scrolls and Christian Origins," in *The Scrolls and Christianity*,
ed. Black, London (SPCK, 1969), 105.

[178] *Op. cit.*, 36; cf. 116.

sect. Rost detects an origin at the end of the 1st c. B.C. in ascetic, possibly Essene, circles of Palestine. E. Preuschen's argument for a Sethian Gnostic origin for interpolations (especially in the Armenian version) has not won acceptance or support. While Ginzberg and Kabisch denied Christian tampering with the Apocalypse of Moses or *Vita*, Wells, Fuchs, Meyer, Torrey, Bamberger Eissfeldt and Denis have acknowledged the existence of some Christian interpolations, at least in the *Vita*. Though Schürer [179] acknowledged the possibility of a Jewish *Grundschrift*, he thought the traces of Hebrew very uncertain. He and O. Stählin found nothing specifically Jewish and looked for a Christian author, or at least editor. Peterson finds traditions of diverse Judaic and Christian origin, with no literary unity.

Evaluations of the Apocalypse of Abraham are rather uniform. Chapters 1-8 are early Jewish haggadic midrash by almost universal agreement. Ginzberg saw the first part as a purely Jewish composition of before 50 A.D., and chh. 9-32 as a product of the last decades of the 1st century which has been subjected to Christian and Sethian interpolations (e.g. through the Apocalypse in the name of Abraham possessed by the Sethians: Epiphanius, *Haer* 39, 5.1). The book as a whole was written in Hebrew or Aramaic in Palestine, thought Ginzberg. James thought it a Jewish work with Christian insertions which Sethians probably used. G. Scholem [180] thinks it a late 1st c. esoteric Jewish work written in Hebrew. For Pfeiffer it was a partly Christian, but largely Jewish, 1st century Aramaic work. Bardenhewer judged it a 2nd century A.D. basically Jewish writing slightly edited by a Christian and known to the author of Clementine Recognitions I, 32. G. Beer thought only cf. 29 to be Christian. Schürer considered it a Jewish apocalypse edited (at least in ch. 29) by a Christian. According to Frey, [181] the first eight chapters are 1st century Jewish, while the rest is a bizarre Jewish apocalypse of the end of that century with a Christian interpolation in ch. 29. Hebrew or Aramaic was the original language. Kohler thought it was written

---

[179] *Geschichte des jüdischen Volkes im Zeitalter Jesu Christi*, Leipzig (J. C. Hinrichs), iii (1909), 396-99.

[180] *Jewish Gnosticism, Merkabah Mysticism and Talmudic Tradition*, New York (Jewish Theol. Seminary, 1960), 23-24, 42.

[181] Bibliographies in Frey, *art. cit.*, 30, 32-33; Peterson, *Encicl. Cattolica* 1 (1948), 122; *The Oxford Dictionary of the Christian Church*, ed. F. L. Cross, London (Oxford Univ., 1958), 7; Bamberger, "Abraham, Apocalypse of," *IDB* 1, 21; Denis, *op. cit.*, 37-39.

in Hebrew or Aramaic soon after 70, and later the latter chapters were intermingled with Christian and Gnostic elements. R. Meyer [182] finds it a Christian reworking of a Hebrew or Aramaic work of the beginning of the 2nd c. A.D. which has a Qumranian angelology. Arie Rubinstein [183] writes: "Several words and phrases ... bear a striking resemblance to linguistic usages peculiar to the Dead Sea Scrolls"; the Palestinian Hebrew original underwent early Jewish Christian interpolation. G. H. Box [184] concluded that it was "composed in Hebrew, with a slight admixture of Aramaic" between 70 A.D. and the first decades of the second century. Its "character, as a whole, is thoroughly Jewish". It is "an Essene production" which "would have appealed to Jewish-Christians in Palestine" and may have been used and slightly modified by Christian Gnostics. It is explicitly referred to in *Clem. Rec.* I, 32, Box claimed. Peterson also views it as a late first century Jewish work with a tendency to gnostic speculation; ch. 29 was revised by a Christian gnostic. B. J. Bamberger finds it a Jewish apocryphon written originally in Hebrew or Aramaic "at the end of the first or beginning of the second Christian century"; it has "quasi-Gnostic touches", and the obscure final chapters "contain manifestly Christian insertions." Bonwetsch imagined that it was written by a Christian before the time of Pseudo-Clement and that the legends which he used in the first eight chapters were mainly of Jewish origin, while those in the rest of the work were Jewish, Christian and gnosticizing. J. Felten thought that it received its Christian and probably Gnostic form between 70 A.D. and the reign of Hadrian; a Jewish writing might underlie it. H. Weinel detected a 2nd century Jewish Christian Gnostic author.

Early 5th century Coptic manuscript fragments, according to the editor, G. Steindorff, [185] contain three apocalypses: one anonymous, one of Zephaniah, and one of Elijah, which was a Christian revision of the one known to Origen (*Comm. in Matth.* xxvii, 9). This Coptic Apocalypse of Elijah has some striking parallels in a Hebrew Apocalypse of Elijah edited by M. Buttenweiser; both he and Bousset

---

[182] "Abraham-Apocalypse", *RGG* 1 (1957), 72.
[183] "Hebraisms in the Slavonic 'Apocalypse of Abraham,'" *Journal of Jewish Studies* 4 (1953), 108; 5(1954), 135.
[184] *The Apocalypse of Abraham*, x, xv-xvii, xx-xxiii.
[185] *Die Apokalypse des Elias, eine unbekannte Apokalypse und Bruckstücke der Sophonias-Apokalypse* (TU 17, 3a), Leipzig (J. C. Hinrichs, 1899); bibliographies in Schürer, *op. cit.*, iii, 369; W. Schneemelcher, "Later Apocalypses," Hennecke-Schneemelcher, *op. cit.*, ii, 752; Denis, *op. cit.*, 166-69, 192-93.

pointed them out. Buttenweiser dated the original, more lengthy text in 261 A.D. in Palestine; it was edited in the 6th and 7th centuries. Schürer thought the Anonymous Apocalypse belongs to the Coptic Zephaniah Apocalypse and that this may be connected with the quotation by Clement of Alexandria (*Strom.* v, 11.77) [186] from a Book of Sophonias. Moreover, the Coptic Elijah fragments are more to be associated with the Zephaniah Apocalypse than with the ancient Elijah Apocalypse known to Origen. This Schürer believed to be a pre-Pauline Jewish apocalypse possibly interpolated by a Christian, whereas the Coptic Elijah is an independent 3rd or 4th century Christian work. According to James, the abridged and interpolated Hebrew Elijah Apocalypse is probably connected with the Jewish work quoted by Origen, Epiphanius (*Haer.* 42, 1), the encratite Epistle of Titus and the two Testaments of the Lord Jesus Christ. The Coptic Elijah and Zephaniah Apocalypses are Christianized, and the latter is probably identical with the one quoted by Clement. Bardenhewer, however, upheld the Christian origin of the Elijah Apocalypse known to Origen; the Coptic Elijah, he held, was a later Christian work unknown to Origen, though possibly based on Jewish traditions; the Coptic Zephaniah Apocalypse was Christian and lacks Clement's quotation. Frey thought that the Elijah Apocalypse known to Origen was probably Jewish and that the Anonymous one was part of a 2nd century Jewish Apocalypse of Zephaniah. Possibly a rather early Jewish Apocalypse of Elijah underlay all the texts, including the Apocalypse of Zephaniah, Frey suggested. F. Spadafora concurs with him, and adds that the Jewish Elijah Apocalypse was mentioned in *Apost. Const.* vi, 16. According to G.-Larraya,[187] the Apocalypses of Elijah and Zephaniah probably formed part of one anonymous apocalypse composed by a 2nd or 3rd century Jew. We would add that the words of 1 Cor. 2:9 which Origen found in the Elijah Apocalypse reappear in the Encratite mid-2nd century Acts of Peter 39(10) and the Gospel of Thomas 17 [188] and in the Acts of Thomas, ch. 36. The latter (chh. 55-58) and the Apocalypse of Peter contain the earliest Christian descriptions of the torments of hell: a subject of

---

[186] J. Ruwet," Clement d'Alexandrie, canon des Écritures et Apocryphes", *Biblica* 29 (1948), 248-251.

[187] *Encicl. de la Biblia* 6 (1966), 788.

[188] See H.-Ch. Puech, "The Gospel of Thomas," Hennecke-Schneemelcher, *op. cit.*, i (1963), 300.

which "the prophet Elijah bears witness in a vision" (Epistle of Titus).[189]

The Greek Apocalypse of Baruch (3 Baruch) was known to Origen (de princip. ii, 3.6). Ginzberg [190] saw it as a Jewish Gnostic work of the beginning of the 2nd century. The author "revered equally the Haggadah, Greek mythology and oriental wisdom," including that of India. "The author was not a Pharisee, since the Pharisees opposed dedidedly such doubtful angel-lore." "Only one passage (ch. 4) can with certainty be considered a Christian interpolation." H. M. Hughes [191] detected a Jewish original near the beginning of the second century; the author's Judaism was tempered by Hellenic-oriental syncretism." The Christian redactor (chh. 11-17) was dated soon after 136. Connections with 2 Enoch and the History of Zosimus are pointed out. James [192] concluded that it was a Christian apocalypse of the 2nd century. That it was a 2nd century Jewish composition edited by a Christian is the opinion of Beer, Torrey, [193] G. Stano [194] (1st decades of 2nd c.), D. S. Russell,[195] Denis and the author of the article in the Oxford Dictionary of the Christian Church. Riessler, J.-C. Picard [196] and Danielou [197] concur, without suggesting a date.

The Lives of the Prophets is a collection of Jewish legends which supplement or embellish scriptural accounts. Theodor Schermann, while admitting the possibility of a Hebrew Grundschrift (as advocated by H. A. Hamaker), viewed it as a Greek Jewish writing emanating from 1st century Palestine and containing subsequent Christian interpolations. Torrey, Pfeiffer and Denis [198] have agreed, except for their affirmative conclusion that Hebrews was the original language. J. Jeremias [199] finds Christian interpolation in a Hebrew or

---

[189] Hennecke-Schneemelcher, op. cit., ii, 158; cf. Denis, op. cit., 169.

[190] "Apocalypse of Baruch (Greek)," Jewish Encyclopedia 2 (1902), 549-50.

[191] In Charles, The Apocrypha and Pseudepigrapha of the O.T. ii, 527.

[192] Apocrypha Anecdota, Texts and Studies v-l (1897), lxxi.

[193] "Apocalypses", Jewish Encyclopedia 1 (1901), 674.

[194] Encicl. Cattolica 2, 937; see bibliography.

[195] The Method and Message of Jewish Apocalyptic, Philadelphia (Westminster, 1964), 65.

[196] Apocalypsis Baruchi Graece, Leiden (E. J. Brill, 1967), 75-78.

[197] Art. cit., Recherches de Science Religieuse 58 (1970), 125.

[198] Op. cit., 89-90. Bibliography in ibid., 85-90; also in Pfeiffer, op. cit., 66, n. 6.

[199] Heiligengräber in Jesu Umwelt, Göttingen (Vandenhoeck & Ruprecht, 1958), 12.

Aramaic work of before 70 A.D. T. Schermann [200] conjectured that this work (Recension A) and the Testaments of the Twelve Patriarchs were interpolated by the same Patripassionist Christian. De Jonge [201] also notes resemblances to the Testaments and detects a Jewish Christian redactor. J. Schoeps [202] thinks that the Jerusalem *Urgemeinde* turned a *Grundstamm* (a collection of traditions) into a prophetic florilegia book for polemical use.

Torrey specified the time of origin as the 3rd quarter of the 1st century; the author was a man of Jerusalem, though he incorporated Christianized Egyptian folklore concerning Jeremiah. The Armenian version [203] refers to the destruction and desolation of Jerusalem (Jonah [Greek also], Zechariah) and the Temple (Habakkuk [Greek also], Zephaniah, Zechariah) by a western nation (Habakkuk [Greek also]), the worship of the Lord in Jerusalem by converts from all nations (Jonah, Zephaniah, Zechariah) and the pending end of the world (Jonah). This may be an historical reference to the rebuilding of Aelia Capitolina in 138 or, more likely, to the entrance of Gentile believers into the new heavenly Jerusalem.

The Fourth Sibylline Oracle was "almost certainly written in the Maeander Valley or not far from it." There is good reason for accepting this conclusion of Sherman E. Johnson.[204] Lines 107-08 tell of the destruction of the of Laodicea (in 60 A.D.), while lines 149-54 emphasize the Maeander River. The command to "wash your bodies in running streams" presupposes their availability nearby. Rome stole the wealth of Asia, but it shall be returned manifold (145-49). Other areas of Asia or the province itself are also of interest: lines 76-79, 97-101 and 109 and 109-13. The Carians, a people of Asia, "shall inhabit Tyre" (90). Italy is "the West" (103, 137), while Egypt is scarcely mentioned (72-76).[205] Most significant is the otherwise unknown explanation (115, 125) of "Jerusalem (Hierosolyma)" as

---

[200] *Propheten und Apostellegenden* (TU 31, 3), Leipzig (J. C. Hinrichs, 1907), 120-21.

[201] "Christelijke elementen in de Vitae Prophetarum, "*Nederlands Theol. Tijdschrift* 16 (1961), 161-78.

[202] *Aus frühchristlicher Zeit*, Tübingen, 1950, 131-32.

[203] Jacques Issaverdens, *The Apocryphal Writings of the Old Testament*, Venice (St. Lazarus, 1900), 186-91.

[204] "Laodicea and its Neighbors," *Biblical Archaeologist* 13 (1950), 17; also "Stray Pieces of Early Christian Writing," *Journal of Near Eastern Studies* 5 (1946), 52. An origin in Asia Minor has been upheld also by J. B. Lightfoot, Hort, Frey, M. Simon and Denis.

[205] Nevertheless, an Egyptian origin has been accepted by Torrey and Noack.

derived from Solyma, a sacred mountain in Lycia. The Jerusalemites seem to be identified with the tribe of Solymi.[206] Justin, who spent some time in Ephesus after he was converted to Christianity there from discovery of fulfillment of prophecies, was the first writer (Apol. I, 20 cf. I, 44) to quote the Fourth Oracle (172-77, concerning the world destruction by fire).

The date can be pinned down rather precisely. Jerusalem and the Temple have been destroyed (115-19, 125-27); the return of Nero is expected (119-24, 137-39); a great earthquake has rocked Cyprus (dated by Eusebius in 76 A.D.) (128-29, 143-44); and, Vesuvius has erupted (130-36). A date of around 80-81 A.D. is almost universally recognized. The Oracle contains nothing specifically Christian, while the evidence that it was written by a Hebrew is strong. The unrighteous are described in lines 25-39; in 135-36 they are called "the blameless people of God," though the folly of the militaristic Zealots is attacked (117-18). The eschatological expectations could be Jewish or Christian. Schürer[207] observed that "it would be hardly possible for a Christian writer to avoid mentioning Christ when writing an eschatology." Thus he rejected the opinion prevailing until a century ago and revived by Johnson,[208] who thinks it could be Christian. An Essene origin has been upheld by Hilgenfeld, Lightfoot and Charles. Ewald, Friedländer and Joseph Thomas[209] held it arose in a Jewish sect with baptist and Essene tendencies or principles.

II Enoch (the Slavonic Book of the Secrets of Enoch) was dated by Charles and N. Forbes: 30 B.C.-70 A.D.; its orthodox, syncretistic Egyptian Jewish author(s) drew upon the Hebrew original of 1 Enoch. It was cited by the Testaments of Levi, Dan and Naphtali, the Book of Adam and Eve, Clement's Apocalypse of Zephaniah, the Epistle of Barnabas, Origen (de Princip. i, 3, 2) and the Zohar, believed Charles and Forbes. Bonwetsch concurred that it was a Jewish Greek composition, but rejected evidence for a Hebrew original underlying some sections. Enno Littmann detected one

---

[206] Montanus named Pepuza and Tymion (Phrygian towns) "Jerusalem" (Apollonius ap. Eusebius, H. E. v, 18. 1). Jewish legends associated Noah and Apamea, Enoch and Iconium (G. Kittel, "Das kleinasiatische Jüdentum in der hellenistisch römischen Zeit," TLZ 69 (1944), 15-16.

[207] Op. cit. (A History of the Jewish People in the Time of Jesus Christ, New York (Charles Scribner's Sons, 1891), ii-iii, 285; cf. H. C. O. Lanchester, "The Sibylline Books," in Charles, The Apocrypha and Pseudepigrapha of the O.T.., ii, 373.

[208] Art. cit., Journal of Near Eastern Studies 5 (1946), 285.

[209] Le Mouvement Baptiste en Palestine et Syrie, Paris (Gembloux, 1935), 46-49.

Egyptian Jewish author of 50 B.C.-70 A.D. writing in Greek, but perhaps basing parts on Hebrew originals; a few interpolations were made, he held. Frey [210] thought it written by a pious Jew in Palestine in Hebrew or Aramaic between 30 and 70 A.D. before being translated in Egypt before the end of the century; direct dependence on 1 Enoch was denied. E. de San Marco largely agrees. L. Gry,[211] in a study of angels' names, argued strongly for an Egyptian Jewish author who knew Hebrew and Aramaic; the Christian interpolator "des premiers âges" knew the same languages. Schürer, Beer, F. R. Tennant, Felten and Plöger have thought there may have been Christian interpolations; Loisy disagreed. Schürer noted Hebrew month names, accepted dependance on 1 Enoch and dated 2 Enoch before 70 A.D. Rost envisions an Egyptian Jewish author of the first half of the 1st c. A.D., while Scholem detects the hand of a Hellenistic Jew of the second half of that century. Tennant admitted Palestinian and Alexandrian affinities. Bonwetsch, Plöger and Eissfeldt concur that it was written in Greek in Egypt before 70 A.D. Bousset saw it as a product of speculative, gnosticizing (but not anti-sacrificial Essene) Palestinian Judaism of 30-70 A.D. Pfeiffer viewed it as a Jewish, but partly Christian, 1st century A.D. work. On the other hand, a Christian origin has been upheld on the basis of its alleged implicit seventh century calendar (Mrs. Maunder, J. K. Fotheringham, F. C. Burkitt) and dependance on the Apocalypse of Peter (T. Silverstein). Eissfeldt admits its present form stems from the seventh century. Jean Danielou [212] judges it a Jewish Christian work from Syria at the end of the first century. A. Vaillant sees it as a Hellenistic, Jewish Christian continuation and counterpart of 1 Enoch; the author knew Hebrew and, like Hermas, imitated Jewish apocalyptic. The writing was later twice revised, according to Vaillant.

Ethiopic or 1 Enoch, was written in Aramaic, or partly in Hebrew and partly Aramaic, according to all past investigators.[213] This judgment is confirmed by the discovery of Aramaic fragments of 1 Enoch (but not of chh. 37-71) or its sources among the Dead Sea

---

[210] *Art. cit.*, 451-52; bibliographies pp. 453-54 and in E. de San Marco, *Encicl. Cattolica* 6, 1407; Russell, *op. cit.*, 61-62; D. Romano, *Encicl. de la Biblia* 3, 36, Eissfeldt, *op. cit.*, 622.

[211] "Quelques noms d'anges et d'etres mysterieux en II Enoch," *RB* 49 (1940), 203.

[212] *Op. cit.*, 27.

[213] Bibliographies in Frey, *art. cit.*, 357-71; H. H. Rowley, *The Relevance of Apocalyptic*, London (Lutterworth, 1947, 2nd ed.), 52ff., 75ff.; Grelot, *ap.* Massaux (ed.), *op. cit.*, 44-45; Russell *op. cit.*, 51-53.

Scrolls. Agreement is almost universal that it is a composite work. Its components have been dated as follows:

Chh. 6-36 (Angels and Universe):
Mid-3rd century B.C. (Milik)
Pre-Maccabean: Charles, Lagrange, Martin, Oesterley
175-164 B.C.: Frey
Soon after writing of Daniel: H. H. Rowley
Before 150 B.C. (O. Eissfeldt)
167-64 B.C. (B. Beer)
164-80 B.C. (Bousset)
133-100 B.C. (Schürer, Causse, Baldensperger)
100 B.C. (Pfeiffer)
110-80 B.C. (Klausner)
103-76 B.C. (Felten)
37-4 B.C. (C. Kaplan)

Chh. 37-71 (Similitudes or Parables):

164 B.C. (Frey)
Before 103 B.C. (Szekely)
100-76 B.C. (O. Holtzmann, Felten, Martin, L. Gry, Pfeiffer)
94-64 B.C. (Charles); 94-63 B.C. (Lods)
80-63 B.C. (Causse); 70-68 B.C. (Klausner)
Before 64 B.C. (Beer)
66-40 B.C. (Lagrange)
49-38 B.C. (E. Sjöberg, M. Black)
37-4 B.C. (Schürer, Baldensperger)
50 B.C.-50 A.D. (P. Volz)
30-70 A.D. (Grelot)
44-66 A.D. (Messel)
115-17 A.D. (J. C. Hindley)
Early Christian origin (Hoffmann, Weisse, Hilgenfeld, Volkmar, Philippi, Colani, Cornill, Koenig, E. Herstein, M. Vermes, Tideman)
Christian interpolations (Drummond, Pfleiderer, Messel, Lagrange, Grelot, Black, R Longenecker)
270 A.D. (Milik)

Chapters 72-82 (Astronomical Book):
Before 250 B.C. (Milik)
150-100 B.C. (Pfeiffer)
Before 110 B.C. (Charles)
110-80 B.C. (Klausner)

Chapters 93:1-10; 91:12-17 (Apocalypse of Weeks):
Pre-Maccabean (Beer, Charles, Martin, Szekely, Eissfeldt)
167-164 B.C. (Pfeiffer)
Shortly after Daniel (Causse)
163 B.C. (Pfeiffer)
152 B.C. (Lagrange)

48 SOURCES

Maccabean Age (Rowley)
Roman period (A. C. Welch)

Chapters 106-07 (Book of Noah):[214]

Before 161 B.C. (Charles)
100-80 B.C. (Pfeiffer)
Before 64 B.C. (Martin, Oesterley)
Christian interpolation (Lagrange)

The Dream Vision (Chapters 83-90) are usually dated between 164 and 95 B.C., while dates from 175 B.C. until the beginning of the Christian era have been suggested for chapters 94-105.

According to Charles,[215] (followed by Martin) "the sections belong to Chasids or to their successors the Pharisees." Klausner[216] believed that Enoch "came forth largely from the circle of the early Essenes." Its origin among the Essenes has been upheld by J. Thomson, E. Hammershaimb, Dupont-Sommer and Grelot.[217] Hilgenfeld found Essene influences except in the Christian gnostic Parables. Charles located "nine direct references" to 1 Enoch in the Testaments of the Twelve Patriarchs. He also called attention to the interdependence of Jubilees and various parts of 1 Enoch.[218]

The following dates have been suggested for Jubilees:[219]

Before 200 B.C. (Krüger, E. Meyer, Zeitlin, Albright)
175-167 B.C. (Finkelstein)
150 B.C. (Frey, Bohn, Russell)
Maccabean age (Rowley)
150-100 B.C. (J. Gutmann, Box, Pfeiffer, S. Tedesche)
135-104 B.C. (Bousset, Charles, Kohler)
135-67 B.C. (Klausner)
120-110 B.C. (S. Klein)
110 B.C. (M. Testuz)
Late 2nd c. (Martin)
100 B.C. (O. Holtzmann, Szekely, Eissfeldt)
63-50 B.C. (Baldensperger, Messel)
50-1 B.C. (Torrey)

---

[214] *Ibid.*, 51, n. 4; N. Schmidt, "The Apocalypse of Noah and the Parables of Enoch," in *Oriental Studies for Paul Haupt*, Baltimore (John Hopkins, 1926), 111-23.

[215] *The Book of Enoch*, Oxford (Clarendon, 1912), xi.

[216] *The Messianic Idea in Israel*, transl. W. F. Stinespring, London (George Allen & Unwin, 1956), 309.

[217] *Art. cit.* in Massaux, *op. cit.*, 48.

[218] *The Book of Jubilees*, London (Adam & Charles Black, 1902), lxviii-lxxi.

[219] Bibliographies in Frey, *art. cit.*, 375-76; J. Gutmann, *Encyclopaedia Judaica*, Berlin, 9 (1932), 507-08; Rowley, *op. cit.*, 84-85; Russell, *op. cit.*, 54.

Early 1st c. A.D. (Felten)
50-60 A.D. (Headlam, Rönsch)
58-60 A.D. (Singer)

The following authorship has been proposed:

Pharisee (Charles, Martin, Bousset, Littmann, Schürer, Pfeiffer; refuted by S.
    Schechter, Box)
Pharisee before complete break with Sadduccees (Klausner)
Strict Pharisee or Levite priest (Tedesche)
Levite priest (Torrey)
Sadduccee (Leszynsky)
Hasid or Sadduccee (Box)
Samaritan (Beer)
Sectarian (Büchler, Finkelstein)
Damascus Document sectarian (Gutmann)
Essene (Jellinek, Milik, Testuz, Eissfeldt, Rost)

The latter hypothesis gains some support from the discovery in three caves near Qumran of eleven fragments of Jubilees in Hebrew.[220] Likewise, the case for a Hebrew original (Schürer, Littmann, Charles, Rönsch, Box, Rost), rather than an Aramaic (Torrey, Pfeiffer), has been strengthened.

    This broad summary of scholarly opinion on the origin of Jewish apocrypha which are to be quoted, serves to illustrate the difficulty of identifying the type of Jewish influences on Paul's opponents (e.g. Essene, Pharisee, Hasidim, Therapeutae, Alexandrian, gnostic, apocalyptic). Sometimes these categories overlap.

    As all of these apocrypha are widely classified as "apocalyptic", the various theories[221] concerning the producers and readers of the apocalypses merit enumeration. The tracing of apocalypse to Old Testament prophecy by H. Rowley and W. Pannenberg gains some support from the intermediate figure of John the Baptist. Were they the esoteric literature of the rabbis (A. Schlatter, J. Jeremias)[222] or a gnosticizing, syncretistic outgrowth of the Wisdom literature (von Rad)? or from conventicles (P. Vielhauer)? or the folk literature of the "pious" poor (W. Baldensperger, A. Causse, M. Friedländer, Bousset,

---

[220] Reinhard Deichgräber, "Fragmente einer Jubiläen-Handschrift aus Höhle 3 von Qumran," *RQ* 5 (1967), 415-22; Maurice Baillet, "Remarques sur le manuscrit du livre des Jubilés de la Grotte 3 de Qumran," *RQ* 5 (1967), 423-33.
[221] Bibliographies in Frey, "Apocalyptique," *Dictionnaire de la Bible*, Supplement I (1928), 342; Grelot, "Apocalíptico," *Encicl. de la Biblia* I, 588; P. Vielhauer, "Apocalyptic," in Hennecke-Schneemelcher, *op. cit.*, ii, 597-98.
[222] The rabbis rejected apocalyptic, according to F. C. Burkitt (*Jewish and Christian Apocalypses*, London, 1914, 11-13); denied by Kohler, *art. cit.*, *JQR* N.S. 11 (1920), 145-47, 153-54.

E. Stauffer)? or the Pharisees (E. Kautzsch, S. Zeitlin),[223] or the Pharisees and their forerunners, the Chasids (Charles)? or the Essenes (Frankel, Graetz, Jost, Herzfeld, L. Loew, Jellinek, Hilgenfeld, Lucius, J. Thomson, Lagrange, Kohler, Ringgren)?[224] Frank Cross writes:[225]

> The Essenes prove to be the bearers, and in no small part the producers, of the apocalyptic tradition of Judaism ... Essene editions of certain apocalyptic works are based on sources composed in the Hasidic 'congregations' or like communities of Maccabean or pre-Maccabean era. Such an explanation evidently obtains in the case of the rich Daniel literature at Qumran, only a portion of which escaped later condemnation by Pharisaic Judaism.

D. S. Russell[226] believes "there are indications that in its origins Jewish apocalyptic was closely associated with the Hasidim," but "the apocalyptic writers were to be found ... throughout many parties, known and unknown, and among men who owed allegiance to no party at all." He conceded that, "If it can be proved that the Qumran Covenanters were a branch of the Essenes, then the argument for Essene influence on the apocalyptic writings is strengthened.[227] Oesterley[228] also believed that apocalyptic arose among the Hasidim.

If the first great apocalyptic book, Daniel, arose among the Hasidim,[229] then we should look among the spiritual descendants of the Hasidim for the writers of later apocalypses. The Hasidean origin of the Pharisees has been widely accepted (e.g. Friedländer, Wellhausen, Schürer, R. W. Moss, Guignebert, J. C. Dancy). Most of the scholars deriving the Essenes from the Hasidim (beginning with Hitzig, Ewald and Lucius)[230] have identified the latter with the *hasayya* or *Essaioi*, the Syriac and Greek terms for "the pious." J. T.

---

[223] Denied by R. T. Herford, *The Pharisees*, London, 1924, 180-85, 190-93 and Kohler, *art. cit.*, *JQR* N.S.11 (1920), 167-68. See W. D. Davies, *Christian Origins and Judaism*, Philadelphia (Westminster, 1962), 19-30.

[224] On the relation of apocalyptic to the Essenes and folk literature see Johann M. Schmidt, *Die jüdische Apokalyptic*, Neukirchen, 1969, 75-77, 139-42, 189-92, 297.

[225] *The Ancient Library of Qumran and Modern Biblical Studies*, Garden City, N.Y. (Doubleday, 1961), 198-200; cf. 44.

[226] *Op. cit.*, 23, 27.

[227] *Ibid.*, 24. For a bibliography on the question of the origin of the Qumran community in the Hasidean movement, see Edmund F. Sutcliffe, *The Monks of Qumran* Westminster, Md. (Newman, 1960), 253, n. 10.

[228] *A History of Israel*, Oxford (Clarendon, 1951), II, 319.

[229] On this movement see B. D. Eerdmans, "The Hasidim," *Oudtestamentische Studien* 1 (1942), 176-257.

[230] See p. 133.

Milik[231] did not identify Hasidim and Essenes, but envisioned a broad Hasidean movement from which Essenes emerged as exiles at Qumran. John Bright and Oesterley and Wayne G. Rollins[232] have traced both Essenes and Pharisees to the Hasidim. W. R. Farmer[233] writes: "The later Pharisees and Essenes probably developed out of rival wings of this postrevolutionary Hasidean party." S. Horodezky[234] suggested that the extremists joined the Essenes and the moderates united with the Pharisees. According to Matthew Black,[235] Pharisaism may have arisen when lay scribes "joined the ranks of the Hasidim during the Seleucid persecution", whereas during the reign of Hyrcanus the priestly wing of the Hasidim became the sect of the *hasayya*, or Essenes. Cross holds that "the Hasidic party broke into two wings": the Pharisees, who "represent the 'continuing' Hasidic movement" and "find a *modus vivendi* ... for a season with the Hasmoneans," rather than in apocalypticism; and, the Essenes "drawn especially from the Zadokite priesthood, together with some lay elements of strong apocalyptic bent" who separated "from the main body of their Jewish brethren."[236] Joseph Klausner[237] traced Pharisees, Essenes and Zealots to the Hasidim. We venture to define the Essenes as: priestly,[238] sectarian, monastic, ascetic, angel-venerating, apocalyptic Hasidim.

It is possible to trace a line of development from Tobit to Daniel to 1 Enoch, Jubilees and the Testaments of Levi and Naphtali (all of which have been found at Qumran in Hebrew or Aramaic) to the rest of the apocalyptic literature already described. Pfeiffer[239] wrote: "By example and by precept the Book of Tobit inculcates the noble religious and moral principles of Judaism of the first third of the second century B.C.", i.e. "of those devout Jews ... who were the precursors of the Pharisees." The incipient angelology, ascetism

---

[231] *Ten Years of Discovery in the Wilderness of Judaea*, transl. J. Strugnell, London (SCM, 1959), 80-82.

[232] "The New Testament and Apocalypse", *NTS* 17 (1971), 463-64. He rightly cautions that "apocalyptic" is a complex and ambiguous term (pp. 458-64).

[233] "Hasideans," *IDB* 2, 528.

[234] *Encyclopaedia Judaica* 5 (1928), 359.

[235] *The Scrolls and Christian Origins*, New York, Charles Scribner's Sons, 1961), 23-24.

[236] *Op. cit.*, 141, n. 66.

[237] *Op. cit.*, 202.

[238] Priestly legitimacy became less of an issue as hopes of recovering control of the Temple became more eschatological and when non-Zadokite recruits came to constitute a larger portion of the Essene communities.

[239] *Op. cit.*, 278, 284.

legalistic piety and mysteries of Tobit reappear in the Book of Daniel, which Pfeiffer [240] regarded as "the manifesto of the Hasidim, issued to encourage the pious Jews persecuted by Antiochus Epiphanes (168-165)." The Hasidim are apparently referred to in Dan. 11:33; 35; 12:3, 10 (cf. 1 Enoch 90:6-7; Macc. 2:42; 7:13).

Whether 1 Enoch, Jubilees and the Testaments of Levi and Naphtali should be labelled as "Essene" or "proto-Essene" or "Hasidean" or treated as products of the Qumran community depends in part upon chronological considerations. The prophecy of "Judas the Essene" during the reign of Aristobulus I(104-03 B.C.) is mentioned by Josephus (*Antiquities* xiii, 11.2; 311-13; *War* i, 3.4.78-80). The same historian (*Antiq.* xiii, 5.9.171) related toward the end of his account of the reign of the Hasmonean Jonathan (160-142 B.C.) that "at this time (κατὰ δὲ τὸν χρόνον τοῦτον) there were three sects (αἱρέσεις) of the Jews", the Pharisees, Sadduccees and Essenes. The religious rupture [241] was apt to have begun when Jonathan became high priest and officiated at the Feast of Tabernacles in 153(152) B.C. The following fifty years is the natural period in which to date the stages by which the Essenes, the Qumran Community, the Damascus Covenanters and other possible sectarians grew out of, or broke away from, the Assideans and Hasmoneans. The evidence of coins and paleography [242] points to the same period for the establishment of the Qumran community. For these reasons historical correlations by Milik,[243] E. F. Sutcliffe,[244] P. Winter [245] and G. Jeremias [246] or those of Cross [247] and G. Vermès [248] concerning Qumran document clues, are potentially convincing. Accordingly, if the Essenes were in the process of separating from their Jewish brethren in the decades following 153-52 B.C., then the earliest portions of 1 Enoch are likely to be (proto-) Hasidean. Several explanations are possible for

---

[240] *Introduction to the Old Testament*, New York (Harper & Bros., 1941), 773.

[241] Milik, *op. cit.*, 66, 83-87.

[242] Cross, *op. cit.*, 58-61, 118-22; "The Early History of the Qumran Community, "*McCormick Quarterly* 21(1968), 249-52; Sutcliffe, *op. cit.*, 37-39; but cf. G. R. Driver, *The Judaean Scrolls*, Oxford (Basil Blackwood, 1965), 410ff.

[243] *Op. cit.*, 47ff.

[244] *Op. cit.*, 42-57.

[245] "Two Non-allegorical Expressions in the Dead Sea Scrolls," *PEQ* 91 (1959), 43-46; "The Wicked Priest," *Hibbert Journal* 58 (1959-60), 53-60.

[246] *Der Lehrer der Gerechtigkeit*, Göttingen (Vandenhoeck & Ruprecht, 1963), 66-78.

[247] *Op. cit.*, 122ff.; *art. cit., McCormick Quarterly* 21 (1968), 261-64.

[248] *Cahiers Sioniens* 7 (1953), 71-74; *Discovery in the Judean ˉDesert*, New York (Desclée, 1956), 90-97.

the absence of later apocalypses (including the ten non-Semitic Testaments of the Patriarchs) from the Qumran library. Were they lost? Were they in oral form (like the Targums or the Gospels according to Matthew) before the destructive rebellion against Rome? Were they written by other spiritual descendants of the Hasidim? Were some written and read among the related Therapeutae of Egypt [249]? The Book of Tobit contains Egyptian traditions,[250] perhaps with the use of Palestinian Essene haggadah. Greek Septuagint manuscripts were found in the Qumran library.[251] The Egyptian Therapeutae had "writings of men of old, the founders of their way of thinking, who left many memorials of the form used in allegorical interpretation" (Philo, *de vita contemplativa* 29). Is this a bit of Philonic circumlocution referring to interpreting apocalyptic symbolism in the revelations and testaments attributed to Adam, Abraham, Isaac, Jacob, Enoch and Job? Or did the Therapeutae translate and edit Palestinian apocalypses?

The presence of some of the above described apocryphal writings in the Qumran library caves- and the absence of others-shed a bit of light on the question of origin of these apocrypha and the Qumran writings in the same Jewish sect. Many texts from the Caves could easily be from extraneous sources and be of extraneous authorship.[252] But their preservation with the rest of the library does indicate a certain acceptability of most of their teachings, and this compatibility further points to common roots. Matthew Black writes: "The later Essene sects were no doubt the descendants of the Hasidim, but the precious Hebrew documents they have preserved represents a large part of the surviving literature of the ancient Hasidim-in particular the literature of the priestly traditions of Israel".[253] The identity of the Qumran sectarian covenanters with Essenes has been generally

---

[249] For comparisons of Essenes and Therapeutae see A. Hilgenfeld, "Die jüdischen Sibyllen und der Essenismus," *Zeitschrift für wissenschaftliche Theologie* 1871, 50-59; W. H. Brownlee, "A Comparison of the Covenanters of the Dead Sea Scrolls with pre-Christian Jewish Sects," *Biblical Archaeologist* 13 (1950), 66-69; Stanley G. Luff, "The Monks of Qumran and St. Benedict's Rule: The Continuity of Monastic Tradition," *Dublin Review* 231 (1957), 313-21; Black, *op. cit.*, 16, 25, 45-47, 107-12; Driver, *op. cit.*, 121-24; bibliography in C. Spicq, "L'Épitre aux Hébreux, Apollos, Jean Baptiste, les Hellénistes et Qumran, *RQ* I (1958-59), 370, n. 30.
[250] Pfeiffer, *History of New Testament Times*, 275; A. Wikgren, "Tobit, Book of," *IDB* 4, 661.
[251] Cross, *op. cit.*, 192, n. 43.
[252] H. F. D. Sparks, "The Books of the Qumran Community," *JTS* 6 (1955), 226-28.
[253] *Op. cit.*, 21-22.

accepted by scholars through the work of E. L. Sukenik, Roland De Vaux, J. T. Milik, A. Dupont-Sommer, J. M. Allegro, F. M. Cross *et alia*. Acceptance of this identity has not been universal, however; among the dissenters are S. Zeitlin, M. H. Gottstein, S. Lieberman, N. Wieder, A. M. Habermann, C. Rabin, J. Teicher, Cecil Roth, H. E. del Medico, K. H. Rengstorf, G. R. Driver, I. Baer, L. Bronner and E. J. Pryke. As most of the evidence for the Essene origin of such apocryphal writings as Jubilees or the Testaments of the Twelve Patriarchs rests upon the assumption that the Qumran writings are Essene, caution is necessary in the use of the term, "Essene." Likewise, scholars noting striking resemblances between New Testament and Qumran literature usually make the facile assumption that the Qumran library was Essene.

The words of caution from B. Noack [254] are to heeded:

> The Essenes must, by virtue of the ancient accounts and the information given in them, be regarded as a larger religious current than the Qumran community. Consequently, I think we might speak of Essenic influence or of allusions to the Essenes, in the Sibylline Oracles and elsewhere, without surmising that the Qumran community is mentioned or that an alleged Essenic influence could, directly or indirectly, be traced back to Qumran.

W. H. Brownlee [255] has argued prudently that "The term 'Essene', as employed by Philo and Josephus, probably covers a multiplicity of small related sects, including the society at Khirbet Qumran." The *caveat* of F. F. Bruce [256] is equally pertinent:

> There are so many hints in ancient writings of a bewildering variety of messianic and baptist groups with their headquarters in the Jordan valley and Dead Sea region that we should be cautious before we can make a complete identification of two of these groups concerning which we are now better informed than we are about the others ... It seems clear that the term "Essenes" was a comprehensive one. Hippolytus distinguishes four parties of Essenes..., and there may have been other groups which were loosely designated by the same name.

J. T. Milik often pointed out that Essene institutions and teachings

---

[254] "Are Essenes Referred to in the Sibylline Oracles?", *Studia Theologica* 17 (1963), 101.

[255] *The Meaning of the Qumran Scrolls for the Bible*, New York (Oxford Univ., 1964), ix; see also Burrows, *More Light on the Dead Sea Scrolls*, 266, 273-74.

[256] *Second Thoughts on the Dead Sea Scrolls*, Grand Rapids, Mich. (Wm. B. Eerdmans, 1964), 134, 135.

evolved and included different tendencies. According to Leah
Bronner [257]

> Many scholars have wrongly identified the various groups with one of
> the well known and established sects...; Hamburger, like Kohler,
> maintains that all the minor factions were but the various splinter
> groups of which the Essene sect was composed.

We have the following Christian lists [258] of divisions within first
century Judaism (and Samaritanism):

Justin (Dial. 80)	Hegesippus (ap. Eusebius, H.E. iv, 22.4 & 7)	Epiphanius (Haer. 9-20)	Philaster (Haer.)	Ps.-Tertullian (Adv. omn. haer. 1)	Ephraem (Evang. Conc. appendix) [259]
		Scribes			
Pharisees	Pharisees	Pharisees	Pharisees	Pharisees	Pharisees
Sadducees	Sadducees	Sadducees	Sadducees	Sadducees	Sadducees
		Herodians	Herodians	Herodians	
Galileans	Galileans				Galileans
	Essenes	Essenes	Essenes		Essenes
		Ossenes			
Baptists	Hemerobaptists	Hemerobaptists			
		Nasaraeans			
Genistai					
Meristai					
Hellenians					Habionenses
					Mazbuthazi
	Masbotheans				Samaritans
	Samaritans	Samaritans (Sabaeans	Samaritans		
	Dositheans	Dositheans	Dositheus	Dositheus	
	Gorathenes	Gorothenes)			

Hegesippus treated the latter two as derivative sects, like followers of
Simon and Cleobius (cf. 3 Cor. ap. Acts of Paul). The lost Σύνταγμα
of Hippolytus probably underlies what is common to the lists of
Epiphanius, Philaster and Pseudo-Tertullian. Because Philo and
Josephus described only Essenes among the baptizing sectarians,
scholars are tempted to broaden the use of the term to include related
obscure groups, or to include Essenes and Qumranians in the larger
sectarian baptist or apocalyptic movement.

In so far as members of any of these groups honored Jesus but

---

[257] *Sects and Separatism during the Second Jewish Commonwealth*, New York
(Bloch, 1967), 117.
[258] Black, *op. cit.*, 49-54.
[259] Ed. Moesinger, pp. 287-88; ed. Leloir, p. 249.

retained objectionable traditional beliefs and practices, Christian heresiologists might view them more as still Jewish heretics than as new church members. Or at least they would be called by their former designations if they converted their Jewish heresy into a Christian heresy (cf. Acts 15:5; 23:6; Phil. 3:5).

The present writer shall try to avoid labelling in the process of presenting parallels between Paul's opponents, apocryphal Jewish literature, Qumran material and ancient literature descriptions of the Essenes. These parallels shall simply be assembled in individual sections, so that each reader may make his own comparisons and designations, if desired.

While the archaeological evidence overwhelmingly supports the identification of the Qumran community and nearby cave library as Essene, the accounts in Philo, Josephus, Hippolytus (and their sources-?) do not always correspond to the Qumran literature. The differences can be partially explained as stemming from insufficient information on the part of ancient writers and from "the Greek tinge and garment" [260] of Josephus and Philo. By identifying their way of life with that of the Pythagoreans, Josephus (*Antiquities* xv, 10.4) misled a number of scholars concerning its origin (Dollinger, Zeller, Schürer, Dietrich, Pfleiderer, Legge and M. I. Levy).[261] In the words of Christian D. Ginsburg,[262] their accounts "are manifestly shaped to exhibit the Jews to the cultivated Greeks in a Hellenistic garb." Or as Helmer Ringgren [263] rhetorically asks, "Has Josephus to some extent manipulated his reports of the teachings of the Essenes in order to make it more understandable and perhaps more appreciated by Greek readers?" The question is most pertinent in regard to eschatology: the resurrection of the dead (cf. Acts 17:32) and apocalyptic catastrophe (cf. 2 Pet. 3:4-7) associated with Messianic expectations (which could be understood to imply the overthrow of the Roman Empire). Josephus and Philo were eager to demonstrate the political loyalty of as many as possible of their coreligionists, especially if they were as apologetically attractive as the noble Essenes. It was sufficient, for these purposes, to laud their power of prophecy and knowledge of secret traditions, and to state their belief in divine determinism

---

[260] Schürer, *A History of the Jewish People...*, ii-ii, 214.
[261] Charles Guignebert, *The Jewish World in the Time of Jesus*, New Hyde Park, N.Y. (University Books, 1959), 175-76.
[262] "Essenes," *DCB* ii, 200.
[263] *Op. cit.*, 151.

(Josephus, *Ant.* xiii, 5.9.172).[264] Their potential militarism [265] was ignored, although Josephus did mention the activity of the Essene general, John (*War* ii, 20.4.557; iii, 2.1.11), and the torture of the Essenes (*War* ii, 8.10.152-55), during the Roman War.[266]

Whatever be the precise relation between the Essenes described in ancient accounts, and the inhabitants of Qumran, and members of the baptist movement, and those whose piety was shaped by apocalypses, the teachings and practices of all of these groups (considered individually) do provide ostensible parallels to those of Paul's opponents. To the extent that these parallels are considered adequately illustrative and to the extent that these groups are considered to belong to the same general non-conformist trend within Judaism, a contemporary pre-Christian stream of thought will have been identified as the major source for Paul's opponents. The classification and history of Judaic sectarianism is not an object of the following study; our purpose is simply to assemble possible and mostly previously noted specific parallels. The assumption is made that if a self-consistent current in Judaism is thus detected, then it is highly probable that Paul's opponents drew upon such a tendency and that many of its Jewish converts were previously sympathetic to this religious outlook. In other words, the advent of Christ crystallized and fulfilled their hopes and they interpreted his mission and person in the light of their earlier expectations. Christianization speeded the convergence of similar Judaic sectarian systems. Other Jews within the same general movement, of course, were more impressed by the deviations of the life and teachings of Jesus from their Messianic expectations, and they remained aloof from his new followers.

If Paul's opponents in 2 Cor., Gal., Rom. 16, Phil. 3 and Col. were Judaizers (an assumption which remains to be proved), then it is proper to inquire what sort of Judaism they subscribed to. If a detailed examination of Pauline epistles (individually or collectively

---

[264] Kohler, *art. cit., JQR* N.S. 11 (1920), 156, 158.

[265] According to Hippolytus (*Philos.* ix, 26), the Zealots were a sect of Essenes.

[266] Literary evidence connects the Qumran library and the defenders of Masada at the end of the war (Y. Yadin, "The Excavation of Masada—1963/64," *Israel Exploration Journal* 15 [1965], 105-08; *Masada*, New York (Random House, 1966), 173-74, 179; John C. Trever, "1Q Dan a. The Latest of the Q Mss.," *RQ* 7 (1970), 282-83; Danielou, *art. cit., Recherches de Science Religieuse* 58 (1970), 116. On Essene participation in the war see Athanase Negoïtsa, "Did the Essenes Survive the 66-71 War?", *RQ* 6 (1969), 517-19.

assessed) uncovers features which were peripheral to normative or rabbinic or Temple Judaism, then these features could be correlated in order to facilitate the identity of the current of Judaism represented by the Apostle's enemies. Not of all these sectarian features (dietary and sexual asceticism, angel veneration, angel Christology, secret revelations and mysteries, apocalyptic eschatology, baptisms, special laws of perfection, etc.) should be expected in every letter. The Pauline Gospel was more threatened by Judaizing (in respect to the Law, the old covenant, circumcision, holy days, purity, sacerdotalism, exclusivism at common meals, etc.) than it was by the sectarian features. If one or more of the sectarian features is detectable in a given epistle and if they cumulatively point to a coherent tendency in Judaism, then it is more likely that Paul's opponents in one epistle are identical with those in another, than it is that he fought on several fronts at once. If his opponents were united against him and if they invaded most of his churches, it would not be realistic to look for two or more distinct groups of rival Judaizing, sectarian "workman," with each attacked in a different epistle. And even if there were, it would still be proper to correlate and compare their teachings and practices. For this reason, at least, it is better to seek the maximum number of common denominators in available information about Paul's opponents, than to be satisfied with individual analyses for each Epistle. Whether such analyses be individual or correlative or both, it is essential to look for contemporary parallels in first and second century Judaism or Christianity.

CHAPTER TWO

JUDAIC LEGALISM

THE LAW

In Galatians is found Paul's foremost polemic against the Judaizers' gospel (1:7-9). They held that a man is justified, reckoned righteous before God and made alive by works of the law (2:16, 21; 3:11, 21; 5:4). The law rests on faith, they claimed; that is, legal obedience and righteousness depend on faith (3:12). Moreover, held Paul's opponents, to receive and to be led by the Spirit are inseparable from the requirement of subjection to the law (3:2, 5; 5:18, 23; 6:1-2).[1] They considered law and grace to be compatible (2:21; 5:4). The inheritance (κληρονομία) promised to Abraham and his offspring-heirs is received through keeping the covenant with Abraham and the law of Moses (3:17-18, 21, 29; cf. 4:30-31). From this it follows that it was by grace that Christ allegedly renewed the covenant based on law. The revelation of faith in Christ does not remove the law as teacher (3:23-25) and guardian (4:2) or redeem from servitude those who were under the law (4:1-5, 30-31). Paul's opponents relied on works of the law (3:10) and led the Galatian converts to desire (θέλοντες) to be under the law of the old covenant (4:21, 24). Paul thus saw them as enslaved to it and to its givers, the angels or στοιχεῖα of the world 3:19; 4:3, 5, 7-10, 24-25, 30-5:1). The Judaizers accused the Apostle of trying to please Gentiles and win their favor by preaching freedom through the Gospel of Christ (1:9-11; cf. 1 Cor. 10:33). In 2:5, 14 ἡ ἀλήθεια τοῦ εὐγγελίου refers to the liberty in Christ from bondage to the law. This freedom through faith, they charged, provides an opportunity for the flesh (5:13, 16ff.) and makes Christ an agent of sin (2:17-18). The law, they held, makes one alive and empowers him to avoid sin (3:21ff.). They sought to impose the law upon Gentile believers by stages; circumcision represented an important level (5:3; 6:13). The Pauline message related by Acts 13:38-39 as having been preached at Pisidian Antioch proved to be the point of attack: "by this man (Jesus) every one that believes is freed from everything from which you could not be freed by the law of Moses."

---

[1] H. Lietzmann, *Der Brief des Apostels Paulus an die Galater* (Handbuch z.N.T.), Tübingen (J. C. B. Mohr [Paul Siebeck], 1932, 3rd ed.), 39; Oostendorp, *op. cit.*, 36).

The Apostle warned the Colossians not to be moved away from the hope of the gospel (i.e. of being presented holy, blameless and irreproachable before God) which they had heard and of which he became a minister (1:22-23). He hoped through his preaching to present every man τελείως in Christ (1:28; cf. 4:12). They had learned of the hope laid up for them when they heard "the word of the truth of the gospel" (1:6). For they were in danger of being beguiled with persuasive, but false, reasonings (παραλογίζηται ἐν πιθανολογίᾳ) (2:4), that is, "by philosophy and empty deceit, according to human tradition, according to the στοιχεῖα of the world, and not according to Christ" (2:8). To follow or serve these στοιχεῖα involved subjection to regulations (δογματίζεσθε), "Do not handle, do not taste, Do not touch ... according to human precepts and doctrines" (2:20-22). These seductive standards, which allegedly promoted divine growth (2:19b) and by which the readers were being judged (2:16), pertained to eating, drinking, feasts, new moons and sabbaths. But, warned Paul, "these are only a shadow of what is to come"; the reality is received only from Christ (2:16-17). Moreover, God had "canceled the bond which stood against us with its legal demands (δόγματα); this he set aside, nailing it to the cross" (2:14). The crucifixion removed the unpayable debt. The hostile ordinances handwritten on the heavenly tablets were rubbed off. Maurice Jones [2] commented on 2:14-15: "Freedom from the Law meant at the same time freedom from the angels who in company with other principalities and powers held the world in thraldom." Both Colossians (1:22-23, 27-28; 2:4-10) and Galatians (2:20-21) attack a legal righteousness which has been replaced in Pauline theology by holiness from the indwelling Christ received through faith. A comparison of the false legal teachings attacked in Colossians and those in Galatians reveals a similar submission to supposedly still valid regulations received from the στοιχεῖα. But, whereas in Galatians Paul was willing to grant the role of God (3:19-21) and Moses (3:17) in giving these laws, in the more developped polemic of Colossians the role of human (cf. Isa. 29:13 LXX; Mk. 7:7) tradition and philosophy in applying and teaching them is attacked. The δόγματα to which the opponents hoped to subject the Colossians were not only revealed (2:14) but also angelic (2:20). and human (2:22). When Paul first encountered the legalists in Galatia, he instinctively used the arguments about justification which

---

[2] *The Epistles of St. Paul to the Colossians*, London (SPCK, 1923), 38.

had served him in rebuking Peter at Antioch (Gal. 2:14ff.). Consequently, Paul may have reacted as if he sensed that the intruders in Galatia were radicals demanding as unconditional a submission to the law as had the Jerusalem messengers (Gal. 2:12; Acts 15:1-2).

In Ephesians, the non-polemical companion writing to Colossians, the view is resisted that salvation is because of works or through self-made faith; such would be contrary to the grace and gift of God, which are taken for granted (2:8-9). This grace is bestowed in Christ (1:6-7; 2:7), who abolished "in his flesh the law of commandments and ordinances" (2:15). As in the case of Gal. 5:18-26, the Christian life was guided by the Spirit (4:1-7, 20-5:18). Its aim is to raise up a τέλειος man, to the measure of the stature of the fulness of Christ (4:12, 15; cf. 2:22; 3:16-19). This sanctification is enhanced by apprehending "the truth in love", but is impeded by "being tossed to and fro and carried about with every wind of doctrine, by the cunning of men" in inventing error (4:14-15).

In Philippians 3 Paul countered boastful Judaizers by asserting his own former zeal for the law (cf. Acts 21:20; 22:3) and his blameless "righteousness under the law" (3:6) while minimizing its value (3:7-8). His desire was to belong to Christ, "not having a righteousness of my own, based on law, but that which is through faith in Christ" (3:8-9; cf. Gal. 3:11-12). His boast was of Christ (3:3). The Apostle's attack on perfectionism, the lack of objects for ἔλαβον, κατειλήφέναι and ἐφθάσαμεν and disagreement on how the τέλειοι should think (3:12-16), imply the existence of a false belief in either a special law for the perfect [3] or in human perfectability through legal obedience, especially circumcision.[4] Perfect righteousness lay in the future in Paul's way of thinking; yet his opponents were confident in pursuing (διώκω) and of apprehending (καταλάβω) it (3:12; cf. Rom. 9:30-31) as a present reality in its legal form. Hence they asked their followers to imitate them in walking (στοιχεῖν) and arriving (φθάνω) (3:16-18); by their teaching and example Paul's opponents demonstrated the path to be followed.

In 1 Cor. Paul stressed that the apostle's duty is to preach the saving Gospel of Christ (9:12, 14, 16, 18, 22-23). In order to gain more converts to the Gospel, he enslaved himself to all men, though

---

[3] A. F. J. Klijn, "Paul's Opponents in Philippians iii," *NT* 7 (1965), 281-82.
[4] Robert Jewett, "Conflicting Movements in the Early Church as Reflected in Philippians", *NT* 12 (1970), 387, n. 5.

he was free from all (9:19). "To the Jews I became as a Jew . . . To the
weak I became weak" (9:20, 22). His insistence that he himself was
not under the law of Moses witnesses to his break with Judaism. "To
those under the law I became as one [i.e. acted as if] under the law"
(9:20). As Clarence Craig [5] commented, "no concession to the Jews
had involved a return to legalism on his part." T. W. Manson [6] asked:
"What criticism is Paul meeting. . .? Was it being urged . . . that
missionaries of Jewish origin were not free to abandon the Law. . .?
Or that all genuine Apostles strictly observe the Law themselves. . .?"
(cf. Gal. 2:14). His behavior among Gentiles (9:21) could be seen as
objectionable and inconsistent [7]. His inward freedom (9:19) inspite of
outward accomodation is explained as part of his ἀπολογία against
those who attacked his apostle ship (9:2-3). "Am I not free? Am I not
an apostle?" (9:1). His right to eat and drink as he chose with
everyone was the ἐχουσία to eat (or avoid) any sort of food (8:9), even
if idolatrous and offensive to his brother (8:13). Paul's liberty was
being criticized (10:29-30). His defense of his apostolic status and
methods was sandwiched between his discussions of eating (chh. 8,
10). C. K. Barrett observes: [8] "The problem of εἰδώλοθυτα. . . possibly
would never have arisen in a Gentile Church like that of Corinth if
Jewish Christians (the Cephas group, perhaps) had not raised it."
"Conscience demanded of the devout Jew the most searching inquiry
before he might eat" [9] food sold in the market. Paul conceded the
Jewish view that heathen idol sacrifices were really offered to demons
(10:14-23). Manson [10] further wrote: "the Jewish conscience was
extremely sensitive about anything connected with idolatry, and there
is an a priori presumption that where this question is raised, Jewish
or Jewish-Christian scruples are involved." He believed that the
question of the decree of the Jerusalem Council (Acts 15) "was raised
in Corinth by the Cephas party, and that Paul's way of dealing with it
is, and is meant to be, a snub." The "weak" were those whose
religious conscience [11] did not allow them to eat food from an

---

[5] In his exegesis in *The Interpreter's Bible*, New York & Nashville, Abingdon, Vol.
10 (1953), 104.

[6] *Op. cit.*, 201, n. 1.

[7] Hurd, *op. cit.*, 128-31.

[8] *Art. cit., NTS* 11 (1965), 146; cf. 150.

[9] *A Commentary on the First Epistle to the Corinthians*, London (Adam & Charles
Black, 1968), 240.

[10] *Op. cit.*, 200; approved by Barrett, *art. cit., NTS* 11 (1965), 150.

[11] Michel Coune, "Le problème des Idolothytes et l'éducation de la Syneidesis,"

idolatrous sacrifice (8:7-13; 9:22; cf. Rom. 14:1; 15:1). Paul saw their scruples as a sign of a weak, fragile faith. He distinguished between the law of Moses and the law of Christ (9:21) for His slaves (7:22; cf. 19, 23). Paul argued on the basis of what was written in the law of Moses with those who opposed his right to be treated as an apostle (9:8-10, 13) and who impressed the church by speaking in tongues (14:21-22).

The threat of Judaizing continued to spread in Corinth. In 2 Corinthians are found echoes of the controversy on legal righteousness versus "the righteousness from God that depends on faith" (Phil. 3:9). Paul disputed his opponents' claim to be "servants (διάκονοι) of righteousness" (2 Cor. 11:15). "Such men are false prophets, deceitful workmen, disguising themselves as apostles of Christ" (2 Cor. 11:14). Evidently their understanding of righteousness differed sharply from Paul's, and their deceitful, self-commended deeds would be condemned. The ironical, "their τέλος will be κατὰ τὰ ἔργα αὐτῶν" (11:15) may well be an application of their principle of judgment according to works. These false prophets were opposing God's gospel and the truth or Christ as preached by Paul (11:7, 10). For he served God through weapons of (evangelical) righteousness (2 Cor. 6:4, 7). Through Christ we "become the righteousness of God" (5:21). According to the Apostle, moreover, the ministry (διακονία) of righteousness" pertains to the glorious life of the Spirit, rather than to the Mosaic order leading to condemnation and death (3:7-9). Paul and Timothy were διάκονοι of a new and superior (καινός) covenant of the life-giving Spirit, rather than of the old written legal code that kills (3:6-7). "Where the Spirit of the Lord is, there is liberty" (3:17). The illumination which comes with accepting Christ is contrasted with the obscurity of Moses (3:13-18; cf. Mt. 13:17). The letter of Christ is superior to the law of Moses, even though the latter is written on tablets of stone (3:3). Plummer [12] commented on 3:7-9: "The inferiority of the Law to the Gospel is shown in three different aspects...; it is a ministration of death, a ministration of condemnation, and a ministration which was designed to be only temporary." The ministration of righteousness through the Spirit is

---

Recherches de Science Religieuse 51 (1963), 503-18. They did not consider themselves weak, of course.

[12] A Critical and Exegetical Commentary on the Second Epistle of St. Paul to Corinthians (I.C.C.), New York (Charles Scribner's Sons, 1915), 89; cf. Oostendorp, op. cit., 39-41.

much more glorious (3:9; cf. 13). "In this argument the Apostle has chiefly in view the Judaizers who made the Law indispensable and superior to the Gospel." [13] The light of the knowledge of the glory of God in the face of Jesus Christ (4:6; cf. 3:18) is the light of the gospel of the glory of Christ (4:4); it is implicitly contrasted with the light of the Law given to the radiant Moses (3:13). As all of these arguments in ch. 3 are given in defense of the Pauline ministry (3:1-3, 6; 4:1-3), it is a reasonable inference that his critics were still entangled in servitude to the old covenant and Jewish ministration. Derk Oostendorp [14] argues Paul was attacked "because of his laxness and unwillingness to introduce the Mosaic law into the Corinthian church" and to enforce strict discipline and wipe out sin (10; 13; 3:1, 4-6).

In light of similar passages in 2 Cor. we may partially grasp the nature of the σκάνδαλα contrary to the doctrine ... learned" by the readers of Romans 16. Paul reassured his readers of his joy in their obedience (ὑπακοή), i.e. of faith and in serving Christ (16:18-19, 26); it was universally known. They were wise as to the good (16:19). Such obedience and wisdom pertain to the Gospel (16:26-27) which they had learned (16:17). Paul's wish that they be wise is parallel to his joy in their obedience (16:19). Yet others, who do not serve Christ, are said to be creating "dissensions and difficulties" by a different teaching concerning the Gospel of Christ. Their doctrine concerning good and evil is contrary to (τὰ σκανδαλα ... ροιοῦντες) Paul's doctrine and deceives the hearts of the guileless ἀκακοι: 16:17-18). The readers, however, are to be innocent (simple, harmless and faultless: ἀκέραιοι) concerning evil, but wise as to the true good concerning the Gospel (16:19). This good, rather than special laws of good and evil (in which matters they are guiltless), is the object of true obedience in Paul's view. The same contrast appears in 1 Cor. 14:20: be mature in your (mental) understanding, but infantlike (νηπιάζετε) or harmless in malice (κακία) (cf. 13:11 Mt. 10:16; Phil. 2:15-16). Satan symbolizes those who deceive the hearts of the ἀκακοι (16:19-20). In 2 Cor. 11:13-14 Satan is portrayed as the deceiver; there are false apostles and deceitful (δόλιοι) workmen who imitate Satan. The passage in Rom. 16 accordingly is to be understood as saying: these deceitful teachers satanically masquerade as apostles, workmen and servants of Christ (16:18). Though they have sufficient authority to divide (διχοστασίας ... ποιοῦντας) the church (16:17), the God of peace will

---

[13] Plummer, *op. cit.*, 92.
[14] *Op. cit.*, 17-51, quoting 80; cf. Plummer, *op. cit.*, 310.

soon crush them (16:20; cf. 2 Cor. 11:15). Their use of fair and flattering words (16:18) corresponds to the methods of "the circumcision" in Titus 1:10 and the Colossian heretics (2:4; cf. 8); i.e. they commended their converts for their growth in understanding, obedience and righteousness. But the Apostle taught a different sort of wisdom and obedience.

Robert E. Osborne [15] ingeniously finds that the wild beasts which Paul fought at Ephesus (1 Cor. 15:32) "are the Simple of Judah who keep the Law." They are called "the beasts" in the Qumran Commentary on Habakkuk 2:17. Hence Paul's opponents were the doers of the Law, the Asian legalists. In the Epistles they are Jewish Christians, and in Acts, Jews, according to Osborne.

In the Pastoral Epistles we find explicit reference to the Ephesian and Cretan churches' problem with a Jewish legalism which was opposed to the normative Pauline teaching:

> Certain persons by swerving from these [a love that issues from a pure heart and a good conscience and sincere faith] have wandered away into vain discussion, desiring to be teachers of the law, without understanding either what they are saying or the things about which they make assertions. Now we know that the law is good, if any one uses it lawfully, understanding this, that the law is not laid down for the just but for the lawless and disobedient ... liars, perjurers, and whatever else is contrary to sound doctrine, in accordance with the glorious gospel of the blessed God with which I have been entrusted (1 Tim. 1:5-11).

> ...good deeds; these are excellent and profitable to men. But avoid stupid controversies, genealogies, dissensions, and quarrels over the law, for they are unprofitable and futile (Titus 3:8-9).

> If anyone teaches otherwise and does not agree with the sound words of our Lord Jesus Christ and the teaching which accords with godlines (εὐσέβεια), he is puffed up with conceit, he knows nothing; he has a morbid craving for controversy and for disputes about words, which produce envy, dissension, slander, base suspicions, and wrangling among men who are depraved in mind and bereft of the truth, imagining that godliness is a means of gain (1 Tim. 6:3-5).

> ...that they may be sound in the faith, instead of giving heed to Jewish myths or to the commands of men who reject the truth (Tit. 1:13-14).

That the νομοδιδάσκαλοι were exegetes of the Torah is indicated by the use of the title for Gamaliel (Acts 5:34). Evidently the false teachers viewed the law as having been laid down for the righteous (1 Tim. 1:9) and the pious (1 Tim. 6:3, 5; cf. Rom. 16:18: ἄκακοι); it was

---

[15] "Paul and the Wild Beasts," *JBL* 85 (1966), 229-30.

not replaced by the Gospel, they taught (1 Tim. 1:3, 9, 11; Tit. 1:14).
They professed to teach legal traditions (Tit. 1:14; cf. Col. 2:21) and
hidden mysteries of the law (1 Tim. 1:7; 6:4; Tit. 3:9; cf. 1 Cor. 8:1b;
Jd. 10a; Col. 2:18), probably in connection with its cosmic
significance (cf. Gal. 4:3, 7-10) and with Jewish myths (Tit. 1:14).
Zahn [16] — deduced that "contrary to the spirit of the gospel, they
considered certain requirements of the Mosaic law binding upon
Christians," though not necessarily as a condition of salvation. Vain
discussions (1 Tim. 1:4, 6; 6:4; Tit. 1:10) and dissensions (1 Tim. 6:4;
Tit. 3:9) arose, i.e. concerning rabbinic exegesis of the Torah.
Disputed legal questions, to judge from the context, included the use
of wine (1 Tim. 5:23), the recognition of good and evil works (1 Tim.
5:24-25) and the proper behavior of Christian slaves; masters were
being despised rather than deemed worthy of all honor (6:1-2).[17] The
true keeping of the law is upheld in 1 Tim. 1:8-10.

The persistence of veneration of the Torah is demonstrated by the
warnings of Ignatius to the Magnesians:

> Be not deceived with strange doctrines . . . For if we still (μέχρι νῦν) live
> according to the Jewish law ('Ιουδαϊσμὸν), we acknowledge that we have
> not received grace (ch. 8).

> Let us not, therefore, be insensible to [Christ's] kindness. For were he to
> reward us according to our works, we should cease to be. Therefore,
> having become his disciples, let us learn to live according to the
> principles of Christianity... It is absurd to profess Christ Jesus and to
> Judaize. For Christianity does not embrace Judaism, but Judaism
> Christianity (ch. 1).

Because the tone of Hebrews is theologically constructive rather
than polemical, the teachings being refuted therein are less clear.
Reminiscent of Col. 2:17 the author teaches: "the law has but a
shadow of the good things to come instead of the true form of these
realities" (10:1). As Hugh Montefiore [18] paraphrases: "The Law cannot
give an accurate embodiment of these heavenly realities. It can only
provide an insubstantial and distorted expression of future promises."
"Christ has obtained a ministry which is as much more excellent than
the old as the covenant he mediates is better, since it is enacted on

---

[16] Op. cit., ii, 105.

[17] Cf. Eph. 6:5-8 and Col. 3:22-25, where slaves' singleness (haplotes) of heart in
fear of the Lord is called for. On this motivation see pp. 116,141-142.

[18] A Commentary on the Epistle to the Hebrews (Harper's N.T.), New York &
Evanston, Ill., 1964), 164.

better promises. For if that first covenant had been faultless, there would have been no occasion for a second" (8:6-7; cf. 7:22). "He is the mediator of a new covenant, so that those who are called may receive the promised eternal inheritance" (9:15; cf. 6:17). "In speaking of a new covenant (the Lord) treats the first as obsolete. And what is becoming obsolete and growing old is ready to vanish away" (8:13; cf. 10:16). Offerings and sacrifices according to the law are abolished with the coming of Christ (9:9-10; 10:5-9). "A former commandment is set aside because of its weakness and uselessness (for the law made nothing perfect); on the other hand, a better hope is introduced through which we draw near to God" (7:18-19; cf. 11, 22, 28; 10:1b; 11:40). The heart is strengthened by grace, rather than by strange food laws (13:9), and we can approach the throne of grace because of the sacrifice of Christ the High Priest (4:14-5:1; cf. 2:9). "To enter the sanctuary by the blood of Jesus" is "the new and living way" (10:19-20; cf. 9:11). "When there is a change in the priesthood, there is necessarily a change in the law (νόμου μετάθεσις) as well" (7:12). The blood of Christ purifies "conscience from dead works to serve the living Lord" (9:14). On the other hand, a greater punishment awaits those who reject the Son than those who violate the law of Moses (10:26-31; 12:18-29). Whereas Paul dealt with the theological problem of the Law as a whole, the author of Hebrews was especially interested in the sacrificial aspect, because of either his own theological perspective or because of the views of his addressees. But both writers were resisting the view that, in spite of the work of Jesus, the old covenant was a permanently valid, immutable, faultless guide to perfect righteousness, if fully obeyed (Gal. 3:3, 10; 4:3).

John the Baptist, as Carl Kraeling observed,[19] made legal demands for supererogatory works which as a whole were not even required for the Day of Atonement: inner and outer purity, fasting and special prayers. He criticized "Jews who relied on the merits of the patriarch for their salvation instead of acquiring merit for themselves by pious observance."[20] "God has sent me to show you the way of the Law..."[21] John's coming "in the way of righteousness" (Mt. 21:32 cf. Prov. 16:31) meant that, under the threat of the fire of just divine punishment, repentance and righteous deeds were necessary. As John

---

[19] Op. cit., 76-77, 81.

[20] Ibid., 77.

[21] From the Slavonic War of Josephus (Robert Eisler, The Messiah Jesus and John the Baptist (London, Methuen, 1931, 224.

intensified Torah-righteousness, Jesus saw him as the culmination of
the Law and the Prophets (Mt. 11:11-13; Lk. 16:16); his fasting
reminded Jesus of an old garment and old wineskins (Mt. 9:14-17;
Mk. 2:18-22; Lk. 5:33-39). Later, Zechariah and Elizabeth were
honored for being "righteous before God, walking in all the
commandments and ordinances of the Lord blameless" (Lk. 1:6).
Zechariah hoped that God would "remember his holy covenant, the
oath which he swore to our father Abraham, to grant us that we ...
might serve him without fear, in holiness and righteousness before
him all the days of our life" (1:72-75). The narrative of the
presentation of Jesus in the Temple has four references to legal
obedience: "their purification according to the law of Moses" (2:22),
"as it is written in the law of the Lord" (2:23), "to do for him
according to the custom of the law" (2:27) and "they had performed
everything according to the law of the Lord" (2:39).

At the Jerusalem Council Pharisee believers urged that Gentile
converts be charged to keep the law of Moses (Acts 15:5). But in Acts
21:20-21 Luke mentions the broad base of Palestinian legalism.
James says to Paul, "You see, brother, how many thousands there are
among the Jews of those who have believed; they are all zealous for
the law." James' loyalty to the Law is clear from Acts 21:24; Gal.
2:12, Hegesippus and Josephus (*Antiq.* xx, 9.1, 201, 203). The
Ebionites insisted upon the complete, literal observance of the law
(Eusebius, *H. E.* iii, 27). Elkesai held that believers ought to live
according to the law (Hippolytus, *Philos.* ix, 14.1). The κερύγματα
πέτρου (ap. Clement, Hom. iii. 51; Epistle of Peter to James 2.4-6)
teaches that not one iota will pass away from the true law (cf. Mt.
24:35).

The Ascension of Isaiah (9:26; cf. 3:18; 4:15-16; 7:23; 8:26)
promises heavenly garments to those who "believe on the words of
that one who ... shall be named, and observe them and believe
therein, and believe in his cross."

The Apocalypse of Peter teaches that evil deeds result from hearing
but not believing preaching about the judgment of God and place of
everlasting torture (Ethiopic 7, 13). Christ will repay everyone
according to his works (1, 3, 6, 13). To blaspheme "the way of
righteousness" (Akhmim 28; cf. Ethiopic 9: "my righteousness") is
among the sins.

The Testament of our Lord Jesus in Galilee separates the righteous
and unrighteous according to legalistic principles. Christ's beloved

are those who follow the commands of His Father and scorn gold, silver and earthly goods(7); but there are "many who hate and scorn the commandments of God", i.e. "the will of my Father" (cf. Mt. 7:21; 12:50), and who persecute the righteous and love the world (8). "Their sin is hidden in the days (of life), but will be revealed on the last day" (2). God "will repay everyone according to his deeds and words" (11; cf. Mt. 12:36; 16:27). "The righteous who have followed the way of justice will inherit the glory of God"; but, "mourn those who have not listened to His commandments" (11).

Apart from Jubilees, the Old Testament apocryphal literature does not manifest a severe legalism. The light of the law given for the illumination of every man, including all the Gentiles living in darkness (T. Levi 14:4). Although the children of Levi promised to choose the light and to walk according to the law of the Lord (T. Levi 19:1-2), their descendents were going to teach commandments contrary to the ordinances of God (14:4). Judah advised his children to "observe all the law of the Lord, for there is hope for all of them who hold fast unto His ways "(T. Jud. 26:1). But God will punish them for their sins until they "repent with a perfect (τελείως) heart and walk in all His commandments" (T. Jud. 23:5). Through the influence of the spirits of error "perisheth every young man, darkening his mind from the truth, and not understanding the law of God, nor obeying the admonitions of his fathers" (T. Reub. 3:8). The Life of Adam and Eve (Vita Adae 29:4-9) presents a theology of history based on a cycle of human obedience and disobedience:

> The Lord will give commandments and statutues ... They will transgress His statutes ... God will stir up for himself a faithful people whom He shall save for eternity, and the impious shall be punished by God their King, the men who refused to love His law. Heaven and earth, night and days, and all creatures shall obey Him, and not overstep His commandment. Men ... shall be changed from forsaking the law of the Lord.

The validity of the law is unchanging. Thus Naphtali tells his sons:

> If ye keep silence in purity of heart, ye shall understand how to hold fast the will of God, and to cast away the will of Beliar. Sun and moon and stars change not their order; so do ye also change not the law of God in the disorderliness of your doings (T. Napht. 3:1-2)

The eternal validity of the law is implicit in the pre-existence of the law on heavenly tablets (T. Asher 2:10; Jub. 1:29; 3:10, 31; 4:5, 32;

5:13; 6:17, 29 etc.). Legal obedience, however, does not remove the need for faith. Righteousness and faith are associated in 1 Enoch 39:6; 58:5; 61:4, 11; T. Levi 8:2. Those who will shine like lightning and stars are "the holy who dwell on earth and believe in the name of the Lord of Spirits for ever and ever" (1 Enoch 43:4).

The legalism of the Qumran texts has been emphasized by many scholars.[22] Admission to the Community required an oath of "to the Law of Moses according to all His commands, with all his heart and all his soul, following all that is revealed of it to the sons of Zadok the priests who keep the Covenant and seek His will ... "(1QS 5.8; cf. CD 15.12; 16.1, 4-5). The members of the Community are "those who volunteer to be converted from all evil and to cling to all His commands according to His will; ... to become a Community in the Law ... under the authority of the sons of Zadok the priests who keep the Covenant" (1 QS 5.1-2). They should "seek God with [all their heart] and [all their soul and] do what is good and right before Him, as commanded by the hand of Moses and all his servants the Prophets" (1QS 1.1-3). All who volunteer to enter should bring all their mind and strength into Community and "wish to practice the precepts of God in the Covenant of Grace, that they may ... behave perfectly before Him according to all the revelations. . ." and "purify their understanding in the truth of the precepts of God" (1QS 1.7-9, 11-12). Strength is a gift to the elect (1QS 11.7) and hymnist (1QH 2.7-8; 1.7, 17, 19), in whom God showed his power (1QH 4.8, 23; 5.15). Those "who volunteer together for His truth and to walk in His will" are contrasted with those perverse men who "have not inquired nor sought Him concerning His precepts in order to know the hidden matters in which they have guiltily strayed" (1 QS 5.10-12). Those who have separated themselves from perverse men follow the way which "is study of the Law which He has promulgated by the hand of Moses, that they may act according to all that is revealed, season by season, and according to that which the Prophets have revealed by His Holy Spirit" (1QS 8.13-16). The Law is to be studied (1QS 6.6-8) and taught (1 QS 9.12-14). Thus the Psalmist prayed: "Grant me understanding, O Lord, in thy Law, and teach me thine ordinances" (11Q PSa 155.9).[23]

---

[22] Herbert Braun, *Qumran und das Neue Testament*, ii, 229-30.
[23] *Discoveries in the Judaean Desert of Jordan IV. The Psalms Scroll of Qumran Cave 11*, ed. J. A. Sanders, Oxford (Clarendon, 1965).

Matthew Black [24] rightly points out that the ideal of a "legalistic perfection" of the sectarians is to be found

> in the absolute and total demands which are made on their obedience to 'the whole Law' as thus secretly divulged by its priestly interpreters ... The sectarians are to be obedient and perfect in *all* that is revealed to them (cf. 1QS i.8-9; v.9; viii.1,15; ix.13, 19), in 'everything which He has commanded' (i.17; v.1, 8; ix.24), to keep *all* the words of God' (i.14; iii.11), to 'depart from *all* evil '(i.4, 7; ii.3; v.1), 'every perversity' (vi.15; viii.18; ix. 21).

The members of the Community are to be instructed in the Mysteries "that they may walk with one another in perfection in all that has been revealed to them" (1QS 9.18-19).[25] To walk in perfection of the way is a recurrent theme (1QS 2.2; 8.10, 18, 20-21; 9.5-6, 8-9; 10.21; 11.2). "Whoever has entered the Congregation of men of perfect holiness" should practice the precepts of the righteous "in accordance with the interpretation of the Law in which the men of perfect holiness walk" (CD 2.2-3, 5-7). In the Council of the Community there were to be twelve men and three priests who were "perfect in all that is revealed of the Law" (1QS 8.1-2; cf. 1QS 6.6-7). All volunteers were to strive to understand the precepts of God and the perfection of His ways (1QS 1.12-13). As the Community understood itself to be "the dwelling of infinite holiness for Aaron" and "the house of perfection and truth in Israel" (1QS 8.8-9), its membership was to be classified and purified:

> And if any man enters the Covenant to act according to these precepts by joining the holy Congregation, they shall examine his spirit in common, (distinguishing) between one and the other according to his understanding and his works with regard to the Law ... And they shall inscribe them [the members] in order, one before the other according to their intelligence and their works ... And they shall examine their spirit and works year by year, in order to promote each man according to his understanding and the perfection of his conduct, or demote him according to the faults which he has committed (1QS 5.20-24).

Expulsion or two-year exclusion from the Community was possible for deviation from "the ordinances in which men of perfect holiness walk"; those who sinned against the Law of Moses, whether

---

[24] *Op. cit.*, 122.
[25] W. D. Davies," 'Knowledge' in the Dead Sea Scrolls and Matthew 11:25-30," *HTR* 46 (1953), 115; B. Rigaux, "Révélations des Mystères et Perfection à Qumran et dans le Nouveau Testament," *NTS* 4 (1957-58), 238-40.

deliberately or carelessly, were to be tested concerning the perfection of their conduct and counsel (1QS 8.20-9.2).

Those who voluntarily entered the Community sought "to practice the precepts of God in the Covenant of Grace, that they may ... behave perfectly before Him" (1QS 1. 7-8). "For all who walk in these (precepts) in holy perfection, obeying all His instructions, the Covenant of Grace is assurance that they will live for a thousand generations" (CD 7.5-6). Those entering this Covenant have remembered the Covenant of the Patriarchs (CD 1.4; 6.2; 8.16-18) and swore to be converted to the Law of Moses (CD 15.8-10; 16.1-2). This New Covenant was made in the land of Damascus among members of the House of the Law (CD 8.21; 19.33; 20.12-13; 1Q p Hab 2.3). There is no separation of law and grace nor of the old and new covenants. The New renewed the Old, following the legal interpreatations of the Teacher of Righteousness. Accordingly, the commentary on Habakkuk 2:4 ("But the righteous will live by his faith") reads:

> The explanation of this concerns all those who observe the Law in the House of Judah. God will deliver them from the House of Judgment because of their affliction and their faith in the Teacher of Righteousness (1Q p Hab 8.1-3).

In other words, deliverance from death to life comes by such faith in the true expounder of the Law as leads one to labor successfully to follow it. Hab. 2:3b is said to concern "the men of truth who observe the Law, whose hands do not slacken in the service of Truth" (1Q p Hab. 7.9-12).

Josephus related concerning the Essenes that "the name of the Lawgiver is, after God, a great object of veneration among them, and if any man blasphemes against the Lawgiver he is punished with death" (War ii, 8.9.145). Hippolytus (*Ref.* ix, 25) concurs, but omits "with death." This legislator may be Moses (cf. Acts 6:11) or the founder who gave the Essenes their regulations;[26] the Slavonic translation reads, "their Lawgiver." "They are diligent concerning the reading aloud of the Law and the Prophets" (Hippolytus, ix, 22; cf. Josephus, *War* ii, 8.7.136: "the study of the writings of the ancient ones"). The apologist Philo praised the Essenes in these terms:

---

[26] Marc Philonenko, "La notice du Josephe slave sur les Esseniens," *Semitica* 6 (1956), 72-73; A. Dupont-Sommer, *The Essene Writings from Qumran*, transl. G. Vermes, Oxford (Basil Blackwell, 1961), 31, n. 3.

They work at ethics with extreme care, constantly utilizing the ancestral laws ... They learn piety, holiness, justice, ... knowledge of what is truly good or bad or indifferent, and how to choose what must be done and how to flee from what must be avoided. In this they make use of triple definitions and rules concerning, respectively, the love of God, the love of virtue, and the love of men (*Quod omnis probus* 80, 83).

For example, they condemned slavery (Philo, *ibid.*, 79; *Apologia pro Judaeis, ap.* Eusebius, *Praep. Evang.* viii, 11.4; Josephus, *Antiquities* xviii, 1.5.21; cf. 4Q 159.3 [27]). A certain perfectionism is implied in the report that "they are divided into four lots according to the duration of their discipline" (Josephus, *War* ii, 8.10.150). "Not [all] observe the ἄσχεσις in the same way, being divided into four parts. For some of them are more austere than they need be" (Hippolytus, ix, 26). "Athletes of virtue" are produced by the Essenes' philosophy, "which propounds, like gymnastic exercises, the accomplishment of praiseworthy deeds as the means by which a man ensures absolute freedom for himself" (Philo, *Quod omnis probus*, 88). The Therapeutae believed that knowledge and εὐσέβεια grew together and were perfected (τελειοῦνται) through the laws and inspired sayings of the prophets (de vita contemp. 25)

RELATIONS TO JUDAISM

In Gal. 1:14 Paul emphasizes: "I advanced in Judaism beyond many of my own age among my people, so extremely zealous was I for traditions of my fathers." He was no fallen or assimilated, Hellenized Jew! Apparently his opponents were teachers who took pride in their progress in learning and practicing the legal traditions of Judaism. However, the Apostle boasted of receiving an independent revelation of Jesus (1:1, 12, 15ff.) and of the true gospel, as distinguished from the perverted gospel (1:6, 7, 11). Paul's gospel was not implicit in the Torah. He urged against this opponents and Peter himself that to walk straight with the truth of the gospel is incompatible with Judaizing (2:13-16). Paul boasted of Jesus Christ, but his opponents gloried in circumcision (6:13-15). Nevertheless, both Pauline and Judaizing Christians belonged to the Israel of God (Gal. 6:16; cf. Rom. 9:6). The issue of the value of the Jewish privileges and legal tradition comes into focus in the question of the

---

[27] G. W. Buchanan, "The Role of Purity in the Structure of the Dead Sea Sect," *RQ* 4 (1963-64), 405-06.

promises and blessings given to the seed (σπέρμα) of Abraham (3:14, 16, 26-29). Are the true sons of Abraham those who keep the law or who believe in Christ? According to Paul, "Abraham 'believed God, and it was reckoned to him as righteousness.' So you see it is the men of faith who are the sons of Abraham" (3:6-7). Because "in Christ Jesus the blessing of Abraham" comes upon the Gentiles (3:14), making them "sons of God, through faith" (3:26), "there is neither Jew nor Greek...; for you are all one in Christ Jesus" (3:28). Propagators of the false gospel apparently were teaching that the priveleges accruing to the seed of Abraham could be received by Gentiles only by obeying the law, and that faith alone did not remove the barriers between Jew and Gentile. Ernest D. Burton [28] found it "evident from the counter argument of the apostle in chapters 3 and 4 that they had taught the Galatians either that salvation was possible only to those who were, by blood or adoption, children of Abraham, or that the highest priveleges belonged only to these (3:7, 9, 14; 4:21-23)." To the Judaizer, whose argument Paul is answering, the "seed of Abraham ... meant the circumcised descendant of Abraham, with whom might also be included the circumcised proselyte; and to these he limited the blessing of the covenant with Abraham and so in effect the blessing of God." [29] In his dispute with Peter at Antioch (2:14-16) Paul conceded the advantage of being Jews by nature (φύσει) rather than Gentile sinners because this origin made it easier to live as a Jew and perform works of the law; but this does not lead to justification.

A similar Pauline message is found in Colossians. "The Father ... has qualified us to share in the inheritance of the saints in light" through the Son (1:12-14), just as Canaan was given to the Jews (Exod. 6:8; Num. 33:53; Deut. 3:18; 1 Chron. 16:18; Ps. 105:11). Through the Son, by making peace, God reconciles to himself all things, including believers "who once were estranged (Ezek. 14:5, 7; cf. 13:9) and hostile in mind, doing evil deeds." But sanctification is contingent upon continuing in the faith and in the hope of the Gospel, of which Paul is a minister (1:20-23). His ministry of preaching fully the word of God in the ἐκκλεσία is a stewardship (οι κονομία) in the house of God (1:24-25). The readers

---

[28] *A Critical and Exegetical Commentary on the Epistle to the Galatians* (I.C.C.), New York (Charles Scribner's Sons, 1920), liv.

[29] *Ibid.*, 158.

"were called in the one body" by "the word of Christ" (3:15-16). They were urged to put off or put to death the old nature and its corrupt practices and to "put on the new nature which is being renewed in knowledge . . . Here there cannot be Jew and Greek, circumcised and uncircumcised. . . , but Christ is all, and in all" (3:5-14). Lightfoot [30] commented on 3:11: "If it is no advantage to be born a Jew, it is none to become a Jew." No superiority stems from circumcision. The phrase, κατὰ τὴν παράδοσιν τῶν ἀνθρώπων (2:8), as A. Lukyn Williams [31] noted, "suggests the essentially Jewish character of the error, for the Jewish leaders always deprecate any supposition of originality, and, even in developing some startling detail of the Oral Law, claim that it is involved in what they have heard from their teachers." Thus even "Kabbala" means "tradition." In Mk. 7:2-13 (cf. Mt. 15:1-9) the traditions of men include the elders' rules against eating with unwashed hands. Zahn [32] thought that the Colossians knew the Hebrew language.

The passage in Ephesians which describes the significance of Christ for the covenants of promise with the Jews is 2:11-19. The Gentiles' alienation from God (cf. Col. 1:21) and from the commonwealth of Israel is overcome and the resultant dividing wall of hostility between Jew and Gentile is broken down through the cross. For Christ made peace "by abolishing in his flesh the law of commandments and ordinances, that he might create in himself one new man in place of the two" (3:12-16). Peace was not accomplished through the Gentiles' submission to the Torah, but through the Crucifixion, whereby the legal barriers to fellowship were overcome. Gentiles are "no longer strangers and sojourners" in the commonwealth of Israel, but "are fellow citizens with the saints and members of the household of God" (2:12, 19). Evidently the contrary view was current that the law continued to exclude non-observant Gentiles from access to God and the community of His people.

In Philippians 3 Paul boasts that he, too, like the evil-workers, had cause for confidence in the flesh, by virtue of circumcision, membership in the people of Israel, Hebrew Palestinian parentage (Εβραῖος ἐξ Ἑβραίων),[33] Pharisaic zeal in following the law, and

---

[30] St. Paul's Epistles to the Colossians and to Philemon, 215.

[31] The Epistles of Paul the Apostle to the Colossians and to Philemon, Cambridge (University Press, 1907), 87.

[32] Op. cit., i, 477.

[33] Walter Gutbrod, Theological Dictionary of the New Testament, ed. Gerhard Kittel and G. W. Bromiley, Grand Rapids, Mich. (Wm. B. Eerdmans), iii (1965), 390.

blameless righteousness under the law (3:3-6). Opposing teachers had reckoned these Jewish priveleges and achievements as gain (κέρδος); they provided the basis of claiming superiority according to the flesh over those converted Gentiles whose legal obedience was deficient. Distinctions within the church were being set up according to Jewish standards. Trusting in them (3:4), the Judaizers tended to think of themselves as already perfected (3:12-13, 15). Doubtless they deemed themselves to be the true sons of Abraham and heirs to the promise. But, countered the Apostle, they were enemies of the cross (3:18; cf. Gal. 2:21; 6:12).

Similarly, in 2 Corinthians 10-13 Paul attacked evil workers (11:13; cf. Phil. 3:2) whose end is destruction (11:15; cf. Phil. 3:19). Having confidence in the flesh (11:12, 18; cf. Phil. 3:4, 19), they boasted of being Hebrews, Israelites and descendants (σπέρμα) of Abraham (11:22; cf. Rom. 11:1). Oostendorp [34] finds their Palestinian origin confirmed by their use of εὐαγγέλιον (cf. Isa. 52:7). They claimed to be more Jewish and better off spiritually than Paul and his converts by virtue of their origin and/or loyalty to the heritage of Judaism. Because the Apostle acquired a widespread reputation among Jews and Hebrew Christians for being a lawbreaker (Acts 21:20-28; cf. 24:5-6), there is a presumption that his opponents at Corinth did not overlook this obvious ground for impugning his Jewishness. But in so doing, they must have prided themselves on observance of the Torah, a foremost distinguishing mark of a Jew. [35] Sharing in the promises to Abraham and in membership among God's people was at stake.

The Epistle to the Hebrews, which is an exposition of the relations between Christianity and Judaism, is of special interest because of its title. It was so-called by Tertullian ("*ad Hebraeos*": *de pudicitia* 20), Pantaenus ("the blessed presbyter") and Clement of Alexandria ("πρός Ἑβραιους": Eusebius, *H.E.* vi, 14.3-4), Origen (Eusebius, *H.E.* vi, 25.11) and by the Alexandrian textual witnesses, P[46] A B Sinaiticus. As Tertullian and the Alexandrians shared neither the same textual tradition nor the same views of the Epistle's authorship, and because no other title for the writing is known, an early date must be assigned to the designation. At the latest the name was given when the full Pauline corpus was assembled somewhere in area where Paul had

---

C. F. D. Moule ("Once More, Who were the Hellenists?, "*Expository Times* 70 [1959], 100-02) finds *Hebraios* a linguistic term.

[34] *Op. cit.*, 9-10.   [35] *Ibid.*, 13 and n. 24, 81.

taught and struggled with Judaizers. If Hebrews were addressed to the Ephesians,[36] considerable value must be attached to the title. Is it coincidental that the "deceitful workers" boasted of being "Hebrews" (2 Cor. 11: 22; Phil. 3:5)? Whether the title were given by the author himself or by a Pauline editorial compiler, the Epistle was deemed relevant to the problems posed by (potentially) sectarian Hebrew Christians. The author assumes that the readers drew inspiration from the examples of faith whom he describes in chapter 11. "We are ... of those who have faith and keep their souls" (10:39). Noah "became an heir of the righteousness which comes by faith" (11:7), and from the faithful Abraham were born innumerable descendants (11:12). Nevertheless, all these witnesses, "though well attested by their faith, did not receive what was promised, since God had foreseen something better for us, that apart from us they should not be made perfect" (11:39-40; cf. 13, 16). That is, Christ is the superior object and promised reward of our faith.

According to Titus 1:10, the false teachers ἐκ τῆς περιτομῆς were especially insubordinate and deceptive. "The circumcision" signifies Jews in Rom. 4:12, and Hebrew believers in Acts 10:45; 11:2; Gal. 2:12 and Col. 4:11. Being "sound in faith" is contrasted with "giving heed to Jewish myths" (Tit. 1:13-14). Timothy is to "charge certain persons not to teach any different doctrine, nor to occupy themselves with myths and endless genealogies which promote speculations" (1 Tim. 1:3-4). "Have nothing to do with godless and silly myths" (1 Tim. 4:7), he is cautioned. "Jewish" and "the circumcision" were terms being used perjoratively because of association with what is contrary to a healthy faith and sound doctrine. A composite picture may be drawn of the Pastor's polemical characterizations: Jewish (i.e. Haggadic and Halachic),[37] βέβηλος (impious, profane, secular, non-supernatural), γραώδης (old womanish, old wives'), μῦθος (non-revealed, legendary, allegorical, imaginative Haggadah, fables, tales, sagas and folklore concerning the creation story,[38] Adam and Eve, Satan's fall[39] and glorified Jewish "history"; cf. Philo, vita Mos. ii,

---

[36] Gunther, op. cit., 152-55.

[37] On Jewish genealogical books, traditions and exegesis see Gerhard Kittel, "Die Genealogia der Pastoralbriefe," ZNTW 20 (1921), 49-69.

[38] Jeremias, Die Briefe an Timotheus und Titus (NT Deutsch), Göttingen (Vandenhoeck & Ruprecht, 1937), 46; cf. W. Michaelis, Pastoralbriefe und Gefangenschaftsbriefe, Gütersloh (Bertelsmann, 1930), 102ff.

[39] Alexander Altmann, "The Gnostic Backgrounds of the Rabbinic Adam Legends," JQR 35 (1945), 373ff.

8.46-48; *de praem. et poen.* i, 1) and endless genealogies (the origin and relationships of listed groups and pedigrees of peoples, tribes, patriarchs and priests),[40] all of which are the subject matter of ζητήσεις (speculative, controversial searchings or questionings which might employ of rabbinic exegesis). Genealogy and myth were components of biographical legends which purported to be didactic and edifying sacred history supplementing and reconciling Scripture. Being associated with, and based on, the law, *"elles avaient pour but de consacrer toutes les institutions de la Loi,"* as Père Spicq comments.[41] As "μῦθοι" is used in a perjorative sense, they must have been less credible than the tales of the rebellion of Jannes and Jambres (2 Tim. 3:8). The Book of Jubilees [42] and Pseudo-Philo's *Biblical Antiquities* and the folk tale-filled Lives of the Prophets illustrate types of Jewish histories. For the Pastor, neither Jewish esoteric lore nor race nor circumcision were esteemed. In Tit. 2:14 our great God and Savior Christ Jesus is said to purify for himself a people of his own (λαὸς περιούσιον); the new and true Israel is his possession.

Later Ignatius warned the Magnesians (8:1): "Be not deceived with strange doctrines nor with old fables, which are unprofitable (ταῖς ἑτεροδοξίαις μηδὲ μυθεύμασιν τοῖς παλαιοῖς ανωφελέσιν οὖσιν). For if we live according to Judaism, we confess that we have not received grace." The Antiochene martyr found certain aspects of Judaism to be heterodox and useless for Christians, especially "myths" which had circulated among the Hebrews from ancient times.

John the Baptist was more concerned with eschatological judgment of individuals than of nations.[43] His warnings, promises and moral exhortations were not nationalistic or racialistic (Lk. 3:8, 14). Nevertheless, his baptism of Jews indicates his intent to prepare a purified remnant of penitent Israelites. In spite of traces of universalism in Lk. 2:10, 31-32, the outlook in 1:14, 16, 32, 33, 54, 56, 68-74, 77; 2:25, 32b, 34, 38 is quite narrow.[44] John's role is limited to saving Israelites (1:16, 68, 74, 77).

[40] Kittel, *art. cit., ZNTW* 20 (1921), 54-55, 57.

[41] *St. Paul: les Épitres Pastorales,* 21; cf. lxiii for the explanations of Ambrosiaster. Spicq held that the opponents were Jewish Christians (lv-lvi).

[42] As suggested by F. J. A. Hort, *op. cit.,* 137; D. G. Wohlenberg, *Die Pastoralbriefe* (Kommentar zum N.T., ed. Zahn), Leipzig (A. Deichert, 1923), 31-37; Spicq, *St. Paul: les Épitres Pastorales.* lx-lxii.

[43] Maurice Goguel, *Jean-Baptiste,* Paris (Payot, 1928), 286-88.

[44] Wink, *op. cit.,* 62.

The Revelation of Peter is to be classified with Jewish apocalyptic even in respect to its teaching about Tartarus (cf. 4 Sib. Oracle 184, 186),[45] Acherusia and Elysium (Ethiopic 13-14).[46] Jesus explains that his parable of the fig tree concerns the house of Israel (Ethiopic 2). The patriarchs are exemplary inhabitants of Paradise (Rainer Fragment; Ethiopic 16).

The Ebionites, according to Irenaeus (*Adv. Haer.* i, 26.2) "persevere in the practices of the law and in a Jewish manner of life to such an extent that they venerate Jerusalem as the house of God."

Pride of the Hebrews in the history of Israel was partly based on the ancestry (T. Napht. 1:9-10) and righteousness of its heroes. Thus Benjamin instructed his children:

> Do ye truth each one to his neighbor, and keep the law of the Lord and His commandments. For these things do I leave you instead of inheritance. Do ye also [therefore], give them to your children for an everlasting possession; for so did both Abraham, and Isaac, and Jacob. For all these things they gave us for an inheritance, saying: Keep the commandments of God, until the Lord shall reveal His salvation to all the Gentiles. [And] then shall ye see Enoch, Noah, and Shem, and Abraham, and Isaac, and Jacob, rising on the right hand in gladness (T. Benj. 10:3-6).

"Jacob fell asleep..., being perfect in every virtue (ἀρετή) and spiritual grace... Blessed is every people (ἔθνος) that shall emulate thy holiness and thy virtues and thy righteousness..." (T. Jacob).[47] The patriarchs were glorified as models worthy of imitation. Benjamin taught his children to "[love the Lord God of heaven and earth, and keep His commandments], following the example of the good and holy man [Joseph]" (T. Benj. 3:1). Issachar relates that he walked in uprightness and singleness of heart and urged his children to do likewise (T. Issach. 3:1-5:8; 2-3); for he was at death "not conscious of committing any sin" (7:1). In their Testaments Reuben, Simeon and Judah narrate their experiences as penitent sinners and

---

[45] Moses Gaster, "Hebrew Visions of Hell and Paradise," *Journal of the Royal Asiatic Society* 25 (1893), 571-611; A. Marmorstein, "Jüdische Parallelen zur Petrusapokalypse," *ZNTW* 10 (1909), 297-300; Moffatt, *op. cit.*, 367, n.; James, *The Lost Apocrypha of the O.T.*, 55-56; *art. cit., JTS* 32(1930-31), 378-80; Klausner, *op. cit.*, 536, index for "Gehenna"; Burrows, *More Light on the Dead Sea Scrolls*, New York (Viking, 1958), 347; Josephus, *War* ii, 8.11; Rev. 21:8; 2 Enoch 10; 37:1(B); 1QS 2.6-8; 4.13& 18.

[46] Erik Peterson, "Die Taufe im Acherusischen See," *VC* 9 (1955), 3-20.

[47] Coptic, 84, 78.

urge their children to follow the wisdom which the patriarchs had gained the hard way.

De Jonge [48] observes that "the author of the Testaments was not primarily interested in the narrative passages of his work, but used them to illustrate his ethical teaching ... The author used examples and illustrations which everybody could understand." Robert Eppel noted that the Haggada of the Testaments of the Twelve Patriarchs correct details of the tradition which were particularly shocking to pious Jews.[49] But often these patriarchal myths entertain with picturesque details which amplify the Biblical tradition. The superhuman strength, swiftness and courage of Simeon (T. Sim. 2:3), Judah (T. Judah 2:2-7), Naphtali (T. Napht. 2:1) and Gad (T. Gad 1:3) were illustrated. The haggadic traditions of this work are often found in Jubilees as well. C. C. Torrey [50] wrote that there is "in Jubilees a large amount of legendary matter that had gradually taken shape in Jewish folklore. A characteristic feature of the book is the omission of such details in the history of the patriarchs as could show any of them in an unfavorable light." The romance of Joseph and Asenath also idealizes Hebrew ancestors. In form Jubilees is a privately transmitted record written by Moses of what "the angel of the presence spoke to Moses according to the word of the Lord" (2:1; cf. 1:26-27) "on Mount Sinai when he went up to receive the tables of the law and of the commandments" (prologue). Thus it supplements what the angel had "written in the book of the first law" (6:22), i.e. the Penteteuch. Its narrative runs parallel to, and is based upon, Genesis to Exodus 14.

The relations of angels with the patriarchs or other angels verge on mythology. Several examples may be cited from Jewish apocrypha: the fall of Satan (vita Adae 12:1-16:4), the role of the archangels in burying Adam and Seth (vita Adae 37:4-40:7), Eve's support by twelve angels and two powers (vita Adae 21:1), Adam's reception of traditions which were not to be revealed to Cain (Apoc. Mos. 3:2), and Noah's marvelous birth as one resembling "the sons of the God of heaven" (1 Enoch 106:5-6). Angels play a prominent role in apocryphal patriarchal stories.[51]

[48] Op. cit., 119; cf. Robert Eppel, Le Piétisme Juif dans les Testaments des Douze Patriarches, Paris (Librairie Félix Alcan, 1930), 147.

[49] Ibid., 36-41; this is especially true of the Greek (versus the Hebrew) text (De Jonge, art. cit., NT. 4 [1960], 197).

[50] Op. cit., 127; cf. Pfeiffer, History of New Testament Times, 69.

[51] J. Michl, "Engel," Reallexicon für Antike und Christentum, ed. Th. Klauser, Stuttgart (Anton Hiersemann), v (1962), 66-67.

Volunteers to join the Qumran Community were generally "born of Israel", as they had to be examined on the basis of their knowledge and observance of the Law (1QS 6. 13-14). They constituted the Aaronic "House of holiness for Israel," "the House of perfection and truth in Israel" (1QS 5.5-6; 8.5, 9; cf. 9.3-4), "Israel, the Community of God" (1QS 2.22; cf. 1.12; 5.20-22; 8.12; 9.6). In the War Scroll the sons of light constitute "Israel" (2:7-9; 10.3, 7, 9), the people of God (1.4; 13.2, 13; 14.4, 8; 17.4-5;18.3) "in the war that it destined to crush the nations" (1QS 1.20-21; 1QM 2.10-14; 16.1ff.).

The Covenanters kept a register of members, "who shall stand at the end of days. This is the accurate list of their names according to their lineage and the time of their existence and the number of the days of their afflictions and of the years of their exile, and the accurate account of their works" (CD 4.1-6; cf. 1QSa I.14-16, 23-25; 1 QM 2.1-4; 3.4, 14; 5.1-2). From Cave 6 comes an unpublished genealogical list of priests, and from Cave 4 a genealogy going back to the Judges with accompanying chronology.[52]

The Genesis Apocryphon from Cave I illustates' the sectarians' interest in edifying apocryphal accounts of the lives of the Patriarchs. An unpublished text from Cave 4 describes the wonders of Noah's birth.[53] Other unpublished materials from this Cave include pseudepigraphic narratives, many of which concern patriarchal times, and a pseudo-history of the Daniel-Esther epoch.[54] From Cave 6 come fragments of a Hebrew historical text related to II Samuel.[55]

The Essenes were numbered among the Jews of Palestine by Philo (*Quod omnis probus* 75). Josephus related that the Essenes "are Jews by race, but in addition they are more closely united among themselves by mutual affection than are the others" (*War* ii, 8.2.119). They probably adopted certain Old Testament figures as prototypes of themselves.[56] Christian D. Ginsburg,[57] on the basis of their doctrines and practices, termed them "Hebrews of the Hebrews."

---

[52] M. Baillet, J. Starcky, "Le travail d'édition des fragments manuscrits de Qumran," "RB 63 (1956), 55, 66; B. Gärtner, *The Temple and the Community in Qumran and the N.T.*, Cambridge (University, 1965), 9, n. 4.

[53] Milik, *op. cit.*, 35.

[54] Strugnell and Starcky, *art. cit., RB* 63 (1956), 65, 66.

[55] M. Baillet, *ibid.*, 55.

[56] Kaufmann Kohler, "Essenes," *Jewish Encyclopedia* v (1903), 230b-31a.

[57] "Essenes" *DCB* 2 (1880), 198b.

CIRCUMCISION

According to Acts 16:3 Paul circumcised Timothy on account of the Jews in Lystra and Iconium. Paul's opponents appealed to this fact and to the circumcision of Titus (Gal. 2:3-5, Western reading) [58] when they accused him of trying to please men (Gal. 1:10). They noted that he was still preaching circumcision (5:11), presumably out of the necessity of accomodation and as a matter of conscience and personal choice (cf. Rom. 14; 1 Cor. 7:25-8:13). But their principles and his were irrenconcilable.

In Gal. 3:3 the Apostle angrily asks: "Are you so foolish? Having begun with the Spirit, are you now ending with the flesh?" From the double contrast, beginning and being perfected (ἐπιτελεῖσθε), Spirit and flesh (σάρξ), we may deduce that Paul was as concerned with the Spirit received by faith in the beginning of the Christian life as his opponents were with such works of law (3:2, 5) as circumcision, whereby the convert's growth was measured. Perfection according to the flesh, they insisted, must be added to faith and is necessary for receiving the full promises to the descendants of Abraham (3:6ff.; cf. Gen. 17:13-14). The uncircumcised belong to a lower stage or grade of Christian, whereas circumcision is "a necessary completion and perfecting of faith in Christ." [59] In 6:12-13 Paul charges; "It is those who want to make a good showing in the flesh that would compel you to be circumcised ... For even those who receive circumcision do not themselves keep the law, but they desire to have you circumcised that they may glory in your flesh" (6:12-13). The use of the present participle (περιτεμνόμενοι) suggests that not all those who were urging circumcision upon others were themselves yet circumcised. They have accepted, or listened sympathetically to, the legalistic plan for perfection and intended to be circumcised, if they hadn't already been. Those who had been persuaded by the missionaries to be circumcised were themselves, like recent converts in general, eager to persuade others to accept their new way of life. But none of the Gentile Galatians who had succumbed to the Judaizing missionaries had yet assumed the full yoke of the Torah. Against those who accepted circumcision as a stage on the road to perfection, Paul argued that they do not keep the whole law (6:13): an

---

[58] See Gunther, op. cit., 51-53.
[59] According to L. Goppelt and D.W.B. Robinson ("The Distinction between Jewish and Gentile Believers in Galatians," *Australian Biblical Review* 13 [Dec., 1965], 46).

impossible task to which they had obligated themselves (3:10). "I
testify again to every man who receives circumcision that he is bound
to keep the whole law" (5:3). As the Judaizers had not yet attempted
to make the Galatians obedient to the whole law, the converts were
unaware of the magnitude and difficulty of the burden of the
justification by the law. They fancied that both circumcision (5:6) and
Christ (5:2, 4, 6) were of profit to them. Those who had taught the
law of circumcision may have been partly motivated by the desire to
avoid persecution for (preaching) the cross of Christ (6:12); i.e. by
preaching circumcision instead of the cross they hoped to attain or
maintain legal status as Jews. Paul protested that he himself was
persecuted for preaching the offense of the cross, though preaching
circumcision should exempt him from persecution (5:11). The
necessity which is implicit in the emotional term ἀναγκάζω (6:12, cf.
2:3, 14) may have sprung more from Paul's admonitory polemics and
from the Galatians' fear of persecution of themselves and/or of the
Jerusalem church [60] than from an alleged Biblical requirement for
salvation.

Following a warning against philosophy according to human
tradition and the στοιχεῖα rather than according to Christ (2:8), the
Letter to the Colossians proclaims: "In him also you were
circumcised with a circumcision made without hands, by putting off
the body of flesh in the circumcision of Christ... And you, who were
dead in trespasses and the uncircumcision of your flesh, God made
alive together with him, ...having cancelled the bond which stood
against us with its legal demands" (2:11, 13-14). The opponents did
not realize that Christ has fulfilled what they claimed was
accomplished by circumcision. These benefits are gained, rather,
through baptism alone. A. Lukyn Williams [61] suggested three motives
for the false teaching of circumcision: as a prophylactic against sins,
especially of the flesh (2:11, 23), and as a way of imitating higher
angels who were born circumcised (Jub. 15:27), and as a means of
delivering the circumcised from the power of evil spirits into the
jurisdiction of higher angels. The "deceivers" (2:8), in addition to a
spiritual circumcision, were seeking a circumcision of the flesh
performed with hands in obedience to spiritual powers (2:8b, 15). The
rite was being taught as salutary and desirable, but not as obligatory

[60] Gunther, op. cit., 34-36; R. Jewett," The Agitators and the Galatian
Congregation", NTS 17 (1971), 198-206.
[61] Op. cit., 90-91.

for salvation. Against the claim of Judaic superiority (cf. Rom. 2:17-29; 2 Cor. 11:22; Phil. 3:3-6) as exemplified by circumcision, Paul reassured the Gentile readers that "in baptism they had received a circumcision which in comparison with that of the Jews is much more comprehensive and sanctifying (2:11-13; cf. 1:21)," as Zahn [62] remarked. For, in the words of S. Lewis Johnson, Jr.,[63] in Colossians "circumcision means the putting off of the fleshly nature of man, or the crucifixion of the old man... (cf. Rom. 6:5-6)." The opponents were making the distinction between the circumcised and uncircumcised among believers (3:11). This separation is clear in Ephesians 2:11-13: "At one time you Gentiles in the flesh, called the uncircumcision by what is called the circumcision, which is made in the flesh by hands, ... were ... alienated from the commonwealth of Israel, and strangers to the covenants of promise ... But now in Christ Jesus you who were once far off have been brought near." Χειροποίητος invariably involves a comparatively negative judgment (Mk. 14:58; Acts 7:48; 17:24; Hebr. 9:24); its fifteen uses in the Septuagint pertain to idols. Such a polemical term would not be used in a non-controversial situation.

In Philippians 3 Paul warns against the evil workmen (cf. 2 Cor. 11:13; Tit. 1:10) who mutilate the flesh (τὴν κατατομήν; cf. Gal. 5:12) and boastfully trust in the flesh (3:2-4). As Marvin R. Vincent [64] commented: "These persons had no right to claim circumcision in the true sense. Unaccompanied by faith..., it was nothing more than physical mutilation." While they defined "the true circumcision (ἡ περιτομή)" outwardly and corporeally, Paul gave the description in terms of worshipping by the Spirit of God (cf. Rom. 2:25-29) and boasting in Christ Jesus (3:3). The Apostle "had already possessed all that upon which the Jews especially prided themselves." [65] The fact that he, too, was circumcised he deemed, not as gain, but as loss on account of Christ (3:5ff.). For the opponents circumcision was an element in legal righteousness (3:6, 9) and perfection (3:12-16).

In 1 Cor. 7 Paul urges that after being called, the circumcised and uncircumcised should remain in their existing state (v. 18).

[62] Zahn, op. cit., I, 464.
[63] "The Complete Sufficiency of Union with Christ," Bibliotheca Sacra 120 (1963), 15.
[64] A Critical and Exegetical Commentary on the Epistles to the Philippians and to Philemon (I.C.C.), New York (Charles Scribner's Sons, 1897), 92.
[65] Ibid., 95. See also D.W.B. Robinson," We are the Circumcision," Australian Biblical Review 15 (1967), 29-32.

Maintaining one's *status quo* is his general principle (vv. 17, 20, 24). As the ascetics had made it sinful to deviate from this rule in matters of marriage (see p. 116), Paul may have extended the application of the law in order to answer the call for circumcision. A. Robertson and A. Plummer [66] commented on vv. 18-19: "Having previously proclaimed the folly of *adopting* circumcision, when the freedom of the Gospel was open to them, ... he points out that the difference between circumcision and uncircumcision is a matter of small moment" (οὐδέν). Could an important issue like this escape the local party strife? Paul downgraded the question as insignificant, because of the pain it had caused him elsewhere (cf. Gal. 5:6; 6:15). Due to party pride, it would be more natural for some to boast of their circumcision or non-circumcision, than to press members of other parties to undo their circumcision or to undergo it. C. K. Barrett [67] notes that "from the Jewish point of view this (7:19) is a paradoxical, or rather an absurd, statement. A Jew would reply, Circumcision is one of God's commandments ... firmly rooted in the Old Testament." Commenting on 7:23, Clarence Craig [68] suggested that "the warning against becoming slaves of men may refer to the discussion concerning parties. Church leaders might seek to tyrannize over them, but they had been set free from such bondage" (cf. 9:19; 2 Cor. 11:20). Paul's moving directly from the topic of circumcision to that of slavery and freedom is parallelled (in reverse) in Gal. 4:21-5:12 (cf. 2:4).

Whereas, unlike Moses, the Spirit of the Lord brings liberty (ἐλευθερία) (2 Cor. 3:17; cf. Rom. 8:15; Gal. 4:4-5; 5:18), the false apostles at Corinth were accused of enslaving members of the church (2 Cor. 11:20). Paul used the same term, καταδουλόω, in Gal. 2:4(cf. 5:1-3) to describe the circumcision of a Greek. In the same context (2 Cor. 11:17-18) Paul accused the false apostles of the confidence of boasting according to the flesh. That this pertains to Jewishness and circumcision is apparent not only from a comparison with Phil. 3:3-5 (ἐν σαρκί) and Gal. 6:12-14, but also from the context. For, in boasting that he, too, is a Hebrew, Israelite and descendant of Abraham (11:22), he is carrying out his intent to glory after the flesh also. As circumcision is a distinguishing religious mark of Jews and the

---

[66] *A Critical and Exegetical Commentary on the First Epistle of St. Paul to the Corinthians*, New York (Charles Scribners, 1911), 146.

[67] *Op. cit.*, 169.

[68] Exegesis in *The Interpreter's Bible*, Vol. 10, 83.

initiatory rite whereby a Gentile enters the covenant of promise to
the children of Abraham, the subject of their boasting must have
included their having been circumcised. Such boasting suggests that
circumcision was treated as a privelege or as a sign of perfection of
advanced converts. Moreover, these "deceitful workmen (ἐργάται)" (2
Cor. 11:13) are characterized like the "evil ἐργάται" who teach
circumcision (Phil. 3:2).

Titus 1:10-11 warns: "There are many insubordinate men, empty
talkers and deceivers, especially the circumcision (party); they must
be silenced, since they are upsetting whole families by teaching for
base gain what they have no right to teach. "Teachers of genealogies
were stirring up quarrels about the law (Tit. 3:9), which must have
spread from the church into family life. In contradicting sound
doctrine (Tit. 1:9, 13; cf. 1 Tim. 1:9-10), many were heeding Jewish
fables and human commandments (Tit. 1:14; cf. Jn. 7:22). Whatever
the racial origin of these troublemakers, it is certain that they taught
and practiced circumcision, the chief badge of Judaism from which
they drew their designation. The polemical language is reminiscent
of passages already discussed: Eph. 4:14; Col. 2:4, 8; 1 Tim. 1:5-7;
6:4-6.

Ignatius cautioned the Philadelphians (6:1): "But if anyone preach
Judaism unto you, do not listen to him. For it is better to hear
Christian doctrine from a man who has been circumcised, than
Judaism from one uncircumcised." Apparently the Judaizers included
Gentile Christians who were so enamored with Jewish practices that
they spoke more about circumcision than about Christ. But
circumcision could be delayed for these converts; submission to it
gave them a higher status (cf. Gal. 6:12-13). Zahn [69] believed that the
most that could be strictly deduced from *ad Philad.* 6:1 is that the
false teachers did not require the circumcision of their converts, as
some of them were uncircumcised. Ignatius characterized preachers
of circumcision as those who "wish to deceive according to the flesh
(κατὰ σάρκα ... πλανῆσαι)" (Phil. 7:1).

When eight days old both John and Jesus were circumcised and
given the names revealed by angels (Lk. 1:59-63; 2:21; cf. 1:13, 31).

Judeans identified by the Western text as "Pharisees who had
believed" came to Antioch announcing, "Unless you are circumcised
according to the custom of Moses, you cannot be saved" (Acts 15:1).

---

[69] *Ignatius von Antiochien*, Gotha (Perthe, 1873), 368-69.

This identity is confirmed in 15:5, where believers from this party said, "It is necessary to circumcise" Gentile converts. Palestinian Hebrews as a whole were upset by the report that Paul was telling Diaspora Hebrews "to forsake Moses, telling them not to circumcise their children" (21:21). The Ebionites (Irenaeus *Adv. Haer.* i, 26.2; Epiphanius, *Haer.* 30.2 and 17), Dositheans (*ibid.*, 13) and Elkesaites (*ibid.* 30.17; 19.5; Hippolytus, *Philos.* 9.14.1) practiced it; according to the latter, "believers ought to be circumcised" (*ibid.*). The *Kerygmata Petrou* was to be read only by circumcised believers (Clementine *Contestatio of James* 1.1).

As it is only in Galatians that we find clear evidence of obligatory circumcision, it appears that there was a change in strategy. Converts were at first allowed to postpone being circumcised (in the way that the emperor Constantine postponed his baptism); then it was made an optional good work for those who were approaching "perfection." By the time of Timothy of Constantinople (Migne, *P.G.* 86, 33B) the Melchizedekians (if related to the Judaizers) "did not circumcise their flesh." There may be a hint that they spoke of spiritual circumcision. The Paris graec. 364 MS. confirms that they shunned circumcision.

Jubilees 15:11-14 paraphrases Gen. 17:9-14 concerning God's teaching to Abraham on circumcision. "This law is for all the generations for ever" (Jub.15:25; cf. 28; 16:14).

> And every one that is born, the flesh of whose foreskin is not circumcised on the eighth day, belongeth not to the children of the covenant which the Lord made with Abraham, but to the children of destruction; nor is there, moreover, any sign on him that he is the Lord's, but (he is destined) to be destroyed and slain from the earth, and to be rooted out of the earth, for he hath broken the covenant of the Lord our God (15:26).

However, it is prophesied that Israelites "will leave their sons uncircumcised as they were born. And there will be great wrath from the Lord against the children of Israel, because they have forsaken His covenant and turned from his word" (15:33-34). Levi did not wish the sons of Hamor to be circumcised, because they had wrought an abomination on his sister. But Jacob "was grieved in that they had received the circumcision and after that had been put to death" (T. Levi 6:3-6). This piece of Haggadah presupposes that circumcision should exempt them from being slain.

The Dead Sea Scrolls have surprisingly few references to circumcision. The spiritual sense is found in two. "In the Community they shall circumcise the foreskin of the (evil) inclination and disobedience in order to lay a foundation of truth for Israel, for the Community of the everlasting Covenant (1 QS 5.5-6). The spiritually circumcised no longer "walks in the stubbornness of his heart to stray by following his heart and eyes and the thoughts of his (evil) inclination" (1 QS 5.4-5) For example, the Wicked Priest who persecuted the Teacher of Righteousness "did not circumcise the foreskin of his heart"; rather, he "walked in the ways of drunkenness to quench his thirst" (1Q p Hab 11, 4.12-14). Drunkenness is evidence of the evil inclination which has not been circumcised. Physical circumcision seems to have been esteemed for effecting delivery from the power of Mastemah and thereby from the evil inclination which was to be symbolically circumcised. For, the Damascus Document (16.4-6), in explaining the oath for entrance into the Covenant, taught: "On the day on which a man undertakes to be converted to the Law of Moses, the Angel of Hostility will depart from him if he fulfills his promises. For this reason Abraham circumcised himself on the day on which he knew". Entrance into the Covenant of the Community was likened to Abraham's acceptance of the covenant which required circumcision. Expulsion of the Angel of Hostility was effected by promised obedience to the law of Moses (as understood by the sect) and to the covenant of Abraham. This expulsion began with the oath of entrance and was gradually effected, just as Abraham circumcised himself (thereby entering the Covenant) on the day on which he knew that he would be delivered from the devil. As CD 16.3-4 had just specified that the Book of Jubilees carefully taught the exact times when Israel would be blind, the same work may be assumed to have inspired the reference in CD 16.6. For, according to Jub. 15:32, Israel, among all the nations, was to be preserved and delivered from the evil angels and spirits by God.[70] The value of circumcision need not have been viewed as *ex opere operato*; rather, he who submits to the covenant of circumcision promises thereby to obey the divine law and to cut away disobedience, and it is this new obedience which drives away the devil and his angels, who arouse the evil inclination.

Hippolytus (*Ref.* ix, 26) told of certain Essenes who were called Zealots or Sicarii. "If they hear anyone διαλεγομένος about God and His law, they will watch such a one until he is alone in some place,

---

[70] Dupont-Sommer, *op. cit.*, 162, n. 2.

and threaten to kill him if he be not circumcised. Whom, if he does not consent, he does not spare, but slays him."

OBSERVANCE OF TIMES AND SEASONS

Paul lamented to the Galatians: "You observe days, and months, and seasons, and years! I am afraid that I have labored over you in vain" (4:10-11) The inclusive nature of the list suggests that the whole Jewish sacred calendar may have been religiously kept: sabbaths, New Years Day (1st of Tishri), Day of Atonement (cf. Rom. 14:5), new moons, the four months of fasting (Zech. 7:5; 8:19), the feasts (καιροι: cf. Lev. 23:4 LXX) of Passover, Booths and Weeks, sabbatical years, Jubilees, etc. These times were already being widely celebrated, though circumcision among the Gentile believers was far from universal (5:2-3; 6:12-13); Jewish practices, such as the festival cycle, which were less socially burdensome and more analagous to pagan observances, were the first to be accepted.[71] This suggests degrees of perfection.

The Colossians were cautioned: "Let no one pass judgment on you ... with regard to a festival or a new moon or a sabbath ... These are only a shadow of what is to come; but the substance belongs to Christ" (2:16-17). The reference to a festival, new moon and sabbath implies annual, monthly and weekly observances (cf. 2 Chron. 2:4; 31:3; Ezek. 45:17; Hosea 2:11). If this be the case, the annual feasts would include Passover, Weeks and Booths. The addressees were being critically judged in terms of their keeping these days holy. The context suggests that special times were sanctioned by heavenly powers (2:8, 15-20), as in the case of Gal. 4:8-11.

In an anti-Judaizing section (chh. 8-9) of his letter to the Magnesians, Ignatius exemplifies coming to the newness of hope (εἰς καινότητα ἐλπιδος) by living according to the Lord's day (κατὰ κυριακὲn)[72] rather than σαββατίζοντες (9:1). The latter belongs to Ἰουδαϊσμὸς (8:1) and living apart from (χωρίς) Jesus Christ (9:2), but the former belongs to living κατὰ him (8:2). The Martyr insists that even the ancient prophets hoped in Christ (9:2) and lived according to him (8:2).

John began to preach in 26-27 A.D. in fulfillment of the prophecy

---

[71] Burton, op. cit., 233, 274.

[72] R. B. Lewis ("Ignatius and the 'Lord's Day', "*Andrews University Seminary Studies* 6 [1968], 46-59) believes that the context favors the translation, "the Lord's life."

of Dan. 9:24ff. and 11Q Melch, i.e. of the 490 year Jubilee interim[73] and Melchizedek's return for vengeance (see below, p. 258). Interest in the sacred calendar is presupposed in his belief in the imminence of the Messiah's coming. The Clementine Homilies (ii. 23-24) state that John chose thirty disciples in order to correspond with 30-day months (i.e. in the solar calendar).

The Sabbath was observed by the Ebionites (Eusebius, *H.E.* iii, 27; Epiphanius, *Haer.* 30.2 & 17) and Elkesaites (*ibid.*, 30.17; 19.5; Hippolytus, *Philos.* 16.3).

The Preaching of Peter (*ap.* Clement of Alex., *Strom.* vi, 5.41; Origen, *On John* xiii. 17) boasts that we do not, like the Jews, serve the month and the moon, or celebrate "the first Sabbath, or new moon, or days of unleavened bread, or the feast, or the great day" (of Atonement).

According to the Gospel of Didymus Judas Thomas (27), Jesus said: "If you do not keep the Sabbath as Sabbath, you will not see the Father."

The Dositheans observed the Sabbath and celebrated Jewish feasts and fasts, according to Epiphanius (*Haer.* 13 & 12). Dositheus taught that "in the position in which a man is found on the Sabbath day, he is to remain until evening" (Origen, *de princip.* iv. 17). The Clementine Homilies (ii, 24) and Recognitions (i, 54; ii, 8) treat him as a rival of Simon (Magus) for the leadership of the sect following John the Baptist and of the school handing down his doctrines (e.g. "there gathered about John thirty eminent persons according to the reckoning of the lunar month": *Hom.* ii, 23). The 14th century Chronicle of Abu-al-Fath [74] confirms that the followers of "Dusis" observed 30-day months. They could not even purify vessels on the Sabbath. On this day their feasts were held. They prepared food for their cattle on Friday.

The Montanists observed a solar calendar (Sozomen, *H.E.* vii. 12, 18; Ps.-Chrysostom, *Epist.* vii; Migne, *P.G.* 59, 747).[75] They introduced feasts and fasted at special times (Hippolytus, *Philos.* viii, 19.2; see below, p. 105).

---

[73] Gunther, *op. cit.*, 19.

[74] James Montgomery, *The Samaritans*, Philadelphia (John Winston, 1907), 252ff; J. M. Fuller, "Dositheus", *DCB* i, 903-04; G. F. Moore, "The Covenanters of Damascus; A Hitherto Unknown Jewish Sect," *HTR* 4 (1911), 362-64."

[75] J. Massingberd Ford, "Was Montanism a Jewish Christian Heresy?, "*Journal of Ecclesiastical History* 17 (1966) 146, n. 11.

The observance of times continued to attract Christians in Phrygia down to the fourth century. The Council of Laodicea ruled:

> It is not right for Christians to Judaize and abstain from labor on the sabbath, but to work on this same day. They should pay respect rather to the Lord's day and, if possible, abstain from labor on it as Christians. But if they should be found Judaizers, then let them be anathema in the sight of Christ (canon 29).
> It is not right to receive from Jews or heretics the festive offerings which they send about, nor join in their festivals (can. 37).
> It is not right to receive unleavened bread from Jews or to participate in their impieties (can. 38).

According to Timothy of Constantinople (Migne, *P.G.* 45, 33B) those who glorified Melchizedek observed the Sabbath. His comment that they were neither Hebrews nor Gentiles (ἐθνιχοί) is perplexing even when related to the assertion of the   Paris graec. 364 manuscript: "They are often found among Jews and they pretend to observe the Sabbath." The fact that they did honor the Sabbath indicates at least that they understood themselves to be in the spiritual lineage of Israel of the Old Covenant; accordingly, they sought friendly relations with local Jews. This deduction accords with Zahn's conclusion [76] that certain canons of the Council of Laodicea were directed against local Christian concessions to Jewish customs.

The Sabbatarian doctrine in Jubilees is especially strict. God hallowed the seventh day for all ages (2:1). He commanded all the angels of the presence and all the angels of sanctification to keep the Sabbath together with the Israelites (2:17-33). The Sabbath is a day even "more holy and blessed than any jubilee day of the jubilees" (2:30). Death is promised to whoever on the Sabbath (cf. Exod. 31:14) lies with his wife, fasts, wars, strikes or kills anything, lights a fire, draws water, travels on a beast or ship, or catches a bird or fish (2:29-30; 50:6-13). The Apocalypse of Moses (43:3) treated mourning on the Sabbath as forbidden; "but on the seventh day, rest and rejoice..., because on that very day, God rejoiceth (yea) and we angels (too) with the righteous soul, who hath passed away from the earth."

The author of Jubilees sought to replace the intercalated lunar calendar with a solar calendar. "God appointed the sun to be a great sign on the earth for days and for sabbaths and for months and for

---

[76] *Introduction to the N.T.*, i, 476-77.

years and for sabbaths of years and for jubilees and for all seasons of
the years" (Jub. 2:9). "And all the children of Israel will forget, and
will not find the path of the years, and will forget the new moons,
and seasons, and sabbaths, and they will go wrong as to all the order
of the years" (6:34), i.e. months, festivals and jubilees (6:36-38).
Similar calendric conclusions had been drawn by the author of 1
Enoch 82:4-7.

The divisions of the days and the feasts of the covenant are written
on heavenly tablets (Jub. 6:17-22, 35; 16:28-29; cf. ch. 49). Likewise
the new moons of the first, fourth, seventh and tenth months are
placed on the heavenly tables; they are ordained "as feasts for a
memorial for ever" (Jub. 6:23-29).

The Testament of Levi (ch. 17) divides the history of the
priesthood into seven Jubilee periods, at the end of which the Lord
will raise up a new priest (18:2).

According to the Qumran Manual of Discipline, "the man of
understanding ... shall do the will of God according to all that has
been revealed, season by season, and he shall teach all understanding
discovered through time, together with the Decree of Time" (1QS
9.12-14). Prayers are to be addressed to God

> in all the beginnings of Time, (in) the fundamental divisions of the
> length and circuit of the seasons (which return) at their appointed hour
> (as established) by their signs for all their dominions, at the appointed
> and certain hour according to the mouth of God and the law decreed by
> Him who is. And this law shall endure without end (1QH 12.7-10).

God is to be praised "according to the Decree which is graven
forever"

> at the seasons' entry, on the days of the new moon,... for the moons are
> renewed and grow according to the infinite holiness of the sign N; ...
> according to the beginning of the seasons for all time to come; at the
> beginning of the months according to the seasons on which they
> depend; and (on the) days of holiness, ... ; at the beginnings of the years
> and in the circling of the yearly seasons; ... (on the) feasts of years
> according to the weeks of years; and at the beginning of the weeks of
> weeks of years, at the time of Release [i.e. sabbatical and jubilee years]
> (1QS 10.3-8; cf. 1QM 2.4)

The Qumran Community had special prayers for feasts (e.g. 1Q 34
and 34 bis).[77] "God established His Covenant with Israel for ever,

---

[77] Milik, *art. cit.*, *RB* 63 (1956), 61.

revealing to them the hidden things in which all Israel had strayed:
His holy Sabbaths and His glorious feasts" (CD 3.13-15). God warned
Moses that the Israelites would violate the Sabbath of the Covenant
[and the feasts] (1Q 22 I, 8). But "those who have entered the New
Covenant in the land of Damascus" were careful "to observe the
Sabbath day according to its exact tenor, and feasts, and the Day of
Fasting" (CD 6.18-19). According to the rule of the Community,
"they shall make no single step from all the words of God concerning
their times; they shall not anticipate their times, nor delay them for
any of their feasts" (1QS 1.14). Profanation of the Sabbath or the
feasts led to a seven-year probation before one could re-enter the
Assembly (CD 12.3-6). Regulations for observance of the sabbatical
year are presented in 1Q 22 3.1-7. The tenth jubilee year has
eschatological significance, according to 11Q Melch. 2.7. The newly
discovered Temple Scroll [78] gives detailed rules for the calendar and
the celebration of the festivals, including the New Wine and the New
Oil. There is considerable evidence [79] that the Qumran Community
followed the solar calendar taught by the Book of Jubilees and 1
Enoch. An unpublished text from Cave 4 which resembles Jubilees
defends a pecular calendar theory.[80] The *mishmaroth* (Book of the
Priestly Courses) from Cave 4 describe the weekly offices of the
priests in relation to solar and lunar calendars with their feasts.

With regard to the observance of the Sabbath, five of the twenty-
eight regulations in the Damascus Document (CD 10.14-11.18) go
beyond the Rabbinic ones,[81] though Pharisee and Qumran Sabbath
laws may have had a common point of origin and influenced each
other.[82] Those in Jubilees pose several points of correspondence.[83]

Essene Sabbath observance is described by Philo in general terms.
"They continually instruct themselves in [these] ancestral laws but
especially every seventh day; for the seventh day is thought holy. On
that day they abstain from other work and proceed to the holy places
called synagogues, where they sit in appointed places..." (*Quod
omnis probus* 81). Hippolytus (ix, 25) is more concrete: "More than

[78] Yigael Yadin, "The Temple Scroll," *Biblical Archaeologist* 30 (1967), 137-38.
[79] Bibliographies in Cross, *op. cit.*, 36, n. 71; Ringgren, *op. cit.*, 224, n. 10; also E.
Ettisch, "Der grosse Sonnenzyklus und der Qumränkalender," *TLZ* 88 (1963), 185-94.
[80] Strugnell, *art. cit.*, *RB* 63(1956), 65.
[81] Black, *op. cit.*, 124; cf. S.T. Kimbrough, "The Concept of Sabbath at Qumran,"
RQ 5 (1966), 483-502.
[82] *Ibid.*, 484, 502.
[83] Dupont-Sommer, *op. cit.*, 152-54, notes.

all the Jews, they arrange to abstain from work on the Sabbath. For not only do they prepare their food one day before, so as not to light a fire, but they neither move an implement nor relieve nature. And some of them will not even get out of bed" (cf. Josephus, *War* ii, 8.9.147). The Slavonic version of Josephus adds that "they observe severely the seventh day, the seventh week, the seventh month and the seventh year," i.e. the Sabbath, the seven-week festival of the Therapeutae,[84] who honor the pure and ever-virgin number of seven (Philo, *de vita contempl.* 65; cf. 30, 36), the month beginning the New Year (Lev. 23:24) and the Sabbatical year.

---

[84] M. Delcor, "Repas cultuels esséniens et Thérapeutes, 'Thiases et Haburoth'," *RQ* 6 (1967), 415.

CHAPTER THREE

ASCETICISM

FOOD AND DRINK RESTRICTIONS

The propriety of Hebrew and Gentile Christians' eating together in violation of Jewish scruples was an issue mentioned by Paul in Gal. 2:11ff. He had to explain the uncomfortable fact that Peter, Barnabas and Antiochene Hebrew believers did withdraw from table fellowship when reprensentatives from Jerusalem came to Antioch. For, whoever ate with Gentiles (Daniel 1:8; Tobit 1:11-12; Judith 12:1-2; Jub. 22:16; cf. Lev. 20:24-26) and sinners (Mt. 9:11) was in danger of defilement. Significantly Paul did not mention the kosher food decrees of the Jerusalem Council (Acts 15:20, 29), which did not suit his arguments. Might we presume that the Galatians were being asked to abstain from meat offered to idols and containing blood because the animal had been strangled? Further inevitable eating questions were inevitable in Galatia from the meritorious observance of Jewish fasts at regular times in service of the στοιχεῖα τοῦ κόσμου (4:8-11; see pp. 172-173). The observance of days may well have included fasting on Tuesday and Thursday (Lk. 18:21; Didache 8:1; Ta 'an 12a) as well as on the Day of Atonement.

In the Epistle to the Colossians questions of food and drink are drink are associated with those which concern feasts (ἑορτή), new moons and sabbaths; they are all shadows of things to come (2:16-17). False teachers were critically judging those who did not observe their regulations in these matters as well as in regard to humility and worship of angels (2:18). Wilfred L. Knox [1] deduced that the opponents "sought to impose on them higher standards of special fasts, enjoined as a means of propitiating the angels." That ταπεινοφροσύνη (2:18, 23) was a catchword of the false teachers may be deduced from Paul's favorable use of the term in a non-technical, moral sense in 3:12, and from the fact that θέλων ἐν ταπεινοφροσύνῃ is a Hebraism. This self-humiliation and -mortification is expressed through fasting,[2] according to Shepherd of Hermas Vis. iii, 10.6; Sim.

---

[1] St. Paul and the Church of the Gentiles, Cambridge (Cambridge University, 1939), 170.
[2] Ernst Percy, Die Probleme der Kolosser- und Epheserbriefe, Lund (C. W. K.

v, 3.7 and Tertullian (*On Fasting* 12; cf. 13, 16). Ταπεινοφροσύνη attracted the attention and aid of the angels. Three goals might be served by communication with the angels through fasting. The first, illumination through visions, is suggested by the conjunction of ideas in Col. 2:16, 18 (ἐν βρώσει καὶ ἐν πόσει, ... θέλων ἐν ταπεινοφροσύνῃ καὶ θρησκείᾳ τῶν ἀγγέλων, ἃ ἑόρακεν ἐμβατεύων). In such a case Paul's opponents would be teaching that, in order to communicate with angels and receive and interpret their revelations through visions or to accept them by faith, a cleansing abstinence from wine and meat was fitting. Moreover, specific dietary ordinances constituted part of the γνῶσις allegedly derived from angelic visions, but described in Paul's perjorative terms as human injunctions and teachings (2:8, 18, 22-23). Secondly, the instinctive reaction of Paul's opponents to suffering (cf. Ecclus. 18:20) might be to attribute it to some violated scruple and to fast in order to be influenced more favorably by the angels; i.e. to escape further chastisement and to propitiate them. The Book of James describes how Joachim, the grandfather of Jesus, dealt with the great shame and sadness which his childlessness brought. Withdrawing into the wilderness for forty days, he said to himself: "I shall not go down either for food or for drink until the Lord my God visits me; prayer shall be my food and drink" (1:4). Meanwhile Anna his wife lamented over her childlessness; she humbled herself and mourned (2:1-2). An angel revealed to Joachim that God had heard his prayer and that Anna had conceived (4:2). An angel likewise revealed to Anna that God had heard and would answer her prayer (4:1). The third purpose of ταπεινοφροσύνη stems from its apparent grammatical connection with τῶγ ἀγγέλων (2:18), since ἐν is not repeated before θρησκεία.[3] If so, it signifies imitation of, or participation in, the angelic life (cf. Lk. 20:36: ἰσάγγελοι) of abstinence from eating and drinking. Be that as it may, the reason which the Apostle gave for letting no one judge the Colossians in matters of eating and drinking is that Christ put off and triumphed over the principalities and powers (2:15-16). Moreover, if the readers have died with Christ from the στοιχεῖα τοῦ κόσμου, they should no longer be subject to the ascetic laws, "do not taste, do not handle" (2:20-21). Religious service to these cosmic spirits included obedience to certain dietary regulations. The connection between 2:21 and 23

Gleerup, 1946), 148-49; Fred O. Francis, "Humility and Angel Worship," *Studia Theologica* 16 (1962), 114-19.

[3] Zahn, *Introduction to the N.T.*, 468-69, 477-78, n. 7.

suggests that certain luxury foods were deemed inherently taboo, or at least dangerous, because they were unclean or were hostile to severe control of the flesh (e.g. wine and supposedly aphrodisiac foods). Paul held that all (πάντα) were created for consumption. The ideal of severity (ἀφειδία) to the body (2:23) is a true mark of asceticism, though such mortification need not imply hatred of the flesh. Such severity in disciplining the body was doubtless deemed a θρησκεία pure and undefiled (καθαρὰ καὶ ἀμίαντος) before God (Jas, 1:27), but it was intended for a higher form of purity than that aimed at by ordinary pious Jews (Levit. 11:33ff.).[4] This self-denial was a private discipline (ἐθελοβρησκία) (2:23) elevating the worshipper toward perfection. It was to be observed whenever purification was felt to be needed, though the perfect might habitually abstain from corrupting foods. The ascetic regulations have the reputation (λόγος) of wisdom, but really deserve no honor (τιμή) (2:23): a term commonly associated with δόξα, glory (Rom. 2:7, 10; 1 Tim. 1:17; Hebr. 2:7, 9; 3:3; 1 Pet. 1:7; Rev. 4:9, 11; 5:12-13; 7:12; 19:1; 21:24, 26).

Paul viewed the regulations, rather, as really for the sake of (πρός) the indulgence or satisfaction of the flesh (2:23): not literally, but in the sense of gratification of a sensuous mind (νοῦς τῆς σαρκός) which was preoccupied with "perfecting" the flesh and which was puffed up (φυσιούμενος) with success (2:18). They enjoyed the struggle and revelled with a worldly pride. Thereby the flesh and mind were being served, and an inverted self-satisfaction experienced. Or, perhaps the aim was to be so "perfect" (fulfill the τέλος of) the flesh that it no longer experienced the torments of desire. Accordingly, the Apostle urged: "Set your minds on (φρονεῖτε) things that are above, not on things that are on earth (τὰ ἐπὶ τῆς γῆς)" (3:2). "If with Christ you died to the elemental spirits of the universe, why do you live as if you still belonged to the world" (2:20). The στοιχεῖα belong to the κοσμος (2:8, 20) and the rules, as human precepts and doctrines, refer to "things which perish as they are used" (2:22). Thus Paul degrades dietary laws in so far as they were motivated by fleshly preoccupations. However, as the Apostle degraded angels of God to στοιχεῖα τοῦ κόσμου (2:8, 15, 18, 23; see pp. 174-179), there may be an ironical, polemical degradation of the opponents' intended "spiritual" program and status to the physical level. Instead of servile expressions of self-humiliation before angels, Paul calls for a confident life in Christ (2:5-7), who had

---

[4] H. Strathmann, *Geschichte der frühchristlichen Askese*, Leipzig (A. Deichert, 1914), i, 310ff.

already brought forgiveness of sins and fullness of life (2:10-15, 19-20a; 3:1-4); the true believer has already risen above the sphere where angelic powers enslave their devotees.

Philippians 3 is illumined by several of the above passages in Colossians. Paul castigated those "whose god is the belly" (3:19). In so doing they thought not of heavenly things (as they claimed) and of Christ, but of earthly things (ἐπίγεια φρονοῦντες), and they found glory (cf. Col. 2:20-23; 3:1-2) in what is really shameful (αἰσχύνη). Its contrast with δόξα links it with the primary reference in the Septuagint to "shame," which divine judgment brings especially to those "who are full of proud confidence and expectancy." [5] Αἰσχύνη in this sense is used in Rom. 9:33; 2 Cor. 9:4; 10:8; Phil. 1:20; 1 Pet. 2:6; 3:16. In Phil. 3:3 (cf. Col. 2:11-13) Paul explains that the true circumcision boast rather in Christ and serve (λατρεύοντες) God spiritually. The same sort of criticism is levelled against materialistic trust in circumcision and in serving the belly; one should glory in neither. Circumcision was among the forms of legal righteousness deemed as refuse or dung (σκύβαλα) by Paul (3:5, 8). In this sense the errorists are to be ashamed of glorying in a material service of the belly. As in the case of circumcision, they were deceived both in believing that they thereby served God and in glorying in their legal righteousness. They attributed too much religious significance to the κοιλία. This "belly-service" had nothing to do with antinomian gluttony or indifference, which would be incompatible with Paul's terminology in this context and with the Judaism of the chapter. In actuality Paul was attacking those who were following special food laws. This polemical meaning was attached to the phrase, ὁ θεὸς ἡ κοιλία (3:19) among Patristic commentators.[6] Reliance on diet, rather than on the cross, resurrection and παρουσία of Christ (3:10-11, 18, 20-21; cf. Col. 2:12-3:4), as the heavenly, righteous way of life, is the shame which often brought Paul to tears (3:18). Such grief would hardly be prompted by his converts' overindulgence in food.

Similarly, in Rom. 16:18 Paul relates that deceivers with a contrary teaching "serve not our Lord Jesus Christ, but their own belly." They were speaking "wisely" concerning good and evil (16:18-19) (see p. 64). As they had to speak about or preach the object of their service, their deceptive words must have dealt in part with the welfare of the belly or of the worshipper obeying dietary laws. But, by

---

[5] R. Bultmann, "Αἰσχύνη," in Kittel (ed.), op. cit., i (1964), 189.

[6] Johannes Behm, "Κοιλία", in Kittel (ed.), op. cit., iii (1965), 788, n. 14.

including diet within the scope of their instruction, they seemed to Paul to devote more attention to food and drink than to Christ (as aids to perfection-?). Paul described strange dietary regulations in the non-controversial letter addressed to Rome. His experience was first-hand and was deemed relevant in the imperial capital. In Rom. 14:1-2, 21 he told of the man of weak faith (cf. 1 Cor. 8:9, 11; 9:22) who "eats only vegetables" and who does not "eat meat or drink wine." Such persons were concerned with what is inherently unclean (14:14, 20) and with the religious observance of one day as superior to another (14:5-6). This suggests persons with Judaic scruples.[7] Sometimes they critically judged those who did not abstain (14:3-4, 10, 13; cf. Col. 2:16). But for Paul "the kingdom of God does not mean food or drink" (14:17). Likewise, in Phil. 3:19 he contrasts the glory in God and the preoccupation with the earthly things pertinent to the belly.

Paul advised the Corinthians not to offend Jews, Gentiles and the church by eating and drinking practices (1 Cor. 10:31-32). All believers, whatever their practice, were to act for the glory of God (10:31). The same advice is given in Rom. 14:6 (cf. 2, 13) concerning vegetarianism. Those who ate meat (especially if coming from idol offerings) were to be motivated by the same desire to honor God which moved those with Jewish scruples. Paul's liberty in partaking by grace was judged by Judaic scruples (1 Cor. 10:29-30).

According to 2 Cor. 10:2-3, the Apostle's opponents claimed to walk, not according to the flesh (as allegedly Paul did), but rather spiritually (cf. Rom. 8:4-8; Gal. 5:16-17). He preferred to say, "according to a different spirit" (2 Cor. 11:4). Their scorn for the carnal manner of life presupposes that even more strongly than he (Rom. 7:5-6; 8:3-4; Gal. 5:19-21) they located sin in the flesh. These ostensibly ascetic opponents were more concerned than Paul with techniques of avoiding the ways of sinful flesh. But he proclaimed that he did not "war according to the flesh," i.e. use carnal weapons of warfare (10:3-4; cf. Clement of Alexandria, *Strom.* iii, 4.26) in order to avoid walking according to the sinful flesh. Carnal weapons are appropriate for those who claim to have so subdued the flesh that they walk spiritually. Such a type of warfare appears elsewhere in the N.T. In 1 Pet. 2:11 we read of the flesh and soul being at war, and in Rom. 7:23 (cf. 6:18-20) of the warfare of the law of sin ("in my

---

[7] For additional reasons see Robert Jewett, *Paul's Anthropological Terms*, Leiden (E. J. Brill, 1971), 44-45.

members") and the law of God. In 1 Cor. 9:26-27 (cf. Phil. 3:12-14)
Paul spoke of subduing his body while preaching the Gospel, while
in Col. 3:5 he exhorts: "Put to death what is earthly in you." W. L.
Knox [8] pointed out that "often Paul is handicapped by the difficulty
of admitting any value in external practices without appearing to
justify the claims of his opponents." Scorning the weakness of the
transient body and flesh, his opponents claimed to be strong (δυνατοί)
(2 Cor. 13:9), while they charged Paul with being weak (10:10; 11:21,
29-30; 12:5, 7-10; 13:4, 9; cf. Gal. 4:13-14), that is, in his flesh (cf.
6:9-10: dying, sorrowful, chastened with a physical weakness, rather
than abounding with their own alleged vitality, joy and grace). But he
replied that his weapons were δυνατὰ τῷ θεῷ (10:4); that is, his
weapons of knowledge of God and obedience to Christ made up for
the weakness of his flesh (10:5). Armed with the weapons of
righteousness, he commended himself by word of truth and the
power of God (2 Cor. 6:7). He was empowered by his faith in the
Gospel of Christ (cf. Eph. 6:10, 14-17), who is the power of God (1
Cor. 1:24; 2:5; 2 Cor. 13:4), rather than by weapons pertaining to the
flesh. Yet he was spry enough to escape in a basket lowered through
a wall (11:32-33), and strong enough to undergo such involuntary but
necessary, hardships as sleepless nights, fastings, thirst and exposure
(2 Cor. 11:27; cf. 6:5) in service of Christ. Could Paul have been
contrasting these to his opponents' self-denial and mortification of
the flesh? By the power of God Paul underwent all kinds of affliction
"so that the life of Jesus may be manifested in our body" (2 Cor. 4:7-
11). Paul's weaknesses and sufferings, such as a thorn in the flesh, are
paradoxically contrasted with mutually claimed visions, revelation
and divine power and grace in 12:1, 5-11 (cf. 1 Cor. 2:3-4). His
opponents may have voluntarily undergone fasts (νηστείαις (11:27),
which elsewhere were a condition for receiving angelic revelations. In
the Shepherd of Hermas, in which fasting and chastity were requisite
for receiving revelations (see pp. 119, 271-272), the visionary is told:
"Because thou wert weaker in the flesh it was not showed unto thee
by the angel; but when thou becamest strong through the Spirit, and
grewest mighty in they strength, so that thou wert able even to see
the angel, then was the building of the tower revealed unto thee by
the church ... Now thou seest (a vision) by means of an angel
through the same Spirit" (Simil. 9:1-2; transl. Hoole). For both
Hermas (and Paul's opponents?), then, he who fasts properly gains

---

[8] Op. cit., 171, n. 1.

strength through the Spirit so that he can subdue his flesh and receive revelations. Another clue to the techniques of walking spiritually is given in 2 Cor. 4:2-3. The "hidden things of shame (αισχύνε)," the avoidance of which constitutes their gospel of practical truth, but which really represent an adulteration (δολοῦντες) of the word of God, is best understood in terms of the food laws of the false teachers in Phil. 3:19, "whose glory is in their αισχύνη." Paul self-righteously proclaimed his renunciation of secret vices (e.g. imbibing; cf. Mt. 11:19). Was it by accident that Paul chose as a parallel term καπελεύοντες (2:17), which suggests the adulteration of wine with water by the κάπελος, or merchant? In the Septuagint of Isa. 1:22 and Gregory of Nazianzus (In Defense of his Flight to Pontus, 46; cf. Lucian, Hermotimus, 59) is found the sense of mixing water with wine.[9] Such a deliberate ascetic practice by Paul's opponents in the name of revealed teaching could serve to resist the flesh. In commending their personal example of following it, they were "proclaiming themselves" (4:5).

The Pastoral Epistles partially confirm this type of asceticism. Some depart the faith by heeding the deceitful spirits, demons and liars who "enjoin abstinence from foods which God created to be received with thanksgiving by those who believe and know the truth. For everything created by God is good, and nothing is to be rejected if it is received with thanksgiving; for then it is consecrated by the word of God and prayer" (1 Tim. 4:1-5; cf. Acts 10:9-16). Some foods were being considered taboo because of the teachings of spirits (διδασκαλίαις δαιμονίων). Since true nourishment is by words of the faith and of good teaching (1 Tim. 4:6), the inference may be drawn that positive food laws were also being taught. After warning Titus' Cretans against "giving heed to Jewish myths or to commands of men who reject the truth," the Pastor continues: "To the pure all things are pure, but to the corrupt and unbelieving nothing is pure" (Tit. 1:14-15). Evidently certain false teachers of the law considered many things to be unclean (cf. Mk. 7:2, 4, 7, 15; Lk. 11:38-41); their minds were preoccupied with defilement. Their commands concerning clean and unclean may have been supported by Jewish

---

[9] R. H. Strachan, The Second Epistle of Paul to the Corinthians (Moffatt N. T. Comm.), London (Hodder & Stoughton, 1935) & New York (Harper & Bros.), 78. Usually the ancient Greeks, Romans and Jews drank wine mixed with water (Everett Ferguson, "Wine as a Table-Drink in the Ancient World," Restoration Quarterly 13 (1970), 141-53.

myths about angels. Timothy was urged (1 Tim. 5:22b-23): "Keep yourself pure. No longer drink only water, but use a little wine for the sake of your stomach and your frequent ailments." The ascetic water-drinkers considered purity and goodness to be evidenced by outward, conspicuous (5:24-25) abstinence from wine.

The author of Hebrews exhorts: "Do not be led away by strange (ξένος) and diverse teachings; for it is well that the heart be strengthened by grace, not by foods (βρώμασιν), which have not benefitted their adherents" (13:9). Special dietary regulations were being regularly followed (περιπατοῦντες) as profitable aids to spiritual growth; perhaps foods were being graded according to the strength which they gave to, or took from, the soul (cf. 1 Cor. 8:8), so that the ardent dieters deemed themselves more strong and perfect (βεβαιοῦσθαι). The references to eating from the altar (13:10) and to true sacrifices (13:15-16) suggest that there were strange teachings about consecrated foods and/or about dieting as a sacrifice. In the reference (9:10) to ἐπὶ βρώμασιν καὶ πόμασιν, Levitical law lies in the background as much as in Col. 2:16. The same conclusion may be drawn from 13:9, since Levit. 11:43 (LXX) refers to unclean foods as ποικίλαι καὶ ξέναι βρόματα. The strangeness of teaching lay in the extended application of the Torah.

"John came neither eating or drinking" (Mt. 11:18), i.e. "eating no bread (Hebrew, *lechem*: bread, meat) [10] and drinking no wine" Lk. 7:33), whereas "the Son of Man came eating and drinking" and was charged with being "a glutton and a drunkard" (Mt. 11:19; Lk. 7:34). Jesus was asked, "Why do John's disciples ... fast (often), but your disciples do not fast?" (Mk. 2:18; Mt. 9:14; Lk. 5:33). Matthew puts this question in the mouth of critical disciples of the Baptist. The Slavonic version of Josephus' *War* (inserted after ii, 9.1.168) adds that he did not even eat unleavened bread at the Passover feast, "saying, 'In remembrance of God who redeemed the people from bondage, in (this) given to eat, and for the flight (only), since the journey was in haste.' But wine and strong drink he would not so much as allow to be brought near [11] him; and every beast he abhorred (for food); ... and fruits of the trees served him for (his) needs." [12] He also ate roots,

---

[10] Otto Böcher, "Ass Johannes der Täufer kein Brot (Luk. vii, 33)?", *NTS* 18 (1971), 90-92.

[11] J. Rendel Harris, *Josephus and His Testimony*, Cambridge (W. Heffer, 1931), 26-27.

[12] See John S. Pryke, "John the Baptist and the Qumran Community," *RQ* 4(1964), 484; translation by H. St. John Thackeray in Loeb Classical Libr., *Josephus* iii, 647-48.

bulrushes and young shoots.[13] As one who "ate locusts and wild honey" (Mt. 3:4; Mk. 1:6), he lived the ascetic life of Bannus, who dwelled in the desert and fed himself on what grew of its own accord (Josephus, *Life* 2). The censorious ascetic ideal which John inculcated in his close disciples lends support to the implication in the Slavonic Josephus that the Baptist was a rigorist in principle rather than a victim of the desert. As his baptism and understanding of divine forgiveness of sins required repentance (Mk. 1:4; Lk. 3:3) and purification of body and soul (Josephus, *Antiquities* xviii, 5.2.118), it is reasonable to deduce that these were (among) his motives for practicing and teaching asceticism. John Scobie [14] calls attention to "the prevailing Jewish conception of fasting, namely that it expressed humiliation before God and symbolized repentance for sin." Moreover, the Baptizer's quest for purity was that of a prophet "with a leather girdle around his waist" (Mt. 3:4; Mk 1:6), like Elijah (2 Kings 1:8). Luke 1:15-17 hints that his asceticism fostered not merely eschatological preparedness but also inspiration with "the spirit and power of Elijah." Or, at least consumption of alcoholic refreshments is incompatible with being filled with the Spirit. The angel revealed to Zechariah, "he shall drink no wine or strong drink, and he will be filled with the Holy Spirit, even from his mother's womb" (Lk. 1:15). Carl Kraeling [15] uncovered the implication that "John's abstinence is of a Nazirite type and that by virtue of his dietary program he can lay claim to an unusual measure of sanctity." Scobie [16] detects a legend that "John was consecrated as a Nazirite before his birth just as Samson was." An affinity of Baptist followers and Nazirites is clear.

The food and drink practices of ancient Hebrew Christians provide some analogy to those already considered. The Gospel of Didymus Judas Thomas gnosticized the saying, "If you fast not (cf. 104, 75) from the world (cf. 56, 80), you will not find the kingdom" (27). Hegesippus (*ap.* Eusebius, *H.E.* ii, 23.5) reported in the fifth book of his Memoirs a tradition that James the Just, the Lord's brother, "was holy from his mother's womb. He drank no wine nor strong drink, nor did he eat flesh; no razor went upon his head; he did not anoint himself with oil, and he did not go to the baths. . ."

---

[13] Eisler, *op. cit.*, 225; S. Szyszman, review of N. Z. Mescerskij, *History of the War of the Jews of Flavius Josephus in Old Russian*, in *RQ* 1(1959), 455.

[14] *Op. cit.*, 139-40.

[15] *Op. cit.*, 10.

[16] *Op. cit.*, 136-37.

This ascetic piety combines certain features of Essene, Rechabite and Nazirite piety as embodied in John the Baptist. Epiphanius (*Haer.* 29.4) called James a Nazirite.[17] He also vowed not to eat bread (i.e. to fast) until he saw Jesus risen from the dead (Hebrews Gospel, *ap.* Jerome, *vir. ill.* 2).[18] Epiphanius related that the Ebionites "abstain from all meat and from every kind of flesh" (*Haer.* 30, 15.3)[19] and include in their Gospel rhetorical words attributed to Jesus,, "Have I desired with desire to eat flesh at the Passover with you?" (*Haer.* 30, 22.4). The Ebionites celebrated the Lord's Supper with unleavened bread and "water of this world" (Irenaeus, *Adv. Haer.* v, 1.3; Epiphanius, *Haer.* 30.16.1; cf. Clem. Hom. xiv. 1; Clementine Contestio of Jas. 4.3). Ebionite abstinence from animal food is illustrated by their tradition in the Circuits of Peter (Epiphanius, Haer. 30.15) that Peter ate "only bread and olives, and rarely vegetables" (*Clem. Hom.* xii, 6).[20] Matthew's diet, according to a Hebrew Christian tradition reported by Clement of Alexandria (*Instructor* ii, i.16), consisted of "seeds, fruits and vegetables, without meat." The Clementine Homilies (viii, 15) lamented that the giants, "on account of their bastard nature, not being pleased with purity of food [manna], longed only after the taste of blood. Wherefore they first tasted flesh," i.e. ate animals. In *Clem. Hom.* ix. 10 Peter explains about demons:

> having desires after meats and drinks and sexual pleasures, but not being able to partake of these by reason of their being spirits, ... they enter

[17] James' wearing of the πέταλον (Epiphanius, *Haer.* 29.4; 78.14) is an indication that he was a Nazirite (J. Viksjaer Andersen, "L'apôtre Saint-Jean grand prêtre," *Studia Theologica* 19 (1966), 22-29. Paul honored the Nazirite vow twice when going to Jerusalem to see James (Acts 18:18-22), once upon the suggestion of James himself (21:23-24).

[18] Hegesippus' Memoirs apparently contained the story of the resurrection appearance to James after "the Lord returned with triumph from the spoil of Tartarus" (Gregory of Tours, *Hist. Francorum* i, 21). James had taken the vow when he saw the crucifixion (*ibid.*; Pseudo-Abdias, *Hist. Apost.* vi, 1). The Son of Man (Jerome) told James to "rise" (Gregory of Tours; James of Voragine, *Legenda Aurea* lxvii, where he attributes the narrative to Jerome and "Josephus"). Jerome and Hegesippus were independent witnesses to the Gospel according to the Hebrews, and Hegesippus recorded as well unwritten traditions of Hebrew believers (Eusebius, *H.E.* iv, 22.8) concerning the relatives of Jesus. On the resurrection appearance to James, see Edward W. B. Nicholson, *The Gospel according to the Hebrews*, London (C. Kegan Paul, 1879), 63-65.

[19] H. J. Schoeps (*Aus Frühchristlicher Zeit*, Tübingen, 1950, 84) explains this as a radicalization of the Mosaic prohibition of eating blood; ritual sacrifice did not guarentee the total drainage of blood.

[20] Peter's accomodating nature is indicated by Acts 11:3; Gal. 2:12. "To the Jews I became as a Jew," admitted Paul also (1 Cor. 9:20).

into the bodies of men, in order that, getting organs to minister to them they may obtain the things that they wish ... Hence, in order to put the demons to flight, the most useful help is abstinence and fasting, ... prayer and petitions, refraining from every occasion of impurity (cf. Rec. ix. 6; iv. 16).

He further explains premature death, periodical diseases, attacks of demons and of madness and all other kinds of afflictions:

Because men, following their own pleasure in all things, cohabit without observing the proper times; and thus the deposition of seed, taking place unseasonably, naturally produces a multitude of evils (Clem. Hom. xix. 22; cf. xi. 28; Rec. ix. 12; viii. 48).

The Elkesaites opposed the eating of flesh by Jews (Epiphanius, Haer. 19, 3.6). Some Sampsaeans, a variety of Elkesaites, abstained from things with souls (empsúchon) (ibid., 53, 1.4). So did the Dositheans (ibid. 13). Their vegetarianism eventually extended to refusal to eat eggs and to drink from springs containing living creatures (Chronicle of Abu-al-Fath). This source and Epiphanius (Haer. 13) concur on the Dositheans' fasting and on the death of Dositheus from hunger during a pious fast in a cave.

Montanus' laws on fasting (Apollonius ap. Eusebius, H.E. v, 18.2) were called καινάς and παραδόξους by Hippolytus (Ref. x, 25; cf. viii, 19.2), because meals consisted of parched foods and radishes. Fasting often on the Sabbath and Sunday were commanded (Hippolytus, Comm. on Daniel iv, 20). Their abstinence from foods served to display their superior virtue (Epiphanius, Haer. 48.8; Origen, de princip. ii, 7.3). In his treatise, On Fasting, Tertullian mentioned criticisms of Montanist prolonging of Wednesday and Friday fasts until evening, keeping their food unmoistened by flesh, juiciness or succulent fruit, and avoiding anything with a winey flavor, and observing xerophagies (ch. 1) twice a year for a week (chh. 2, 9, 10, 13-15). Jerome (Ep. 41, ad Marcell. 3) charged them with having three forty-day Lenten fasts (cf. Comm. on Haggai 1; Comm. on Matth. 9:15).

According to the Ascension of Isaiah (2:9-11), he, Micaiah, Joel, Habakkuk and many of the faithful withdrew to the desert. "And they all put on sackcloth and all were prophets; they had nothing with them, but were naked ... And they had nothing to eat except wild herbs ... and after they had cooked them, they ate them in the company of the prophet Isaiah."

The Testament of our Lord Jesus in Galilee has him teach: "Through the prophets I have already told their fathers neither to eat carrion nor to drink the blood of corpses" (8; cf. Lev. 17:14). "My people have eaten flesh and drunk wine; they have become thick and fat (cf. Deut. 31:20; 32:15; Neh. 9:25; Isa. 22:13) ... The priest and prophet are mad because of wine (cf. Isa. 28:7). But Jonadab, son of Rechab, and his descendants have been everlastingly blest, for they never drank wine and they observed the commandments of their fathers." Eating flesh and drinking wine are treated as desires of the flesh (9) and as sins of joyful indulgence (8, where Isa. 22:12-14 is quoted). The Old Testament roots of this abstinence are striking.

The Narrative (Apocalypse) of Zosimus concerns a man "who for forty years ate no bread, and drank no wine, and saw not the face of man" (1). He visited the blessed ones (1), the children of Rechab the son of Jonadab; following his command, "we ate no bread from the fire, and drank no vessel of wine nor honey nor strong drink" (7; cf. 8, 9). "For the earth produces most fragrant fruit, and out of the trunks of the trees comes water sweeter than honey" (10; cf. 11). Their casting away garments from their bodies (7, 8) apparently meant replacing them by "wearing skins of the cattle of the earth" (5). Their avoidance of civilization is confirmed by their lack of silver and gold (10).

In the *Conflicts of the Holy Apostles*, Matthew, in his section,[21] tells Peter and Andrew of his experience in a city of the country of rejoicing in Syria, where Gabriel and 144, 000 martyrs "who had not defiled their garments in the world" appeared. Matthew learned: "We want neither gold nor silver in our land, neither do we eat flesh or drink wine; but we feed on honey and drink of the dew ... from the leaves of trees growing in gardens. Neither do we wear garments made by the hand of man." Commodian, probably relying on a common Jewish source, described a hidden holy (*sanctus*), heavenly people fulfilling the whole law (*Instructions* ii-1, 20, 24, 28, 35) and the mysteries of Christ (15-16). "They uprightly (*candide*) obey the whole law, ... living purely" (*Carmen Apologeticum* 956-57). They eat no living thing with blood, but only vegetables" (*ibid.*, 951-52).

Canon 14 of the Council of Ancyra ruled that if priests and clerks "βούλοιντο (βδελύσσοιντο?) meat, so that they will not eat even vegetables cooked with meat," they are to be excluded from the ranks

---

[21] Malan, *op. cit.*, 44.

of the clergy.[22] Nothing is known of the background or theology of these Galatian ascetics in 314 A.D. However, one might suppose that blood was among the meat juices which were thought to contaminate the vegetables.

For the possible background of the Judaizing ascetics we turn first to the Testament of Isaac, where it is related that the Patriarch "three times a year fasted without eating for forty day periods." Moreover, he used to fast every day until sunset. He rose for prayer in the middle of the night and spent half of the night praying to God.[23] He never touched fruit nor slept on a courch (bed or mattress). "He ate no flesh and drank no wine for the length of the days of his life." [24] Motivations for fasting according to other apocrypha were less plainly ascetic. Fasting and prayer drive away demons (Testament of Jacob,[25] Apocalypse of Elijah 23:5; cf. variants of Mt. 17:21 and Mk. 9:29). In the Testament of Joseph (4:8) the Patriarch relates that he "gave himself yet more to prayer and fasting that the Lord might deliver" him from the Egyptian woman who had adulterous intentions. According to the Apocalypse of Elijah, "The Lord who created the heavens ordered the fast for the welfare of men on account of their passions and lusts ... Whoever fasts all the time sins not: in him there is no concupiscence or struggle. The pure man may fast. But whoever fasts except to be clean, angers the Lord and also the angels" (22:4-23:3).[26]

Fasting as an expression of expiatory penitence appears both in the Old Testament (e.g. Judges 20:26; 1 Sam. 7:6; 1 Kings 21:9, 12, 27; Dan. 9:3ff.; Jonah 3:5; Joel 2:12) [27] and in the Testaments of the Twelve Patriarchs (T. Reub. 1:10; T. Sim. 3:4; T. Jud. 15:4; 19:2). Prayer with fasting in humility (ταπείνωσις) of heart is necessary if the Lord is to dwell among you (T. Jos. 10:2). Ταπεινόω signified the mortification appropriate for the Day of Atonement (Lev. 16:29-31; 23:27, 29, 32). Self-abasement through fasting is mentioned also in Psalm 35:13; Isa. 58:3-5. Daniel, in order to be prepared for a

---

[22] Charles Joseph Hefele, *A History of the Christian Councils*, transl. William R. Clark, Edinburgh (T. & T. Clark, 1871), i, 213.

[23] Sleepless vigils are commended for the faithful who are strong enough (Coptic, 71; Arabic, 149.

[24] Coptic, 63; Arabic, 143.

[25] Coptic, 87-88; Arabic, 153.

[26] Steindorff (ed.), *TU* 17, 3a, 157. Otto Böcher, *Dämonenfurcht und Dämonenabwehr*, Stuttgart (W. Kohlhammer, 1970), 273-74, 278-88.

[27] Among the rabbis, see Adolph Büchler, *Types of Jewish Palestinian Piety from 70 B.C.E. — 70 C.E.*, London (Oxford University, 1922), 139, n. 4.

revelation, "ate no delicacies, no meat or wine for three full weeks" (10:3; cf. 9:3).[28] That is, he mourned (10:2; cf. Ps. 35:14; Mt. 9:14-15) and humbled himself (10:12). Priests were to drink no wine when entering the inner court (Lev. 10:8-9; Ezek. 44:21). Fasting as an element in such spiritual preparation is found frequently in Jewish writings (Exod. 34:28; Lev. 16:29, 31; Deut. 9:9, 18; 1 Sam. 28:20; 1 Kings 19:8; II [Syr.] Baruch 5:7; 9:2; 12:5; 21:1; 43:3; 47:2; II Esdras [IV Ezra] 1:2-3; 5:13, 20; 6:31, 35; 9:23-27; 12:51-53). In the Apocalypse of Abraham (ch. 9) the Patriarch is instructed to "abstain from every form of food that proceedeth out of fire, and from the drinking of wine" for forty days before he is shown mysteries through a heavenly ascent. He explains that he went without bread and water for forty days "because my food was to see the angel who was with me, and his speech- that was my drink." Adam and Eve had the food of angels rather than of animals before the expulsion from the Garden (Vita Adae 4:1-2; cf. Psalm 78:25; Wisdom Sol. 16:20).

Several of the Patriarchs served as models of abstinence. Isaac "ate no flesh and drank no wine for the length of the days of his life." [29] Issachar "drank not wine, to be led astray thereby" (T. Iss. 7:3). Joseph fasted for seven years and, when his master was away from home, drank no wine. He "appeared to the Egyptians as one living delicately, for they that fast for God's sake receive beauty of face" (T. Jos. 3:4-5; cf. 9:2; 10:1-2). The T. of Judah (13:6-16:5) presents an eloquent diatribe against the dangers of drinking wine:

> Be not drunk with wine; for wine turneth the mind away from the truth, and inspires the passion of lust, and leadeth the eyes into error ... For if a man drink wine to drunkenness, it disturbeth the mind with filthy thoughts [leading to fornication], and heateth the body to carnal union ... He who is drunken reverenceth no man ... After I had drunk wine I reverenced not the commandment of God, and I took a woman of Canaan to wife. For much discretion needeth the man who drinketh wine ...; and herein is discretion in drinking wine, a man may drink so long as he preserveth modesty. But if he go beyond this limit the spirit of deceit attacketh his mind, and maketh the drunkard to talk filthily, and to transgress and not be ashamed, but even to glory in his shame, and account himself honourable ... But if you would live soberly do not touch wine at all, lest ye sin in words of outrage, and in fighting and

---

[28] The Armenian Lives of the Prophets (Daniel) adds that he ate only vegetables for 21 years, and he bade Nechuchadnezzar "to draw near to God eating moist pulse and vegetables" "in the time of his repentance" (Greek text).

[29] Coptic 63; Arabic 143.

slanders, and transgressions of the commandments of God, and ye perish before your time. Moreover, wine revealeth the mysteries of God and men...[30]

Stories concerning Adam and Eve may contain ascetic mysteries. The fruit of the forbidden tree "was like the appearance of a bunch of grapes of the vine" (Apocalypse of Abraham, ch. 23).[31] "The vine which the angel Sammael planted ... led Adam astray" and God cursed the plant (3 Baruch 4:8). Moreover,

As Adam through this very tree obtained condemnation, and was divested of the glory of God, so also the men who now drink insatiably the wine which is begotten of it, transgress worse than Adam, and are far from the glory of God, and are surrendering themselves to the eternal fire ... Those who drink it to surfeit do these things: neither does a brother pity (his) brother, nor a father (his) son, nor children (their) parents, but from the drinking of wine come all (evils), such as murders, adulteries, fornication, perjuries, thefts and such like. And nothing good is established by it (3 Baruch 4:16-17).

Adam received, after his expulsion, seeds for food and fragrant herbs for offereing his sacrifices to God (Apocalypse of Moses 29:3-6). "The Lord God sent divers seeds by Michael the archangel and gave to Adam and showed him how to work and till the ground, that they might have fruit by which they and all their generations might live" (Vita Adae 22:2).

Continued and habitual abstinence from meat may have arisen from scrupulous observance of the Lord's command to Noah not to eat flesh with its blood, i.e. its life (Gen. 9:4-5; cf. Lev. 7:27; 17:10-14; Deut. 12:23-24). Jubilees (6:7, 10-14; 7:28-32) stresses its importance. "And Noah and his sons swore that they would not eat any blood that was in any flesh (Jub. 6:10). "The man who eateth the blood of beast or of cattle or of birds during all the days of the earth, he and his seed shall be rooted out of the land" (6:12). "Woe to you, ye obstinate of heart, who work wickedness and eat blood," echoes 1 Enoch 98:11. The giants drank blood (1 Enoch 7:5).

The story of Daniel 1:8-16 may have inspired the insights that a diet of vegetables and water was healthier than one of rich food and wine and that with such a diet it was possible to eat with Gentiles without defiling oneself. To the four youths subsisting on such a diet

---

[30] On the rabbinic views of the holiness of abstinence, see Büchler, op. cit., 53, n. 1; 63.
[31] Ginzberg, The Legends of the Jews, i(1912), 97, n. 70; Charles, The Apocrypha and Pseudepigrapha of the O.T., ii, 535.

God gave "learning and skill in all letters and wisdom; and Daniel had understanding in all visions and dreams" (1:17; cf. 20).

The Damascus Document (CD 12.11-15) gives the following dietary regulations:

> Let no man defile himself with any animal or creeping creature by eating them, from the larvae of bees to all living creatures which creep in water. And as for fish, let them not be eaten unless they have been split alive and their blood spilt. And as for all the locusts in their various species, let them be put into fire or water alive; for such is the ordinance according to their nature.

In principle there was no prohibition of eating meat. But the laws of defilement regarding the eating of animal life were rigid. Eating blood was a prime sin of the sons of Jacob in Egypt (CD 3.5-6). That the inhabitants of the Qumran community occasionally ate meat at sacramental feasts is indicated by the excavation of partially burned and carefully buried goat, sheep, lamb and cattle bones.[32] The sectarians possessed herds which they followed to pasture (CD 11.5-6).

Wine (tirosh) was blessed by a priest at the community's meals (1QS 6.4-6) in anticipation of the Messianic banquet (1QSa II, 17-21). It is uncertain whether or not the drink (mishqeh) at the Banquet of the Many (1QS 6.20; 7.20) was tirosh, which, strictly speaking, means unfermented grape juice, but could mean fermented wine.[33] Both water decanters and wine flasks have been unearthed at Qumran.[34] M. Delcor[35] has accepted the appealing suggestion of Joseph M. Baumgarten[36] that "the production of ritually pure fermented wine was ... difficult. Tirosh, on the one hand, aside from its benefits with regard to sobriety..., has the considerable advantage of assured purity if the grapes are squeezed shortly before the priest pronounces the blessing." If the Zadokite priests of Qumran saw themselves prophesied in Ezek. 44:15-31 (CD 3. 21-4.2) and if their meals had a sacrificial character, then they would have been obliged to abstain from wine (Ezek. 44:21; cf. Levit. 10:9).[37]

---

[32] R. de Vaux, "Fouilles de Khirbet Qumrân. Rapport III," *RB* 63(1956), 549-50; cf. Gärtner, *op. cit.*, 13, n. 1.

[33] Ringgren, *op. cit.* 219.

[34] Cross, *op. cit.*, 69.

[35] "Repas cultuels esséniens et Thérapeutes, Thiases et Haburoth," *RQ* 6(1967-68), 414-15, n. 67.

[36] "The Essene Avoidance of Oil and Laws of Purity," *RQ* 6(1967-68), 191-92, n. 42.

[37] Yadin, *The Scroll of the War of the Sons of Darkness*, transl. B. & C. Rabin, London (Oxford University, 1962), 200; Delcor, *art. cit.*, RQ 6 (1957-58), 412-18.

Judas Maccabeus with nine companions withdrew into the desert
and lived in the mountains in the manner of beasts, feeding on a
vegetarian diet (σιτούμενοι διετέλουν) in order to avoid defilement (2
Macc. 5:27; cf. 1 Macc. 2:27ff.).

The significance of food laws for the Essenes is illustrated by
Josephus' report that no Roman torture could "compel them either to
blaspheme against the Lawgiver or to eat forbidden food" (*War* ii,
8.10.152). Hippolytus (ix, 26) wrote of their refusal to speak ill of the
Law or eat what has been offered to an idol. A readiness to face death
in preference to eating forbidden food is also shown by the behavior
of the individual who was expelled from the Essene community.
"Being bound by the oaths and customs, he cannot take food with
(παρά) other people "(Hippolytus ix, 24; Josephus, *War* ii, 8.8.143).
Josephus adds that the outcast may perish from having to eat herbs
alone. "Before touching the common food" the initiate "makes
solemn vows before his brethren" (Josephus, *War* ii, 8.7.139). The
Essenes "choose virtuous men to ... gather the various products of
the soil, and priests to prepare the bread and food" (Josephus,
Antiquities xviii, 1.5.22). When the members are quietly seated in the
refractory, "the baker serves out the loaves of bread in order, and the
cook serves only one bowlful of one dish to each man" (*War* ii,
8.5.130; cf. Hippolytus ix, 21: "bread ... and then some one kind of
food, from which each has a sufficient portion"). The cause of their
silence at meals is "their invariable sobriety and the fact that their
food (τροφή) and drink are so measured out that they are satisfied and
no more" (*War* ii, 8.5.133; cf. Hippolytus ix, 21: "eating and drinking
all things by measure [μέτρο])". This moderation is really continence,
as the postulant must prove his ἐγκράτεια for one year (*War* ii,
8.7.138; Hippolytus ix, 23). Philo (*de vita contempl.* 34-35) lauded
the Therapeutae, who:

> lay down ἐγκράτεια as a foundation, as it were, for the soul and then
> proceed to build up the rest of the virtues upon it. Accordingly none of
> them would think of taking food before sundown ... A number of
> them, in whom the thirst for wisdom is implanted, to a greater degree,
> remind themselves of their food but once in three days, while a few ...
> fare so sumptuously at wisdom's banquet of teachings ... that they ...
> even after six days barely take a mouthful of the most necessary food.

Vegetarianism is suggested by the references to bread and herbs and
products of the soil. The Therapeutae described by Philo (*de vita*

contempl. 37, 73, 81) lived on a meagre fare of only necessary
quantities of water, and bread seasoned with salt and hyssop. Their
table contained nothing having blood in it (*ibid.*, 73). "For just as
right reason bids priests to make offerings free from wine and blood,
so does it bid these sages live. For wine is a drug that brings on
madness, and costly seasonings rouse up desire, the most insatiable of
beasts" (*ibid.*, 74). The hermit Banus "had no other food than what
grew of its own accord" (Josephus, *Life* 2). Pious priests whom Felix
sent to Rome in bonds lived on figs and nuts (*ibid.*, 3). Jerome [38]
lauded the Essenes for abstaining from wine and meat: "*ab uxoribus
et vino et carnibus semper abstinuerint et quotidianum ieiunium
verterint in naturam*" (adv. *Jovin.* ii, 14). A likely connection of the
Essenes and Rechabites existed.[39] If the Essenes drank wine, certainly
it was mixed with water and consumed sparingly. Their possession in
common of various types of cattle (Philo, *ap.* Eusebius, *Praep. Evang.*
viii, 11.8; cf. 4) seems to have been motivated by usage for plowing,
transportation, fleecing and provision of food (cheese, curds, milk)
and hides. Seemingly the killing of animals was deemed unnecessary.
It would have been a luxury for the Essene community to eat one of
its few valuable assets except on special festive occasions. Elpidius
Pax [40] notes that Jews in general ate meat mostly at such times
anyway. He further holds that the diet at Qumran was more that of
the pious poor of the desert than of rigorous ascetics.

Sexual Abstinence

Paul dealt with Judaizing ascetics as tactfully as possible in Gal.
5:13-6:8. It must be kept in mind that, as Paul himself treated his
body severely (ὑπωπιάζω) (1 Cor. 9:27) and viewed virginity as an
ideal (1 Cor. 7:1-38), he was in no position to oppose its proponents
for reserving special disciplines for the "mature." It was charged that
Paul's converts used their "freedom as an opportunity for the flesh"
(5:13). It was agreed that "the desires of the flesh are against the
Spirit, and the desires of the Spirit are against the flesh; for these are
opposed to each other" (5:17) as ways of life. Moreover, it was plain to

---

[38] Doubted by Schürer, *op. cit.*, ii-ii, 201 (ET).

[39] Kohler, *art. cit., Jewish Encyclopedia* v(1903), 230b; Schoeps, *op. cit.*, 247-52,
255; Black, *op. cit.*, 58.

[40] " 'Essen und Trinken.' Steiflichter aus neutestamentlicher und nachbiblisher
Zeit," *Bibel und Leben* 10(1969), 286-87, 290-91.

all that the works of the flesh included immorality, impurity,
licentiousness, ... drunkenness and carousing ... Those who do such
things shall not inherit the kingdom of God" (5:19-21). Self-control
(ἐγκράτεια) is opposed to the indulgence in sex and wine (1 Cor. 7:9;
cf. 9:25) as fostered by the flesh. "But," objected Paul, "if you are led
by the Spirit, you are not under the law" (5:18); freedom from the law
did not necessarily lead to works of the flesh. There was also
disagreement whether self-control was generally given by the Spirit
through faith (5:21) or whether it was a work of the law whereby the
Spirit was received (3:2-5) and obedience was gained (5:23b). The
Apostle's opponents would hardly agree that "those who belong to
Christ Jesus have crucified the flesh with its passions and desires"
(5:24) and that the law of love (5:14; cf. 6:2) suffices. The Galatians
were commended for running well (5:7), i.e. making proper use of
their Christian liberty (5:1-6, 13-14). The boastful pride of the
πνευματικοὶ (5:26; 6:1, 3-4) presupposes a more arduous abstinence
than that from fornication and drunkenness. In teaching that male
and female, like Jew and Greek, "are all one in Christ Jesus" (3:28),
Paul may have been resisting some anti- femininism (cf. 1 Pet. 3:7:
συγκχηρονόμοις).

In Colossians the opponents' slogan, "do not touch (ἅψη) ... do not
handle ... severity (αφειδία) to the body ... satisfaction (πλησμονή) of
the flesh" (2:21, 23)[41] cumulatively suggest asceticism in sex (cf. 1
Cor. 7:1: γυναικὸς μὴ ἅπτεσθαι) as well as in diet because of
uncleanness (2 Cor. 6:17). Thereby would be gained freedom from
the body and communication with the spiritual world.
Ἅπτομαι implies a more temporary than permanent abstinence; i.e.
women were taboo under certain conditions or circumstances.
Φιλοσοφία (2:8) among the Greek Fathers beginning with Origen
signified the ascetic principles of an anchorite life.[42] In response Paul
asked his readers to focus their attention, not on such earthly matters,
but on their new life in Christ (3:1-4), in consequence of which (οὖν)
they should "put to death what is earthly in (them): immorality,
impurity, passion, evil desire (ἐπιθυμία) and covetousness. . ." (3:5).
Here, as in Gal. 5:19-21 (cf. Eph. 5:3-5), the Apostle begins his list
with sexual sins, as if they were considered the more basic ones. The
false teachers were preoccupied with resolving these problems of the

[41] Percy, op. cit., 140-43. R. Leaney," Col. ii.21-23 (the use of πρὸς)," Exp. Times
64(1952-53), 92.
[42] Hort, op. cit., 121.

flesh by physical methods of "mortification." Above all, the readers should put on love, which is the bond of perfection (σύνδεσμος τῆς τελειότητος) (3:14). "Whatever you do, in word or deed, do everything in the name of the Lord Jesus ... Wives, be subject to your husbands, as is fitting in the Lord. Husbands, love your wives..." (3:17-19). While Paul believed that sexual behavior should be regulated according to the believer's new life in Christ, his opponents perhaps sought to imitate and participate in the life of the angels, who do not marry and after whose life the resurrection state is patterned (Mt. 22:30; Mk. 12:25; Luke 17:26-27; 20:33-36). Virginity was compared to the angelic life of perfection by Cyprian (hab. virg. 22), Methodius (Conv. 2, 7; 8, 2), Eusebius (Comm. in Ps. 102), Cyril of Jerusalem (Catech. Myst. 12.34), Ambrose (de Virgin. i, 9.52-53) and the Cappadocian Fathers, Gregory of Nyssa (virginit. 13; Migne, P.G. 46, 381) and Basil (virginit. 51; cf. 68).[43]

Ephesians 5:22-23 also describes the proper relationship between husbands and wives. "Husbands should love their wives as their own bodies. He who loves his wife loves himself. For no man ever hates his own flesh, but nourishes and cherishes it, as Christ does the church, because we are members of his body. 'For this reason a man shall leave his father and mother and be joined to his wife, and the two shall become one'" (5:28-31). A man should love his woman with the same sacrificial love that unites Christ with his church, for which he gave himself, "that he might sanctify her, having cleansed her,... that she might be holy and without blemish" (5:25-27). Did such language reflect a reaction against ascetic scorn for marriage and the female and the accompanying desire to remain καθαρός while growing toward perfection? It was agreed, however, that no fornicator or unclean (ἀκάθαρτος) person "has any inheritance in the kingdom of Christ and of God" (5:5).

Could Hebrews 13:4 ("Let marriage be held in honor ἐν πᾶσιν," i.e. in every way and respect and under all conditions) have been addressed to the same situation?[44] Were ascetics denying that marriage is honorable and that the bed (sexual relations) sometimes could be undefiled? Our author specifies fornication and adultery as defilement, and promises that God will judge offenders. Since 13:1-5 concern different types of love, it is implied that marital relations

---

[43] J. Danielou, The Angels and their Missions, David Heimann, Westminster, Md. (Newman, 1957), 89-91, 101; Michl, art. cit., Reallexicon f. Ant. u. Chr., v, 156-57.

[44] Spicq, art. cit., RQ 1(1958-59), 388.

should be honored as an expression of love. Zahn [45] commented that
the exhortation of 13:4 "does not mean that those in the married
state are to regard it as holy,—that is not considered until the
following sentence,—but that all, especially those who are unmarried
and are inclined to despise marriage, are to honour this state." There
is no additional hint in ch. 13 of ignorance of, or opposition to, the
law. Nevertheless, ἐν πᾶσιν suggests the existence of both positive
legal disobedience and asceticism.

In 1 Cor. 7 Paul answers the Corinthians' questions about virginity.
The readers (v. 25) wished to follow the commandment of the Lord
on the subject and probably (unlike the Apostle) had learned the
tradition (7:7) behind Mt. 19:10-12. He quoted, but proceeded
decisively to qualify (cf. 8:1-4), their slogan, καλόν ανθρώπω γυναικός
μὴ ἄπτεσθαι (7:1); i.e. it is morally best (ideal, perfect) to avoid sexual
contact with all women (cf. Gen. 20:4, 6; Prov. 6:29). The restriction
applied to both the married and unmarried.[46] "There was an ascetic
tendency or group at Corinth which was suspicious of all sexual
relations." [47] Paul replied that each man should be allowed to have
his wife sexually (ἐχέτω: cf. 5:1), and each woman her own husband
(7:2). They should not make a habit of sexually depriving each other
without agreement (7:5). Paul's concession or allowance (συγγνώμην)
contrasts with the ascetics' command (7:6); he permitted them the
right to physical relations. An anti-feminine bias may be implied in
the equality and reciprocity of rights and obligations as commended
by Paul in 7:4 and 10-11. Married ascetics would be repelled by his
teaching that authority over one's own body rests not with oneself,
but with one's mate (7:4). The Apostle reassuringly states (7:28) that
there was no sin when either a man or a virgin marries. His
statement, as F. W. Grosheide notes,[48] "is intelligible only if there
were some at Corinth who considered marriage sinful." If anyone
thinks he is behaving dishonorably toward his virgin, "let him do as
he wishes: let them marry—it is no sin" (7:36). This ασχημονειν (cf.
12:23; Rom. 1:27; Rev. 16:15) involved some sort of sexual contact
and was thought inappropriate for either an engagement or spiritual

---

[45] *Introduction to the N.T.*, ii, 333.
[46] Hurd, *op. cit.*, 156-64; William F. Orr, "Paul's Treatment of Marriage in 1
Corinthians," *Pittsburgh Perspective* 8(1967), 6-8; Barrett, *op. cit.*, 154-55.
[47] Hurd, *op. cit.*, 158.
[48] *Commentary on the First Epistle to the Corinthians* (New International Comm.),
Grand Rapids, Mich. (Wm. B. Eerdmans, 1953), 176.

marriage.[49] Probably some engaged couples had postponed marriage indefinitely; others may have carried out their marriage plans with the announced intent not to touch each other. Yet neither Paul nor the ascetics favored the contracting of any marriages.[50] The proponents of asceticism apparently counselled each man not to marry, but to keep his virgin as she is (7:37). In verse 26, which is directed to the same problem,[51] he again quotes the Corinthians' slogan and qualifies it. "It is καλὸν for a person to remain as he is." This was their ideal for the unmarried: the bachelors, widowers and divorced (7:27-28). Their insistence on the *status quo* is clear from verse 39. Paul teaches that a widow is free to marry any believer she chooses; second marriages are as permissible as first ones (cf. 7:8-9). Nevertheless, on grounds of expediency alone, Paul sometimes recommended celibacy, and on other occasions marriage.

The existence of a party of ascetics at Corinth was fostered by the teachings of the false apostles who arrived, teaching carnal laws of perfection for the strong and criticizing Paul for not eliminating sexual sinners from the church (2 Cor. 12:21). C. K. Barrett [52] suggests that it was being taught at Corinth that "the continent man is strong; he proves his strength by dispensing with a wife." In 2 Cor. 11:2-3, where Paul states that he has betrothed the Corinthians to Christ as a παρθένος ἀγνή to one husband, he defines virgin purity in terms of a single-purposed devotion (ἀπλότης) to Christ as manifested by a continued acceptance of his gospel about Christ (11:4, 7). But Paul feared that the Corinthians' minds would be seduced (φθαρῇ) by preachers of another Jesus (11:3-4). Was he making use of the language of his opponents, who considered pure virgins as those who walk in ἀπλότης? Was Eve's deception by the cleverness of the serpent (11:3) a major reason for their avoiding women? i.e. because their thoughts are more readily seduced (cf. 1 Tim. 2:14).

That ascetic proponents of spiritual marriage were appealing to the the image of the eschatological marriage of Christ and his Church, is

---

[49] Hurd, *op. cit.*, 172.

[50] A spiritual marriage would still involve worldly cares (7:28, 31, 33-34). Γαμησάτωσαν (7:9) and γαμείτωσαν (7:36) imply no existing marriage. During the brief time after Paul's departure would spiritual marriages arise between persons with strong passions (ὑπέρακμος) unless the pair had already loved each other and hoped to get married, -even before hearing ascetic preaching? Would virgins live together if they had not already been thinking of marriage? On the question see Hurd, *op. cit.*, 170-80.

[51] *Ibid.*, 177-78.

[52] *Art. cit.*, *BJRL* 46(1963-64), 285.

evidenced by the Revelation of John (19:7ff.; 21:2, 9ff.; 22:17). "The 144,000 who had been redeemed from the earth" are the spotless first-fruits; "it is these who have not defiled themselves with women, for they are παρθενοι" (14:3-5; 19:14). By implication even sexual relations in marriage are contaminating.[53] John the Prophet-Seer was perpetually virgin, according to the Acts of John (63, 107, 113).

I Timothy tells of hypocrites (cf. Mt. 7:15) "who forbid marriage" (4:2-3); it counsels: "while bodily training (γυμνασία) is of some value, godliness is of value in every way" (4:8). Perhaps physical exercise was considered a healthy substitute for sexual activity and a means of mortifying the flesh or disciplining the body and its impure desires. Or, ascetic self-control was being defended by the analogy of athletic training (cf. 1 Cor. 9:24-27). In any case the Pastor considered the opponents' self-discipline to be excessive and to be more physical than religious. "So I would have (βούλομαι) younger widows marry, bear children" (5:14; cf. Tit. 2:4-5). Although Eve (rather than Adam) "was deceived and became a transgressor," as the anti-femininist ascetics apparently noted, "yet woman will be saved through bearing children, if she continues in faith and love and holiness. . ." (1 Tim. 2:14-15). Church officers were to be once-married; their children were to be well-behaved believers (1 Tim. 3:2, 12; Tit. 1:6): a compromise between celibacy and re-marriage. The ascetics ostensibly opposed all marriages on the part of bishops, elders and deacons, and re- marriage by younger widows.

The Ascension of Isaiah is world-negating. "The world of the flesh" (8:23) is corrupted (8:26); in it there is much darkness (8:24). This alien world (6:9) is contrasted with "the world which is hidden from (all) flesh" (6:15), where "the remembrance of this world is not known" (7:24). Beliar has ruled this (lower) world since it came into being (4:2; 10:12). But during his ascension to heaven Isaiah observed: "Nothing of the vanity of that world is here named" (7:25). For, love of office and of honor of this world, respect for persons, covetousness, boasting, jealousy and fornication characterize contemporary church leaders; in becoming worldly, they have become lawless and abandoned apostolic purity (3:21-30). But Jesus "will bring rest to the pious" (4:15) and destroy with fire the impious (4:19). "Many will exchange the glory of the garment of the saints for

---

[53] C. H. Lindijer, "Die Jungfrauen in der Offenbarung des Johannes xiv 4, in "Studies in John Presented to J. N. Sevenster, Leiden (E. J. Brill, 1970), 125-27.

the garment of the covetous" (3:25). Conversely, in his ascent from the body, Isaiah received the garments allowing him to resemble the angels (8:14-15; 11:34-35). Garments are stored for the saints in the seventh heaven (4:16; 8:26; 9:17, 25-26; 11:40). Isaiah "saw all the righteous from Adam ... stripped of the garment of the flesh, and saw them in their higher garments, and they were like the angels" (9:7-9; cf. 4:17). In this dualism of heaven and earth, all material, corporeal values are scorned as inappropriate for the pious who are striving for angelic purity. Naturally Joseph "did not approach Mary, but kept her as a holy virgin, although she was with child" (11:5). Later the Ascension of Isaiah was admired and used by such ascetics as Hieracas (a Melchizedekian) (Epiphanius, Haer. 67.3), the Messalians, Bogomiles and Cathari.[54]

The virginity of John the Baptist may be deduced from his being "strong in spirit" and living in the desert until he manifested himself (Lk. 1:80). The Slavonic version of Josephus (after War ii, 9.1.168) relates that his ways were not human, for he lived as a fleshless spirit. He charged Herod Antipas with "satisfying fleshly lusts and committing adultery." [55]

James the Lord's brother was a virgin, according to Epiphanius (Haer. 78.13). He wore the highpriestly πέταλον (ibid. 29.4; 78.14). like the John who died at Ephesus (Polycrates, ap. Eusebius, H.E. v, 24); i.e. both were Nazirites.[56] Philip's four daughters who prophesied were virgins (Acts 21:8-9).

Some Dositheans remained virgins, while others lived in continence after their wives had children (or died?) (Epiphanius, Haer. 13).

In the Pseudo-Clementine Epistles concerning Virginity, virgins "live a divine and heavenly life, like the holy angels"; therefore "God will give them the kingdom of heaven, as to the holy angels" (I, 4). Virgins worthy of imitation included Jesus, John the Baptist, John the disciple, Paul, Timothy, Elijah and Elisha (I, 6; cf. I, 14-15).

The Apocalypse of Peter reveals the torture reserved for maidens not retaining their virginity before marriage (Ethiopic 11), homosexuals defiling themselves (10) and for fornicators, including

---

[54] Charles, The Ascension of Isaiah, xi, xliv, 67; André Vaillant, "Un apocryphe pseudobogomile: La Vision d'Isaïe," Revue des Études Slaves 42 (1963), 110, 119-21.
[55] In Josephus' Slavonic War (Eisler, op. cit., 230, 601).
[56] J. V. Andersen, "L'apôtre Saint-Jean grand-pretre," Studia Theologica 19 (1966), 22-29.

women who plait their hair so "that they might ensnare the souls of
men to destruction" (7). According to Sibylline Oracle iv, 33, the
pious do not "set their foul affection on another's bed."

In the Gospel of Didymus Judas Thomas (114) Peter says: "Let
Mary go out from among us, for women are not worthy of life" (cf.
Gospel of Mary P. Berol. p. 18).

Hegesippus (ap. Eusebius, H.E. iii, 32.8; iv, 22.4) records a
Palestinian tradition that "the church continued ... as a pure and
uncorrupt virgin" until the heresies arose. Thus virginity was a
standard for purity which was deemed analogous to the marriage of
Christ and the Church.

Montanists called Priscilla a virgin and reported that their
prophetesses (she and Maximilla) left their husbands when they were
filled with the Spirit. Montanus taught dissolutions of marriages
(λύσεσις γάμων) (Apollonius ap. Eusebius, H.E. V, 18.2-3). The
forbidding of marriage was reminiscent, for Origen (de princip.
ii.7.3), of teachings attacked in 1 Tim. 4:1-3 (cf. Tertullian, On
Fasting ii, 14-15) [57] Remarriage was prohibited (Epiphanius, Haer.
48.9; Tertullian, On Modesty 1; On Monogamy 3, 4, 9, 11, 14, 15).
Virginity was deemed best (Tertullian, To His Wife i, 1, 3 & 8, 9).
Those who abstain from marriage "are already counted as belonging
to the angelic family" (ibid., i, 4). Prisca (ap. Tertullian, On
Exhortation to Chastity 10) preached: "The holy minister knows how
to minister sanctity ... For purity is harmonious, and they see
visions; and turning their face downward they even hear secret
voices. . ." Tertullian comments that the exercise of carnal nature has
a dulling effect on spiritual faculties even in the first marriage.
According to Epiphanius (Haer. 49.2), "Often in their assembly one
sees seven virgins enter, bearing torches and dressed in white, who
come to prophesy before the people."

In the Book of James (10:1; 13:3; 15:2-3) virginity is a sign of
purity before God. In the Shepherd of Hermas (Vis. ii, 2.3) the angel
asks the visionary to live thereafter with his wife as with a sister
(ἀδελφῃ). In a dream he slept "in the midst of virgins as a brother, and
not as a husband" (Sim. ix, 10.7.11.7).[58] Such abstinence increased the
likelihood of receiving revelations. If widow(er)s "remain unmarried,

---

[57] J. Massingberd Ford ("A Possible Liturgical Background to the Shepherd of
Hermas," RQ 6(1969), 538ff.) thinks the background is a sectarian celebration of
Tabernacles.
[58] Similarity to Galatian opponents was also charged.

they gain greater honor and glory with the Lord ... Guard your chastity and purity, and you will live to God" (*Mand.* iv, 4.1). According to the Melchizedek section of 2 Enoch, "Nir the priest did not sleep with her (Sopanima, his wife), nor knew her from the day that the Lord appointed him to serve before the face of the people" (iii, 2).

According to the legendary Life of St. Conon, Michael,[59] dressed in a white robe, revealed to Conon "the mystery of truth" and the excellence of ἁγνεία. Henceforth he lived with his wife in ἁγνεία and in prayer, as the apostle of Isauria (a district of Lycaonia).

In the Narrative (Apocalypse) of Zosimus, the self-control of the Rechabites is described in these terms:

> Neither do any of us take to themselves wives, except for so long as to beget two children, and after they have produced two children they withdraw from each other and continue in chastity, not knowing that they were ever in the intercourse of marriage, but being in virginity as from the beginning. And one child remains for marriage, and the other for virginity(10).

In the Conflicts of the Holy Apostles, Matthew relates what he heard from the inhabitants of a city visited by Gabriel and 144,000 martyrs: "We do not look upon our wives with the lust of sin, and all our first-born sons we present unto the Lord as an offering, to serve in His holy temple all the days of their life from three years ... No man marries two wives ... Our women dwell with us, they neither corrupt us or we them." [60]

The Testaments of the Twelve Patriarchs warn sternly against the dangers of fornication (T. Reub. 4:6-11; 5:5; 6:4; T. Levi 9:9; T. Jud. 13:2-3; 15:1-2; 17:1-2; T. Jos. 4:6).[61] Among the seven spirits of deceit is "the power of procreation and sexual intercourse, with which through love of pleasure sin enters in" (T. Reub. 2:8). "Beware, therefore of fornication, for fornication is the mother of all evils, separating from God, and bringing near to Beliar" (T. Sim. 5:3). On the other hand, "he that hath a pure mind in love, looketh not after a woman with a view to fornication; for he hath no defilement in his heart, because the Spirit of God resteth upon him (T. Benj. 8:2). "The

---

[59] M. R. James, "Le livre de la prière d'Aseneth," in Pierre Batiffol (ed.), *Studia Patristica*, Paris, i (1889), 33-34.

[60] Malan, *op. cit.*, 44.

[61] Otto Böcher, *Der Johanneische Dualismus im Zusammenhang des Nachbiblischen Judentums*, Gütersloh (Gerd Mohn, 1965), 61-63.

wickedness of the ungodly hath no power over them that worship God with chastity (σωφροσύνη)" (T. Jos. 6:7). "[If ye follow after chastity and purity with patience and prayer with fasting in humility of heart, the Lord will dwell among you, because He loveth chastity] "(T. Jos. 10:2; cf. 9:2-3). Joseph "guarded himself from a woman, and purged his thoughts from all fornication, and found favor in the sight of God and men" (T. Reub. 4:8; cf. T. Jos. 4:1-2). [62]

Another example of chastity was Issachar. To his children he said: "When I was thirty- [five] years old, I took to myself a wife, for my labour wore away my strength, and I never thought upon pleasure with women" (T. Iss. 3:5). "Except my wife I have not known any woman. I never committed fornication by the uplifting of my [eyes] "(7:2). The Lives of the Prophets laud Daniel (v. 2): "In his manhood he was chaste, so that the Jews thought him a eunuch." The chastity of Adam was also the subject of legends. According to R. Meir, "Adam was very *hasid*, and when he saw that death was decreed against him and the human race, he spent 130 years in fasting and separated himself from his wife for 130 years, during which time he was covered by the leaves of a fig tree" (Erubin 18b). Irenaeus echoes the myth: "He showed his repentance by wearing the girdle of fig leaves as a bridle of continence upon himself and his wife" (Adv. Haer. iii, 23.5). [63] The penance of Adam and Eve also included standing for forty days in the Jordan River and the Tigris, respectively (Vita Adae, chh. 6-7). Eve relates in the Apocalypse of Moses (19:3) that "Satan went and poured upon the fruit the poison of his wickedness, which is lust, the root and beginning of every sin, and he bent the branch on the earth and I took the fruit and I ate." Thus Eve was condemned to cry out in childbirth: "I will never again indulge in carnal pleasure" (Apoc. Moses 25:3-4); her sin was one of the flesh. Adam was punished because he listened to Eve (Apoc. Mos. 34:1). Satan "seduced Eve, but did not touch Adam" (2 Enoch 31:6). Her beauty deprived him of reasoning; "It is better for me to die than to part from the woman ... I cannot live without her." [64] In this spirit Reuben warned:

---

[62] Strathmann, *op. cit.*, I, 61-82; on similar rabbinic views see Büchler, *op. cit.*, 42-48, 53-55. Such restraint could be associated with humility. Joseph is called a παρθένος by the story, *Joseph and Asenath* (4:9; 8:1). Noah's abstention also was holy (Buchler, 50-51, n. 3).

[63] Further references in Charles, *Apocrypha and Pseudepigrapha of the O.T.*, ii, 137, note on 18:3; Ginzberg, *op. cit.*, v (1925), 106; Büchler, *op. cit.*, 52, n. 1.

[64] Armenian *Narrative of the Creation and Fall of Adam*, ch. 8, *ap.* E. Preuschen,

Evil are women, my children; and since they have no power or strength
over man, they use wiles by outward attractions that they may draw him
to themselves. And whom they cannot bewitch by outward attractions,
him they overcome by craft.[For], moreover, concerning them, the angel
of the Lord told me, and taught me, that women are overcome by the
spirit of fornication more than men, and in their heart they plot against
men; and by means of their adornment they deceive first their minds,
and by the glance of the eye instil the poison, and then through the
accomplished act they take them captive (T. Reub. 5:1-3).

An angel revealed to Judah (T. Jud. 15:5-6) that "for ever do women
bear rule over" men and take away their glory, might and sustenance.
"Pay no heed, therefore, [my children], to the beauty of women, nor
set your mind on their affairs, but walk in singleness (ἁπλότης) of
heart in the fear of the Lord." (T. Reub. 4:1; cf. 3:10; T. Jud. 17:1).
Silly women lead astray the ἁπλότης of their husbands (T. Job 26:6)
"And if you wish to be pure in mind, guard your senses from every
woman. And command the women likewise not to associate with
men, that they also may be pure in mind" (T. Reub. 6:1-2).

Chastity was an aid in receiving revelations. The command to
Jeremiah (16:1-4) was based on the dreadful coming Judgment.
Enoch told of his two dream visions (concerning the collapse of
heaven and a bull's emergence from the earth) before he took Edna
to be his wife (1 En. 83:2; 85:3-4).[65] In 4 Ezra (2 Esdras) Uriel says:

"Die apokryphen gnostischen Adamschriften aus dem Armenischen...," in *Festgruss
Bernhard Stade*, Giessen (J. Ricker, 1900), 191.

[65] The Armenian *Gospel of Seth*, however, stated that "Enoch did not marry" nor
"eat of the vineyard ... He wore on his head an iron helmet, that he should not look
up into the fruits of the trees ... When the other children of Seth ... saw that Enoch,
on account of his purity and fasting, was taken up into Paradise, many of them ...
retired to mountains, and devoted themselves to purity and mortification" (Issaverdens,
op. cit., 65). "There were five hundred and twenty single men devoted to an austere life
... But young women of Cain's seed invented the artifice" of painting their faces, eyes,
eyebrows, hands and feet, decking their hair with curls, wearing ornaments, inventing
musical instruments. "And with trimmed garments and with all kinds of music
dancing joyfully, they went up into the mountain; and with clapping of hands and
sounding trumpets, and making long gyrations and singing ..., they mixed with" the
five hundred and twenty solitary men, and "only Noah remained virgin; all the others
... became ... more lascivious than dogs" (66-67). When an angel "told Noah to take a
wife" in order eventually to repopulate the earth, he protested: "Why for a transitory
dream should I contaminate my virginity?" But the angel "said; 'It is the Lord's
command,'" and directed him to the sole remaining pure virgin (67). See Preuschen,
ibid., 200, 219-20: Giorgio R. Cardona, "Sur le Gnosticisme en Armenie: les livres
d'Adam," *in Le Origini dello Gnosticismo. Colloquio di Messina 13-18 Aprille, 1966*,
Leiden (E. J. Brill, 1967), 645-48.

These things came I to show thee this night. If therefore thou wilt ...
fast seven days more, I will tell thee yet again greater things than these
... The Mighty One hast seen thy rectitude, and marked also thy
chastity (*pudicitia*) [66] which thou hast had ever since thy youth.
Therefore has he sent me to show thee all these things (6:32-35).

The ascetic inclination of the writer is confirmed in 7:122 and 125.
"The glory of the Lord is to defend them who have led a pure life."
"The faces of such as have practiced *abstinentia* shall shine above the
stars." Did he exclude himself? Job in his Testament (xi, 12-14, 22-
27) describes his gift to his daughters of glorious girdless (of chastity;
cf. Joseph & Aseneth 14:16: λαμπρὰν τῆς παρθενίας·) [67] for the sake of
prophecy.

It appears from the Testament of Issachar (chh. 1-2), as Robert
Eppel [68] observed, that "les relations conjugales ne sont permises que
dans la mesure ou elles sont nécessaires à la conservation de la race."
Because the barren Rachel did not eat the mandrakes (i.e. love apples
inducing fertility), but rather offered them in the house of the Lord,
He hearkened to her and visited her. "For he knew that for the sake
of children she wished to company with Jacob, and not lust for
pleasure" (2:3). "Then appeared to Jacob an angel of the Lord, saying:
'Two children shall Rachel bear, inasmuch as she hath refused
company with her husband, and hath chosen continency (ἐγκράτεια)" '
(2:1). Likewise, according to Tobit 6:16-22; 8:4-9, Tobit had relations
with Sara his wife, moved by the love of children for posterity rather
than by fleshly lust. The Testament of Naphtali (8:8) places another
restriction: "There is a season for a man to embrace his wife, and a
season to abstain (ἐγκράτεια) therefrom for his prayer." The Book of
Jubilees (50:8) promises death for whoever desecrates the Sabbath by
lying with his wife.[69] According to Niddah 38a, "the pious old men
performed their marital duty on Wednesday only, in order that their
wives should not be led to a desecration of the sabbath" (i.e. as a 271-
day pregnancy had been calculated).

That marriage and the procreation of children (descendants) were
permitted among the Qumran Covenanters may be deduced from
1QH 17.14; CD 7.3, 6-8; 16.10; 19.3-5 (cf. 4.21-5.11); 1QSb 3.4; 1QS

---

[66] See Box's note in Charles, *Apocrypha and Pseudepigrapha of the O.T.*, ii, 577.

[67] James, *Apocrypha Anecdota* (Texts and Studies v-1) (1897), xcv.

[68] *Op. cit.*, 155, n. 2.

[69] Kohler, *art. cit.*, *Jewish Encyclopedia* v (1903), 225b; Charles, *Apocrypha and Pseudepigrapha of the O.T.*, ii, 81-82; Büchler, *op. cit.*, 33.

4.7,[70] 4Qp Ps 37 [71] and 1QSa I, 4.9-10. But an uncle could not marry his niece (CD 4.7-11), and no man was permitted to "marry two women during their lifetime" (CD 4.20-5.2); i.e. he could not re-marry if his first wife were still alive. F. M. Cross [72] finds many vague references to celibacy. The cemetery of the newly found settlement on the shore of the Dead Sea ten miles south of Qumran contains the tombs of twelve men, seven women and a seven year old boy.[73] The presence of families in the Qumran community has been confirmed by the discovery of the skeletons of young women and children near the central cemetery.[74] Were they wives, or widows or virgins caring for children adopted by the community? However, the apparent presence of only men among the more than a thousand or so burials in the central cemetery indicates that there were mostly celibate males at Qumran and that they probably worshipped separately. F. F. Bruce [75] finds it "difficult to see how those who devoted themselves to the full rigours of community life at Qumran can have been able to discharge the normal obligations of marriage and fatherhood." On the other hand, Hans Hübner [76] observes that the Qumran priests had to marry in order to insure hereditary succession. Celibacy was patterned after that of the consecrated Israelite warrior in an eschatological holy war (1QM 7.4-6; cf. Exod. 19:10-15, 22; Deut. 20:7; 23:9-14; Judg. 20:26; 1 Sam. 7:6; 14:24; 21:5-6; 2 Sam. 11:11).[77] A priestly community in the presence of angels (1QM 7:4-6; 1QSa 2:3-9; see pp. 203-204, below) required cultic purity.[78]

---

[70] Hans Hübner, "Zölibat in Qumran?", NTS 17 (1971), 158-61.

[71] Ibid., 164-66.   [72] Op. cit., 42, 79.

[73] Reuters dispatch from Jerusalem, Mar. 13, 1969. Similar to Qumran are its architecture and Hebrew script.

[74] De Vaux, art. cit., RB 63 (1956), 569-72; S. H. Steckoll, "Preliminary Excavation Report on the Qumran Cemetary," RQ 6 (1967-68), 335; cf. Driver, op. cit., 45-46. Alfred Marx, "Les racines du celibat essénien," RQ 7 (1970), 334-35.

[75] Second Thoughts on the Dead Sea Scrolls, Grand Rapids, Mich. (Wm. B. Eerdmans, 1964), 117.   [76] Hübner, art. cit., N.T.S 17(1971), 161-64.

[77] Black, op. cit., 17, 29-31, 72; "Hasidaean-Essene Asceticism," in Aspects du Judéo-Christianisme. Colloque de Strasbourg, 23-25 avril 1964, Paris (Presses Universitaires, 1965), 25-28; W. R. Farmer, "Essenes," IDB 2, 147-48; E. Nielson, "La Guerre consiḍerée comme une religion à la Religion comme une guerre. Du chant de Débora au Rouleau de la Guerre de Qoumran?," Studia Theologica 15 (1961), 93-112; Buchanan, art. cit., RQ 4 (1963-64), 402; A Marx, "Les racines du célibat essénien," RQ 7 (1970), 339-42; Anton Steiner, "Warum lebten die Essener asketisch?", Biblische Zeitschrift 15 (1971), 24-27.

[78] Ibid., 15-16; Johann Maier, Die Texte vom Toten Meer, Munich (Ernst Reinhardt), ii (1960), 78.

Fornication was naturally scorned (QS 1.6; 4.10; CD 2.16; 4.15-18). The intensity of the sectarians' reaction against the dangers of passion is illustrated by "The Wiles of the Wicked Woman" (4Q 184).[79] "Her heart's perversion prepares wantonness, and her emotion[. . .]. In perversion they seized the fouled (organs) of passion, they descended the pity of her leg to act wickedly" (2-3). She seeks to seduce righteous men (12-17). The young man growing up in the community was not allowed to approach "a woman to know her sexually unless he is twenty years old" (1QSa 1.8-12); marriage was to be postponed until judgment concerning good and evil had sufficiently matured. Sexual intercourse was further restricted to places outside Jerusalem (or Qumran)[80]: "Let no man lie with a woman in the city of the Sanctuary for the fear of defiling the city of the Sanctuary with their defilement" (CD 12.1-2). Yigael Yadin[81] reports that the recently discovered Temple Scroll contains rules of purity and uncleanness pertinent to sexual intercourse which were to be observed in Jerusalem.

Pliny the Elder (*Natural History* v, 17.4) described the celibacy of the Essenes[82] living to the west of the Dead Sea in these terms: "They are ... without women and renouncing love entirely (*omni venere abdicata*) without money, and having for company only the palm trees." Life leads many, "wearied by the fluctuations of fortune, to adopt their customs." Philo (*Apologia pro Judaeis, ap.* Eusebius, *Praep. Evang.* viii, 11. 14-17) is more descriptive:

> Providing against the sole or principal obstacle threatening to dissolve the bonds of communal life, they banned marriage at the same time as they ordered the practice of perfect continence. Indeed, no Essene takes a woman because women are selfish, excessively jealous, skilful in ensnaring the morals of a spouse and in seducing him by endless charms. Women set out to flatter, and wear all sorts of masks, like actors on the state; then, when they have bewitched the eye and captured the ear, when, that is to say, they have deceived the lower senses, they next lead the sovereign mind astray ... The husband, bound by his wife's spells, or anxious for his children from natural necessity, is no more the same toward the others, but unknown to himself he becomes a different man, a slave instead of a freeman.

Some reservation in accepting this account *in toto* is necessitated

---

[79] John M. Allegro, *Palestine Exploration Quarterly* 96 (1964), 53-55.
[80] Hübner, *art. cit., NTS* 17 (1971), 167.
[81] *Art. cit., Biblical Archaeologist* 30 (1967), 139.
[82] On Essene asceticism, see Strathmann, *op. cit.,* i, 83-100.

from the possible inclusion of Eusebius' own misogynous views. Nevertheless, Pliny and Philo agree that there was a communal celibacy motivated by the desire to abandon the worldly responsibilities associated with marriage. Josephus confirms their scorn for womanly weakness as a motive for continence:

> The Essenes renounce pleasure as an evil, and regard continence and resistance to the passions as a virtue. They disdain marriage for themselves, but adopt the children of others at a tender age in order to instruct them ... It is not that they abolish marriage, or the propagation of the species resulting from it, but they are on their guard against the licentiousness of women and are convinced that none of them is faithful to one man (*War* ii, 8.2.120-21).

Hippolytus (ix, 18) adds that "they turn away from every deed of concupiscence, holding it hateful even to listen to such things," that they do not forbid their adopted children to marry, and that "they admit no women." Elsewhere Josephus (*Antiquities* xviii, 1.5.21) observes that "they take no wives" and "live among themselves" because they "consider marriage as leading to discord." Presumably they viewed women as more quarrelsome than men. But they did not in principle condemn marriage itself. They attributed the longevity of most of their members to their ἐγκράτεια, measured serving (of food), control of anger and piety to God (θεοσέβεια) (Hippolytus ix, 26; cf. Philo *ap*. Eusebius, *Praep. Evang.* viii, 11.7). In other words, they saw asceticism as beneficial to both body and soul. The Theapeutae saw satiety as inimical to soul and body alike (Philo, *de vita contempl.* 73); as pleasure, desire, passions and vices are also injurious, the Therapeutae healed both souls and diseases (*ibid.*, 2). For the same reason the Essenes studied ancient writings on the healing of diseases (e.g. through the therapeutic value of plant roots and stones); for they were especially interested in works "which tend to be useful to body and soul" (Josephus, *War* ii, 8.6.136; cf. Hippolytus ix, 22; Jubilees 10:10-14; Tobit 6:16-22).[83] They considered their zealous and lengthy training to be "more agreeable to body and soul ... than athletic games," whereas they "hated luxury as a plague for body and soul" (Philo, *ap*. Eusebius, *Praep. Evang.* viii, 11.7 and 11).

However, unity of opinion was lacking on the subject; one was free to choose between celibacy and marriage:

---

[83] G. Vermès, "The Etymology of 'Essenes'," *RQ* 2(1959-60). 440-43.

Now there is another order of Essenes making use of their customs and ways of life, but they differ from these in the one [point of] marriage; saying that those who reject marriage do a fearful thing. And they declare that this comes to a taking-away of life, and that one must not cut off the succession of children, and that if everyone thought like this, the whole race of men might easily be cut off ... They try their wives ... When they have had three purifications, so as to prove that they can bear children, they wed them. But they do not company with them when pregnant, proving [thereby] that they do not marry for pleasure but from the need of children (Hippolytus ix, 28; cf. Josephus, *War* ii, 8.13.160-61).[84]

Their abstinence from the pleasure of intercourse except when conducive to reproduction indicates that these celibates were wary of ἡδονή. As long as one remained married he could not enter the ranks of the highest degree of discipline (ἄσκησις) or holiness (Josephus, *War* ii, 8.10.150).

Kaufmann Kohler [85] concluded that the Essenes were:

rigorists ... whose constant fear of becoming contaminated by either social or sexual intercourse led them to lead an ascetic life, but whose insistence on maintaining the highest possible standard of purity and holiness had for its object to make them worthy of being participants of 'the Holy Spirit', or recipients of divine revelations, and of being initiated into the mysteries of God and the future. 'Woe to the wives of these men.' 'exclaimed Zipporah, the wife of Moses, when she heard that Eldad and Medad had become prophets, for this meant cessation of conjugal intercourse (Sifre, Num. 99).

When God revealed Himself to Moses and to the people of Israel they were enjoined to abstain from sexual intercourse, Israel for the time being, Moses for all time (Shab. 87a; Ab. R.N. ii, based on Ex.xix [.15]; Deut. v. 27). Those in hope of a divine revelation consequently refrained from sexual intercourse as well as other impurity.[86]

Emil Schürer [87] commented: "Since the act of marriage as such made an individual unclean and necessitated a Levitical bath of purification [Lev. 15:16-18; Josephus, *Contra Apion* ii, 24], the effort to attain to the highest degree of purity might well lead to the entire repudiation

---

[84] Dupont-Sommer, *op. cit.*, 35, nn. 2-3.

[85] Kohler, *art. cit., Jewish Encyclopedia* 5 (1903), 230a; cf. Büchler, *op. cit.*, 51-52.

[86] Kohler, *art. cit., Jewish Encyclopedia* v (1903), 226a; *art. cit., JQR* 11 (1920), 159.; cf. Böcher, *op. cit.*, 293-95. See Yebamoth 62a.

[87] Schürer, *op. cit.*, ii-ii, 211 (ET); cf. Conybeare, "Essenes," *A Dictionary of the Bible*, ed. James Hastings, Edinburg (T. & T. Clark), i (1898), 769b; Wilfried Paschen, *Rein und Unrein*, München (Kösel, 1970), 59-63; Böcher, *op. cit.*, 293.

of marriage." Matthew Black [88] concurs: "Since everything connected
with sexual functions and relations was unclean, total renunciation
alone meant complete holiness, especially in a priestly sect." Priests
"shall not marry a harlot", widow, defiled or divorced woman; "for the
priest is holy to his God" (Lev. 21: 7, 13-14; Ezek. 44:22).

The Essenes renouncing a love life may have consisted in large
measure of older persons.[89] Both Josephus (War ii, 8.10.151; cf.
Hippolytus ix, 26) and Philo (ap. Eusebius, Praep. Evang. viii, 11.13)
commented on their longevity; such might statistically be expected if
those admitted were already of mature years. Pliny (Nat. Hist. v, 17.4)
stated that most of their recruits had been wearied by life (vita fessi)
and tossed about by the fluctuations of fortune (fortuna fluctibus
agitat). Many of the Therapeutae recruits were elderly (Philo, de vita
contempl. 13, 67). Philo (ap. Eusebius, Praep. Evang. viii, 11.3)
confirms:

> There are no children of tender age among the Essenes, nor even
> adolescents or young men, since at this age the character, because of its
> immaturity, is inconsistent and attracted to novelty; but they are men of
> ripe years already inclining to old age who are no longer carried away by
> the flux of body nor drawn by the passions, but enjoy true and
> unparalleled liberty.

Perhaps the married Essenes or those living in towns would tend to
adopt the monastic life in order to seek perfection after such a
change in fortune as the death of their mate. They would not remarry
and would bring their children with them into the community,
though the offspring could not be initiated until they had matured.
Perhaps they were adopted only when the parents were Essene and
had died. The Therapeutae accepted both men and women into their
ranks (Philo, de vita contempl. 32-33, 83), though they were
separated for worship and sacred dancing. "Women also share in the
banquet, most of whom have grown old in virginity, preserving their
purity (ἀγνεία) . . . through their zealous love (πόθος) of wisdom" (ibid.,
68). Asenath was a παρθένος ἀγνή (Joseph and Asenath 15:1; 19:2; cf.
4:9; 8:1).

---

[88] Op. cit., 29. See also Steiner, art. cit., Biblische Zeitschrift 15 (1971), 11-24. Seven
days before the Day of Atonement, the high priest had to leave his house (Yoma I, 4a).

[89] Black, op. cit., 31; their high rate of mortality (Driver, op. cit., 48) supports this
assumption.

HOLINESS

Paul commended himself to the Corinthians in every way so that no fault could be found in his ministry. Among his weapons of righteousness were watchings (ἀγρυπνία), fastings, purity, knowledge, forebearance, kindness, a Holy Spirit, unfeigned love, truthful speech and the power of God (2 Cor. 6:3-7). In spite of this blameless standard of sanctity and his sufferings, Paul was treated as an unknown imposter who was punished, grieved and dying (6:8-10). Again, in 2 Cor. 11:23-29 he defends his ministry against Hebrew Christian rivals by appealing to his watchings, fastings, famine, thirst, cold, nakedness and other sufferings. They could excel him in none of his hardships. Paul and his readers and critics alike viewed vigils and fastings as among the weapons of the righteousness of a minister of God (6:4) and of Christ (11:23), or a minister of righteousness (11:15). Paul's holiness and sincerity had been questioned, however. "Our boast is this, that the testimony of our conscience that we have behaved in the world, and still more toward you, with holiness and godly sincerity, not by earthly wisdom but by the grace of God. For we write you nothing but what you can read and understand" (2 Cor. 1.12-13). His claim to εἰλικρίνεια in 2:17 (cf. 4:12) is opposed to corrupting the word of God. The opponents evidently meant that he had made God's word unintelligible (2:13-14) and non-spiritual (2:12b); in 1 Cor. 2:4-5, 13-14 human wisdom is contrasted with spiritual truths taught by the Spirit. They, like Paul, assumed that ἁγιότης καὶ εἰλικρίνεια τοῦ θεοῦ were associated with the grace, power and Spirit of God.

From 1 Cor. 7:34 C. K. Barrett [90] concludes "that in 'that she may be holy both in body and in spirit' we have words quoted from the Corinthian ascetical party. Paul approves the sentiment, though he would not himself confine it to the unmarried ... He believes that all Christians, married or unmarried, must be holy in body; see Rom. vi. 12; xii. 1", etc. J. A. "Bengel remarks that ἅγια here means more than it does in v 14: what is set apart from the world for God ought to conform to the purity of God and not to the defilements of the world."[91] Paul's view is that the believer sanctifies an unbelieving mate, and their children are holy rather than unclean; that is, believers are not contaminated by sexual contact with ἄπιστοι. Some

---

[90] Op. cit., 181.
[91] Robertson and Plummer, op. cit., 158.

at Corinth who were moved by Old Testament distinctions of pure and impure,[92] had apparently recommended divorce (7:12-13, 15). At stake was the question whether purity or impurity overcomes the other.

The opponents in Philippians 3 were eager to be blameless (v. 6) and perfect (12-15) in terms of legal righteousness (9). In their zeal for the Law (v. 6) they did not imagine themselves subject to Paul's charge of being "dogs" (2; cf. Mt. 7:6) preoccupied with σκύβαλα (8) and ἐπίγεια (19) to their shame (19). For, they were holy men.

Paul warned and taught every man in order to present them τελείως in Christ (Col. 1:28). By his crucixion he could present them holy (ἁγίους) and blameless and irreproachable before himself (1:22), provided they did not move away from the hope of thhe true gospel. A preaching contrary to Paul's (1:23) would not make them holy in Christ's sight.

For the author of Ephesians holiness implies the indwelling of Christ, the possession of faith and knowledge, and being filled with all the πλήρομα of God (3:17-19). Those who are chosen in Christ are holy and blameless before him (1:4). They are new men (4:24) and belong to a holy and unblemished church (5:27; cf. 4:12). Their knowledge of the Son of God and their love grow to maturity and fullness; they grow into Christ in all respects and become complete men measurable by the stature of Christ's fullness (4:13, 15). But this holiness presupposes unity of faith and freedom the influence of seductive erroneous teaching (4:13-14)), which does not bring men to such sanctity.

The ascetic sabbatarians irenically described by Paul in Romans 14 dedicated their observances to God. They judged one day to be above another day and ate only vegetables because of thanksgiving to God and honor to the Lord (τὴν ἡμέραν κυρίω ... φρονεῖ ... μὴ ἐσθίων κυρίω) (14:2-6).

Before warning against the teachings of spirits and against those who forbid marriage and the consumption of certain foods, the Pastor sets forth a confessional hymn of the church as the mystery τῆς εὐσεβείας (1 Tim. 3:16). There are further hints that asceticism was being viewed as an expression of godliness. In 1 Tim. 4:6-8 the words of the faith and of good teaching are set against profane, old-womanish myths, while life-giving training in piety is contrasted with

[92] E.-B. Allo, St. Paul. Première Épitre aux Corinthiens, Paris (J. Gabalda, 1935), 166-67.

physical training or self discipline. True εὐσέβεια is distinguished from the false in terms of orthodoxy in Tit. 1:1, where Paul's apostolate is defined in terms of the faith of God's elect and their full knowledge of truth according to piety. Likewise, in 1 Tim. 6:3-6 τῇ κατ᾽ εὐσέβειαν διδασκαλία is a correlate of the sound words of Christ; whoever teaches otherwise is conceited, lacking in understanding (μηδὲν ἐπιστάμενος), and is morbidly concerned about questionings (ζητήσεις; cf. 1:4 and Tit. 3:9, where it is linked with myths and genealogies) and verbal battles about the Law. Possessing a corrupted mind which is bereft of the truth, and supposing εὐσέβεια to be a means of profit, these wranglers teach their γνῶσις for the sake of base gain (cf. Tit. 1:10-15, where those of the circumcision professionally teach Jewish myths and human ascetic commandments). However, responds the Pastor, great gain is really found in εὐσέβεια μετὰ αὐταρκείας, which comes through pursuing righteousness, εὐσέβεια, faith, love, endurance, ὑπομονή and meekness (1 Tim. 6:6, 11). Thus we conclude that for the opponents, true εὐσέβεια was manifested by obeying ascetic laws after growth in knowledge and understanding of the myths and genealogies of the law-giving spirits.

John was a "righteous and holy (ἅγιον) man": a reputation known even to Herod (Mk. 6:20). The Baptist's exhortation to δικαιοσύνη toward one another and εὐσέβεια πρός τὸν θεόν (Josephus, *Antiq.* xviii, 5.2) corresponds to the Essene oath of εὐσεβήσειν τὸ θεῖου and τὰ πρὸς ἄνθρώπους δίκαια (*War* ii, 8.7).

In the (Jerusalem-) Caesarean source of Acts, Dorcas was praised for being "full of good works and acts of charity" (9:36) and Cornelius as "a εὐσεβής man who feared God ..., gave alms liberally to the people, and prayed constantly to God" (10:2; cf. 4, 7, 22, 31).

According to *Clem. Hom.* xi. 16, a θεοσεβής "really performs the deeds of the law ... If one acts impiously (ἀσεβήσε), he is not εὐσεβής."

In Sibylline Oracle IV the ideal of righteousness is described by the terms, εὐσέβεια, εὐσεβής and εὐσεβειν (lines 26, 35, 42, 45, 133, 148, 151, 162, 165, 181, 183).

In the Testaments of the Twelve Patriarchs εὐσέβεια signifies righteousness or honoring the words of the law and the prophets (T. Levi 16:2). It includes keeping the truth, loving the Lord and every man, and doing deeds of mercy (T. Iss. 7:5). He who is a fornicator or a lover of money resents the words of εὐσέβεια; he can neither obey

God nor hearken to a prophet (T. Judah 18:5). "For in fornication there is neither σύνεσις nor εὐσέβεια" (T. Reub. 6:4). In the Septuagint (Prov. 1:7; Isa. 11:2; 33:6) εὐσέβεια can be a translation for "fear of the Lord." Benjamin (T. Benj. 3:1; cf. 5:4-6) instructed his children to "follow the example of the good and holy (ὅσιος) man Joseph."

Members of the Qumran community numbered themselves among "the saints" (1QH 4.25; 1QSb 3.26; 1QM 3.5; 6.6; 10.10; 12.8; 16.1; 4Qp Ps 37 II.8).[93] They were men of holiness and perfection, or of perfect holiness (1QH 15.23; 1QS 8.17, 20-23; 5.18; 9.2, 8; CD 4.6; 20.2, 5, 7); they were following precepts of holy perfection (CD 7.5; 20.30). Through conversion and baths they had "purified their way to be separated from perversity and walk in perfection of way" (1QS 5.13-14; 9.9). The holy have recognized the Covenant of God and are counted in it (1QS 5.18-19). The saints in the Covenant belong to "the Council of Holiness" (1QH 7.10; 1QM 3.4; 1QSa 2.9), "the House of holiness" (1QS 8.5, 8; 9.6), "the holy Congregation" (1QS 5.20; 1QSa 1.9, 13; cf. 2.16). IQSb I, 1-2 blesses "those who fear (yr') [God and do] His will, who observe His commandments and cling firmly to his holy Covenant and walk perfectly [in all] His [ways of truth]." Those who are holy (qwds) manifest kindness (chesed) (1QS 2.24-25; 8.6; 10.4).[94] But the apparent reluctance of the members of the Qumran community to call themselves "chasid" suggests that the word could be used in a perjorative or derogatory sense, or that the Hasidim were by no means restricted to, or identical with, them or the Essenes.[95] Qumran piety expressed itself through prayers at sunrise, midday and sunset (1QS 10.1; 1QH 12.4-7) and through vigils for studying the law (1QS 6.7).

The first oath of the Essene was "to practice piety towards the Deity (μὲν εὐσεβήσειν τὸ θεῖον; then to observe justice towards men" (Josephus, War ii, 8.7.139). "Their piety (εὐσέβεια) towards the Deity takes a particular form: before sunrise they speak no profane word but recite certain ancestral prayers to the sun as though entreating it to rise" (War ii, 8.5.128). According to the Slavonic version of the same passage, "Towards the Deity they are especially pious. They rest little, and they rise at night to sing praises to God and to pray.[96]

---

[93] F. Nötscher, "Heiligkeit in den Qumranschriften," *RQ* 2 (1959-60), 328-32.

[94] On the etymology, see Büchler, *op. cit.*, 7.

[95] *Ibid.* 19, 33, 39, 43, 73, 78, 107, 127, 257-59, 264.

[96] Philonenko, *art. cit*, *Semitica* 6 (1956), 69-70; Arie Rubinstein, "The Essenes according to the Slavonic Version of Josephus' *Wars*, *Vetus Testamentum* 6 (1956), 308.

Philo (de vita contempl. 183-87) described the Therapeutae's vigil (παννυχὶς) from supper until prayers at sunrise. Communal vigils and sunrise prayers (cf. Joseph and Asenath 2:14; 12:1) were an expression of piety. Studying the law day and night is commanded in Josh. 1:8 and Psalm 1:2. The Essenes saw their lofty θεοσέβεια as one of the forms of self-discipline which fostered longevity (Hippolytus ix, 26). Josephus (War ii, 8.2.119ff.), after describing the Essenes as those "who intend to cultivate a particularly saintly (σεμνοι) life," goes on to explain asceticism. Menahem the Essene set before the young Herod the ideal of loving righteousness, piety (εὐσέβεια) toward God and gentleness towards his citizens (Josephus, Antiquities xv, 10.5.375). The goal (τέλος) of the Therapeutae's ideas, expressions and sacred dancing was εὐσέβεια (Philo, de vita contempl. 88). Joseph was θεοσεβής (Joseph and Asenath 4:9; 8:5-7, etc.) The Therapeutae believed that through hymn singing and the study of the law and prophets, εὐσέβεια would grow and be perfected (τελοῦνται) (ibid., 25). Εὐσεβής is closely associated with ὅσιος in 2 Macc. 12:45 and Philo (Decal. 119). Porphyry (ap. Cyril Alex., Contra Julian. V, Migne, P.G. 76,776) mentioned the Essenes' πρὸς ἀλήθειαν καὶ εὐσέβειαν ἀσκήσεως and their διαφόροις ἁγνείαις.

Thus the Essenes saw themselves as saints or holy ones who expressed their piety toward God through ascetic safeguards of purity, in conformity with their interpretation of His law. It is not surprising that this overarching ideal was apparently incorporated in the very name, "Essene." The "pious" or "holy" ones were the "hasidim", a Hebrew term which is cognate to "hasayya" (Aramaic, Syriac, Palmyrene). It is equivalent to the Greek "ὅσιοι," [97] from which Philo (Quod omnis probus 75, 91; Apologia pro Judaeis, ap. Eusebius, Praep. Evang. viii, 11.1) derived their name, and to Epiphanius' 'Οσσαῖοι (Haer. 30 & 53; cf. 10 & 19),[98] though he treated the Essenes and Ossenes as different sects. While Pliny called them "Esseni" and Philo, "Εσσαῖοι," Josephus used both 'Εσσηνοί and "Εσσαῖοι." Hippolytus (ix, 18, 28) spoke of the "'Εσσηνοί." [99]

---

[97] Schürer, op. cit., 191 (ET); Klausner, op. cit., 202; Cross, op. cit., 51-52, n. 1; K. G. Kuhn; "Zum heutigen Stand der Qumrānforschung, "TLZ 85 (1960), 654; Hans G. Schonfeld," Zum Begriff, 'Therapeutai' bei Philo," RQ 3 (1961-62), 240; Milik, op. cit., 80, n. 1; W. F. Albright, "Qumran and the Essenes: Geography, Chronology and Identification of the Sect," in Sect," in The Scrolls and Christianity, ed. Black, 108, n. 12; cf. Vermès, art. cit., RQ 2 (1959-60), 428-29.

[98] Schürer, op. cit., 213, n. 102 (ET).

[99] Ibid., 190.

CHAPTER FOUR

SACERDOTAL SEPARATISM

Washing Away Pollution

A legalistic, perfectionist, ascetic Judaic piety required repentance and remedies for physical, moral and ritual contamination. Purification of flesh and spirit (cf. 2 Cor. 7:1) through the cleansing power of water provided the most natural remedy.

In Colossians the spiritual experience of participation in the death, burial and resurrection of Christ through baptism is stated to be the Christian replacement of circumcision and the regulations for the body as imposed by the στοιχεῖα τοῦ κόσμου (2:11-12, 20-21; 3:1-3). While the legal demands have been cancelled (2:14), those baptized have already been made alive and forgiven (2:13); their "life is hid with Christ in God" (3:3). Not even the act of baptism is effective in forgiveness of trespasses (2:13) unless there is "faith in the working of God" (2:12). The use of the term, "βαπτισμός," (2:12), rather than the customary βάπτισμα, suggests the ritual washing of eating utensils (Mk. 7:14). This usage suggests further that Christian baptism is the new counterpart of the ceremonial washing of cups, pots and vessels. Ascetic rules for food preparation and consumption (2:22) were meant to avoid contact with impure, defiling objects.[1]

In Ephesians 5:26-27 the corporate, rather than the individual, sanctification of believers is described in terms of cleansing the church, so as to be glorious and holy, without spot, wrinkle or blemish. This purification from defilement is effected "by the washing (λουτρόν) of water with the word." In the Septuagint λουτρόν is the term used for "laver," the bronze bowl employed for ritual cleansing. In this context the reference seems to the bride's bath before her marriage. Eph. 4:5 insists on only one baptism. The soteriological nature of the cleansing taught in Ephesians could be a constructive response to proponents of ablutions and to opponents of marriage.

Hebrews 5:11-6:12 was addressed to those who, having become dull of hearing (5:11; 6:12), were in danger of drifting away from the

---

[1] Norbert Hugedé, *Commentaire de l'Epître aux Colossiens*, Geneva (Labor et Fides, 1968), 155; cf. Lev. 5:2-3; 11:8, 24, 31, 39; 15:7; Num. 19:11-12, 19; 31:19.

Gospel (6:4, 6-8; cf. 2:1). Being "unskilled in the word of righteousness" (5:13) and in the distinction of good and evil (5:14), they had been unable to progess beyond the elementary rudiments which marked the beginning of their Christian life: namely, "repentance from dead works and . . . faith toward God, . . . ablutions, the laying on of hands, the resurrection of the dead and eternal judgment" (6:1-2). These initial requirements, which by themselves do not foster "the full assurance of the hope unto the end" (6:11), are ostensibly more Jewish than specifically Christian. The readers' understanding of Christ was germinal, undeveloped. They were preoccupied with eschatological judgment (cf. 6:5b, 7, 9) and with the means of escaping condemnation (cf. 6:6, 8), namely, repentance, washings and faith in God. The immature practice of purificatory βαπτισμοι appears to be a survival from the addressees' Judaic background. Hebrews 10:19-39 return to most of the themes of 5:11-6:12. "Let us draw near with a true heart in full assurance of faith, with our hearts sprinkled clean from an evil conscience and our bodies washed (λελουσμένοι: a perfect participle) with pure water. Let us hold fast the confession of our hope without wavering" (10:22-23). Christian baptism is favorably compared to the ablutions of the old covenant. The preacher, having explained the saving work of Jesus as the Melchizedekian High Priest (6:19-10:21), now supposes that his addressees have gone on to maturity of knowledge of the Son, confidence (10:19, 35) and full assurance of faith (10:22, 39; cf. 6:11). "By a new and living way" (10:20) condemnation has been escaped by the purification and washing of an evil conscience through faith. A partial explanation of this is found in Hebr. 9:6-10:2. According to 9:9-10, "Various ablutions (βαπτισμοι), regulations for the body imposed until the time of reformation, . . . cannot perfect the conscience of the worshipper." For if the sprinkling of defiled persons . . . sanctifies for the purification of the flesh, how much more shall the blood of Christ . . . purify your conscience from dead works to serve the living God" (9:13-14). "Since the law has but a shadow of the good things to come . . . , it can never by the same sacrifices which are continually offered year by year, make perfect those who draw near . . . If the worshippers had once been cleansed, they would no longer have any consciousness of sin" (10:1-2). Such is the shortcoming of all Levitical rituals. A major theme of the Epistle is announced at the outset: the Son "made purification for sins" (1:3).

In Philippians 3 Paul taunts his opponents as dogs (v. 2) who are preoccupied with matters which Paul classifies as rubbish (8) and earthly shame (19). They had sought instead purity by their legal righteousness (6-7) and food laws (19). But Paul felt impelled to write down his warnings in order to make the Philippians "safe" (1) from the corrupting "dogs."

In dealing with the problem of marriage to unbelievers, the Apostle advises the Corinthians that the believing wife sanctifies the unbelieving husband and that their children are holy. There was concern lest their children be unclean (ἀχάθαρτά) (1 Cor. 7:14). The virgins sought to be holy in both body and spirit (7:34). Holiness and purity were correlates for them. The church factions were concerned about their baptisms (1:12-17).

The Pastoral Epistles reflect the same concern over being clean. Whereas those ascetics "whose minds and consciences are corrupted" find that "nothing is pure," Titus is informed: "To the pure all things are pure" (1:14-15). The αντίθεσις of the false γνῶσις (1 Tim. 6:20) may have referred to the contrast of clean and unclean or of flesh and the spirit, as they did for Marcion (Tertullian, *Adv. Marc.* 1, 19). The Pastor describes purity from the positive, rather than the negative, point of view. Thus Timothy is exhorted to ἀγνεία, i.e. being an example of right speech, behavior, love and faith (1 Tim. 4:12), of a chaste view toward younger women (1 Tim. 5:2), and of a right attitude toward wine (1 Tim. 5:22b-23). "With a clean conscience (ἐν καθαρᾷ συνειδήσει)" Paul worshipped God (2 Tim. 1:3) and deacons must hold the mystery of the faith (1 Tim. 3:9). From a clean (καθαρός) heart and consciensce comes love, which is the τέλος of the true law (1 Tim. 1:5; cf. 3-4, 6-8). Christ "gave himself for us to redeem us from all iniquity and to purify for himself a people of his own who are zealous for good deeds" (Tit. 2:13-14). Commenting on this passage Fred D. Gealy writes:[2]

> After liberation from the power of evil, purification follows. As Moses sealed the people of Israel with the blood of the covenant (Exod. 24:8), so Christ with his own blood purified for himself a people of his own (Exod. 19:5; Deut. 14:2; ... Hebr. 9:14-22; 1 Pet. 1:2), a 'special' people belonging to him because redeemed by him. As Israel was formerly God's peculiar people, so now is the church; as Israel was zealous for the law (Deut. 26:18; Gal. 1:14; Acts 21:20), Christ's new people are to be zealous for good deeds. . .

---

[2] "Titus," *IB* 11 (1955), 540-41.

"He saved us, not because of deeds done by us in righteousness, but in virtue of his own mercy, by the washing (γουτρόν) of regeneration and the renewal in the Holy Spirit" (Tit. 3:5), i.e. through baptism.

As a vegetarian living off the countryside and as a locust-eater (Lev. 11:21-22) John ate only ceremonially clean food. He did not eat with sinners and tax collectors, as did Jesus (Mt. 11:18-19; Lk. 7:33-34). This ostensible concern for the Mosaic laws of purity led him to say to Herod, who had married his brother Philip's wife, "It is not lawful for you to have your brother's wife" (Mk. 6:17-18; Mt. 14:3-4; Lk. 3:19-20). "If a man takes his brother's wife it is impurity" (Lev. 20:21; cf. 18:16). Moreover, his avoidance of populous areas was partly motivated by his desire for purity. Whoever was responsible for John's religious training in the wilderness probably had withdrawn there for similar reasons. At an earlier age his father was bound to teach him principles of priestly purity. Finally, John's concern for cleanness appears in the refining or purgative aspects of the coming eschatological fire (cf. Mal. 3:2) and Spirit (cf. Mt. 12:28). Only a prophet so preoccupied with purification could have offered fellow Jews something new:[3] a baptism of repentance which prepared them for the rapidly approaching eschaton; through God's forgiveness they would be spared from a fiery destruction. His baptism was "to mark them out as belonging to the true and purified Israel," in the words of John Robinson [4] i.e. "a pure and purifying remnant." As the chief priests did not believe John (Mt. 21:23, 32; Mk. 11:27-33; Jn. 1:19), and as his disciples disputed with a Jew concerning purification (Jn. 3:25), it is reasonable to deduce from the contexts that there was resistance to claims that John's penitential baptism was uniquely efficacious for eschatologically-oriented purification from sins. His baptism of repentance for the remission (εἰς ἄφεσιν) of sins (Mk. 1:4; Lk. 3:3) "would be acceptable to God if it were used, not for the pardon (παραιτήσαι) of certain sins, but for the purification of the body, provided that the soul had been thoroughly cleansed beforehand by righteousness" (Josephus, *Antiquities* xviii, 5.2). In other words, sins were not remitted without seeking and obtaining bodily purification, which in turn was conditional upon inward cleansing. Such requirements far exceeded those for proselyte baptism; but close resemblances to Qumran's rite of initiation have

---

[3] Roland Schütz, *Johannes der Täufer*, Zurich & Stuttgart (Zwingli Verlag, 1967), 14, 44-45, 52.

[4] *Twelve N. T. Studies*, 19, 21.

been often noted.[5] In John's background lie the prophetic calls to cleansing (Isa. 1:16; Jer. 4:14; Ezek. 36:25-28; cf. Ps. 51) and priestly ritual lustration before service in the Temple.[6] Hence priests and Levites were sent to question him (Jn. 1:19). John Robinson [7] argues that it was not John who disavowed the efficacy of external washings (Mk. 7:1-15) (the βαπρισμοι of "all the Jews": 7:3-4) and the repeatability of baptism (Hebr. 6:2, 4-6). Is it reasonable to argue from Christian analogy and *ex silentio* that John the Washer, desisted from all traditional and scriptural washings because his rite of initiation was an adequate safeguard and preparation for the eschaton? Was he no longer concerned about his disciples' state of purity when his activities brought his circle into contact when the crowds from populated areas, including tax collectors, harlots and soldiers? Dwelling near baptismal waters, would he dispense with the usual mode of dealing with moral contamination? In answering these questions, how much weight should we give to the closest analogies, namely, the Essenes, the Jordan baptizing sects (including the Elchesaites) and the desert hermit Bannus (who used frequent ablutions of cold water, both by day and night, for the sake of purity [πρός ἀγνειανl: Josephus, *Life* 2)? Clementine Homily ii, 23 states that John was a Hemerobaptist. To admit that John used lustrations as need arose, however, is not equivalent to the less attractive assertions that he adopted a schedule of daily ablutions and that these did not differ in form from his eschatological, penitential rite of initiation.

The Hemerobaptists used daily ablutions. They did not eat unless they washed. "Unless they cleanse their beds and tables or platters and cups, they do not make use of any of them" (Apostolic Constitutions vi. 6). Epiphanius (*Haer.* 17) explained that the Hemerobaptists "bathe themselves daily in water, to release and purify themselves from every fault (πάσης αἰτίας)." Hegesippus (*ap.* Eusebius, *H. E.* iv. 22) mentioned Hemerobaptists and Masbotheans (a doublet of Baptists in Graecized Aramaic) [8] in his list of Hebrew semi-Christian heretics, which included followers of Simon, Cleobius

---

[5] *Ibid.*, 18-20; H. Braun, *op. cit.*, ii, 2-3.

[6] Mathias Rubinstein, "Le baptême de Jean," *Revue des études juives* 84 (1927), 66-70; Joachim Gnilka, "Die essenischen Tauchbäder und die Johannestaufe, *RQ* 3 (1961), 207.

[7] *Twelve N. T. Studies*, 17-18.

[8] Marcel Simon, *Les sectes juives au temps de Jesus*, Paris (Presses Universitaires, 1960), 77; also Thomas, *op. cit.*, 41-42.

(see 3 Cor., *ap*. Acts of Paul) and Dositheus. Justin (*Dial*. 80) in his list of αἱρέσεις amongst the Jews included Pharisees [and] Baptists.[9] Whether or not John himself had a relation with the Baptists, their contact with his followers in the Jordan Valley was inevitable. Some Daily Baptists honored Jesus.

The twelve disciples at Ephesus knew John's baptism of repentance (Acts 19:4-5; cf. 13:24). But the Apostle convinced them to be baptized "in the name of the Lord Jesus" (19:5). The Western Text addition, "for the remission of sins", accords with both the Johannine and Christian baptism. But Paul had to convince them that sins were forgiven in the name of Jesus; the "Baptists" water baptism had not been sufficiently effective. The twelve had sought purification through repentance and its fruits and by water. Their willingness to accept re-baptism would have been greater if they were accustomed to repeated ablutions.

The Ebionites practiced daily ablutions (Epiphanius, *Haer*. 30.16 & 21) and avoided touching outsiders (30.2). The Bishop of Salamis (30.15) reports their use of the Clementine Circuits of Peter, in which Cephas is represented as being "daily baptized for the sake of purification, as they themselves also are." Thus in the derivative Clementine literature we read that he daily practiced voluntary (θελήσασι; *volentibus*) ritual ablutions in running waters (*Rec.* v. 36) and bathed in the sea, streams or water reservoirs before prayer and meals (*Rec.* iv. 3; viii. 1; *Hom.* viii. 2; ix. 23; x.1, 26; xi. 1, 1, 3). A man must keep himself pure by washing after sexual intercourse and by avoiding it during his wife's monthly periods (*Hom.* xi. 28, 30, 34). Because καθαρεύειν belongs to the worship of God, "cleanse your hearts from wickedness by heavenly thoughts ... and wash your bodies with water" (*Hom.* xi. 28; cf. *Rec.* vi. 11). Elkesai taught a second baptism for the forgiveness of sins (βαπτίσματι λαμβάνειν ἄφεσιν ἁμαρτιῶν). All clothes were to be left on. One was to purify and sanctify himself and to vow before seven angelic and cosmic witness to sin no more. Those suffering from consumption and demon possession were "to baptize themselves in cold water forty times in seven days" (Hippolytus, *Ref.* 9.13.4; 9.15-16.1; Epiphanius, *Haer*. 30.17.4).[10] The Elchesaites ritually washed their fruits and vegetables

---

[9] Black, *op. cit.*, 51-52.

[10] O. Cullmann, *Le problème littéraire et historique du roman pseudo- clémentin*, Paris (Felix Alcan, 1930).

and had to grow their own food.[11] The Sampsaeans honored God by their βαπτισμοις (*Haer.* 53.1). The Dositheans prayed in water and hid their bodies while bathing (Chronicle of Abu-al-Fath); they avoided human contact (Epiphanius, *Haer.* 13).

According to the Apotolic Tradition of Hippolytus, which Danielou and Black [12] believe to show Qumran influence, those who are to be baptized are to undergo purificatory washings on the previous Thursday, and menstruating women are to be baptized on some other day.

The Melchizedek-glorifiers known to Timothy of Constantinople (Migne, *P.G.* 86, 33B-C) were referred to as "'Αθίγγανοι" because, in his words,

> they do not allow themselves to be touched, but if anyone give them bread or water or anything else, they are not permitted to take it their hands. They ask those who bring them things to put them on the ground, and only then do they approach and take them. They do the same when they give something to someone else.

The Paris. graec. 364 manuscript echoes this report that the Melchizedekians refused to touch other men. Their shunning of direct contact with others presupposes fear of some type of contamination from those outside their sect who were less pure than themselves. Yet they apparently did not avoid Jews as scrupulously as they did others (see p. 91). If so, Jewish law must have been one of the sources of their concern for cleanness.

The Adam literature and Testaments of the Twelve Patriarchs manifest a special concern for purity. As it should be specially exemplified in priestly functions, defilement in this area was loathsome. Levi prophesied a priesthood in which there "shall be such pollution (μιασμός) as I cannot express before men" (T. Levi 17:8). "The temple, which the Lord shall choose, shall be laid waste through your uncleanness (ἀκαθαρσία), and ... ye shall be an abomination unto (all nations), and ye shall receive reproach and everlasting shame from the righteous judgment of God" (T. Levi 15:1-2). "For seventy weeks ye shall go astray, and profane the priesthood and pollute the sacrifices. And ye shall make void the law, and set at nought the words of the prophets by evil perverseness... And your

---

[11]   A. Hinrichs and L. Koenen, "Ein griechischer Mani-codex, "*Zeitschrift für Papyrologie und Epigraphik* 5 (1970), 144-45, 148, 159.

[12] *Op. cit.,* 99-101, 114-15; F. F. Bruce (*op. cit.,* 150) is of similar opinion. The reference is found in the G. Dix edition, pp. 31-32

holy places shall be laid waste... And ye shall have no place that is clean" (T. Levi 16:1-2, 4-5; cf. 14). The need for ritual purity is emphasized in Isaac's teaching: "Before entering into the holy place, bathe; and when thou offerest the sacrifice, wash; and again, when thou finishest the sacrifice, wash" (T. Levi 9:11; cf. Jub. 21:16; T. Isaac [13])

Purity is lost through transgressing against the Lord and his commands (T. Levi 14:1-4, 7; T. Ash. 2:6-7). Thus Adam and Eve could confess, "Our lips are unclean from the awful and forbidden tree" (Vita Adae 6:1). The exhortation of Naphtali illustrates the inner source of outward uncleanness. "Be ye, therefore, not eager to corrupt your doings through covetousness or with vain words to beguile your souls; because if ye keep silence in purity of heart, ye shall understand how to hold fast the will of God and to cast away the will of Beliar" (T. Napht. 3:1). III Baruch (8:4-5) teaches that the sun's "rays have been defiled upon the earth ... because it beholds the lawlessness and unrighteousness of men, namely, fornications, adulteries, ... idolatries, drunkenness, ... divinations and such like, which are not well pleasing to God." Most examples of defilement lie in the area of sexual relations: fornication, incest, adultery, marrying Gentiles (T. Reub. 1:6; 4:8; T. Levi 7:3; 9:9-10; 14:6; T. Jud. 14:5-6; T. Ash. 4:4; T. Jos. 4:6), looking at a woman lustfully (T. Iss. 4:4; T. Benj. 8:2), or even associating with them (T. Reub. 6:1-2). "He that hath a pure mind in love, looketh not after a woman with a view to fornication; for he hath no defilement in his heart ... For [as] the sun is not defiled by shining on dung and mire, [but rather drieth up both...]; so also the pure mind, though encompassed by the defilement of the earth, rather cleanseth (them), and is not itself defiled" (T. Benj. 8:2-3).

The good mind "hath one [disposition], uncorrupt and pure, concerning all men ... [And he cleanseth his mind that he be not condemned by men as well as] by God. And in like manner the works of Beliar are twofold, and there is no singleness (ἁπλότης) [14] in them" (T. Benj. 6:5, 7). Ἁπλότης is contrasted in T. Reub. 4:1 with heeding the beauty and affairs of women (cf. T. Iss. 3:4-5). But it is also contrasted with jealousy and envy, covetousness and insatiable

---

[13] Coptic, 64-65; Arabic, 144.
[14] Danielou, Histoire des Doctrines..., 418-21; 362-65 (ET); Jacob Amstutz, Aplotes. Eine begriffsgeschichtliche Studie zum jüdisch-christlichen Griechisch, Bonn (P. Hanstein, 1968).

desire (T. Sim. 4:5; T. Iss. 4:1; 6:1) and is manifested by walking according to the law (T. Levi 13:1; T. Iss. 4:6; 5:1; cf. 3:2-8). The kinship of purity and ἁπλότης is shown by T. Iss. 4:4-6: the man walking in singleness of soul "beholdeth all things in uprightness [of heart] and does not pollute his mind by worldly desires and errors. They are altogether clean who walk "in zeal for the Lord and abstain from what God also hateth and forbiddeth by His commandments, warding off the evil from the good" (T. Ash. 4:5).

Legal obedience is but one path to purity. Joseph, after recounting his own success, exhorts:

> Ye see, therefore, my children, how great things patience worketh and prayer with fasting. So ye too, [if ye follow after chastity and purity (ἁγνεία) with patience and prayer with fasting in humility of heart, the Lord will dwell among you, because He loveth chastity] (T. Jos. 10:1-2).

Yet he who commits adultery and fornication, though he fast by abstaining from meats, is half clean, but in very deed unclean (T. Ash. 2:8-9). The Testament of Isaac [15] contains the following prayer to God as "the treasury of purity": "Cleanse me by thy mercy, ... for I am a thing of flesh and blood fleeing to Thee ... I know my filthiness and do Thou cleanse me ... I know my sins, so cleanse me, that I may enter into they presence with modesty." In the same spirit the Patriarch teaches: "Keep thy body that it may be pure, for it is the temple of the Spirit of Holiness that dwelleth in it. Take heed to thy 'vile' body that it may be pure and sanctified."

Ablutions play a role in the Adam and Eve literature. Their standing neck-deep in the Jordan and Tigris (Vita Adae 6) illustrates the teaching in Yoma 78a that for ritual purification one must sit in water until it reaches the neck.[16] Adam prophesies that when men shall love and obey God's law, they "shall be purified by water from their sins. But those who are unwilling to be purified by water shall be condemned" (Vita Adae 29:10). At his own death he was thrice washed in the Acherusian Lake (Apoc. Mos. 37-39). Sibylline Oracle IV (161-65) exhorts: "Wretched mortals, repent ye of these things ... Wash your bodies from head to foot in running streams and lift up your hands to heaven, asking forgiveness for former deeds, and make propitiation for your impiety with gifts."

Rules of cleanliness and uncleanness are found in the Temple

---

[15] Coptic 64-65; Arabic 144-45.
[16] Ginzberg, op. cit., v (1925), 115, n. 66.

Scroll of the Qumran library.[17] Purity is the most common subject of the legal prescriptions found in four unpublished Cave 4 manuscripts.[18] Those who entered the Covenant were obligated "to distinguish between the unclean and the clean" (CD 6.17) "and to be separated from all uncleanness according to their ordinance, and not to defile each man his Holy Spirit according to the distinctions which God has made for them" (CD 7.3-4). Members of urban communities "shall distinguish between the clean and unclean, ... the sacred and the profane" (CD 12.19). From the battle on the Day of Vengeance were to be excluded all who were physically impure; volunteers for the battle "shall be perfect in spirit and body ... Nothing shameful nor ugly shall be visible in the surroundings of all their camp" (1QM 7.4-7; cf. Deut. 23:11-15; CD 15.15-17; 4QFlor. 1.3-4).[19] "The property of the men of holiness who walk in perfection" shall "not be mingled with those of the men of deceit who have not purified their way to be separated from perversity" (1QS 9.8-9).

The primary mode of purification was through bathing in the pools at Qumran.[20]

> Whoever scorns to enter the ways of God ... shall not be brought into the Council of the Community. For his silence (is invaded) by confusion of wickedness and defilements (are hidden) within his calm ... He shall not be absolved by atonement, nor purified by lustral waters, nor sanctified by seas and rivers, nor cleansed by all the waters of washing. Unclean, unclean shall he be for as long as he scorns the ordinances of God and allows not himself to be taught by the Community of His Council. For by the Spirit of true counsel concerning the ways of man shall all his sins be atoned when he beholds the light of life. By the Holy Spirit of the Community, in His truth, shall he be cleansed of all his sins ... By his soul's humility towards all the precepts of God shall his flesh be cleansed when sprinkled with lustral water and sanctified in flowing water (1QS 2.25-3.9).

Thus the purifying waters alone are insufficient for atonement and sanctification; the Spirit and humiliation (cf. 1QS 1.16-26) are also requisite. The prior requirement of conversion is manifest also from the regulation in 1QS 5.13-14; "Let not (the wicked) enter the water to touch the Purification of the holy, for a man is not pure unless (ki

---

[17] Yadin, *art. cit.*, *Biblical Archaeologist* 30 (1967), 137, 139.
[18] J. Strugnell, *art. cit.*, *RB* 63 (1956), 65.
[19] Gärtner, *op. cit.*, 6.
[20] Cross, *op. cit.*, 67-68.

im) he be converted from his malice. For he is defiled as long as he transgresses His word." There were certain regulations for ritual washings: "Let no man bathe in dirty water or in a quantity too little to cover a man completely. Let no man purify a vessel with this water. And any pool in a rock in which there is not enough water to cover (a man) completely, if an unclean person has touched it he defiles the water of the pool (as) he would defile the water in a vessel" (CD 10.11-13). A liturgical fragment from Cave 4 deals with purification before eating bread.[21] From the same cave comes a manuscript of prayers for every morning and evening of the month; the verso gives directives (including prayers) for a rite of purification.[22]

The pure things, the purity or purification (*tohorat*) of the Many or of the men of holiness (from which the unclean were to be separated and excluded as a punishment) is sometimes altogether obscure (1QS 6.25; 7.3, 16; CD 9.21). The offending member who is punished for two years, "during the first year shall not touch the Purification of the Many, and during the second year shall not touch the Banquet of the Many" (1QS 7, 19-20). For, "no man among the members ... of the Covenant of the Community who has turned aside from all that is laid down, in any way whatever, shall touch the Purification of the men of holiness ... until his deeds are purified of all perversity and he walks in perfection of way. Then he shall be made to approach the Council ... according to this ordinance for all those who join the Community" (1QS 8.16-19). The readmission rules thus resembled the regulations for initiation: "when he approaches the Council of the Community, he shall not touch the Purification of the Many until he has been examined concerning his spirit and deeds, and until he has completed one full year" (1QS 6.16-17). Concerning this admission into the Covenant it was decreed that only the penitent convert could "enter the water to touch the Purification of the holy" (1QS 5.13). Evidently this Purification included the lustration of the initiate or expelled member at the end of one year's trial; after he had proven himself to be inwardly purified, he was ready to be washed ritually and to (re-) join the Community. Full membership for the new volunters, as evidenced by touching the Banquet, required another year (1QS 6.20-21). The Purification of the Many, whether for new recruits or older penitents, was the culmination of the first, rather

---

[21] Starcky, *art. cit., RB* 63 (1956), 67.
[22] C. -H. Hunzinger, *ibid.*

than the second, year of probation. Whether such a washing was one of initiation or a regular preparation for daily meals cannot yet be ascertained. It is clear, however, that since an unclean person would defile the waters of the pool (CD 10.13), no one could be washed in it who had not passed sufficient tests of sanctification.

The defilement of those outside the Community was moral (1QS 5.13-15, 18-20; CD 5.8-12); such persons were to be avoided (1QS 5.17-18). "They have defiled their Holy Spirit, and with a blaspheming tongue have opened their mouth against the precepts of the Covenant, saying, They are not true" (CD 5.11-12). "To the Spirit of perversity belong ... abominable deeds committed in the spirit of lust, and the ways of defilement in the service of impurity" (1QS 4.9-10). Yet ultimately, though the world

> has defiled itself in the ways of wickedness under the dominion of Perversity until the time of final Judgment, then God will cleanse by His Truth all the works of every man, and will purify for Himself the (bodily) fabric of every man, to banish all Spirit of perversity from his members, and purify him of all wicked deeds by the Spirit of holiness; and He will cause the Spirit of Truth to gush forth upon him like lustral water. All lying abominations shall come to an end, (and) defilement by the Spirit of defilement (1QS 4.19-22).

In the meanwhile, the members of the Qumran sect were "the good ones," "the pure ones" (11Q Psa 154.3 [cf. 18]; 11Q Psa Zion, 9).

The Essenes practiced various ablutions in order to counteract pollution. They married only women who had mentruated and purified themselves three times (Josephus, *War* ii, 8.13.160; Hippolytus ix, 28). "They regarded oil as a defilement, and should any of them be involuntarily annointed, he wiped his body clean" (Josephus, *War* ii, 8.3.123; cf. Hippolytus ix, 19). Joseph M. Baumgarten [23] deduces that, in their concern for levitical purity, they feared oil as a carrier of defilement; e.g. pagans may have touched it. Following prayers at sunrise they worked until the fifth hour, when, according to Josephus (*War* ii, 8.5.129; cf. 13.161; Hippolytus ix, 21, 28):

> they reassemble ... and, girded with linen loin-cloths, bathe themselves thus in cold water. After this purification they reassemble in a special building to which no one is admitted who is not of the same faith; they themselves only enter the refractory if they are pure, as though into a holy precinct.

---

[23] Art. cit., RQ 6 (1967-68), 183-92.

Schürer [24] pointed out that "the common meals. . . , the food for which was prepared by the priests, were a guarentee to the Essene that only clean food would by set before him." At least when they were eating (Hippolytus ix, 21), they welcomed into their houses only those who shared their beliefs (Philo, *Quod omnis probus* 85). Kaufmann Kohler [25] and Joseph Klausner [26] identified the Essenes and the "Tobele Shacharit":

> They that wash at dawn say: We protest against you, O Pharisees, that ye mention the Name at dawn without washing. The Pharisees say: We protest against you, O washers at dawn, that ye mention the Name out of a body wherein is defilement (Tosephta, Yadaim ii. 20; cf. Ber. 2b, 22a).

For the Essenes, contamination could be physical, moral and ritual.

> When they wish to evacuate, they dig a pit a foot long . . . and covering it on all sides with their cloak, sit down, affirming that they must not insult, the rays. Then they throw back the excavated earth into the pit. And this they do choosing the most deserted places, [and] when they have done this they straightway wash, as if the secretion were polluting (Hippolytus ix, 25; cf. Josephus, *War* ii, 8.9.148-49; Deut. 23:12-14).

Among the oaths taken by an Essene for admission was one "to keep his hands pure from theft and his soul pure from wicked gain" (Josephus, *War* ii, 8.7.141; cf. Hippolytus ix, 23: "nor soil [μολύνειν] his conscience with unlawful gain"). The stages of the novitiate were determined by standards of purity.[27] The postulant, "having proved his continence" for one year, "draws closer to the way of life and participates in the purificatory baths at a higher degree, but he is not yet admitted into intimacy . . . His character is tested for another two years" (Josephus, *War* ii, 8.7.138; cf. Hippolytus ix, 23). F. C. Conybeare [28] astutely observed:"That the waters of purification in their purer quality were denied to novices, proves that the water of the bath was ceremonially cleansed, and probably exercised." The Essenes were "divided into four lots according to the duration of their discipline, and the juniors are so inferior to their elders that if the latter touch them they wash themselves as though they had been in

---

[24] *Op. cit.*, ii-ii, 211 (ET); also Paschen, *op. cit.*, 103-06, 112-14, 198.

[25] *Art. cit., Jewish Encyclopedia* v (1903), 230b.

[26] *Op. cit.*, 208; also Kohler. More simply J. B. Lightfoot (*St. Paul's Epistle to the Colossians* . . . , 402) identified the Tobele Schacharit with the Hemerobaptists. See also Thomas, *op. cit.*, 44; Bronner, *op. cit.*, 115-16.

[27] Baumgarten, *art. cit., RQ* 6 (1967-68), 190-91.

[28] *Art. cit., Dictionary of the Bible*, ed. J. Hastings, i (1898), 769a.

contact with a stranger" (*War* ii, 8.10.150; cf. Hippolytus ix, 26).[29]

That the Essenes were dominated by the ideal of purity is indicated by their wearing of white garments (*War* ii, 8.3.123; 7.137). The Therapeutae (Philo, *de vita contempl.* 66; cf. Joseph and Asenath 5:6) were also clad in white robes. According to Daniel 12:10 (cf. 11:35), "Many shall purify themselves, and make themselves white, and be refined." White is the color of the apparel of angels (1 Enoch 71:1; Mt. 28:3; Jn. 20:12; Acts 1:10) and of the saints in heaven (Rev. 3:4-5, 18; 4:4; 6:11; 7:9,13-14; 19:14) and of priests (Exod. 39:27-29; 2 Chron. 5:12). Isaiah (Ascension Isa. 9:9) "saw Enoch and all those who were with him ... in their higher garments, and they were like the angels who stand there in greater glory." If the Essenes lived in a state of apocalyptic readiness, their earthly attire was a copy of the heavenly, and the ideal of angelic purity motivated them in their service of God. Christian D. Ginsburg [30] saw the Essene manner of living as dictated by laws of cleanliness:

> As ... contact with any one who did not observe the rules of purity, or even did not observe them to the same degree, rendered the faithful followers impure, the Essenes had to form themselves into a separate society or community. Moreover, as contact with things manufactured or prepared by anyone who did not keep the same rules, likewise produced impurity, the Essenes were also obliged to cultivate and manufacture all the articles of food and dress which their commonwealth required.

EXCLUSIVE SACRED MEALS

If there were a schism in any church, it would manifest itself in the celebration of the Agape meal or Lord's Supper. In Galatians 4:17 Paul warns against those who "are envious of you, but not with an honest envy; what they really want to do is to bar the door (ἐκκλεῖσαι) to you so that you may come to envy them" (NEB). That is, they wished to exclude from fellowship all who were "lawbreakers." Erwin R. Goodenough [31] noted Jewish opposition to Paul's teaching in so far as it promoted "the breakdown of the segregation of their group." The Apostle described the split in the church at Antioch when Peter withdrew from eating with Gentiles (2:11ff.); for, the event was

---

[29] Josephus was apparently alluding to the married and/or the immature adopted children; the first year postulants; the two year novices; and, those permanently accepted as members.

[30] *Art. cit., DCB* ii (1880), 199a.

[31] *Jewish Symbolism in the Roman Period, I. The Archaeological Evidence from Palestine*, New York (Pantheon, 1953), 41.

relevant to the controversy in Galatia. In 5:20 he includes among the works of the flesh, διχοστασίαι (cf. 1 Clem. 46:5; 51:1; Hermas, *Simil.* viii, 10.2) and αἱρέσεις.[32] The other evil works which are most closely associated with divisions and sects are enmities, strife, jealousy, anger, rivalries (ἐριθεῖαι) and envying (φθόνοι). The mention of party splits would be most relevant if they were the correlate of exclusions by the Judaizers. The same conclusion may be drawn from the mutual biting and eating (5:15), provocations and envying (5:26).

The divisions which result from the exclusivism of Judaizing or ascetic Christianity are alluded to in Rom. 16:17, where Paul accuses the false teachers of διχοστασίας ... ποιοῦητες. The expectation that the God of peace would crush Satan (16:20) indicates that the peace of the church had been disturbed by "belly-servers" (16:18). The Pauline command to turn away (ἐκκλίνετε) from an opponent (16:17; cf. 1 Cor. 5:9, 11; 2 Thess. 3:6, 14) includes separation at church common meals.

The Clementine literature portrays a vegetarian (*Hom.* xii, 6) Peter who did not eat with the unbaptized and unpurified (*Rec.* i, 19; ii, 7).

In the Pastoral Epistles a αἱρετικός ἄνθρωπος, who is to be avoided (παραιτοῦ) after two warnings, is by definition perverted and self-condemned in his sins (Tit. 3:10-11). ζητήσεις, genealogies and the law are the subject matter of unprofitable and vain dissensions and fights. Αἵρεσις is the expression of the futility of the quarrels. At an early date in the Corinthian church the problem became acute in the eating of the Lord's Supper (1 Cor. 11:18ff.). The σχίσματα and αἱρέσεις when the Corinthians came together at the Lord's Supper reflected different attitudes toward food and drink consumed there [33]. The command, παραιτοῦ, suggests not merely exclusion from church offices (1 Tim. 5:11; cf. 3:6-7) but outright rejection and avoidance (1 Tim. 4:7; 2 Tim. 2:23) of the merely formally pious. They had their own professional teachers (1 Tim. 6:5; Tit. 1:11), whom the bishop had to be able to refute convincingly (Tit. 1:9).

Ignatius forewarned the Philadelphians to flee from division (μερισμός) and evil doctrine (2:1; 7:2) because of the danger of many wolves who are seemingly worthy of credence (ἀξιόπιστοι) (2:2). In a possible ironic reference to vegetarianism, he goes on to counsel

---

[32] Heinrich Schlier, *Der Brief an die Galater* (Meyers Komm.), Göttingen (Vandenhoeck & Ruprecht, 1951), 185.

[33] T. W. Manson, *Studies in the Gospels and Epistles,* Manchester (University, 1962), 202-03.

abstinence (ἀπέχεσθε) from the bad herbs (βοτάνη) which are not cultivated by Jesus Christ, lest there be division (μερισμός) through following a maker of schism (σχίζοντι ἀκολουθεῖ); set against this are the unity of the church and living according to Jesus Christ (ch. 3). Ignatius continues: "Take heed to have but one Eucharist. For there is one flesh of our Lord Jesus Christ and one cup in the unity of his blood; one altar, as there is one bishop" (4:1). That there was a schismatic Eucharist may be inferred also from *ad Magn.* 7:2: "Πάντες ὡς εἰς ἕνα ναὸν συντρέχετε θεοῦ ὡς ἐπὶ ἓν θυσιαστήριον ἐπὶ ἕνα Ἰησοῦν χριστόν..." The unity of the altar was being undercut by a dual Eucharist.

Much earlier the Epistle to the Hebrews had inveighed against "forsaking the assembling of ourselves, as is the habit of some" (10:25). A fearful punishment will be deserved by "the man who has spurned the Son of God, and profaned the blood of the covenant by which he was sanctified" (10:29). Absence from the Eucharist thus is the worst aspect of neglecting the meetings of the church. But to attend assemblies is a mark of holding fast to the confession of hope (10:23-25). "Since we have confidence to enter the sanctuary by the blood of Jesus, ... let us draw near with a true heart in full assurance of faith" (10:19-22). This exhortation to those whose body and conscience have been cleansed through baptism (10:22) signifies an approach with confidence unto the throne of grace in order to receive mercy and grace (4:16). In 13:12-13 the exhortation to go forth to him who sanctified the people through his own blood follows a reminder that the heart is strengthened by grace rather than by foods and that we have an altar at which priests of the old covenant have no right to eat. In 12:22-25 the reminder that the readers had come to the heavenly Jerusalem to the assembly and ἐκκλησία of the firstborn, and to Jesus, the mediator of a new covenant, and to his sprinkled blood,- is followed by the command: "See to it that you do not refuse him who is speaking, ... who warns from heaven." The fearful punishment awaiting him who does not heed this call of Jesus and does not ˇthereby "offer to God acceptable worship, with reverence and awe" (12:28), resembles the terrible fate of him who spurns the Son of God at the Eucharist (10:26-31). Accordingly Johannes Betz [34] has not erred in finding a liturgical import in all of these passages.

---

[34] *Die Eucharistie in der Zeit der griechischen Väter*, Bd. II/I: *Die Realpräsenz des Leibes und Blutes Jesu im Abendmahl nach dem Neuen Testament*, Freiburg im

The eating of foods offered at the altar is mentioned in Hebr. 9:9ff. The food and drink (ἐπὶ βρώμασιν καὶ πόμασιν) pertain to gifts and sacrifices (9:9) which priests serving in the tabernacle have a right to eat (13:10; cf. Lev. 6:26; 10:12-15; 1 Cor. 9:13), including the first fruits of grain, wine and oil (Num. 18:8ff.; Deut. 18:24; Ezek. 44:30; Jub. 15:2; T. Levi 9:14) and the bread of the presence and the wine offered in thanks on the table in the holy place (9:2). These regulations for service and purification (9:9-10, 13) under the first covenant (9:1,6) are earthly and transitory (9:10; cf. 7:16); they have been replaced by sanctification through the sacrifice of Christ (9:10-15; 13:10-12). Apparently the readers were interpreting the Lord's Supper more in light of the priestly eating of food offerings than in light of the sacrifice of the Cross.

While John preached to soldiers (Lk. 3:14), he apparently did not baptize Gentile converts. He preached to tax-collectors (Lk. 3:12-13), and tax-collectors and harlots believed him (Mt. 21:32) and were baptized by him (Lk. 7:29). Yet he stayed in the wilderness and did not eat with tax collectors and sinners (Mt. 11:18-19).[35] He gathered an inner group of disciples whom he taught to pray at fixed times (Lk. 11:1) and with whom he fasted (Mk. 2:18) often (Lk. 5:33); presumably these penitents hoped to belong to the eschatological remnant of Israel. John was apparently a separatist who condemned Pharisees and Sadducees (Mt. 3:7) and sought to attract a select group of purified disciples while preaching publicly. His dwelling in the deserts from childhood (Lk. 1:80) probably would have been possible only through association with a group of ascetic separatists. As W. H. Brownlee [36] rhetorically asks, "How did he live out there? Who took care of him? How could he receive there proper training for his prophetic mission?" Whatever their identity be, such a wilderness community inculcated in the young prophet ideals of purity which led him to condemn the sins of the masses of people and of the religious leaders.

Members of the Jerusalem church disputed with Peter after he visited the uncircumcised and ate with them (Acts 10:24, 28; 11:3).

Breisgau (Herder, 1961), 154-66; cf. J. Coppens, "Les affinités qumrânniennes de l'Épître aux Hebreux. II.," "Nouvelle Revue Théologique 84 (1962), 268-70; Paul Andriessen, "L'eucharistie dans l'Épître aux Hebreux," Nouvelle Revue Theologique 94 (1972), 269-77.

[35] W. R. Farmer, "John the Baptist," IDB 2, 957.

[36] "John the Baptist in the New Light of Ancient Scrolls," ap. Stendahl (ed.), op. cit., 35; Steinmann, op. cit., 60.

At Antioch, after representatives from James arrived, Cephas withdrew from eating with the Gentiles, due to fear of the circumcised (Gal. 2:12). Justin (*Dial.* 47.3) knew of Hebrew Christians who compelled Gentile believers "to live in accordance with the law appointed by Moses, or choose not to have communion with them."

In the Testament our Our Lord Jesus in Galilee there appears to be no allowance for a Lord's Supper with wine [37] representing the blood of Jesus poured out as a sacrificial offering for our sins. Rechabites were commended for not drinking wine (9). Believers are not to drink the blood of corpses and think carnal thoughts of Jesus. He does not wish blood libations in his name offered on account of their sins. He is not to be treated as an idol (8). Communion with Jesus would have to be, not with his material flesh and blood, but with his glorified body, or at least the form in which he gave his post-resurrection teachings (as set forth in this document). "I will become an altar for them, but they will become a temple for me" (7). Parallel to this spiritual mediation and fellowship is a spiritual concept of sacrifice (9; quoting Ps. 51:17). Their Lord's Supper was essentially an Agape at which eschatological expectations (as outlined in this writing) were heightened.

Loyalty to the law resulted in Jewish exclusiveness in Jubilees 22:16-17:

> And do thou, my son Jacob, remember my words,
> And observe the commandments of Abraham, thy father:
> Separate thyself from the nations,
> And eat not with them:
> And do not according to their works,
> And become not their associate;
> For their works are unclean,
> And all their ways are a pollution and an abomination and uncleanness.
> They offer their sacrifices to the dead. . .
> And they eat over the graves. . . .

Holiness, as well as contamination, could lead to separation at meals. The angel of the Lord thus said to Judah: "The Lord chose him [Levi] rather than thee to draw near to Him, and to eat of His table [and to offer Him the first-fruits] of the choice things of the sons of Israel"

---

[37] The Ebionites' common meal consisted of unleavened bread and water (Irenaeus, *Adv. Haer.* v, 1, 3; Epiphanius, *Haer.* 30, 16.1), while Justin (*Apology* i, 65, 67) described the Eucharist as consisting of bread and a cup of wine mixed with water. cf. Hippolytus, *Apostolic Tradition* 23.1; Clement, *Paedagogus* ii, 2.23-24; Cyprian, *Epistle* lxii, 2.11 & 13.

(T. Jud. 21:5). Levi saw in a vision an angel, or man in a white robe, who "fed him with bread and wine (even) the most holy things" during his consecration to the priesthood (T. Levi 8:5). M. Delcor [38] accepts the reading, ἅγια ἁγίων, and associates it with the Septuagint of Levit. 2:3, 10 ("And what is left of the cereal offering shall be for Aaron and his sons; it is a most holy part of the offerings by fire to the Lord"). Accordingly, he finds the passage to pertain to the priestly meal at which part of the sacrifice was eaten;[39] if it is a gloss, it was not from Christian hands. Such an interpretation accords well with the sense of T. Jud. 21:5. Its significance for Christian readers of the Testaments would be that the Lord's Supper is comparable to Levitical sacrificial meals. Delcor [40] observes that a meal is sacred if the food is consecrated or if a cultic sacrificial meaning is attached to the meal. Joseph and Aseneth (8; 5, 9; 15:5; 16:6, 14) affirms that the plous elect receive the bread of life and cup of immortality, apparently at sacred kosher meals [41] or at a mystery rite of intiation [42]; thereby they commune with angels. Sibylline Oracle IV, 25-27 illustrates the importance attributed to blessings at meals: Happy "shall be they who love to bless the great God before taking food and drink, trusting in the way of godliness (εὐσέβεια)"

The communal cultic meal at Qumran is described in 1QS 6.2-5:

> And in every place where there are ten persons of the Council of the Community, let there not lack among them ... a priest ... And they shall eat in common, bless in common ... When they set the table to eat, or (prepare) the wine to drink, the priest shall first stretch out his hand to pronounce a blessing on the first fruits of bread and wine.

The analogous Messianic banquet is characterized in these terms:[43]

> And [when] they gather for the Community tab [le or to drink w] ine, and arrange the Community table [and mix] the wine to drink, let no man [stretch out] his hand over the first-fuits of bread and [wine] before

---

[38] Art. cit., RQ 6 (1967-68), 420.

[39] "The rabbis required the priests to handle their heave offering ... given to them of various kinds of produce by the farmers, as being of a holy character, also at home in due levitical purity" (Büchler, op. cit., 35).

[40] Art. cit., RQ 6 (1967-68), 402.

[41] Christoph Burchard, Untersuchungen zu Joseph und Aseneth. Überlieferung-Ortsbestimmung, Tübingen (J. C. B. Mohr, 1965), 121-33; Karl Georg Kuhn, "The Lord's Supper and the Communal Meal at Qumran," in The Scrolls and the New Testament, ed. Krister Stendahl, New York (Harper & Bros., 1957), 75-77.

[42] Marc Philonenko, Joseph et Aseneth. Introduction, texte, critique et notes, Leiden (E. J. Brill, 1968), 89-98, 104-06.

[43] Kuhn, ap. Stendahl (ed.), 65-72.

the Priest; for [it is he who] shall bless the first-fruits of bread and w[ine, and shall] first [stretch out] his hand over the bread. And after [wards], the Messiah of Israel shall [str] etch out his hands over the bread. [And afterwards], all the Congregation of the Community shall [bl] ess, ea [ch] according to his rank. And they shall proceed according to this rite at every mea [l where] at least ten persons [are as] sembled (1QSa II.17-22).

Matthew Black [44] rightly points out that this is not an ordinary meal which is being described, "but a special cult-meal in which only sectarians of the highest rank, the Council, are permitted to participate; these were, no doubt, the 'full members' of the Sect." The obligations of the Many (rabbim) to eat, worship, deliberate and keep study vigils together (1QS 6.2-3, 7-8) are set forth apart from the duties of members of the Council of the Community to deliberate, study and eat together (1QS 6.3-7). Such a distinction might imply that not both of the daily meals were cultic, or that only on certain days (e.g. at Pentecost, when the covenant renewal feast was celebrated)[45] there were sacred meals. But more likely it signifies that only the community leaders celebrated the daily cultic meal; the hierarchical principle is emphasized in the description of the Messianic banquet (1QSa 2.11-17, 21-22). Perhaps the Many did not receive the first-fruits and wine, and ate only after the Council began to eat. Nevertheless, even the regular meal remained sufficiently sacred for the novitiate to be excluded. "He shall not touch the Banquet of the Many until he has completed a second year in the midst of the members of the Community" (1QS 6.20-21). Those who were in bad standing might lose this privelege. One who betrayed the truth to outsiders was to be punished for two years; "during the second year he shall not touch the Banquet of the Many and shall be seated after all the members of the Community" (1QS 7.18-20).

Essene exclusiveness based on holiness is illustrated by their bringing offerings to the Temple separately (see pp. 169-170) and by the elders' purifications after touching the juniors, "as though they had been in contact with a stranger" (Josephus, War ii, 8.10.150). Only the initiated could partake of the common table at communal meals (Josephus, War ii, 8.7.139; cf. Philo, Quod omnnis probus 91; Apologia pro Judaeis, ap. Eusebius, Praep. Evang. 5.12). "Before the meal the priest says a prayer and no one is permitted to taste the food before the prayer; and after they have eaten the meal he recites

---

[44] Op. cit., 104.
[45] Delcor, art. cit., RQ (1967-68), 415-16; John H. Groh, "The Qumran Meal and the Last Supper," Concordia Theological Monthly 41 (1970), 283-87.

another prayer. At the beginning and at the end they bless God as the Giver of life. Sacred garments are worn for the meal" (Josephus, *War* ii, 8.5.130; cf. Hippolytus ix, 21). That this was a sacred cultic meal is indirectly confirmed by Philo's description of the Therapeutae's holy banquet:

> The young men bring in the tables on which is set the truly purified meal of leavened bread, seasoned with salt mixed with hyssop, out of reverence for the holy table enshrined in the sacred vestibule of the Temple on which lie loaves and salt without condiments, the loaves unleavened and the salt unmixed. For it was meet that the simplest and purest food should be assigned to . . . the priests (*de vita contempl.* 81-82)

Matthew Black [46] comments that:

> The parallel which Philo draws between the 'tables' of the Therapeutae and the table of the Shew-bread in the Temple is intended to remind us that, though the Therapeutae were a lay order, their sacred meal had the same cultic character as the offering of the Shew-bread by the priests in the Temple of Jerusalem; the bread was consecrated bread, the Table was a 'holy' table. . .

Doubtless those persons who were deemed impure were not permitted to be present.

PRIEST, SANCTUARY AND SACRIFICE

The author of Hebrews and his readers (since he is too skilled in rhetoric to bypass meaningful allusions) are disinterested in the Jerusalem Temple and its cultus.[47] Held in higher esteem and deemed more relevant to the work of Christ is the tabernacle (σκηνή). The wilderness tabernacle (9:1, 6, 8-9, 21) is patterned after the divine, heavenly prototype (8:2, 5; 9:11; cf. 9:1-3, 8, 24; 13:10). The principle of shadow and copy of heavenly things applies not only to the sanctuary (8:5), but also to sacrifices (9:23; cf. 9), the law (10:1) and Jerusalem (11:10; 12:22; 13:14). The readers are expected to take the difficult concept for granted, without necessarily drawing the same conclusions therefrom. The divine presence is understood to

---

[46] *Op. cit.*, 108.

[47] R. E. Brown ("Second Thoughts: X. The Dead Sea Scrolls and the N.T., "*Expository Times* 78 [1966], 22b) writes: "The theme of the Christian replacement of the Tabernacle (not of the Temple) could well have been expressed to a group like that of Qumran, where the Jerusalem Temple was rejected and the sectarians modelled themselves on the Exodus community grouped around the Tabernacle."

dwell in the heavenly tabernacle. A further replacement of the idea of the Jerusalem Temple as God's special earthly "residence" is found in the view of the church as the house of Christ, i.e. the house of God over which Christ rules, since Christ indwells its members (3:6; 10:21); but the readers were in danger of not retaining the latter teaching (3:6). A third form of God's true dwelling is described in 12:22-25:

> But you have come to Mount Zion and to the city of the living God, the heavenly Jerusalem, and to innumerable angels in festal gathering, and to the assembly of the first-born who are enrolled in heaven, and to a judge who is God of all, and to the spirits of just men made perfect, and to Jesus, the mediator of a new covenant, and to the sprinkled blood that speaks more graciously than the blood of Abel. See to it that you do not refuse him who is speaking.

Bertil Gärtner [48] comments: "Zion is manifested in the Christian Church, the ultimate goal of which is to be incorporated into the heavenly reality." Believers have already entered into fellowship with the spirits of the righteous, the angels, God, Jesus and his blood as found in the heavenly Jerusalem. But this "new cultic fellowship with the heavenly world" [49] has been made possible through the mediation of a new covenant by the blood of Jesus. This blessing from the new covenant is contrasted with the dreadful upheavals which terrified Moses when the old covenant was revealed to him on Mount Sinai; he could approach God only with fear and trembling (12:18-21).

Because perfection was unattainable through the Levitical priesthood, it was necessary for a High Priest after the order of Melchizedek to appear (7:11-12). The prominence attributed to this title suggests that the addressees were familiar with Jewish traditions about Melchizedek and that they valued the office of true high priest. In Hebr. 13:15-16 appears a spiritualized understanding of sacrifice which is pleasing to God, namely, continually confessing and praising God with our lips, doing good and sharing. While denying that animal sacrifice takes away sins (10:4-6, 11) or perfects the conscience (9:9, 12-14), the author appeals to the Torah in stating, "almost everything is purified with blood, and without the shedding of blood there is no forgiveness of sins" (9:22). Alexander C. Purdy [50] comments on this passage: "Despite protests against bloody sacrifices,

---

[48] *Op. cit.*, 90.
[49] *Ibid.*, 89.
[50] "The Epistle to the Hebrews," *IB* 11 (1955), 695.

the efficacy of blood was axiomatic not only in Judaism, but by and large in the ancient world." On this assumption Hebrews teaches the once for all sanctification by the sacrifice of Christ (7:27; 9:12, 14, 23-28; 10:1-14, 19-20, 29; 12:24; 13:12, 20), the spotless (ἄμωμος) victim (9:14) who offered his body (σῶμα) (10:5, 10) to bear and make propitiation for the sins of many (2:17; 9:28) through a sprinkling of blood (12:24). Through his sacrifice Christ has been manifested (πεφανέρωται) (9:26).

I Peter repeats much of Hebrews' sacrificial language. The church is the spiritual house (οἶκος πνευματικὸς) of God (2:5; 4:17), "a holy priesthood, to offer spiritual sacrifices acceptable to God through Jesus Christ" (2:5), i.e. "a royal priesthood, a holy nation, God's own people, that you may declare the wonderful deeds of him who called you out of darkness into his marvelous light" (2:9). Here we see the spiritualization and Christianization of the Old Testament cultus. To quote Gärtner again:[51]

> The οἶκος πνευματικός, in a context in which are also mentioned priests, sacrifices and the 'corner-stone', can hardly refer to anything but the temple. It is 'spiritual', the implication being that it belongs to the new sphere created by the pouring out of the Spirit ... The fact that the 'house' in 1 Peter 2:5 is said to be 'spiritual' ... stresses the new level on which the temple and its cultus have been placed through the person and work of Jesus. The Holy Spirit is the new sphere of reality to which the Church and the company of Christians belong.

Behind this temple symbolism lies the divine promise to Israel (Exod. 19:5-6; cf. Jubilees 16:18): "If you will obey my voice and keep my covenant, you shall be my own possession among all peoples; ... and you shall be to me a kingdom of priests and a holy nation." The condition of obeying the Mosaic covenant is replaced in 1 Pet. 2:5, 9-10 by the responsibilities (a) of those who are already God's own people to proclaim the divine mercy of Him who called them into His marvelous light, and (b) to offer spiritual sacrifices acceptable to God through the self-sacrifice of Jesus Christ (cf. Hebr. 13:5). The addressees had been ransomed "with the precious blood of Christ, like that of a lamb without blemish or spot (ἄμωμος)" (1:19); that is, they were "sanctified by the Spirit for obedience to Jesus Christ and for sprinkling with his blood" (1:2; cf. Exod. 24:7-8). Like the Levitical scapegoat, "he himself bore our sins in his body..."

---

[51] *Op. cit.*, 73, and n. 1.

(2:24). He died once for all for sins (3:18). In the midst of a passage mentioning his precious blood and resurrection, 1 Pet. 1:20 teaches: He "was made manifest at the end of the times for your sake" (cf. Hebr. 9:26).

The Revelation of John contains similar imagery. The church is a kingdom of priests to God (1:6; 5:10; 20:6). The Christian martyrs serve God "day and night within his temple" (7:15). This heavenly or spiritual temple is mentioned sixteen times (e.g. 11:19). In this temple there is an altar which recalls the altar of holocausts (6:9; 8:3; 14:18; 16:7) as well as another which corresponds to the altar of perfumes (8:3; 9:13). An angel cares for each altar (8:3, 5; 14:18). The new Jerusalem will come down out of heaven from God (3:12; 21:2, 10ff.). He and the Lamb will be the only temple therein (21:22). Jesus is referred to twenty-seven times as the Lamb, who was slain (5:6, 9, 12; 13:8) and ransomed us from our sins by his blood (1:5; 5:9; 7:14; cf. 12:11).

In Galatians (4:25-27) Paul assumes that his readers, including those influenced by the Judaizers, accepted the existence of a heavenly Jerusalem, which is both an eternal pattern in the mind of God and the church to which all believers aspire to belong. The opponents, however, did not accept Paul's contrast of Zion in Jerusalem with Mt. Sinai as symbols, respectively, of the freedom of the new covenant and the bondage of the old covenant.

Colossians 2:17 follows Hebr. 8:5; 9:9, 23; 10:1 in treating the old cultic law as but a shadow of coming things; "but the substance (σῶμα) belongs to Christ." In him all the fullness of the Godhead was pleased to dwell bodily (σωματικῶς) (1:19; 2:9). Thus the divine presence lived in a person rather than in such a place as a temple. The thought continues: ". . . and through him to reconcile to himself all things, . . . making peace by the blood of his cross" (1:20). That Christ is the ideal temple (in whom believers are bound together) is implied in 2:7: "built up in him (ἐποικοδομούμενοι)". He is the community's center of unity: "And let the peace of Christ rule in your hearts, to which indeed you were called in the one body" (3:15). The suggestion of blood sacrifice (1:20) appears also in 1:14 ("in whom we have redemption, the forgiveness of sins") (cf. the reading, "through his blood" in 1:14; Eph. 1:7; Hebr. 9:22) and 1:22 ("present you without blemish: ἄμωμος").

Ephesians presents a Christological interpretation of traditional terminology. The church is "the household of God"; the chief

cornerstone is "Christ Jesus himself. . ., in whom the whole structure
is joined together and grows into a holy temple in the Lord."
Believers, whether Hebrew or Gentile, "are built into it for a dwelling
place for God in the Spirit" (2:19-22).[52] "There is one body and one
Spirit, just as you were called to the one hope that belongs to your
call" (4:4). Christ has broken down the middle wall of the partition
which divided Jews and Gentiles, as in the Jerusalem temple, so that
they may become one body (2:14, 16). "But now in Christ Jesus you
who were once far off have been brought near in the blood of Christ"
(2:13). "In him we have redemption through his blood" (1:7). "Christ
loved us and gave himself up for us, a fragrant offering and sacrifice
to God" (5:2; cf. Levit. 1). As προσάγειν in the Septuagint is often
associated with sacrifices in the Temple,[53] it is proper to give a
similar cultic interpretation to 2:18: through Christ "we both have
access (προσαγωγή) in one Spirit to the Father." That is, through
Jesus' self-offering Gentiles are no longer aliens to the Spirit-formed
and -filled household of God, though they were excluded from the
Jerusalem Temple. The citizenship (συνπολῖται) and fellowship of Jew
and Gentile in God's heavenly city church-house-temple (2:19) is
made possible only by the work of Christ on the cross and in
establishing the church through his Spirit.

   In 2 Corinthians 2:14-17 Paul commends himself (3:1) on his
apostolic ministry; or, rather, he thanks God "who in Christ always
leads us in triumph" (2:14). "As commissioned by God, in the sight of
God we speak in Christ" (2:17). The references to the hawkers of
God's word and their letters of recommendation (2:17-3:1) confirm
that the Apostle was defending himself. He does so by using the
image of burning sacrificial incense (cf. Rom. 15:16; Phil. 2:17). To
speak sincerely and to reveal knowledge of Christ gives the sweet
odor which is pleasing to God and bringing life and salvation to
some. Paul's Gospel message concerning Christ is a fragrant offering
to God, even when rejected by those who are perishing (2:15-16).
Paul's opponents charged that Paul's gospel was veiled both to those
who were perishing and those being saved (4:3); thus he could not
commend himself in the sight of God (4:2-3; cf. 2:17-3:1). The
hawkers of God's word, however, claiming to be strong, felt
themselves sufficient (2:16; 3:5) to present a pleasing aroma to God

---

[52] *Ibid.*, 60-66.
[53] *Ibid.*, 61, nn. 1-2.

by their preaching of the law (3:3, 6) as servants of righteousness (11:15).

According to 1 Timothy 3:15 (the) "church of the living God is (the) house (οἶκος) of God: the term generally used for the Temple in the Septuagint. Appropriate behavior is, therefore, necessary. Ἐκκλησία θεοῦ is compared to an οἶκος in the need for careful rule (1 Tim. 3:5). But ἐν μεγάλη οἰκία there are vessels of varying degrees of honor (2 Tim. 2:20). The context and the lack of a definite article in these passages suggest that the references are to a local community. But the individual church is closely associated with truth and Christ (1 Tim. 3:15-16), since it is "the pillar and foundation of the truth" as embodied in the credal mystery about Christ. The οἶκος of God, then, is not a stone building or dead idol, but the community which is the bulwark of the Gospel. It is taken for granted that God's dwelling has been understood spiritually even by those who reject true Christology. Timothy's need correctly to rule the church and to conduct his own personal life is so grave that the charge is given before God and Jesus Christ and the elect angels (1 Tim. 5:21), who watch over and judge the community's affairs.

In the midst of a polemic against interpretations of the Old Testament which resulted in a defective understanding of the crucifixion and resurrection of Christ, Ignatius wrote to the Philadelphians (9:1): "The priests indeed are good (καλοὶ καὶ οἱ ἱερεῖς), but the High Priest is better, to whom the holy of holies has been committed, and who alone has been trusted with the secrets of God." Ostensibly the Judaizers honored priests as transmitters of divine gnosis (see p. 279).

John denounced the Sadducees *inter alia* as vipers requiring works of repentance if they were to escape the coming wrath (Mt. 3:7-8). Jerusalem priests and Levites were sent to examine him at the outset of his ministry (Jn. 1:19). The chief priests and elders did not believe him (Mt. 21:23, 32; Mk. 11:27-33). As a desert ascetic with an apocalyptic message, John had little patience with their worldly priveleges[54] and undeveloped eschatology. They had willfully misused their holy office and failed in their responsibilities. At times the chief priests deprived the poorer one of their tithes and caused starvation (Josephus, *Antiq.* xx, 8.8.181; 9.2.207; Pesachim 57a).[55] As the son of a rural priest, John could have looked forward to only two weeks of

---

[54] Scobie, *op. cit.*, 32-33.
[55] Kraeling, *op. cit.*, 48-50, 150; Wink, *op. cit.*, 74. See Malachi 3:8-10.

Temple service per year. As his parents were of advanced age at the time of his conception (Lk. 1:7), it is statistically probable that Zechariah died or at least that John was left destitute before he was able to enter the priesthood. Spending his youth in the deserts (where sectarian influences were stronger than Sadducean ones), John decided to abandon his hereditary responsibility to serve as a priest in the (polluted-?) Temple. His apocalyptic expectations and scorn for Sadducean "vipers" kept him from following a petty career; he had been called instead to be a prophet preparing the way of the Lord. He could, of course, have served his two weeks in the Temple and carried on a wilderness ministry the rest of the time. But he did not esteem the Temple cultus sufficiently to have anything to do with it. That he did not repudiate the institutions of Temple and priesthood is indicated by the veneration in which they were held by the circles in which Luke 1-2 took shape. Carl Kraeling writes:[56] "In the birth story it is a priest, officiating in God's presence, to whom it is revealed that God's plan of national deliverance is about to be put into execution," through his own son. He becomes "an instrument of God." Kraeling [57] calls attention to the analogy in Jubilees and the Testaments of the Twelve Patriarchs. The large number of priests who "obeyed the faith" (Acts 6:7) doubtless included those rural ones who honored John and formulated Luke's opening narratives. They were interested in priestly genealogy; they deemed it significant that Zechariah belonged to the divisions of the Zadokite Abijah (1 Chron. 24:10) and that Elizabeth was one of the daughters of Aaron (1:5) [58] The Temple altar of incense was recognized as an appropriate place for seeing visions (1:8-11, 21-23). Zechariah served here, burning incense; there is no hint of his association with the cultus of animal sacrifice. Anna is praised for not departing from the temple, worshipping with fasting and prayer night and day" (Lk. 2:37).

Hippolytus' lost Σύνταγμμα, as reflected in Epiphanius (Haer. 14), Ps.-Tertullian (Haer. 1) and Philaster (Haer. 5.1), associated Dositheus with the Sadducees, i.e. Zadokites.[59]

---

[56] Op. cit., 21.

[57] Ibid., 22.

[58] E. P. Blair ("Mary Mother of Jesus," IDB 3, 290b) writes: "Elizabeth, 'of the daughters of Aaron' (Luke 1:5), is called Mary's "kinswoman (συγγενίς: Luke 1:36)'. If the kinship was of blood and not from marriage, Mary would seem to be of Levitic descent. It is not, of course, impossible that both lines lay behind her," i.e. the Davidic line as well.

[59] That "Sadducee" means "Zadokite" is the opinion of R. McL. Wilson ("Simon,

Hegesippus (*ap.* Eusebius, *H.E.* ii.23) pictured James the brother of the Lord as one for whom it was lawful to enter into the Holy of Holies. He wore linen (like a priest). He entered the temple alone and "was always kneeling. . . , worshipping God and asking forgiveness for the people." He was buried "on the spot by the temple, and there his monument still lies, by the temple." [60] He functioned as the high priest for the church, apparently. As he was being stoned, "one of the priests of the sons of Rechab (the son of Rechabim),[61] spoken of by Jeremiah the prophet, cried out and said: 'Stop! What are you doing?' " This narrative was shaped in circles with a piety like that found in Luke 1-2. The good priests were Rechabites; like James they were dedicated to abstaining from wine.

According to the Testament of our Lord Jesus in Galilee, "the sacrifice for God is a gentle spirit, and God despises not a contrite and pure heart" (9; cf. Ps. 51:17). But "there are many who maintain the sacrificial killing and pouring out (of blood) of animals to be my will, and who shed blood in my name as an oblation which they offer on account of their sins. In so doing they treat me as an idol" (8). To believers Jesus promised: "I will become an altar for them, but they will become a temple for me" (7).

In the Testament of Levi (8:1-10) the Patriarch tells of his consecration to the highpriesthood.[62] In a vision he "saw seven men (i.e. the archangels: cf. 3:5; 5:6-7) in white raiment saying unto me: Arise, put on the robe of the priesthood, and the crown of righteousness, and the breastplate of understanding (σύνεσις), and the garment of truth, and the plate (πέταλου) of faith, . . . and the ephod of prophecy" (8:2). As these highpriestly garments (cf. Exod. 29:5-6) are interpreted spiritually, it appears that the highpriesthood is a type of the priesthood of the saints (cf. Eph. 6:13-17). The Apostolic Constitutions (viii, 5) transmit the teaching that Abel, Seith, Enos, Enoch, Noah, Job, Abraham and the rest of the patriarchs and Moses were priests.[63] The Melchizedek portion of 2 Enoch gives the names

---

Dositheus and the Dead Sea Scrolls," *Zeitschrift für Religions- und Geistesgeschichte* 9 [1957], 24, 28), Danielou ("L'étoile de Jacob et la mission chrétienne à Damas," *VC* 11 [1957], 131) and Black (*op. cit.,* 63). Abu-al-Fath called him "bene Zadok."

[60] Note the similarity to references to burial places in the Lives of the Prophets.

[61] Eisler (*op. cit.,* 245) noted a rabbinic tradition (Jalqut on Jerem. 35:12) that Rechabites married the daughters of priests and their grandsons ministered as priests in the Temple.

[62] De Jonge, *op. cit.,* 43-44.

[63] Goodenough, *By Light, Light,* New Haven (Yale University, 1935), 330-31.

of the great high priests who had reigned continuously since Seth (ii.34; cf. i.4, 15; ii.4, 13, 19, 29, 31). The Testament of Isaac [64] relates that "Isaac in old age became a priest of the Lord as a consolation." Louis Finkelstein [65] observed that Jubilees and the Testaments of the Twelve Patriarchs abolish all distinctions between the Levites and Aaronids. The superiority of the Levitical priesthood to the laity is described in these terms: to Levi the Lord gave "[the things in the heavens. As the heaven is higher than the earth, so is the priesthood of God higher than the earthly kingdom. . .] For the Lord chose him . . . to draw near to Him, and to eat of his table" (T. Jud. 21:2-5). G. Beasley-Murray [66] deduced that "the priesthood was more important than the sovereignty because in the Messianic age . . . the Temple would be the focal point of all the world's life."

The eschatological New Jerusalem appears not infrequently in Jewish apocrypha (e.g. Tobit 13:10-23; 1 Enoch 90:28-36; Test. Dan 5:12-13; Apoc. Abr. ch. 29; 2 Esdras 7:26; 10:26, 54; 13:36; cf. Psalm 87). The Messianic temple as the house of God is mentioned in 1 Enoch 90:28-29; 19:13; Jub. 1:28-29; Vita Adae 29:6; T. Benj. 9:2-4. The pattern of the tabernacle shown to Moses on Mount Sinai (Exod. 26:9, 40; cf. Num. 8:40) was a pattern for Solomon's temple (Wisd. 9:8). An angel opened to Levi in a vision the gates of heaven and he "saw the holy temple, and upon a throne of glory the Most High" (T. Levi 5:1). In the times of the priestly Messiah "the heavens shall be opened, and from the temple of glory shall come upon him sanctification" (T. Levi 18:6). The seed of Abraham "shall live and be established through sacrifices and gifts of righteousness and truth in the Age of the righteous and shall rejoice in Me (God) continually" (Apoc. Abr. 29).

Bloody animal sacrifices on earth are to be practiced (Jub. 6:14; Apoc. Abr. chh. 9, 12, 25; 2 Enoch 59:1-2), both for sin offerings and charity offerings consecrated to the poor (T. Job iv. 2, 6; x. 10-11), along with first fruit and drink (wine) offerings and frankincense (Jub. 15:2; T. Levi 9:14; cf. 2 Enoch 42:6). Yet there was concern about the pollution of Temple sacrifices (T. Levi 16:1; Apoc. Abr. ch. 25), especially when the priesthood is profaned (T. Levi 16:1), i.e. when it "[falleth away through sin from the Lord and is dominated by the

---

[64] Coptic, 64; Arabic, 144.

[65] Louis Finkelstein, "Pre-Maccabean Documents in the Passover Haggadah. Appendix. The Date of the Book of Jubilees," *HTR* 36 (1943), 22-23.

[66] "The Two Messiahs in the Testaments of the Twelve Patriarchs," *JTS* 48 (1947), 9.

earthly kingdom" (T. Jud. 21:4). In many circles attachment to the Jerusalem sacrificial cultus was replaced by the pious practices of penitence, abstinence and good works. Prayers and thanksgiving came to be seen as sufficient sacrifice to God (Justin, *Dialogue* 117.2; Aristeas 234). The lost Apocalypse of Adam [67] taught, "But to us he speaks thus: 'The sacrifice of God is a contrite heart; a savour of sweetness to the Lord is a heart glorifying Him that hath formed it" (cf. 2 Enoch 45:3-46:2, 61:4-5, 66:2). Isaac, by his daily fast until sundown, was "offering up his sacrifices" (T. Isaac).[68] The same writing commends the pious exercise of "bringing an offering of a little incense in the Lord's name on the memorial day of Isaac".[69] The Apocalypse of Moses tells of the origin of such sacrifices to God. The Lord "bade Adam to go in and take sweet spices and fragrant herbs from paradise" (29:3-6). Eve and Seth returned bearing with them herbs of fragrance, i.e. nard, crocus, calamus and cinnamon (43; 2; cf. 40:1). Jubilees (3:27) narrates that "on that day on which Adam went forth from the garden he offered as a sweet savour an offering, frankincense, galbanum, and stacte, and spices in the morning with the rising of the sun from the day when he covered his shame." This offering may have been patterned after one in heaven. For, Eve "beheld golden censers, between your Father [Adam] and the chariot, and all the angels with censers and frankincense came in haste to the incense-offering and blew upon it and the smoke of the incense veiled the firmament" (Apoc. Mos. 33:4-5; cf. 4 Baruch 9:1-4; T. Job 32:8: censers of the fragrant assembly). Likewise the T. of Levi 3:5-6 tells of the archangels in the sixth heaven "who minister and make propitiation to the Lord for all the sins of ignorance of the righteous; offering to the Lord a sweet-smelling savour, a reasonable and bloodless offering". M. De Jonge describes the intent—of the author as follows:[70]

> He wanted to emphasize that in heaven bloody sacrifice did not take place. Consequently the sacrifices on earth had to be 'reasonable' too. We now understand the connection between vs. 6 and vs. 7: While Angels of the Presence offer a prayer to God for the sins of the righteous, prayers and/or good deeds are brought to heaven as the sacrifices of mankind. Vs. 8 fits admirably into this context, for praise of

---

[67] James, "Notes on Apocrypha," *JTS* 16 (1915), 409-10; *Lost Apocrypha of the O.T.*, 1-2.

[68] Coptic, 63.

[69] Arabic, 149.

[70] *Op. cit.*, 49.

God is regarded by early Christian authors as a θυσία αἰνέσεως (see Hebr. 13:15f. . . .)

Without rejecting bloody sacrifices the author of Jubilees compares the Levitical service to that of the two highest angelic orders in heaven: the Lord caused Levi and his seed, "from among all flesh, to approach Him to serve in His sanctuary as the angels of the presence and as the holy ones" (31:14). The rank of the angels offering heavenly sacrifices appears in Jub. 2:2: on the first day God created "the spirits which serve before Him-the angels of the presence, and the angels of sanctification" followed by the angels controlling nature.

The priestly atmosphere of Qumran Community[71] may have stemmed from the fact that the Teacher of Righteousness was a priest (1Q p Hab 2.8; 4Qp Ps 37 2.15). Its members, for purposes of the annual census, were divided into the priests, the Levites and all the people (1QS 2.29-22). In the assembly of the Many they were seated according to rank: the priests, the elders and all the people (1QS 6.8-9). The author of the Damascus Document (3.21-4.4) understood Ezek. 44:15 to refer prophetically to these groups: "The priests are converts of Israel who went out of the land of Judah; and (the Levites are) those who joined them. And the sons of Zadok are the chosen of Israel." Instead of a threefold classification of the members of the Community, a twofold division sometimes appears: Aaron and Israel (1QS 8.5-6, 9; 9.6), or priests and people (4Q p Isa fr. 1). However they were classified, it is obvious that the community was "organized as an ideal priestly theocracy," in the words of Frank M. Cross.[72] The claim of legitimacy for their priesthood is implicit. In the Council of Community there were to be twelve men and three priests "to guard the faith, . . . and to expiate iniquity . . . and to undergo distress of affliction" by their perfect knowledge and behavior (1QS 8.1-4). The ten judges[73] of the Congregation were to consist of "four for the tribe of Levi and Aaron, and for Israel, six" (CD 10.4-6). The Covenanters were gathered in various places in groups of at least ten, one of whom had to be learned priest or, if necessary, a Levite. His orders were to be obeyed (CD 13.1-4; 1QS 6.3-4). The priests having authority over most of the Community members are identified as the sons of Zadok (1QS 5.2, 9); they instruct the people in God's laws (1QSb 3.22-24).

---

[71] Gärtner, op. cit., 14.

[72] Op. cit., 128; cf. 98: "The community takes the posture of a priesthood standing in the presence of God."

[73] Gärtner, op. cit., 10.

"The sons of Aaron alone shall command in matters of justice and property" (1QS 9.7). Priestly prerogatives included judgment in case of leprosy (CD 13.4-7) and the voluntary return of unlawfully obtained property (CD 9.13-14). They blessed the first-fruits of bread and wine (1QS 6.4-5; 1QSa 2.18-20), while both the priests and Levites conducted the ceremony of entering the rule of the Community (1QS 1.18ff.). The elevated status of the priesthood is manifest from the blessings of the high priest and the sons of Zadok the priest in the Book of Blessings (1QSb 2-4). Because lineal descendants of Zadok were needed for the Community's vital functions, probably celibacy among them was discouraged.

It is not surprising that a priestly-oriented and -led community conceived of itself as a spiritual Temple.[74] Its members sought "to lay a foundation of truth for Israel, for the Community of everlasting Covenant; that they may atone for all who are volunteers for the holiness of Aaron and for the House of truth in Israel, and for those who join them to live in community..." (1QS 5.5-6). The members of the Community were separated into "the House of holiness for Aaron that infinite holiness may be assembled together, and (into) the House of community for Israel for those that walk in perfection" (1QS 9.6). The Council of the Community

> is the House of holiness for Israel and the Company of infinite holiness [Holy of Holies?] for Aaron ... It is the tried wall, the precious corner-stone; its foundations shall not tremble nor flee from their place. It is the Dwelling of infinite holiness [Holy of Holies?] for Aaron ... the house of perfection and truth in Israel (1QS 8.5-9).

The spiritualization of the true Temple implies dissatisfaction with the existing Jerusalem Temple and its cultus. Such was the case with the Qumran Community.[75] The three nets of Belial are affirmed to be lust, riches and "defilement of the Sanctuary" (CD 4.15-18). Two specified types of impurity defiling the Temple in Jerusalem were lying with a menstruating woman (CD 5.6-7) and lying with a woman in the city of the Sanctuary (CD 12.1-2). The importance of Temple desecration for the origin of the sect is apparent in CD 20.22-24: the House of Separation (peleg) "are those that went out of the Holy City and leaned upon God at the time when Israel was unfaithful and

---

[74] Ibid., 16-44.

[75] J. M. Baumgarten, "Sacrifice and Worship among the Jewish Sectarians of the Dead Sea (Qumran) Scrolls," HTR 46 (1953), 142-44.

defiled the Sanctuary and were converted to God" (cf. 3:21-4:2). In Jerusalem "the Wicked Priest committed abominable deeds and defiled the Sanctuary of God" and "he stole the goods of the Poor" in the towns of Judah" (1Q p Hab 12.7-10). The Wicked Priest, "when he commanded over Israel, ... abandoned God and betrayed the precepts because of riches, ... and he took the riches of the people, ... and he followed the ways of a [bo] mination in every kind of unclean defilement" (1Q p Hab 8.8-13). The sect's continuing oppostion to the Jerusalem priesthood in power is reflected in the charge that the last priests of Jerusalem "heap up riches and gain by plundering the peoples" (1Q p Hab 9.4-6). The sect's opposition to the defiled priesthood and Temple cultus was longstanding: "None of those who have entered the Covenant shall enter the Sanctuary to kindle His altar in vain, but they shall close the door; as God said [Mal. 1:10], "Who among you will close his door? And you shall not kindle my altar in vain" (CD 6.11-14). A community of priests, in order not to offer defiled sacrifices, had vowed not to enter the Temple any longer. The exile of these Convenanters with their books of the Law and the prophets to Damacus under the leadership of the Interpreter of the Law is alluded to in the Damascus Document (7.14-19). In this passage Amos 5:26-27 is quoted, and these prophetic words immediately follow a denunciation of offerings and sacrifices by unrighteous men. In this spirit CD 11.18-22 warns:

> Let there be sent to the altar of holocaust neither offering nor incense nor wood by the hand of a man defiled by any defilement whatsoever, permitting him thus to render the altar unclean; for it is written, 'The sacrifice of the wicked is an abomination, but the prayer of the just is like a delectable offering.' And whoever enters the House of Prostration, let him not enter in a state of uncleanness; let him wash himself.

Since the Covenanters considered themselves ritually cleaner than the Temple priests by virtue of their superior understanding and observance of the law and prophets,[76] they must have considered themselves or their messengers alone as fully qualified to present offerings in the Jerusalem Temple. Whether they actually sent offerings and entered the Temple is not certain;[77] but their "zeal in guarding the sanctity of the Temple and the Holy City" makes it unlikely that they would offer sacrifice elsewhere, as Joseph M.

---

[76] Yadin, *op. cit.*, 198-99, 201.
[77] Bibliography in Gärtner, *op. cit.*, 20, n. 2.

Baumgarten [78] points out. On the other hand, the excavation at Qumran of burned animal bones carefully placed in jars suggests that at some time there were sacrifices at Qumran,[79] or that the bones were brought there.[80]

The Damascus Document contains several regulations for performing actual sacrifices: the sin offering of the ram (9.14), the Sabbath burnt offering (11.17-18) and free-will offerings (16.13). The Aaronic portion of the Community was "to make offerings of sweet savour" (1 QS 8.9). The Blessing of the High Priest (1QSb 3.1-2) includes a prayer for the acceptability of his offerings to God. As the benedictions in the Book of Blessings pertain to the priests and laity of the convenanted Community, the Covenanters must have had for a time, or anticipated having, their own High Priest who would have charge of a purified sacrificial cultus. The War Scroll, after classifying the High Priest, chief priests and chiefs of the classes, Levites and tribes, directs: "These shall be in office for the holocausts and sacrifices. They shall prepare incense of pleasant odor to (obtain) the lovingkindness of God; they shall expiate for all His congregation and shall feed before Him perpetually at the table of glory" (2.5).[81] Possibly the Community carried on its own sacrifices for the Day of Atonement; but more likely the sacrifices mentioned in the War Scroll were reserved for the final times.[82] The Description of the New Jerusalem (2Q 2.4) also mentions the eschatological altar of holocausts (frags. 5-8) and priests eating a sacred meal at the table (frags. 3-4), which is before the Lord (Ezek. 41:21-22). The Damascus Document (3.21-4.2) quotes Ezek. 44.15 and refers it to the Community: "The priests and Levites and the sons of Zadok who kept the charge of my sanctuary while the children of Israel went astray from me shall come near [to me to serve me and shall stand

---

[78] Art. cit., HTR 46 (1953), 146.

[79] Cross, op. cit., 60-70.

[80] S. H. Steckoll, "The Qumran Sect in relation to the Temple of Leontopolis," RQ 6 (1967-68), 55-56.

[81] The table of glory is that on which the Bread of the Presence was placed, before the Holy of Holies. This showbread was continually "set before the Lord" (Exod. 25:30; Lev. 24:8; 1 Chron. 9:32; 2 Chron. 2:4; Neh. 10:33). The offering "shall be for Aaron and his sons, and they shall eat it in a holy place, since it is for him a most holy portion out of the offerings by fire to the Lord, a perpetual due" (Lev. 24:9). Flagons for the drink offering were also placed on the Table of the Presence (Exod. 25:29; Num. 4:7), which resembled an altar of wood (Ezek. 41:22). Possibly the Qumran Covenanters compared to this table their own refectory table (see pp.151-154).

[82] Ringgren, op. cit., 216-17.

before me to offer] me fat and blood." This seems to refer to the New Jerusalem of Messianic times, which in Aramaic fragments from five caves [83] is described together with the New Temple and its ritual as based on the final nine chapters of Ezekiel. 4Q Florilegium I.1-12 and unpublished Manuscripts from Caves 4 and 11 describe the House into which at the end of days only the saints shall enter and above which God will appear constantly. "He has commanded a sanctuary (made by hands) of man (*miqdash 'adam*) to be built for Himself, that there may be some in this sanctuary to send up the smoke of sacrifice in His honour before Him among those who observe the Law" (6-7). This eschatological Temple may be the non-Herodian one for which building and sacrificial instructions are given in the Temple Scroll.[84] Whether these dimensions correspond to those of the heavenly archetype measured by the visionary in the Cave 5 Description of the New Jerusalem, remains to be seen. The Temple Scroll [85] also gives detailed regulations for the sacrifices and meal offerings for various festivals.

The "Angelic Liturgy" reveals, in the words of J. Strugnell, an "interest in the heavenly sacrificial cult, the priestly quality of the angels and the structure of the heavenly Temple." [86] "The Heavenly Temple is portrayed on the model of the earthly one and in some way its service is considered the pattern of what is being done below."[87] Another spiritualization of sacrifice [88] pertains to the righteous life of the earthly Community.

> They shall expiate guilty rebellion and sinful infidelity and (procure) lovingkindness upon earth more than by the flesh of burnt offering and the fat of sacrifice, but the offering of the lips in accordance with the law shall be as an agreeable odor of righteousness, and perfection of way shall be as the voluntary gift of a delectable oblation (1QS 9.4-5).[89]

In spite of the difficulties of translation of this passage, it appears that

---

[83] See 1Q32, 2Q24, 5Q15; M. Baillet, J. T. Milik, R. De Vaux, *Les 'Petites Grottes' de Qumrân. Exploration de la Falaise. Les Grottes 2Q, 3Q, 5Q, 6Q 7Q, à 10Q. Le Rouleau de Cuivre. Discoveries in the Judean Desert of Jordan III*, New York (Oxford University, 1962) and Oxford (Clarendon), 184-86.

[84] Yadin, *art. cit.*, *Biblical Archaeologist* 30 (1967), 137-39.

[85] *Ibid.*, 137.

[86] "The Angelic Liturgy at Qumran-4Q Serek Šîrôt 'ôlat Haššabbāt," in *Congress Volume*, Oxford, 1959. VT Suppl. 7 (1960), 335.

[87] *Ibid.*, 320.

[88] Gärtner, *op. cit.*, 44-46.

[89] Millar Burrows, *The Dead Sea Scrolls*, New York (Viking, 1955), 383.

both physical and spiritual sacrifice are approved,[90] but the latter moreso. Their quotation of Prov. 15:8 ("The sacrifice of the wicked is an abomination, but the prayer of the just is like a delectable offering") (CD 11.20-21) reveals the basic belief of the sectarians. Their prayers were superior to the polluted existing Temple offerings. The supreme importance of praising God at the appointed times is manifest from 1QS 9.26-10.17:

> [And in all that be] falls, he shall bless Him who did it, and in all that befalls he shall tell [of His deeds] and shall bless Him [with the offering] of the lips ... With the offering of the lips I bless Him ... at the beginnings of the years and in the circling of the yearly seasons ... and at the beginning of the weeks of weeks of years, at the time of Release. For the whole of my life the graven Decree shall be upon my tongue as a fruit of praise and the offering (menat) of my lips ... And I will bless Him with the offering of that which issues from out of my lips because of the table laid for men, and before I lift my hands to nourish me with the delicious fruits of the earth.

A Syriac Psalm (11 Q PSa 154.10-11) commends the man who makes known the glory of God: "And a man who glorifies the Most High he accepts as one who brings a meal offering, as one who offers he-goats and bullocks, as one who fattens the altar with many burnt offerings, as a sweetsmelling fragrance from the hand of the righteous."

According to Philo (*Quod omnis probus* 75), the Essenes did "not offer animal sacrifice (οὐ ζῶα καταθύοντες)." The text of Josephus' *Antiquities* xviii, 5.19) on the subject is much disputed, although the bracketed negative has but slight support:[91]

> When sending to the Temple their gifts dedicated to God, they do [not] offer sacrifices with differences of purifications to which they are accustomed, and for this reason, being excluded from the common court, they offer the sacrifices by themselves.
>
> εἰς δὲ τὸ ἱερὸν ἀναθήματα στέλλοντες θυσίας [οὐκ] ἐπιτελοῦσι διαφορότητι ἁγνειῶν, ἃς νομίζοιεν καὶ δὶ αὐτὸ εἰργόμενοι τοῦ κοινοῦ τεμενίσματος ἐφ αὐτῶν τὰς θυσίας ἐπιτελοῦσιν.

Irrespective of the text, the sense [92] is that the Essenes made offerings according to their own rules of purification, rather than presenting them throught the "impure" priestly rites of the Temple. Assuming that ἀναθήματα,[93] θυσίας ἐπιτελοῦσι and τὰς θυσίας

---

[90] Gärtner, *op. cit.*, 45.
[91] Black, *op. cit.*, 40, n. 1.
[92] Bibliography in Gärtner, *op. cit.*, 20, n. 2.
[93] Though it may have included Essene handicrafts given to the Temple.

ἐπιτελοῦσιν are parallel references to the same offerings, we deduce that the Essenes sent to Jerusalem some of their agricultural first fruits and presented them in the Temple directly to the Lord, lest they be defiled by contact with the crowds, the sanctuary, the established priesthood and their ritual. This privelege was made possible by the existence of the Essene gate (πύλη) in the Temple (Josephus, *War.* v, 4.2); indeed, if they had been able to acquire the privilege of their own gate, they probably would have been granted their own small chapel and altar for vegetable and incense offerings. In this way at least the sectarians' loyalty to Jerusalem and the Temple was preserved, in contrast to the Samaritan disloyalty. In the Talmud (Sheqalim V, 6) we read of the Temple Chamber of the Hassaim, "who put their gifts therein in secret" for the support of the poor. Even the court of the Temple was not "off limits" for the Essenes, for, one of their seers, Judas, foretold the death of Antigonus when he saw him pass through the area (Josephus, *War* i, 3.).

A goodly portion of the Dead Sea colony consisted of farmers sowing and working the fields (Philo, *Quod omnis probus* 76; *Apologia pro Judaeis, ap.* Eusebius, *Evang. Praep.* viii, 11.8; Josephus, *Antiquities* xviii, 5.19). Their obligation to present the first fruits of the ground (Exod. 22:29; 23:16, 19; 34:26; Num. 18:12-13; Deut. 18:4; 26:2) remained.[94] Because Philo (*ap.* Eusebius, *Evang. Praep.* viii, 11.8; cf. 4) also mentions the existence of shepherds and herdsmen in the Essene colony, one cannot exclude the possibility of an occassional, optional animal sacrifice as well. A large scale or regular, mandatory sacrificial cultus is made unlikely by their apparent vegetarianism and by Philo's explicit exclusion of *animal* sacrifice (*Quod omnis probus* 75). There is no evidence of the condemnation of animal sacrifice in principle. The first fleece of their sheep (Deut. 18:4) may also have been offered in Jerusalem.

Frank Cross [95] pointed out that "ἀναθήματα; (Hebr. *ḥērem* ... "could be given to the Temple without the donor's entering into the cultus or recognizing the legitimacy of the priesthood..." Considering the Temple priesthood to be impure, the Essenes were afraid of contracting defilement by giving their offerings as did other Jews.[96] In their communal life they had their own priests "to prepare

---

[94] George W. Buchanan (*art. cit., RQ* 4 [1963-64], 397, n. 3) thinks it unlikely that the legalistic Essenes would have neglected tithes and heave offerings.

[95] *Op. cit.,* 101, n. 118.

[96] Lightfoot, *St. Paul's Epistles to the Colossians and to Philemon,* 87.

the bread and the food" [97] (Josephus, *Antiquities* xviii, 1.5.22) and to offer prayer before and after each meal (*War* ii, 8.5.131). Conybeare [98] reasonably supposed that the Essenes "regarded their common meals as of the nature of a sacrifice ... Only thus can we explain the fact that they elected priests to prepare those meals; for a priest implies a sacrifice to be offered". The priests could have merely been present for supervision if it were simply as matter of ensuring the observance of kosher laws. The Essene dining hall would not have been considered a sanctuary (ἄγιον τι τέμενος) (Josephus, *War*, ii, 8.5.129), moreover, unless the priestly function were sacrificial.

Kohler [99] wrote of the Essenes: "Successors to the ancient Hasidim who instituted the liturgy (Midr. Teh. xvii. 4: 'hasidim ha-rishonim'), they laid all possible stress on prayer and devotion, opposing the priesthood in the Temple out of mistrust as to their state of holiness and purity rather than out of aversion to sacrifice (Tosef. Ned. i. 1; Ker. 25a)." Philo (*Quod omnis probus* 75) thus stated their sentiment that it was "more fitting to render their minds truly holy than to offer animal sacrifice" (cf. 1 Sam. 15:22; Ps. 40:6-8; 50:8ff.; 51:16-17; 69:30-31; Prov. 21:3; Eccles. 5:1; Isa. 1:11ff.; Jer. 7:21-24; Hos. 6:6; Mic. 6:6-9; Amos 5:22-24).[100] This obligation is well summarized by the Essene oath (Josephus, *War* ii, 8.7.139-42). The Therapeutae likewise served God by worship, worthy thoughts and heavenly love, rather than by priestly external sacrifice (Philo, *de vita contempl.* ii, 12).

W. F. Albright [101] thinks "the claim was being made that the sect went back in origin to Solomon's Temple and the original Zadok ... Here ... may be the source of the assertion by Pliny [*Nat. Hist.* v. 17] and Solinus [*Coll. Rer. Mem.* xxv, 9.12] that the Essene sect was of high antiquity." The fact that they had their own priests suggests a claim to a legitimacy not possessed by the official priesthood.

---

[97] Schürer, *op. cit.*, ii-ii, 203, n. 74 (ET).
[98] *Art. cit., Dictionary of the Bible*, ed. J. Hastings, i (1898), 769b.
[99] *Art. cit., Jewish Encyclopedia* v (1903), 230b.
[100] Baumgarten, *art. cit.*, HTR 46(1953), 150n.
[101] *Art. cit., The Scrolls and Christianity*, ed. Black, 21-22.

CHAPTER FIVE

ANGELOLOGY

Paul recalled that the Galatians had received him "as an angel of God, as Christ Jesus," when he preached the gospel for the first time. Yet, he warned that if "an angel from heaven should preach to you a gospel contrary to (παρά) that which we preached to you, let him be accursed" (1:8). Evidently the readers were concerned about fresh revelations (e.g. interpretations of the Torah) from angels, or, at least they were receptive to them. Analogy may be found in the revelations to Daniel by "the man Gabriel"(9:21-27) and by the one having the appearance of a man (10:16, 18; cf. 10). As a premise in an anti-legal argument the Apostle can state that the mosaic law "was ordained by angels through an intermediary" (3:19). Along with its curse (3:10-13) of condemnation to transgressors (3:10, 19, 22), the law was transmitted by angels through Moses as a middleman or agent to Israel.[1] The plurality of agents is contrasted with the unity of God (3:20). Thus the law does not put the observant in direct communication with God; it does not give life in accord with His promises (3:21). George S. Duncan [2] has commented on this passage: "Undue devotion to the ordinances of the Law seemed to Paul to imply a worship of angels rather than of the living God, and thus to have affinities with paganism." The contrast between the Gentile Galatians' worship of God as Christians and their earlier, immature devotion and service to the στοιχεῖα τοῦ κόσμου and their laws is made explicit in 4:2-4, 8-10. Similarly, Jews, though heirs, have been slaves to the Torah in their pre-Christian "childhood" (3:24, 29-4:3, 7). For the Gentile readers to begin to "observe days and months, and seasons and years" (4:10) would be to turn back again (πάλιν ἄνωθεν) to slavery, to the στοιχεῖα, "beings that by nature are no gods" (4:8), but which control time. Pagan feast days were often sacred to the gods. Control over the heavenly bodies by the στοιχεῖα implies their control

---

[1] On the role of angels in the revelation of the law, see W. D. Davies, "A Note on Josephus, Antiquities 15:136," *HTR* 47(1954), 135; Michl, *art. cit., Reallexicon f. Ant. u. Chr.*, v(1962), 67-68, 72.

[2] *The Epistle of Paul to the Galatians*, New York & London (Harper & Bros., 1934), 115. See Klaus Wegenast, *Das Verständnis der Tradition bei Paulus und in den Deuteropaulinen*, Neukirchen (Kreis Moers, 1962), 37-40.

of the sacred calendar. Paul opposed reversion to bondage to either the στοιχεῖα or to the Torah (4:9; 5:1, 3; cf. 2:4), i.e. to heathenism or Judaism, respectively. Pre-Christian bondage to the tutelage of the στοιχεῖα and to the law are placed in parallel in 4:1-5 (cf. 3:23-25). The personality of the στοιχεῖα is suggested by their being compared to guardians and stewards (4:2-3) and lords (4:3) who have the nature of gods (4:8). Στοιχεῖα and angels are not explicitly identified, but both give laws concerning special times which enslave their immature observants. Unless his readers assumed at least the similarity of the angels and στοιχεῖα, Paul's thought in 3:19-4:10 would be less coherent.[3] "But when the time had fully come, God sent forth his Son, born of woman" (4:4) in order to redeem us from the bondage and curse of the law (3:13; 4:5; 5:1) and to liberate us from the στοιχεῖα (4:3, 8-9, 11-13). The opponents of Paul honored and served both the law and the spirits who gave and enforced it. Gal. 1:4 redefines the liberation brought by Christ: he gave himself on behalf of our sins, in order to deliver us out of the present evil age (cf. 6:14-15: crucified to the κόσμος, or old creation). The evil of this αἰών stems from bondage to death, sin, the flesh, circumcision, the law and hostile cosmic powers who crucified the Lord of glory (1 Cor. 2:6, 8).

Colossians presents a similar picture. "Let no one disqualify you, insisting on self-abasement (ταπεινοφροσύνη) and worship (θρησκεία) of angels (2:18)". Theodore of Mopsuestia[4] understood this verse to imply that the law had been given through the ministry of angels and that they watch over (φυλάττειν) the observance of the law. Because the indignant angels do not tolerate any contempt (καταφρόνησις) of the law when it is not observed, Paul's opponents feared them. (-)ρησκεία and ταπεινοφροσύνη, in Theodore's understanding, thus meant little more than what we would term a "healthy respect." Since elsewhere in the New Testament (Acts 20:19; Eph. 4:2; Phil. 2:3; 1 Pet. 5:5) ταπεινοφροσύνη is a virtue, the use of the word[5] here may have been derived from the opponents. The use of the terms, ἐθελοθρησκεία and ταπεινοφροσύνη, in 2:23 is naturally referred back to verse 18. While Paul deemed this external religious observance and practice to be inappropriate, unnecessary and irrelevant for the new

---

[3] Bo Reicke, "The Law and the World according to Paul," *JBL* 70(1951), 261-63.

[4] Ed. H. B. Swete, Cambridge, i(1880), 294.

[5] Bibliography on its interpretation in Francis, *art.cit.*, *Studia Theologica* 16(1962), 111.

life in Christ, he does not accuse the false teachers of failing to honor
the Father or believe in the Son. The role of angels was apparently
one of mediation or intercession when human need arises. Thus
Theodoret [6] explained that it was taught that God was so exalted that
men must come into contact with Him through angels. G.
Macgregor [7] located the heart of the Colossian heresy in "giving to
the στοιχεῖα, as mediators between God and man, the place which
can belong only to Christ." The false teachers also followed certain
religious customs out of reverence for angels. In this sense Aristides
in his *Apology* [8] criticized the Jews: "In the methods of their actions
their service is to angels and not to God, in that they observe
Sabbaths and new moons and the Passover and the great fast and the
feast and circumcision and cleanness of meats" (cf. The Preaching of
Peter, *ap*. Clement of Alexandria, *Strom*. vi, 5.40; Origen, *Comm. in
Jn*. xiii, 17). Now, in Col. 2:8-23 Paul criticizes similar observance of
Jewish laws under the guise of following the στοιχεῖα τοῦ κόσμου and
demonstrating ταπεινοφροσύνη καὶ θρησκείκ τῶν ἀγγέλων. Α λόγος
σοφίας in promoting devotion to angels is manifested by subjection to
ascetic taboos decreed by the στοιχεῖα τοῦ κόσμου (2:20-21) and
interpreted "according to human precepts and doctrines" (2:22). Verse
2:8 is a parallel passage: "See to it that no one makes a prey of you by
philosophy and empty deceit, according to human tradition,
according to the στοιχεῖα τοῦ κόσμου, and not according to Christ."
The prefex, ἐθελο- (2:23), suggests a worship taught by men rather
than by God. A reverence for humanly interpreted and transmitted
teachings and command which are set against Paul's gospel is also
attacked in Gal. 1:1, 6-2:9. Angels and στοιχεῖα are alike as recipients
of humility and "worship" (2:18, 20-22), as rivals of Christ (2:16-21),
as teachers of oppressive ascetic laws (2:16-18, 20-21) and as subjects
of human speculations and traditions. But the question as to the
extent of the overlapping of these heavenly spirits may be left open. [9]
By almost equating these categories and by referring to human
teachings (2:8, 22) and τοῦ κόσμου, Paul indicates that a

[6] Migne, *P.G.* 82, 613.
[7] "Principalities and Powers: The Cosmic Background of Paul's Thought," *NTS* 1(1954), 22.
[8] Ch. 4 of the Syriac transl. by J. Armitage Robinson, *Texts and Studies* i-1(1891), 48.
[9] Günter Bornkamm equated those mentioned in both Galatians and Colossians ("Die Häresie des Kolosserbriefes," in *Das Ende des Gesetzes*, München (Chr. Kaiser), i (1952), 140; so does Hugedé (*op. cit.*, 116-17).

fundamentally Jewish view of angels and the law has been assimilated to current pagan cosmology, at least as far as terminology is concerned. Moreover, the fact that the spiritual powers teach laws and, as bearers of revelations, require self-abasement suggests that they are to be feared. Disobedience of such laws led to human judgment (μὴ κρινέτω, μηδεὶς καταβραβευέτω: 2:16, 18) as a counterpart of the divine. This fearful attitude is confirmed in 2:14-15: God through Christ has "cancelled the bond which stood against us with its legal demands ... nailing it to the cross. He disarmed the principalities and powers and made a public example of them, triumphing over them in him." His resurrection through the working of God (2:12; cf. 2 Cor. 13:4) stands in contrast to the weakness of the feared spiritual powers. Their personal nature is indicated by the use of the masculine, αὐτούς, in 2:15. Because Christ has wiped out a legal servitude which was ὑπεναντίον ἡμῖν through his humiliating military conquest (cf. 2 Cor. 2:14) of the archons and ἐξουσίας, it appears that certainly Paul and possibly the Colossians had viewed these spiritual powers as still powerful and oppressive in their reign [10] over the lives of even their Christian devotees. Indeed, as MacGregor [11] urges, Christ on the cross stripped off from himself (ἀπεκδυσάμενος) the evil spirits to which he had subjected himself (cf. Mt.16:22-23; Lk. 4:1-13; 22:53; Rom. 8:3; 2 Cor. 5:21; Gal. 3:13; 4:4), even unto his crucifixion (1 Cor. 2:8), in order to win a cosmic redemption (Col. 1:20; cf. Rom. 8:22, 38-39). Differing views were held, however, on the laws of diet and holy days (2:16) and chastisements and accusations brought by the angels holding the book in which are recorded sins καθ' ἡμῶν.[12] Paul argued that these cosmic powers have lost their right to condemn for infractions of the law, because Christ has rubbed off, taken away and nailed to the cross their handwritten accusations. Maurice Jones rightly observed: "the whole world, the Jewish with its law and its angels, and the Gentile with its astral religions, is a world in bondage, and can only attain to freedom and life through the victory accomplished in the death of

---

[10] Angelic authority is illustrated in the Shepherd of Hermas (*Simil.* 8.3), where it is the "great and glorious angel" Michael who "beholdest all things, ... who giveth the law into the hearts of them that believe. He observeth, therefore, those to whom He hath given it, to see whether they have kept it ... As many as have been obedient unto the law and kept it, he hath them under his own authority" (transl. C. H. Houle).

[11] *Art. cit., NTS* 1 (1954), 23.

[12] Andrew John Bandstra, *The Law and the Elements of the World*, Kampen (J. H. Kok, 1964), 158-68.

176   ANGELOLOGY

Christ on the Cross. . ." [13] "The Cross had brought the reign of the law to a definite close, and consequently the angels who, according to tradition, had presided over its introduction and were its guardians and the administrators of its decrees, share in this dethronement, and had now ceased to exercise power or to possess rights over men." [14] As the power of sin is the law (Cor. 15:56), Christ's breaking of this power meant the overthrow of the cosmic spirits, although all ἀρχή, ἐξουσία and δύναμις will not be abolished until the end (τέλος) (1 Cor. 15:24-26). Hence believers must no longer humble themselves before angelic powers and the laws by which they judge. Such θρνσκεία should have no part in the new age of freedom inaugurated by Jesus. Rescue from their condemnation may be described in 1:13-14: God "has delivered us from the ἐξουσία of darkness (cf. Eph. 6:12: κοσμοκράτορες τοῦ σκότους τούτου; Gal. 1:14) and transferred us to the kingdom of his beloved Son, in whom we have redemption, the forgiveness of sins." That is, "You have come to fulness of life in him, who is the head of all rule and authority (ἡ κεφαλὴ πάσης ἀρχῆς καὶ ἐξουσίας)" (2:10). Through Christ believers rise above angels, who do not bring fulfillment and who are sometimes hostile. Christ's supremacy is more fully described in 1:16: "In him all things were created, in heaven and on earth, visible and invisible, whether thrones or dominions or principalities or authorities (ἀρχαὶ εἴτε ἐξουσίαι)." The terms found in this verse may well reflect the classification, by Paul's opponents, of all the angelic orders, which dwell in the seven regions of heaven (cf. 2 Cor. 12:2; Eph. 4:10; 6:12; Hebr. 4:14; Asc. Isa. 7:21, 27; 8:8). Interest in the harmonious order of the heavenly hierarchy is indicated by τὰ πάντα ἐν αὐτῷ συνέστηκεν (1:17), τάξις and στερέωμα (2:5) [15] The use of εἴτε . . . εἴτε . . . εἴτε (cf. Eph. 1:21) indicates Paul's disinterest, if not impatience and irritation, toward an attempted subjective classification of angels. [16] In 1:20 τὰ (πάντα) ἐν τοῖς οὐρανοῖς are equated with the spiritual τὰ πάντα ἐν τοῖς οὐρανοῖς (1:16); the personal nature of the former is indicated by their need to be reconciled and pacified by the blood of Christ. Moreover, as they are compared to the sinful readers who need to be reconciled (1:21), the creatures in heaven must be, or at least include,

---

[13] M. Jones, "St. Paul and Angels," *Expositor* viii-15(1918), 415.

[14] *Ibid.*, 413.

[15] Henry Chadwick, "All Things to All Men (1 Cor. ix. 22)", *NTS* 1(1954-55), 273.

[16] Lightfoot, *St. Paul's Epistles to the Colossians and to Philemon*, 150; cf. Goodenough, *By Light, Light*, 307, 324, 344, quoting *Apostolic Constitutions* vii, 35.3; viii, 12.27.

fallen beings. Paul's emphasis on "πάντα" in describing the work of Christ (1:16, 20) was not in agreement with the notions of his opponents; they were able to practice θρησκεία τῶν ἀγγελων without sufficient reference to Christ. Moreover, while they, too, sought release from bondage to hostile spirits, presumably through Christ, they did not understand this release to consist partially of a liberation from the angel-regulated law through the Cross. Rather, the law-angels were given some of the honor due Christ as source of "growing with the growth of God" (2:19).

Do στοιχεα τοῦ κόσμου belong to this classification? As teachers, guardians and enforcers of the law, they bring devotees into religious bondage and judgment. The qualifications, "weak and beggarly" (Gal. 4:9) accords with Paul's attitude toward the κόσμοσ,[17] i.e. temporary, and ineffectual in overcoming sin, and belonging to the present age only. Such a polemical characterization of the στοιχεῖα ran counter to the overestimation of their power, divine authority and world rule which stemmed from their association with the law and which required self-abasement by the Jewish "angel-worshipper." To their Gentile devotees, the στοχεῖα were like cosmic gods (Col. 2:8). Generally associated with the στοιχεῖα in ancient usage was δύναμις, power or force.[18] As agents of God, the στοιχεῖα rule the moral, natural and physical orders. As cosmic spirits and representatives of God they control the sacred calendar (Gal. 4:9-10; Col. 2:15-16) by animating and governing heavenly bodies.[19] Such an interpretation of τοῦ κόσμου is supported by the fact that the term refers to material things.[20] Maurice Jones[21] cogently observed that στοιχεῖα is a more comprehensive term than the angels of the law. Reverence for angels required adoption of their sacred calendar.

The angelology of Daniel offers clarifying parallels. Yahweh, the Prince of the host who receives the daily burnt offering (8:1), is the Prince of princes (8:25). Among the chief of these are the princes in charge of the Persians, Greeks and Jews (i.e. Michael) (10:13, 20;

[17] Bandstra, op.cit., 48-57.
[18] Ibid., 39-46.
[19] Schlier, op. cit., 134-36; Joseph Huby, Saint Paul. Les Épîtres de la Captivité, Paris (Beauchesne, 1947), 60-66; Joseph Blinzler, "Lexikalisches zu dem Terminus' τὰ στοιχεῖα τοῦ κόσμου' ", Studiorum Paulinorum Congressus Internationalis Catholicus 1961 (Rome [Pontif. Inst. Bibl., 1963], ii, 432-39; bibliography in Bandstra, op. cit., 26-29, 41-44.
[20] Ibid., 17, n. 50 for bibliography.
[21] Art. cit., Expositor viii-15(1918), 414-15.

12:1; cf. Deut. 32:8-9 [22]; Jub. 15:31). The host of heaven, or the host
of stars (8:10), consists of the celestial bodies, i.e. sun, moon and stars
(cf. Gen. 2:1; Deut. 4:19; 17:3; Nehem. 9:6; Pss. 33:6; Isa 48:12), who
were entrusted by God with rule over day and night (Gen. 1:14-19; 1
Enoch 80:1). But in other contexts the "heavenly host" signified
angels (1 Kings 22:19; 2 Chron. 18:18; Lk. 2:13; cf. Job 38:7; Rev.
19:14), or both angels and heavenly bodies (Ps. 148:2; Acts 7:42). In
any case, they were considered rulers of the cosmos (i.e.
κοσμοκράτορες), since earth and heaven are closely related. The Lord
of hosts will punish not only the host of heaven (including moon and
sun) but also the heathen kings of the earth (Isa. 24:21-23). On the
other hand, "those who are wise shall shine like the brightness of the
firmament; and those who turn many to righteousness, like the stars
for ever and ever" (12:3; cf. 7:10; 8:10). Even pagan celestial deities
could be included among the hosts of Yahweh (Exod. 15:11; Pss.
29:1-2; 82:1; 89:5-8). Those whom the heathen worship with idols
(Rev. 9:20) and sacrifices (1 Cor. 10:20; cf. 2 Kings 23:5) are classified
as demons. It is not surprising that Paul included Jewish angels and
Hellenistic astral deities among "στοιχεῖα τοῦ κόσμου", i.e. cosmic
angels. Due to his negative view of the enslaving and condemning
law and the cosmos in the present age, the Apostle looked upon law-
giving and -enforcing angels and law-giving, nature-controlling
στοιχεῖα in a more hostile light than did his opponents. The Apostle
worshipped God for His mercy as revealed in Christ, while the
Judaizers revered God for His justice as mediated through angels.[23]
Andrew J. Bandstra perceptively notes:[24]

> Paul could view both the angelic mediators and the demonic accusers as
> belonging to the old situation that threatens man before and outside of
> Christ. This fact may also throw light on such a passage as Rom. 8:38,
> 39. Rather surprisingly, the ἄγγελοι, ἀρχαί and δύναμεις are mentioned
> along with other created but less personal forces that threaten to separate
> us from God's love. Significantly this is set in the context of accusation
> and condemnation (vv. 31, 33- note the καθ' ἡμῶν, the ἐγκαλέσει κατά
> and the κατακρινῶν).

How far Paul, his Gentile readers and his Judaizing opponents agreed
on the relation between angels, στοιχεῖα and ἀρχαί cannot be
determined. Yet all seem to have agreed that their functions were at

---

[22] Albert Vanhoye, *Situation du Christ. Hébreux 1-2*, Paris (Cerf, 1969), 131.
[23] Bandstra, *op. cit.*, 152-53.
[24] *Ibid.*, 160.

least analagous and that astral powers belonged to all three categories.
Paul considered both the Gentiles and Judaizers to be guilty of
serving the στοιχεῖα [25]; he was even ambiguous on the question
whether they were elect or fallen angels. Yet he did discredit the
angels who appeared to Moses, by associating them with the astral
and cosmic rulers; for, both groups were agents of the law concerning
times and seasons. By virtue of their enslaving and accusing of men,
these spirits were viewed more negatively by Paul than by his
opponents.

Ephesians presents a similar view of the relations between Christ
and angelic powers. "We are not contending against flesh and blood
but against the principalities (ἀρχαί), against the powers (ἐξουσίαι),
against the world rulers of this present darkness, against the spiritual
hosts of wickedness in the heavenly places" (6:12). They are agents of
the devil, the tempter (6:11, 16). His angels, then, are unfriendly
spirits who tempt, imprison, accuse and probably punish men.[26] The
Christian's weapons of spiritual warfare include truth, righteousness,
faith, the gospel of peace and the Spirit (6:14-17); thereby he is made
strong in the Lord and stands fast (6:10-11, 14). The κοσμοκράτορες, as
hostile astral spirits which rule the cosmos, resemble the στοιχεῖα τοῦ
κόσμου. As rulers of "this darkness" (6:12), they function in such a
way that they have to be resisted. He is dead in his sins who walks
according to the αἰών of this world, "following the prince of the
power (ἐξουσία) of the air, the spirit that is now at work in the sons of
disobedience" (2:1-2). Thus Paul could speak of delivery through
Christ "out of the present evil age (αἰών)" (Gal. 1:4) and "out of the
authority (ἐξουσία) of darkness" (Col. 1: 13). According to Eph. 3:9-11,
"the plan of the mystery hidden ἀπὸ τῶν αἰώνων and the eternal
purpose realized in Christ Jesus is that "through the church the
manifold wisdom of God might now be made known to the ἀρχαί
and the ἐξουσίαι in the heavenly places." Thus hostile angels learn by
observing the church that "the unsearchable riches of Christ" have
delivered believers from their grasp and that they stand fast through
the armaments of spiritual warfare. Accordingly, now in Christ "we
have boldness and confidence of access through our faith" (3:12); this
had formerly been hindered by the angelic powers. No longer must
these angels be propitiated if there is to be confidence in
approaching God; Christ is the new mediator for the church. As

---

[25] Percy, op. cit., 166.
[26] Thereby evil is not attributable to God.

Francis W. Beare [27] comments on 3:10: "The Christian had no need
to resort to magic or to seek means of propitiation, either to secure
their aid or to avert their hostility." In 1:9-10 the divine mystery, plan
and purpose set forth in Christ is defined as "to unite all things in
him, things in heaven and things on earth." As the latter category
includes hostile angels, they, too, are to be gathered into the unity of
Christ. According to 4:8-10, when Christ "ascended far above all the
heavens," he "led a host of captives" (i.e. his enemies, such as hostile
spirits, sin and death, as distinguished from ἄνθρωποι) "that he might
fill all things." As the authority of Jesus Christ was thereby extended
to all things in heaven, the implication is that he triumphantly led
the conquered angels of death and sin upward in captivity. The verse
is most naturally interpreted in terms of 1:20-23: God raised Christ
"from the dead and made him sit at his right hand in the heavenly
places, far above all rule (ἀρχή) and authority (ἐξουσία) and power and
dominion and above every name that is named, not only in this age
but also in that which is to come; and he has put all things under his
feet and has made him head over all things for the church." By his
resurrection and ascent the tyrannical angels, through whose sphere
he passed, have been subdued (ὑπέταξεν). Over all things not they,
but Christ, reigns; such is God's great gift to the church. J. B.
Lightfoot [28] commented on καὶ παντὸς ὀνόματος ὀνομαζομένων (1:21):

> In this catalogue St. Paul does not profess to describe objective realities,
> but contents himself with repeating subjective opinions ... He brushes
> away all these speculations without inquiring how much or how little
> truth there may be in them, because they are altogether beside the
> question.

None of these angels is worthy of the reverence due Christ in both
this age and the next. Conybeare [29] reasonably suggested that "every
name that is named" implies exorcism with the names of angels and
patriarchs.

The promise in Romans 16:20 that the God of peace would soon
crush satan under the readers' feet implies that the devil has been at
work through the heretical teachers (v. 17). The hearts of the guileless
were open to deception (vv. 18-19) by Satan. Paul found these
teachers to be Satanic because they deceived ἄκακοι just as the devil

---

[27] "The Epistle to the Ephesians," *IB* 10 (1953), 672.
[28] *St. Paul's Epistles to the Colossians and to Philemon*, 150.
[29] *Art. cit., JQR* 8 (1895-96), 585.

had misled Adam and Eve, in consequence of which his head was crushed by man's heel (Gen. 3:15).

In 2 Corinthians the deceitful workmen transforming themselves into apostles of Christ are compared to Satan transforming himself into an angel of light (11:13-14). It is natural to interpret this passage in terms of 11:3, according to which the serpent deceived Eve by his cleverness. As the function of the false apostles and ministers of righteousness (11:15) is to preach their "gospel" (11:4-5), and as light is a symbol of divine revelation (Jn. 3:20-21; Acts 9:3, 7; 22:6, 9; Eph. 5:13; 2 Tim. 1:10), the angel of light is probably to be seen as a teacher. This interpretation accords well with Gal. 1:8 ("Even if ... an angel from heaven should preach to you a gospel contrary to that which we preached to you, let him be accursed"). To detect true preaching is difficult in cases of both deceiving angels and apostles. In 12:7 the intent of the ἄγγελος σατανᾶ is to buffet Paul through a thorn in the flesh (cf. 1 Cor. 5:5) in order to hinder his ministry (1 Thess 2:18), which had been aided by revelations of the Lord. The Corinthians' reception of a spirit different from the one received by Paul (11:4) is associated with their accepting a "different gospel" from preachers of "another Jesus." The situation is again analagous to that of Gal. 1:6-9. But should the deceiving angel of Gal. 1:8 and 2 Cor. 11:14 be related to πνεῦμα ἕτερον? The angelic role in Gal. 3:19 is to ordain the law; in 2 Cor. 11:3, 14 it is to circumvent the law by false interpretation. The "different spirit" apparently "leads astray from a sincere and pure devotion to Christ" (11:3-4). In Rom. 8:14-15 (cf. Gal. 4:4-10, 21-26) Paul distinguishes between the Spirit of God or the spirit of adoption and "the spirit of slavery [i.e. to the law, the flesh, or στοιχεῖα] to fall back into fear." In 1 Cor. 2:12 he distinguishes between the Spirit from God (interpreting the wisdom of God which was unknown by the angelic ἄρχοντες τοῦ αἰῶνος τούτου) (2:8) and the πνεῦμα τοῦ κόσμου (for understanding human wisdom). These parallel passages suggest that Paul's opponents followed either a spirit of bondage or an angelic spirit comparable to the στοιχεῖα τοῦ κόσμου (Col. 2:8, 20-23). In defending his ministry of preaching Paul charges that the god of this world (ὁ Θεὸς τοῦ αἰῶνος τούτου) has blinded the minds of unbelievers to enlightenment by the Gospel (2 Cor. 4:3-4). The πνεῦμα ἕτερον, πνεῦμα τοῦ κόσμου and ὁ Θεὸς τοῦ αἰῶνος τούτου all impede the Gospel. The presence of angels in the Corinthian church is presupposed in 1 Cor. 11:10 (where women are asked to wear a veil "because of the angels") and 13:1-2 (where speaking with the tongue of angels is related to prophetic understanding of mysteries).

In Philippians 3 the opponents were preoccupied with the upward calling of God (v. 14) to citizenship in heaven with a glorious body (vv. 19-21). Their confidence about their progress toward perfection (12-16) may well have been fostered by a foretaste of heavenly citizenship, namely, through contact of holy men with angels But Paul viewed them as enemies of the cross (18) because their eschatological fulfillment was not centered in the fellowship of his suffering (10), his laying hold of them (12), his giving them a resurrection body and subduing all things to himself (20-21). The opponents did not grasp the fullness of his lordship and role in bringing them into contact with heaven. Who were his rivals, if not angels?

In his excellent Commentary on the Epistle to the Hebrews, Hugh Montefiore [30] has written:

> The references to angels, coming as they do in such a prominent place at the beginning of the Epistle, may be presumed to have a bearing on the dangerous situation of its recipients ... Such effort is expended by the writer of this letter to show the Son's superiority to angels that he cannot be concerned only with making an 'academic' point ... Our author was not one to prolong his argument unnecessarily, especially at the beginning of the Epistle.

While there is no polemic against angels or angel worship, the fact that they were chosen as the first standard of comparison with the Son does indicate that the readers were interested in angelology, and that they were receptive to the comparison of Jesus with angels. The author builds upon his readers' assumptions that the angels are of excellent name (1:4), that they all minister in serving those who are to be saved (1:14) (i.e. like priests offering sacrifices: 10:10-12) and that the authoritative word of the law has been spoken through them (2:2), apparently on Mount Sinai (1:7; cf. Deut. 4:11).[31] Yet "he wished to avoid the title 'God' or 'son of God' for angelic beings," [32] and the unique superiority of the Son is categorically upheld against

---

[30] Op. cit., 40-41.

[31] Y. Yadin, "The Dead Sea Scrolls and the Epistle to the Hebrews," Scripta Hierosolymitana 4(1958), 39-40.

[32] M. de Jonge and A. S. van der Woude, "11Q Melchizedek and the New Testament," NTS 12 (1965-66), 315; cf. Vanhoye, op. cit., 223: he even avoids calling them servants of God sent by God, in his desire to prove their absolute inferiority (ibid., 149-51).

all rivals for whom such claims were made (1:4-2:10). They were merely servants (λειτουργός, λειτουργικὰ πνεύματα: 1:7, 14), rather than rulers (1:6, 8, 13). Canon Montefiore shows how the author of Hebrews used five quotations from Psalms, as well as 2 Sam. 7:14 (LXX) and Deut. 32:43 (LXX) as proof texts for this superiority. The angels were not to be considered sons of God in the sense that Jesus is Son (1:5; cf. 2:10). All angels are to worship the Son (1:6). The Son's word is all the more authoritative (2:1-4); it leads to salvation and gifts of the Holy Spirit. Revelation by Christ is superior to that by angels (i.e. of the law).[33] Transgression of the law mediated by angels receives a just recompense; their work is associated with the old covenant. "It was not to angels that God subjected the world to come" (2:5). But God has left nothing that is not subject to the Son (2:8). Evidently some of the readers attributed to angels eschatological powers independent of those of Jesus.[34] He is the mediator (μεσίτης) of the new covenant (8:6, 9; 9:15; 12:24; cf. 7:22) and the author (ἀρχηγός) of salvation (2:10). Paul Andriessen [35] believes that the greater tent through which Christ entered the Holy Place (9:11-12), is the heaven of the angels through which he ascended to the Father; thereby he was raised above the angels (1:6; 4:14; 7:26; 8:1-2; 9:24). Jean Danielou [36] calls attention to 12:22-24, where the liturgy of the church is presented as a participation in, and reflection of, the heavenly liturgy of the angels. Ronald Williamson [37] notes the implication that "in heaven men are co-equal with the angels in the celestial choir." Fred O. Francis [38] has found that in both Hebrews and Colossians "observation of and participation in the angelic liturgy of heaven was itself a significant representation of salvation."

According to 1 Timothy 4:1-3 the false teachers of asceticism were paying attention to misleading spirits and the teachings of demons, who were thus responsible for error. In contrast to the elect angels in 1 Tim. 5:21, these spirits and demons belong to lower orders of angels in the view of the Pastor, who used perjorative terms in order

[33] Ronald Williamson, *Philo and the Epistle to the Hebrews*, Leiden (E. J. Brill, 1970), 189.

[34] *Ibid.*, 40, 45.

[35] "Das grössere und vollkommenere Zelt (Hebr. 9, 11)," *Biblische Zeitschrift* 15(1971), 83-86.

[36] *The Angels and their Mission*, 63; Spicq, *L'Épître aux Hébreux*, ii, 50-61.

[37] *Op. cit.*, 191.

[38] "Visionary Discipline and Scriptural Tradition at Colossae," *Lexington Theological Quarterly* 2 (1967), 77.

to characterize the beings whose teaching was authoritative
(προσέχοντες) for the errorists (4:1). That ascetic laws were a satanic
snare is implied in 1 Tim. 5:14-15: younger women should marry
and bear children, lest they give the adversary an occasion for slander
(λοιδορία). Since διάβολος means "accuser, calumniator, adversary or
slanderer" (cf. 3:11; 2 Tim. 3:3; Tit. 2:3), and as Satan is mentioned in
5:15, ἀντικείμενος is best understood in these terms. Some had already
strayed after him and thus had given him occasion for accusation.
Their turning aside (ἐκτρέπομαι) behind (ὀπίσω) him is parallel to
turning aside (ἐκτρέπομαι) from the παραγγελία of faith and love to the
vain talking of the law-teachers who attend to myths (1 Tim. 1:4-7).
Herein lay the devilish seduction and snare for younger widows:
trying unsuccessfully to follow ascetic laws taught by misleading
spirits; for Satan stimulates evil desire and wantonness against Christ,
and then calumniates his victims for violating the ascetic pledge (1
Tim. 5:11-12). Hence the church had to refuse enrollment to younger
widows (1 Tim. 5:9, 11). The spiritual motives of the women
themselves were more apt to be mixed than purely "orthodox."
Teachings of demons in a more general sense included all harmful
mysteries illegitimately revealed by angels (e.g. "magic" and
incantations). According to 1 Tim. 5:21 final judgment is before God,
Jesus Christ and the elect angels. Presumably these angels standing
before the heavenly thrones (Lk. 1:19; Rev. 1:4; 3:1; 4:5) have been
chosen for a role in accusing and punishing sinners (Mt. 13:41-42;
16:27; 25:31; Mk. 8:38; Lk. 12:8-9; 2 Thess. 1:7; Jd. 14; Rev. 12:10).[39]

In his Revelation (19:10; cf. 22:8-9) John relates that he fell down
to worship the angel who had given him revelations (cf. 1:1; 22:6,
16). But the angel rebuked him: "You must not do that! I am a fellow
servant with you and your brethren who hold the testimony of Jesus.
Worship God." The seer refers to several angels associated with
natural phenomena (7:1; 9:14; 14:18; 16:5; 19:17), and to the seven
stars (1:16, 20), the seven angels (8:2; 15:8; 17:1; 21:8), the seven
spirits of God (1:4; 4:5; 5:6) and "him who has the seven spirits of
God and the seven stars" (3:1). These angels resemble the στοιχεῖα τοῦ
κόσμου. Angels mediate [40] between Christ and his churches (1:20; 2:1,
8, 12, 18; 3:1, 7, 14; 22:16) and stand at the heavenly altar offering up
the prayers of the martyred saints (8:3; cf. 5:8-9; 6:9-10) for prompt

[39] Michl, *Reallexicon f. Antike u. Chr.*, v. (1962), 75-76.

[40] William Ramsay, *The Letters to the Seven Churches of Asia*, London (Hodder &
Stoughton, 1904), 67-72.

divine judgment. The twenty-four elders are intercessory angels.[41] or at least the elders and angels worship together in a heavenly liturgy (4:4-11; 5:8-14; 7:9-12; 11:16-18; 19:1-8). The overthrow of the devil and his angels is described in the following terms. "Now the salvation and the power and the kingdom of our God and the authority of our Christ have come, for the accuser of our brethren has been thrown down, who accuses them day and night before God. And they have conquered him by the blood of the Lamb. . ." (12:9-11). Visions of the angelic adoration [42] of God and of the Lamb are described in chapters 4 and 5. Only the Lamb was worthy, among all in heaven, on earth of under the earth, to open or look upon the scroll which sealed the woes to fall upon the earth (5:2ff.). And John "heard every creature in heaven and on earth and under the earth and in the sea, and all therein, saying, 'To him who sits upon the throne and unto the Lamb be blessing and honor and might for ever and ever." (5:13). Some of the thought of Colossians and Ephesians has been expressed in liturgical and apocalyptic language. In 14:2-4 John heard the sound from heaven of harps and harpers offering a song intelligible only to the 144,000 virgin martyrs; i.e. it was in the tongue of angels.

According to 1 Peter 3:22, Jesus Christ "is at the right hand of God, with angels, authorities (ἐξουσίαι) and powers subject (ηυποταγέντων) to him." "To him belong glory and dominion (τὸ κράτος) for ever and ever. Amen" (4:11). The liturgical nature of at least the latter passage suggests that the local church wished to emphasize the transcendence of Christ in relation to all angels. Moreover, the angels longed to peer into the things pertinent to the Gospel; but instead these blessings have been revealed through the Holy Spirit sent from heaven and have been preached to the readers of Asia Minor (1:12). The angels learned the Gospel through men, rather than vice versa (cf. Eph. 3:10). The new revelation had been concealed from the angels.[43]

As Palestinian Jews associated the wilderness with demonic powers (Lev. 16:8-10; Tob. 8:3; 1 Enoch 10:4-5; 4 Macc. 18:8; Mk. 1:13; Mt. 12:43; Lk. 8:29) and God's angels (Gen. 16:7; 21:14-20; 1 Kings 19:4-8; Mk. 1:13), John the Baptist could have expected spiritual

---

[41] Charles, *A Critical and Exegetical Commentary on the Revelation of St. John* (ICC), New York (Charles Scribner's Sons, 1920), i, 128-33.

[42] On these heavenly liturgies, see Leonard Thompson, "Cult and Eschatology in the Revelation of John," *Journal of Religion* 49 (1969), 334-42.

[43] Danielou, *Histoire des doctrines Chrétiennes avant Nicée. . .* , 159.

encounters there. As a desert dweller he was accused of being demon-possessed rather than being an inspired prophet (Mt. 11:9, 18). He prophesied the opening of heaven and the ascent and descent of angels on the Son of Man (Jn. 1:51). Those around John were also cognizant of the closeness and influence of the spirit world. The angel Gabriel was sent to Zechariah and Mary to bring them good news. He was received in fear; it was a duty to believe his words Lk. 1:11-13, 18-20, 26, 30, 34, 38, 45). The subject matter for angelic revelations was eschatological (1:16-17, 33, 68-79).

The guidance of angels is a common motif in the (Jerusalem-) Caesarean source of Acts (8:26; 10:3, 7, 22, 30; 11:13; 12:7-11). Angels sometimes appeared in a vision (10:3; 12:9). They were addressed as "Lord" (10:4, 14; 11; 8). Later, before the capture of Jerusalem during the rebellion against Rome, "all the disciples were warned beforehand by an angel" (Epiphanius, *de Mens.* et *Pond.* 15).

In his important study *Il Simbolismo dei Giudeo-Christiani*, P. E. Testa [44] has uncovered the significance of the mysterious sacred numbers, letters, signs and names in Palestinian funeral inscriptions. They were used as talismans or potent passports for souls during their ascent from the tomb across the cosmic regions to the presence of God. In this mystical journey through the cosmic ladder [45], the soul is enabled to meet different angels in each of the seven heavens. In the second heaven [46] it knows the severity of God against the angels fallen from the fifth; in the fourth it beholds the harmony of the heavenly liturgy; in the sixth it is taught the works of angels for the good government of men; in the seventh it can enjoy the glory of all the angels and all the saints." Angelic soul escorts accompany the souls of the righteous in their ascent of the cosmic ladder, the sole way to reach the regions of light [47].

In the Gospel of Didymus Judas Thomas (88), Jesus says: "The

[44] (Studium Biblicum Franciscanum 14), Jerusalem (Tipografia dei Franciscani, 1962), 84-95, 117ff. Their doctrine of angels and the cosmic scale threatened the Pauline one of Christ's absolute primacy (p. 570).

[45] See Bagatti, *op. cit.*, 230-38, for a summary of literary evidence (T. Levi, 2 Enoch, Asc. Isa, 3 Baruch) and archaeological finds (including angelic names associated with the cosmic ladder). The rosettes on ossuaries probably symbolized angels (pp. 239, 242; cf. 155-56).

[46] A (fiery) hell in heaven appears in 2 Enoch 10; Rev. 12:7-9; 21:8; Apoc. Peter 11 (Akhmim), T. Jacob 153 Arabic. T. Isaac 146-47.

[47] Ignazio Mancini, *Archaeological Discoveries Relative to the Judaeo-Christians*, transl. G. Bushell, Jerusalem (Franciscan Printing Press, 1970), 168; Testa, *op. cit.*, 253-56.

angels come to you, and the prophets, and they shall give you what belongs to you; and you also, give them what is in your hands. . ."

The Ascension of Isaiah refers to the devil as Beliar (2:4; 3:11-13; 4:2; 5:1, 15), "the prince of this world" (1:3; 10:29), "the god of that world" who "will stretch forth his hand against the Son" (9:14; cf. 11:19), and as "the great prince, the king of this world who has ruled it since it came into being," who will descend as Nero and persecute the church (4:2-3). He will be punished together with "his angels, authorities and powers" (1:3; cf. 2:2) when "the Lord will come with his angels and with the hosts of the saints from the seventh heaven . . . and will drag Beliar with his hosts into Gehenna" (4:14; cf. 7:12). "The voice of the Beloved will in wrath rebuke . . . the angels of the sun and of the moon and all things wherein Beliar manifests himself and acts openly in this world" (4:18). Christ will "judge and destroy the prince and his angels and the gods of this world which is ruled by them" (10:12; cf. 11:16). Angels populating each of the seven heavens (10:17-27; 11:25-32) are differentiated from both the angels of death (10:14) and the angels of this firmament, the princes and powers of this world, the angels of the air, or angels of the glory of this world (6:13; 7:2; 10:11; 11:23; 15:30). For, this is an alien (6:9), vain (7:25), corrupted world of flesh and darkness (8:23-27). Christ's descent into this world was concealed from all the angels (9:13-15; 10:11; 11:15, 24, 26). As to the benenevolent spirits, the angelic heavenly liturgy is described in 7:13-10:5; the seer Isaiah himself joined in the chorus of praise (7:37; 8:17; 9:28, 31, 33). Though he was told to worship the angel of the Holy Spirit (9:36; cf. 40; 11:33), he wrongly addressed his companion as "my Lord" (8:4; cf. Dan. 10:16; Rev. 7:14) and was permitted to "worship neither angel nor throne which belongs to the six heavens" (7:21; cf. Apocalypse of Abraham, ch. 17; Shepherd of Hermas, *Sim.* vi, 3.1). Such warnings presuppose abuse by those who venerated angels.

The Testament of our Lord Jesus in Galilee promises "to those who have loved my name more than their own": "I will place them among my angels and they will rejoice for countless millenia" "For they have endured amidst the seductive world and have hated every state of rest" (7). Apocalyptic or eschatological dualism is further illustrated in chapter 4 and 5, where the approaching tempter-Satan-Antichrist, whose voice will be heard by the four quarters of the earth, is luridly described. With the advent of the Lord, "the angels will depart from harvest, rivers, abysses and trees" and the crops will be burned by heat. (4). These seem to be "the angels who are over rivers and sea, and who are over the fruits of the earth, and the angels who are over every grass, giving food to all and every living thing" (2 Enoch 19:4). Their responsibility for preserving order in heaven and on earth may be deduced from chapter 11. Jesus, in describing the "signs and wonders that would happen in heaven and on earth before the end," mentions great stars visible in the daytime, stars falling down like fire, a star appearing in the East like fire, the sun and moon fighting against each other and losing their illumination, continual thunder, lightning and earthquakes, the disappearance of water in the abysses, streams, rivers and seas (4, 11). Their drying up is parallel to the heat's drying of fruits (4), while the breakdown of order in the heavens is apocalyptically parallel to the breakdown in human relations; relatives and neighbors will forsake each other out of hatred and jealousy (11). In the Synoptic Gospels' prophecy of the universe's disintegration, the powers in (Mk. 13:24) or of (Mt. 24:29; Lk. 21:26) the heavens which shall be shaken are cosmic angels.

The Akhmim fragment of the Apocalypse of Peter describes the beauty and glory (7-11; cf. Ethiopic 15) of the faithful and righteous brethren who had departed from the world (3, 5, 13). "The inhabitants of that place were clad with the shining raiment of angels . . . Angels walked there amongst them. All who dwell there had an equal glory, and with one voice they praised God the Lord . . . (who) said unto us, 'This is the place of your high-priests < brothers? >, the righteous men!" (17-20). The righteous on earth, then, aspired to be like angels and to dwell among them. Jesus will give the elect a "portion of righteousness with my holy ones" (Rainer Fragment). At the Judgment "the angels will bring my elect and righteous which are perfect in all righteousness, and shall bear them in their hands and clothe them with the garments of eternal life "(Ethiopic 13). Angels will sit with Christ upon the throne of his glory (Ethiopic 6). Uriel, who has been set over the resurrection of the dead, and Ezrael the angel of wrath, shall cooperate in bringing them forth on Judgment Day, casting sinners into a pit of darkness and the stream of fire, and showing their punishment to their victims and to the righteous (Ethiopic 4, 6, 7, 9, 10, 11, 12). The angel Temlakos cares for slain children (Ethiop. 8; Clement of Alexandria, *Eclog.* 48.1), but the angel Tatirokos intensifies torments (Ethiop. 13). Unnamed angels bring forward sins and prepare a place of punishment (Ethiop. 6), where angels of punishment "kindle upon them the fire of their torment" (Ethiop. 7; Akhmim 23). A spirit of wrath shall chastise them will all manner of torment (Ethiop. 9).

The kinship between stars, angels and the calendar is illustrated in the Book of Elkesai:

> These are evil stars of godlessness ... Beware of the days of their dominion, and do not make a start on your works in their days! Baptize neither man nor woman in the days of their authority, when the moon passes through from them and travels with them. Await the dday when it departs from them, and then baptize and make a beginning with all your works! Moreover, honor the day of the Sabbath, for it is one of these days! But beware also not to begin anything on the third day of the week, for again when three years of the emperor Trajan are complete, ... the war between the godless angels of the north will break out (Hippolytus, *Ref.* 9, 16.2-4; transl. Hennecke-Schneemelcher, II, 750).

Hippolytus charged the Elkesaites with devoting themselves to the tenets of the mathematicians and astrologers (9.14). These calculations applied both to daily lives and the coming of the eschaton. Their baptism (ἐπί τε τῶν στοιχείων ὁμολογία-Theodoret, *Haer. Fab.* ii. 7) "is connected with the Cabbalistic magic, which commands the aid of good angels, and brings evil ones into subjection, which controls the forces of nature, and makes the elements of the world subservient:[48]

> I call to witness the heaven and water and the holy spirits, and the angels of prayer and the oil and the salt and the earth. These seven witnesses I call to witness, that I will sin no more ... (Hippolytus 9.15).

Elkesaite witnesses, according to Epiphanius (19.1.6; cf. 19.6.3; 30.17.4), included the air and winds. The Clementine Letter of Peter to James (4.2 & 4) requires the recipient of secret writings to call to witness heaven, earth, water and air.

The Gospel of Bartholomew (IV, 24-35, 44-47, 52-59) presents a thorough angelology (creation, fall, names, numbers [in the seven heavens and outer firmament] and functions) as revealed to the Apostle by Beliar himself; in turn, his awesome physical appearance is described (IV, 13-14). The narrative framework is of later origin than the angelology. Of special interest are the angels who are set over the four winds (31-34), the sea (35), hail, snow, thunder and lightning (45), as well as "the avenging angels, who stand by God's

---

[48] "Elchasaites", *Dictionary of Sects, Heresies, Ecclesiastical Parties & Schools*, ed. John H. Blunt, Philadelphia (J. B. Lippincott, 1874), 142.

throne" (I, 24-27; IV, 29). Chairum "has in his hand a fiery rod, and restrains the great moisture which the wind has, so that the earth should not dry up" (IV, 31), whereas Naoutha "has a rod of ice in his hand and puts it in his mouth, and quenches the fire which comes from his mouth. And if the angel did not quench it at his mouth, it would set the whole world on fire" (IV, 34). "The spirits were made subject to Solomon himself" (IV, 21).

In the Narrative of Zosimus we learn that "an angel of the Lord was sent saying to him, Zosimus, man of God, behold I am sent by the Most High, the God of all, to tell thee that thou shalt journey to the blessed, but shalt not dwell with them" (1; cf. 5, 20). Later an angel of God came and said, "Behold, Satan is coming to tempt thee, but the Lord will fight for thee, for the glory of thy faith must bind Satan" (18). "When the angels of God ascended, the Devil came, having a fierce shape, and possessed with anger and gall" and promised to destroy him and all who received God's commandment, "so that they may not be without sin ... Saying these things the Devil departed from me, and after eight days he brought with him one thousand three hundred and sixty demons ... and they beat me, tossed me about between them, for forty days" (19-20). But Zosimus through prayer vanquished the Devil. Before his temptation, Zosimus had "spent the night with the angels of God" (18). Allegedly, "the angels of God dwell with us [the children of Rechab] every day, and tell us all things concerning you (who are there in the world), and we rejoice with the angels over the works of the just, but over the works of the sinners we mourn and lament" (11). "Men of righteousness ... are brothers of the holy angels" (16). The angels taking up the soul of the deceased " sing a song and hymn, making melody to God ... When the angels sing above, we being below listen to them, and again we sing and they listen in heavens above, and thus between us and the angels there arises a giving of praise in hymns" (15).

According to the Apostolic Tradition of Hippolytus,[49] it is necessary for all believers, after washing their hands, to rise and pray at midnight, "because in this hour every creature hushes for a brief moment to praise the Lord; stars and plants and waters stand still [in that instant]; all the hosts of the angels minister [ing] unto Him together with the souls of the righteous praise God."

---

[49] Ed. Dix, pp. 65-67; "the tradition of the elders" is explicitly cited. Joseph narrates that nature stood still at the birth of Jesus in a gloss on the Book of James 18:2 (see Hennecke-Schneemelcher, op.cit. i, 372.

Jeremiah" prophesied (4 Baruch 9:14) that the Son of God would make the unfruitful trees of Paradise to bear fruit, and "the fruit will remain (μενει) with the angels."

Irenaeus (*Adv. Haer.* ii, 32. 4-5) explained that visions, prophetic sayings and foreknowledge of the future were wonders performed in the church "not by invocation of angels or incantations or other deprived methods of magic," but rather by "directing prayers cleanly, purely and openly to the Lord ... and also invoking the name of our Lord Jesus Christ." Celsus brought these accusations against the Jews: they "worship the heaven and the angels who dwell therein" (*Contra Cels.* v. 6 & 8) "They worship angels and are addicted to sorcery, in which Moses was their instructor" (i. 26). Stephen (Acts 7:42-43) accused the Jews of worshipping the host of heaven. Preaching of Peter (*ap.* Clement of Alexandria, *Strom.* vi, 5, 41; Origen, *On John* xiii. 17) proclaimed that we do not worship God as do the Jews, who serve angels and archangels. On the other hand, according to Justin (*Apol.* i, 6), "we worship and adore the good angels."

Angelolatry survived in parts of Asia Minor until at least the fourth century. The Council of Laodicea (canon 35) decreed:

> It is not right for Christians to abandon the Christ of God and go away and invoke (ὀνομάζειν) angels and hold conventicles; for these are forbidden. If therefore any one is found devoting himself to this secret idolatry, let him be anathema, because he abandoned our Lord Jesus Christ and went after idolatry.

As Jesus is given the name of Christ and Lord (Rom. 15:20; 2 Tim. 2:19), and since all the angelic powers are given names (Eph. 1:21), it is reasonable to infer that ὀνομάζειν signifies both the identification and invocation of angels. Their adoration and service at the expense of Christ was seen as a violation of the first two commandments of the Decalogue. Theodoret of Cyrus, commenting on Col. 2:18,[50] noted that this Council forbade "praying (προσεύχεσθαι) to the angels" and that oratories of Michael were still to be found in Phrygia and Pisidia. The next canon (36) condemns clergy who are "magicians or enchanters or mathematicians or astrologers" or who make amulets. Evidently they controlled demons and prepared calendars and horoscopes.

The hermit Archippos of Hierapolis, after fasting ten days, received this revelation in a place of prayer consecrated to Michael:

---

[50] Migne, *P.G.* 82, 613; cf. 620 (in Col. 3:17).

I am Michael, the ἀρχιστρατηγός of the power of God ... Every illness
will be healed in this sanctuary, and whoever turns to God and his
ἀρχιστρατηγός Michael and invokes their names, will be content with my
power and the grace of God.[51]

According to the Paris graec. 364 manuscript,[52] those who declared
Melchizedek was God practiced divination and magic and knew the
names of such evil demons as Saron, Sechan and Ache. They believed
that human lives were subjected not only to the influence of demons
but also of stars. Their astrological beliefs are described in the
manuscript. Commodian (*Carmen Apologeticum* 954) told of a holy
people upon whom the stars (γένεσις) exercised no evil influence
(*impia vires*). The Clementine Recognitions (ix, 19; cf. viii.48)
described a chaste far eastern people, the Seres, whom the
conjunction of planets did not compel to adultery and murder and
whose liberty of will was not compelled by the configuation of
γένεσις. It was from a man of Seres in Parthia that Elkesai had
received his book of revelations (Hippolytus, *Philos* 9.13.1).

In the Testament of Solomon (cf. Wisdom 7:17-21; Josephus,
Antiquities viii, 2.5) we read the repeated question of Solomon, "Tell
me, o demon, to what zodiacal sign thou art subject" (ii, 2)[53].
Demons live on a star (v, 4; vi, 7; vii, 6) or in a phase of the moon (iv,
9). A female demon reveals one of her secrets: "Oftentimes ... do I
consort with men in the semblance of a woman, and above all with
those of a dark skin. For they share my star with me; since they it is
who privily or openly worship my star" (iv, 6).[54] Seven beautiful, evil
female spirits (deception, strife, jealousy, error, etc.) identify
themselves thus: "We are of the 33 elements of the cosmic ruler of
darkness (στοιχεῖα κοσμοκράτορες τοῦ σκότους) ... Our stars are in
heaven ... And we are called, as it were, goddesses (θεοί)" (viii, 2.4).[55]
Thirty six spirits or decani (δέκανος) also reveal their identity: "We
are the 36 elements, the world rulers of this darkness (στοιχεῖα οἱ
κοσμοκράτορες τοῦ σκότους [τοῦ αἰῶνος] τούτου" (xviii, 2).[56] Each does a
different kind of harm to men. The first of the 36 said: "I am the first
δέκανος of the zodiacal circle and am called Ram" (xvii, 4).[57] Kronos-

[51] James, *art. cit.*, *ap.* Batiffol, *op. cit.*, i, 32-33.
[52] Bardy, *art. cit.*, *RB* 36 (1927), 38, 39.
[53] Transl. from Conybeare, *art. cit.*, *JQR* 11 (1898), par. 10.
[54] *Ibid.*, 16-17.
[55] *Ibid.*, 34.
[56] *Ibid.*, 73.
[57] *Ibid.*, 72.

Enepsigos has her abode in the moon and for that reason has three forms. Their measure (μέτρον) of the στοιχεῖα is inexplicable and undefinable (xv, 5).[58] These references indicate that the στοιχεῖα or κοσμοκράτορες were demonic powers having stars and zodiacal signs in heaven; both the demon and the associated star might be worshipped. These spirits rule this lower world as στοιχεῖα or elements. Demons could fall from heaven like stars and lightning (cf. Isa. 14:12; Lk. 10:18) at night and set cities and fields afire (T. Solomon xx, 16-17). Chester C. McCown [59] in his study of the Testament deduced:

> It would seem that astrological influences are operative, not of themselves, but through the demons that "dwell" in each star or sign. In other words, the astral deities of paganism have become demons . . . The author seems to think of the influence of the stars as wholly baleful.

In Jewish angelology prophets (2 Chron. 36:15-16; Isa. 44:26; Haggai 1:12-13; cf. Justin, *Dial.* 75),[60] priests (Malachi 2:7), kings (2 Sam. 14:17, 20; 19:27; Zech. 12:8), patriarchs (Prayer of Joseph, *ap.* Origen, *Comm. in Jn.* ii, 31), Moses (Assumption of Moses 11:17; 12:5-6; cf. 3:13; "mediator") and the son prophesied in Isa. 9:6 (LXX: "angel of great counsel") could be referred to as *"malak"* or *"ἄγγελος."*[61] As mediators between God and the people,[62] the leaders of Israel could be likened to angels because God worked through them. In 1 Enoch the righteous are compared to angels. "These are the names of the holy who dwell on earth and believe in the name of the Lord of Spirits for ever and ever," explained an angel to the visionary who had seen the parable of lightnings and stars called by name (43:4). To the righteous it is promised: "You shall shine as the lights of heaven . . . and the portal of heaven shall be opened to you . . . You shall have great joy as angels of heaven . . . You shall become companions of the hosts of heaven" (104:2, 4, 6; cf. 39:6-7; Dan. 12:3; Mt. 13:43; 22:30). Righteous angels themselves exemplify legal

---

[58] *Ibid.*, 64.

[59] *Op. cit.*, 46.

[60] Including John the Baptist (Mt. 11:10; Mk. 1:2; Lk. 7:27).

[61] Davies, *art. cit.*, HTR 47 (1954), 138-39; Michl, *art. cit.*, *Reallexicon f. Ant. u. Chr.*, v(1962), 73; cf. 74.

[62] Paul Billerbeck, *Die Briefe des Neuen Testaments und die Offenbarung Johannis Erläutet aus Talmud und Midrasch*, München (C. H. Beck, 1926), 673 (vol. 3 of Strack-Billerbeck); Mowinckel, *He that Cometh*, transl. G. W. Anderson, New York and Ashville (Abingdon, 1954), 318.

sanctity. For, "all the angels of the presence and all the angels of sanctification" have been created circumcised (Jub. 15:26-27) and they keep the sabbath (Jub. 2:18). The feast of weeks "was celebrated in heaven from the day of creation till the days of Noah" (Jub. 6:17-18). Levites approach the Lord "to serve in His sanctuary as the angels of the presence and as the holy ones" (Jub. 31:14). The kinship of the worlds of the angels and the saints is described in the Testament of Isaac: humans' "angelic service is the type (τύπος) that they shall perform in the heavens. And the angels shall be their companions because of their perfect faith and their purity." [63] This service consists of priestly offerings and sacrifices. Reference is made to the angel liturgy.[64] "All the heavenly ones sang a hymn, crying out and saying: 'Holy, holy, holy, Lord Sabaoth; heaven and earth are full of thy holy glory.'"[65] At sunset all the angels worship God (T. Abraham 4, shorter). The angelic singing of praises to God is mentioned also in 1 Enoch 40:3-10; T. Levi 3:5-8 (by θρόνοι and ἐξουσίαι); Apoc. Abr., ch. 17; Apoc. Sophonias (ap. Clement of Alex., Strom. v, 11.77); Apoc. Moses 7:2; 17:1; 22:3; Vita Adae 28:2; 2 Enoch 17; 19:6). According to the Apocalypse of Adam quoted by George Cedrenus Chronicle; Migne, P.G. 121, 41),[66]

> Adam in the 600th year, having repented, learned by revelation ... concerning the prayers that are sent up to God by all the creatures at every hour of the day and night, by the hand of Uriel, the angel that is over repentance ... In the second hour is the prayer of angels ... in the sixth the assembly of angels ... in the seventh the entering in of angels to God and their going out, in the eighth the praise and sacrifice of angels.

Job's three daughters sang angelic hymns and praises to God in the voice of angels, i.e. in the dialects of the archontes and the cherubim (T. Job 48.2—51.1). With timbrel and song they blessed holy angels and glorified God in the holy dialect (T. Job xii, 3, 6-7; cf. the angelic hymns of 48.3). Tobit said: "Blessed is God ... and blessed are all his holy angels" (Tob. 11:14).

The mediation of angels between man and God was a widespread

---

[63] Coptic 66; cf. Arabic 145-46.

[64] Arabic 149-50.

[65] Coptic 73.

[66] James, Lost Apocrypha of the O.T.., 2; cf. Ernest Renan, "Fragments du livre gnostique," Journal Asiatique v-2 (1853), 452-54; James, Apocrypha Anecdota (Texts & Studies ii-3, 1893), 139-40; Michael Kmosko, "Testamentum Patris Nostri Adam," Patrologia Syriaca, ed. R. Graffin, Paris (Firmon-Didot), i-2 (1907), 1319-37.

belief.[67] Presumably this intercession was possible because they were sinless beings.[68] To the holy ones of heaven "the souls of men make their suit, saying, 'Bring our cause before the Most High'" (1 Enoch 9:3). Michael, who "holds the keys of the Kingdom of heaven," "comes down to receive the prayers of men" (3 Baruch 11:2, 4) and "presents the merits of men to God" (3 Baruch 11:9; 14:2; cf. ch. 12). According to Tobit 12:12, 15, the archangel Raphael is one of the seven who offer to the Lord the prayers of the saints. In the T. of Levi (5:5, 7) the Patriarch asks the name of the angel whom he has met on his ascent to heaven in order to be able to call upon him in the day of tribulation; for he is "the angel who intercedes for the nation of Israel and all the righteous." Dan urged his children: "Draw near unto God and to the angel that intercedeth for you, for he is a mediator (μεσίτης) between God and man" (T. Dan 6:2).[69] In the sixth heaven" are the archangels, who minister and make propitiation to the Lord for all the sins of ignorance of the righteous" (T. Levi 3:5). Enoch learned that it is the role of Gabriel to "(pray) and (intercede) for those who dwell on the earth and (supplicate) in the name of the Lord of the Lord of Spirits" (1 Enoch 40:6, 9). Michael and Raphael may seek to intercede when God's judgment is severe (1 Enoch 68:2-4). Less specifically, Enoch had another vision in which the righteous angels "petitioned and interceded and prayed for the children of men" (1 En. 39:5; cf. 47:2; 99:3). All the angels made supplication on behalf of Adam for his pardon (Apoc. Mos. 29:2; 33:5-6; 35:2; Vita Adae 9:3).

In Joseph and Aseneth the archangel Michael, after eating a piece, gives to Aseneth the heavenly honeycomb (the bread of life), which "the angels and all the elect of God and all sons of the Most High do eat" (16:14; cf. 19:5). This food of paradise is partaken in a spiritual banquet of men and angels.

According to the Testament of Jacob,[70] "it was his custom (συνήθεια) daily to speak with angels," While he was "making his

---

[67] Bibliographies in Charles, *Apocrypha and Pseudepigrapha of the O.T.*, ii, 531-532; Pfeiffer, *History of New Testament Times*, 282, n. 57; Hans Bietenhaard, *Die Himmlische Welt im Urchristentum und Spätjudentum*, Tübingen (J.C.B. Mohr [Paul Siebeck], 1951), 133-35; Danielou, *The Angels and their Mission*, 78; Michl. *art. cit.*, *Reallexicon f. Ant. u. Chr.*, v(1962), 72-73, 88, Richard N. Longenecker, "Some Distinctive Early Christological Motifs," *NTS* 14 (1967-68), 530-31.

[68] W. O. E. Oesterley, *The Jewish Doctrine of Mediation*, London (Skeffington, 1910), 37-49.

[69] De Jonge, *art. cit.*, *NT* 4(1960), 235, n. 1.

[70] Coptic, 76-77.

prayers unto God day and night, angels came to seek after him, watching over him, saving him, giving him strength in all things." It was likewise customary for Isaac and the holy angels to converse daily (T. Isaac).[71] Abraham, too, was "companion of the holy angels" (T. Abr. 16, longer). The archangel Michael spoke to Seth after he and Eve prayed (Apoc. Moses 13:1-14:1; Vita Adae 41:1-43:2). The powers who supported Eve (Vita Adae 22:1; cf. 33:1; Apoc. Moses 7:2) functioned as guardian angels. An angel of the Lord guided Levi and Judah against Dan (T. Dan 5:4). Raphael was sent to remove the white film from Tobit's eyes "that he might see the light of God with his eyes" (Tob. 3:16). The angel of peace guides the soul of the good man (T. Benj. 6:1) and leads his soul into eternal life when he dies (T. Asher 6:4, 6; T. Abr., *passim*; T. Job xi, 22). Job's throne is among the holy ones (*chasidim*) at the right hand of the Savior in the heavens (T. Job vii, 36-37; cf. x, 19, 21).

Jacob asked that his sons be blessed by the angel that had redeemed him from all tribulations (θλῖψις) (T. Jacob).[72] An angel of God rescued Daniel and his three companions (Dan. 3:25, 28; 6:22). The angel mediating between man and God stands up "for the peace of Israel against the kingdom of the enemy" (T. Dan 6:2). Raphael and the good angels sometimes bind the devil and his cohorts (1 Enoch 10:4, 12; Jub. 10:7, 11; Tobit 8:3; cf. 12:14-15). The belief that good angels frustrate the mischief of evil angels underlies the magic recorded in the Testament of Solomon, which reveals the names and roles of both groups. The demons are frustrated by the names of specific good angels. Angels "explained to Noah all the medicines of their diseases, together with their seductions, how he might heal them with the herbs of the earth. And Noah wrote down all things in a book as we instructed him concerning every kind of medicine. Thus the evil spirits were precluded from (hurting) the sons of Noah" (Jub. 10:12-14). Maurice Jones [73] sagely commented concerning the thought world of Jewish apocalyptic: "The world in which the righteous were subjected to oppression, tyranny and persecution can only be explained as a world under the dominion of evil and in bondage to evil spirits." They corrupt and seduce (Jub. 7:27; 11:4-5), blind, lead astray and destroy (Jub. 10:1, 2, 5, 8) men. Thus Abraham prayed: "Deliver me from the hands of evil spirits

---

[71] Coptic 58; Arabic 140.
[72] Coptic, 81.
[73] *Art. cit., Expositor* viii-15 (1918), 419-20.

who have sway over the thoughts of men's hearts, and let them not lead me astray from Thee, my God" (Jub. 12:20). I Enoch teaches that they lead men astray (69:4-6). The archangel Phanuel, who is in charge of repentance, fends off the satans, "forbidding them to come before the Lord of Spirits to accuse them who dwell on earth" (40:7, 9). However, as God's agents in executing just judgments, the good angels are the ones who record both good deeds and sins in the Book of Life (Ps. 56:8; Dan. 7:10; 1 Enoch 89:62-64, 70; 90:14, 22; 100:10; 104:1, 7; Apoc. of Zephaniah 3:5; 14:1 [74]; 2 Enoch 19:5; Jub. 30:20; cf. 4:5-6; T. Levi 19:3; T. Abr. 12-13, longer; 10 shorter) and punish sinners (1 Enoch 1:9; 48:9; 53:3; 54:6; 56:1; 62:11; 63:1; Apoc. Mos. 27:1-4; 29:1; T.Abr. 12-13, longer; 9 shorter; 4 Baruch 8:9; cf. 4 Esdras 16:67) and evil spirits under Beliar (T. Levi 3:3; 1 Enoch 54:6). Like men, angels bless the righteous and curse sinners (T. Napht. 8:4, 6; cf. Jub. 15:31-32). Fallen angels also punish: "When the soul departeth (life) troubled, it is tormented by the evil spirits which also it served in lust and evil works" (T. Asher 6:5). On Judgment Day spirits of retribution afflict the unrighteous with fire, snow and ice (T. Levi 3:2).

Deception characterizes evil angels. Adam relates: "The hour drew nigh for the angels who were guarding your mother to go up and worship the Lord, and I was far from her, and the enemy knew that she was alone" (Apoc. Mos. 7:2). Eve explained to her children: "And instantly he hung himself from the wall of paradise, and when the angels ascended to worship God, then Satan appeared in the form of an angel and sang hymns like the angels. And I bent over the wall and saw him, like an angel" (Apoc. Mos. 17:1). Later, "Satan transformed himself into the brightness of angels and went away to the River Tigris to Eve, and found her weeping ..." (Vita Adae 9:1); he then induced her to step out of the river and end her penance. In the T. of Abraham (16-17 longer; 13, shorter) the angel of Death, in order to carry out his mission of taking the Patriarch's soul to heaven, appears in the garb of an archangel of light. In the T. of Job Satan disguises himself as a beggar (6:4), a bread seller (23:1-2) and as king of Persia 17:2. *Clem. Hom.* viii. 12-13 grants angels of the lowest heaven an ability to metamorphose themselves into "every nature", including fishes, birds, gold, pearls and purple. A different sort of deception lay in the illegitimate revelation by fallen angels of divine

---

[74] Ed. Steindorff, *op. cit.*, *TU* 17, 3a, 150, 154.

secrets which are harmful to men (1 Enoch 7:1; 8:1-4; 9:6, 8; 10:7;
13:2; 16:3; 64:2; 65:6-10; 67:4; 69:1, 4-14; Apoc. Abr. 13; Clem.
Hom. viii. 14; cf. Jub. 4:15; 8:3). It was Mastema, the Enemy, rather
than God, who tempted Abraham by suggesting the sacrifice of Isaac
(Jub. 17:16; 18:9, 12).

Two account of the fall of angels are presented: the Watchers' lust
for beautiful women (1 Enoch 6:1-7:5; 12:4ff.; 15:9; 19:1; 69:4-5;
106:13-14; Jub. 4:22; 5:1; 7:21; 10:5-11; T. Reub. 5:5-7; T. Napht.
3:5; Clem. Rec. i. 29; *Hom.* vii, 12-15), and the angels' jealousy when
Michael made them worship Adam (Vita Adae 12:1-16:4; cf. 2 Enoch
29:4-5 A). Their chief is usually designated by the name of Beliar (T.
Sim. 5:3; T. Levi 3:3; 18:12; 19:1; T. Issach. 6:1; 7:7; T. Dan 5:1; T.
Napht. 3:1; T. Benj. 3:4; 6:1; Jub. 1:20; 15:33; Lives of the Prophets,
Daniel & Nathan), who is otherwise referred to as the prince of the
Mastema [75] (Jub. 18:9, 12; 48:9, 12, 15; cf. 17:16; 48:2), the prince of
deceit (T. Jud. 19:4; T. Sim. 2:7), **Satan**, the prince of the spirits of
wickedness (T. Dan 5:6; T. Asher 6:4) and the devil (e.g. T. Napht.
8:4). Under him are the chiefs of tens, fifties and hundreds, many of
whose names are revealed (1 Enoch 6:7-8; 69:2ff.). The T. of Reuben
(2:1-2; 3:2-8) describes the eight spirits of deceit or error which
afflict, especially, the minds of young men. Sometimes the heavenly
angels with whom the demons associate amidst the stars are simply
called, "ἀρχαὶ καὶ ἐξουσίαι καὶ δύναμεις," as in the T. of Solomon (xx,
12-15; cf. 1 Enoch 61:10), though this work is a storehouse of
esoteric names which are useful in magic. On the other hand, 2
Enoch, which divides "all the heavenly hosts" into ten ranks (20:3),
locates the lordships (κυριώτετες), principalities (ἀρχαί) and powers
εξουσίαι) in the seventh heaven, along with the great archangels,
incorporeal powers, cherubim, seraphim and thrones (xx, 1). [76]

The Jewish roots [77] of angelic cosmology are traceable to Psalm
104:4: the Lord God "makes his angels into winds, his ministers into
a flaming fire." The horses and chariots of fire and the whirlwind
which carried Elijah into heaven (2 Kings 2:11; cf. 6:17) functioned
as angels. Their fiery nature is taught in 2 Enoch 29:1; Dan. 7:10.
The thunder, lightning, smoke, fire and clouds which accompanied

[75] Yadin, *op. cit.*, 233-34.

[76] Charles. *The Book of the Secrets of Enoch*, 25.

[77] Otto Everling, *Die Paulinische Angelologie und Dämonologie*, Göttingen, 1888,
passim, especially 71-73; Wilhelm Lueken, *Der Erzengel Michael in der Überlieferung
des Judentums*, Marburg, 1898, 6-7, 52-56. Bietenhard, *op. cit.*, 101ff.; Vanhoye,
op.cit., 171-75.

the giving of the Law of Moses (Exod. 3:2; 19:9, 16-19; 20:18; Deut. 4:11-15; 5:22-26; Hebr. 1:7) could be seen as manifestations of the presence of angels at Sinai. These natural phenomena also accompany the Lord's theophany as Judge (Pss. 18:10-16; 97:2-5; Habak. 3:3-5, 14-15) or in a storm (Pss. 29:3-9; cf. 77:16-20). Fire, water, earth, the sun, moon and stars are worthy of honor, but are not to be called "god," who has made everything (Apoc. Abr. 7). Jubilees 2:2 teaches:

> On the first day He created the heavens which are above and the earth and the waters and all the spirits which serve before Him- the angels of the presence, and the angels of sanctification, and the angels [of the spirit of fire and the angels] of the spirit of the winds, and the angels of the spirit of the clouds, and of the darkness, and of the snow and of hail and of hoar frost, and the angels of the voices and of the thunder and of the lightning, and of the angels of cold and of heat, and of winter and of spring and of autumn and of summer. . .

1 Enoch 60:12-21 describes the operations of some of these natural phenomena. Thus, "the spirit of the hoar-frost is his own angel, and the spirit of the hail is a good angel . . . And when the spirit of the rain goes forth from its chamber, the angels come and open the chamber and lead it out" (vv. 17, 21; cf. 2 Enoch 5:1-2). The spirit enforces the pause between the lightning and thunder (v. 15). Enoch saw "lightnings and the stars of heaven . . . and their revolution according to the number of the angels, and (how) they keep faith with each other"; the Lord of the Spirits "called them all by their names and they hearkened unto Him" (1 Enoch 43:1-2). Angels prepare the sun for daybreak and draw it around (3 Baruch 6:16; 7:4); four angels take the crown of the sun and bear it up to heaven and renew it (3 Baruch 8:4). Angels also pull the chariot of the moon (3 Baruch 9:2-4). The relations between the sun, moon, stars, the flying elements of the sun (Phoenixes and Chalcydri), angels and the calendar are explained in great detail in 2 Enoch 4:1-2; 11:1-16:8; 19:1-6; 23:1; 30:14; 48:1-4; the twelve signs of the zodiac appear in 21:6, 30:6. Elemental angels are described also in 3 Enoch 14:3-4 (ed. Odeberg, p. 37)

From 2 Enoch we learn that God planned to lay the foundations (24:5). He commanded light above the Throne to be the foundation for things on high (25:4-5), and He commanded angels to be foundation for things below (26:3). 1 Enoch mentions the foundation of the heaven before setting forth and angelic meteorology (60:11ff.).

Hermas in a Vision (iii, 13.3) beheld a young woman sitting on a
stool. "That means her position is one of strength, for, just as a seat
stands firmly on four feet, so the earth is maintained by means of
four στοιχεῖα.

The angels or powers which rule over natural phenomena and
bodies are truly personified powers. The spirits of the water and of
the winds "give thanks before the Lord of Spirits, and glorify (Him)
with all their power" (1 Enoch 69:22, 24). The Lord set the angel
Uriel over the host (i.e. all the luminaries) of heaven. Names are
given to the leaders of the orders of the stars and leaders who divide
the seasons, the months and the days (1 En. 75, 82; cf. 61:10). The
stars and luminaries "proceed before the face of the holy ones" (1
Enoch 71:4). But for transgressing the commandment of the Lord
seven stars were bound together in "the prison of the angels" (1 En.
21). On the other hand, spirits in the lowest heaven are to inflict
retributions of fire, snow and ice on the unrighteous on the Day of
Judgment (Test. Levi 3:1-2). On the positive side, Judah relates to his
children: "The Lord blessed Levi, and the Angel of the Presence, me;
the powers of glory, Simeon; the heaven, Reuben; the earth, Issachar;
the sea, Zebulon; the mountains, Joseph; the tabernacle, Benjamin;
the luminaries, Dan; Eden, Naphtali; the sun, Gad; the moon, Asher"
(Test. Jud. 25:2). The belief in blessings by cosmic angels is recorded
in an inscription found on a wall of the theatre of Miletus; the seven
unnamed archangels presiding over the seven planets are invoked to
protect (φυλάσσεται) the city.[78] Such intercession could also be
personal. For, Eve begged the luminaries of heaven to bear her
message to Adam (Vita Adae 19:3; cf. 43:2), and the sun and moon
fell down and prayed on behalf of Adam (Apoc. Mos. 35-37). The
visionary's ascent to heaven could even by guided by natural forces.
In the words of 1 Enoch 14:8, "And the vision was shown to me thus:
Behold in the vision clouds invited me and a mist summoned me,
and the course of the stars and the lightnings sped and (hastened) me,
and the winds in the vision caused me to fly and lifted me upward,
and bore me into heaven."

The Testament of Adam (iv) [79] teaches the nature, attributes and
offices of the various orders of heavenly beings. For example, the

---

[78] William Ramsay, *The Church in the Roman Empire before A.D. 170*, London
(Hodder & Stoughton, 1893), 480.

[79] Renan, *art. cit., Journal Asiatique* v-2 (1853), 458-60; Kmosko, *art. cit., Patrologia
Syriaca* i-2 (1907), 1353-60.

principalities control weather, the powers govern the sun, moon and stars; thrones are placed at the entrance of the holy of holies.

Masashi Takahashi [80] points out that in the Old Testament angels are called "sons of God" (Gen. 6:2, 4; Job 1:6; 2:1; 38:7; Ps. 89:6; Dan. 3:25), gods (Ps. 82:1, 6, 97:7; 138:1; Dan 2:11; 11:36), "holy ones" (Ps. 89:5, 7), "the congregation (of divine counsel) of God" (Job 15:8; Ps. 82:1; 89:7; Jer. 23:18, 22).

In the Qumran documents angels are referred to as "sons of heaven" (1QS 4.22; 11.8; 1QH 3.22; cf. 1 Enoch 6:2), "the heavenly host" (1 QH 3.35; cf. 11.13), "the valiant ones" (1QH 8.11; 10.34; cf. 3.35-36), "some of gods" (1QH fr. 2.3), "the holy ones" (1QH 3.22; 4.25; 10.35; 11.12; CD 20.8; 1QSb 3.26; 4:1; 4 Q Flor. 5; 1QS 11.8),[81] "the holy ones of God . . . in the midst of gods" (11 Q Melch 9-10) and "gods (elim) (1QM 1.10-11; 14.15-16; 15.14).[82] As head of the celestial hierarchy God is addressed as "Prince of the gods and King of the venerated beings, and Lord of every spirit and Master of all creatures" (1QH 10, 8). The archangels named in the War Scroll (9.15-16; 17.6-7) are Michael (the might ministering angel), Gabriel, Sariel and Raphael.[83] No name [84] ostensibly is given to the Prince of Lights (urim), who aided Moses and Aaron (CD 5.18); as the Spirit of truth and of light, he has dominion over the righteous, who walk in the ways of light, and over all the spirits of truth (1QS 3.18-20; 1QM 13.9-10). He has helped the sons of light (1QS 3.24-25). Presumably he establishes righteousness in Israel by teaching truth (i.e.Law). Light is coupled with the divine law in Pss. 43:3; 119:105; Prov. 6:23; Isa. 51:4. It belongs to the Spirit of light "to enlighten the heart of man, and to level before him the ways of true righteousness, and to set fear in his heart of the judgment of God" (1QS 4.2-3). "The spirit of truth . . . angel of truth will help all the children of light from the power of Belial" (4Q 177, 1.12-13). The Liturgy of the Sabbath Offering from the Fourth Cave is especially rich in angelic titles and group names, many of which, as J. Strugnell [85] points out, were derived by minute angelological exegesis of Biblical texts.

---

[80] "An Oriental's Approach to the Problems of Angelology," *Zeitschrift für die Alttestamentliche Wissenschaft* 78 (1966), 345. See also Robert North, "Separated Spiritual Substances in the Old Testament," *CBQ* 29 (1967), 124, n. 40.

[81] Nötscher, *art. cit., RQ* 2 (1959-60), 322-25.

[82] Yadin, *art. cit., Scripta Hierosolymitana* 4 (1958;, 47-48; Ringgren, *op. cit.*, 83-84.

[83] On their names see Yadin, *op. cit.*, 237-40.

[84] *Ibid.*, 235-36.

[85] *Art. cit., Congress Volume,* Oxford (1959), 320-21, 330-34.

In this "Angelic Liturgy", for every Sabbath of the sect's calendar year there is a "song of Sabbath sacrifice" [86] in which all the angels under their various names are exhorted to praise God in their special ways.

> The seventh among the chief princes will bless in the name of His holiness all the holy ones among those who establish knowledge with seven words of His wondrous holiness, and will bless all those who exalt His judgments with seven words of wonder ... And all the wondrous chief princes will bless the God of the godly ones (*elim*) ... (4Q S1 39 L1 21-28).[87]

N. Kehl [88] supposes that "the *maskil*, who invokes the angels to begin to sing the hymns,... leads an earthly liturgy in which the angels participate and in which the whole community is translated into the presence of angels." Strugnell writes:[89]

> After the standard exordium of a *syr*, the exhortation of the angels to praise God with all conceivable types of praise, and introduced by a transition such as 'Thus laud all the foundations of the Holy of Holies, and the columns which support the heights of the heaven sing',-comes a description of the heavenly temple. This is ... a description of the heavens incidental to a description of the liturgy performed by the angels in various parts of heaven.

An illuminating parallel is found in the Samaritan Memar Marquah(iv. 1):[90]

> The forces of the unseen were linked together, ten of them-the great glory, the angels, the light, the darkness, the wind, the fire, the foundations, the two luminaries and the stars- all these magnifying him... The foundations (*yasad*) sinking down before him.

That these foundations are divine beings or angels is apparent also from 4 Q S1 39 and 40, line 17, where it is stated that (the fourth) "among the chief princes ... shall bless the foundations [or founders, establishers] of majesty with seven words of wonder, and he shall bless all the godly ones (*elim*) who exalt His faithful knowledge." From these passages we may conclude that their role is to uphold the

---

[86] *Ibid.*, 320.

[87] *Ibid.*, 323.

[88] "Erniedrigung und Erhöhung in Qumran und Kolossä, "*Zeitschrift fur Katholische Theologie* 91 (1969), 389.

[89] *Art. cit., Congress Volume, Oxford (1959)*, 335-36.

[90] John Macdonald, *Memar Marquah*, Berlin (Alfred Toepelmann, 1963), ii, 138. These were seen by Moses, "to whom his Lord revealed what He had never before revealed to anyone" (*ibid.*, 135).

heavens, i.e. the realm of holiness;[91] they serve God by so doing and by their liturgy of praise. The foundations of the earth are mentioned in 1QH 3.30-31; they will be consumed in the universal confligation, like the στοιχεῖα in 2 Pet. 3:10.

That the "Angelic Liturgy" from Cave 4 pertains to worship within the Qumran community in which angels are asked to participate, may be deduced from references in other documents. "Praise be to all His holy angels ... His holy angels are found in your congregation" (11Q Ber 4-5, 14).[92] Physically handicapped persons were not allowed entrance "to take their place in the midst of the Congregation of men of reknown, for the Angels of holiness are [in] their Congregation" (1QSa II, 8-9; cf.1QM 7.6; 4Q Flor. 3-5). To those whom He has chosen God "has granted a share in the lot of the Holy Ones, and has united their assembly, the Council of the Community, with the Sons of Heaven. And the assembly of the holy Fabric shall belong to an eternal planting for all time to come" (1QS 11.7-9; cf.8.5). Three hymns express this kinship of men and angels:

> I knew there was hope for him whom Thou hast shaped from the dust for the everlasting assembly. Thou has cleansed the perverse spirit from great sin that he might watch with the army of the Saints and enter into communion with the congregation of the Sons of Heaven.And Thou has cast an everlasting destiny for man in the company of the Spirits of Knowledge, that he might praise Thy Name in joy [full] concord and recount Thy marvels before all Thy works (IQH 3.20-23).[93]

> And Thou hast cleansed man of sin because of Thy glory that he may be made holy for Thee..., that he may be joined wi[th] Thy sons of truth and with the lot of Thy Saints; that this vermin that is man may be raised from the dust to [Thy] secret [of truth] and from the spirit of perversity to [Thine] understanding; and that he may watch before Thee with the everlasting host and together with [Thy] spirits [of holiness], that he may be renewed ...with them that know, in a common rejoicing (1QH 11.10-14; cf. 4:24-25; 1QM 12.1-8).

> And all the nations shall know Thy truth and all the peoples, Thy glory. For Thou has caused [them] to enter Thy [glo]rious [Covenant] with all the men of Thy counsel and into a common lot with the Angels of the Face (1QH 6.12-13).

---

[91] According to 1 Enoch 18:2-3 the winds stretching out the vaults of heaven are the pillars (κίονες στῆλαι) of heaven. See Delcor, art. cit., RQ 5 (1965-66), 524.

[92] A. S. van der Woude, "Ein neuer Segensspruch aus Qumran (11Q Ber)" in Bibel und Qumran, ed. S. Wagner, 253, 255.

[93] Jean De Caevel, "La connaissance religieuse dans les hymnes d'action de grâces de Qumran," Ephemerides Theologicae Lovanienses 38 (1962), 458. On the communion with angels see Peter von der Osten-Sacken, Gott und Belial, Göttingen (Vandenhoeck & Ruprecht, 1969), 222-32.

"The just will comprehend the Knowledge of the Most High, and the perfect of way will have understanding of the wisdom of the Sons of Heaven. For God has chosen them for an everlasting Covenant" (1QS 4.22). The priests of the Congregation are blessed through the promise of likeness to angels:

> Thou shalt be as an angel of the Face in the dwelling place of holiness for the glory of Elohim of ho[sts . . . and thou shalt] be in the company of God, ministering in the royal palace and decreeing fate in the company of the Angels of the Face . . . And may He make of thee an object of holin[ess] in the midst of His people and a torch [. . . to shine] upon the world in Knowledge and to enlighten the face of many (1QSb 4.25-27; cf. 3.25-28).

Likeness to the angels in knowledge probably was thought to be derived from intimate relations with "the knowers" (1QH 11.14), "the spirts of knowledge" (1QH 3.23). The War Scroll (10.10-11) asks rhetorically: "Who is like . . . the people of the saints of the Covenant and of those who are learned in the Precept, and of those with intelligent under [standing. . .] who hear the voice of the venerated (Being) and see the angels of holiness; and of those whose ear is opened and who hear profound things?" It is a divinely appointed function of "the host of knowledge to recount . . . the true precepts unto him that is born [of woman] "(1QH 18.23).[94] There is no intermediary or interpreter (*melis*)[95] between men and the Angels of the Face (1QH 6.13). But angels bring prayers to God, according to Fragment 19 of Cave 1.

The birth of Noah to elderly parents is described in the Genesis Apocryphon. Lamech laments: "I thought in my heart that the conception was from the Watcher, and that from the holy ones was the [. . .] and that to the Giants [. . .]" (2.1). He is reassured by his wife, however, that Noah arose "neither from any of the Watchers nor from any of the sons of Heav[en]" (2.16). "This seed is truly from thee and this conception. . . This childbearing is truly from thee" (2:15-16). It was taken for granted that conception could arise through the agency of either men or angels; in the latter case the analogy of the birth of giants was in the author's mind. According to the Hebrew Book of Noah, "he was not like a son of man . . . but (like) the glorious ones." He illumined the rooms of the house "like rays of sun" (1Q19.3). His glory is described in song (1Q19.13-14).

[94] De Caevel, *art cit.*, *Eph. Theol. Lov.* 38 (1962), 446-48.
[95] Ringgren, *op. cit.*, 86-87.

Unpublished fragments from Cave 4 [96] gives the baby's weight and narrate his precocious behavior. There is an evident kinship of these Qumran fragments with the "Book of Noah" mentioned in Jub. 10:13 and partially preserved in 1 Enoch 106. Here Lamech says to Methuselah: "I have begotten a strange son, diverse from and unlike a man, and resembling the sons of God in heaven; and his nature is different and he is not like us ... It seems to me that he is not sprung from me but from the angels" (106:5-6; cf. 10, 12). Yet the fact that again Lamech is said to be the real father demonstrates the potential closeness of the human and angelic worlds.

On the negative side, a basic assumption of the Community was that their age was one of wickedness (CD 15.7; 1Q p Hab 5.7-8). The world "has defiled itself in the ways of wickedness under the dominion of [the Spirit of] perversity until the time of final Judgement" (1QSa 4.19-20)

> All dominion over the sons of perversity is in the hand of the Angel of darkness; they walk in the ways of darkness. And because of the Angel of darkness all the sons of righteousness go astray; and all their sin and iniquities ... are because of his dominion...And all the blows that smite them ... are because of the dominion of his malevolence. And all the spirits of his lot cause the sons of light to stumble (1QSa 3.20-24; cf. 4.9-11)

"All the spirits of his lot are angels of destruction; they walk in decrees of darkness and their [de] sire tends towards darkness in one movement" (1QM 13.11-12). Elsewhere (1 QM 15.14; 1 QH fr.v. 4 & 6) they are called the "spirits of wickedness" or "spirits of error." Their ruler, the Angel of hostility, is named Belial (1QM 13.11; cf. 1QSa 1.18, 23-24; 2.5; CD 4.13-18; 5.18; 8.2; 1 QH 3.28-32, etc.)[97] or Satan (11QPsa Plea. 15). Persons who are "governed by the spirits of Belial" are apt to utter words of rebellion (CD 12.2-3.). Eschatological divine punishment will be inflicted by the hand of Belial (CD 8.2-3) and the fiery angels of destruction acting as agents of God's wrathful judgment (CD 2.5-6; 1 QS 4.11-13; 4Q 185.8-9). While the Watchers fell because of stubbornness and disobedience (CD 2.18; cf. 4Q 180; 4Q 181), Belial was created by God for the Pit (1 QM 13.10-11). God made the Spirits of light and of darkness and founded every work upon them (1 QSa 4.25; 1QH 1.8-9). His rebellion is not alluded to.

---

[96] Milik, op. cit., 35; J. A. Fitzmyer, "4Q Mess ar. The Aramaic 'Elect of God' Text," CBQ 27 (1965), 371.

[97] Von der Osten-Sacken, op. cit., 73-78.

The Qumran community was naturally interested in escaping domination by the Angel of hostility. He was expelled by obedience to the Mosaic Law (CD 16.5); but the Spirit of perversity is not banished from all men until Judgment Day (1 QSa 4.20-21).

What will happen "in the time of affliction" (8) is explained by 4Q 177.12-13. "All the children of l[ight] shall be gathered together" in Jerusalem (10-11). "The great hand of God will be with them to help them from all the spirit[s. . .]" (9). His angel of truth will help all the children of Light from the power of Belial" (7) in his anger (4), so that the spirit of truth "might prevail over" Belial (5-6).

Astronomical roles were assigned to angels. In the War Scroll (10.11-12) God is praised for having created the expanse of the heavens, the host of the heavenly luminaries, the duties of the spirits and the spheres of dominion of the holy ones, and the storehouses of water (hail-?) and the clouds. Hymn 1 (lines 9-13) is more explicit:

> It is Thou who hast spread out the heavens for thy glory [and] hast [created] all [their hosts] according to thy will together with the mighty winds according to the laws which governed them before they became [Thine] angels of holi[ness]; and to the everlasting spirits in their dominions [hast Thou entrusted] the heavenly lights according to their mysterious (laws), [the clouds and the rain] according to the office which they fulfill, the thunderbolt and lightnings according to the service appointed to them, and the providential reservoirs according to their functions, [and snow and hailstones] according to their mysterious (laws).

Thus we have angels or spirits of the winds and heavenly lights to whom have been assigned specific dominions and mysterious laws. The angelic rule, like the divine laws, may have extended to the heavenly reservoirs, snow, hail, clouds, thunder and lightning. God has glorious, unchangeable designs and statutes for all things (1QS 3, 15-17). The Decree of time was to be praised in song "when the (heavenly) lights appear from out of the realm of holiness, (and) when they vanish toward the dwelling-place of glory" (1QS 10:1-3).

The recently published Hebrew horoscope (4Q 186)[98] assumes that body and soul are influenced by signs of the zodiac. The spirit of one born under Taurus (the second sign of the zodiac) "has six (parts)

---

[98] John M. Allegro, "An Astrological Cryptic Document," *Journal of Semitic Studies* 9 (1964), 291-94; Jean Carmignac, "Les Horoscopes de Qumran," *RQ* 5 (1965-66), 199-217; M. Delcor, "Recherches sur un horoscope en langue hébraïque provenant de Qumran," *RQ* 5 (1965-66), 521-42. On zodiacal signs in 1st c. Palestinian Judaism see J. Danielou, *Primitive Christian Symbols*, transl. Donald Attwater, Baltimore (Helicon, 1964), 132-34.

in the House of Light, and three in the House of Darkness" (2.7-8).
The spirit of someone born under another sign has "[ei]ght parts in
the House [of Darkness] and one from the House of Light" (3.5-6).
Moreover, the shapes of the thighs, toes (2.5-6; 3.4-5), head, teeth and
fingers (3.2-3) are determined by the same astronomical
consideraions. If the physical and moral makeup of persons was so
under the control of heavenly bodies, then the angels associated with
them had indirect power over individuals. Another horoscope from
Cave 4 [99] mentions Cancer and Gemini.

Josephus relates that upon final initiation the Essene swore to
preserve exactly as received the names of the angels (*War* ii, 8.7.142).
Dupont-Sommer [100] has commented that "this shows the importance
attached by the sect to the revelation of the names of the Angels, a
revelation which secured for the initiates knowledge of the loftiest
secrets of the divine world." The accurate transmission of Essene
doctrines is included also in the oath "to conceal nothing from the
members of the sect, and to reveal nothing to outsiders" (*War* ii,
8.7.142). The names of angels were among the most closely guarded
secrets. The defiled outsider has no right to such knowledge. He who
accurately invokes the angels by name has a power which could be
misused by the defiled outsider. But, as the Essene's primary oath was
"to practice piety toward the Deity, then to observe justice toward
men" (*War* ii, 8.7.139), it may be deduced that knowledge of the
names of angels aided the devotee's piety and justice; that is, that the
angels were mediators who fostered obedience to the will of God.
The Slavonic translation of the same passage adds a congruous detail:
the initiates took as witnesses to their vows the seraphim and
cherubim watching everywhere and the whole heavenly host. This
role of observing and recording human behavior generally implies
the added role of participating in the judgment of men. It may be
deduced further that, as the names of individual angels were
significant, there was some "division of labor" in the celestial
hierarchy; that is, individual angels had special functions.

It is possible that the special Essene interest in the sun was
associated with γνῶσις concerning the motions of the sun under
angelic impetus. "Their piety towards the Deity takes a particular
form: before sunrise they speak no profane work but recite certain
ancestral prayers to the sun as though entreating it to rise" (*Josephus,*

[99] Milik, *op. cit.*, 42.
[100] *Op. cit.*, 31, n. 2.

War ii, 8.5.128).[101] The Therapeutae also prayed at dawn: for sunlight
and inward illumination (i.e. truth, the heavenly light and keeness of
spiritual vision [ὀχυρία λοψισμός.]) (Philo, *de vita contempl.* 27, 89). R.
Judah (Berakhoth vii. 6) in the middle of the 2nd century said:
"When one pronounces a blessing over the sun, he is (following) a
heterodoxy." Saul Liebermann [102] has considered this a reference to
Essene prayer having to do with the sun. Epiphanius (Haer. 53.2)
related that the Sampsaens, the "sun people" (from *shemesh*, Hebrew
for sun) reverently observed its circuit from east to west. When the
Essenes obeyed the call of nature they squatted and covered their
excreta "so as not to offend the rays of God (τὰς αὐγὰς τοῦ θεοῦ) (*War*
ii, 8.9.148). Possibly for the same reason they did not expose their
private parts when bathing (*War* ii, 8.5.129; 13.161). Although "sun
worship" would be too strong a term to use (cf. Psalm 19:4-6; Ecclus
42:17; Wisdom 16:28; Clement of Alex., *Proph. Eclog.* 56), the
motions of the sun were deemed religiously important and its light
was more associated with the heavenly than the earthly world. A solar
calendar might be expected. M. Delcor thinks that the sun occupied
a central place in the Essenes' daily life because "the postion of the
sun in the zodiac played a great role in deriving (*tirer*) the
horoscopes.[103] Also in his study of a Qumran horoscope he finds
evidence of astrological determinism in Josephus' statement
(*Antiquities* xiii, 5.9.172) that "the sect of Essenes declares that Fate is
the mistress of all things and nothing befalls men unless it be in
accordance with her decree." Martin Rist [104] observes: "According to
astral beliefs, the zodiac with its constellations was a heavenly tablet
or book predetermining the deeds and fate of mankind."

The belief that the Deity "is the cause of no evil" (Philo, *Quod
omnis probus* 84) presupposes a demonology. Their interest in "what
is good for soul and body" and their reputation for "curing ailments"
was apt to lead to exorcism of evil spirits (Josephus, *War* ii, 8.6).

---

[101] Kohler (*art. cit.*, Jewish Encyclopedia v[1903], 226b) mentioned the Watikim
who finished reciting the Shema at sunrise.

[102] "Light on the Cave Scrolls from Rabbinic Sources," *Proceedings of the American
Academy for Jewish Research* 20 (1951), 395-96, 399-400. See also Bronner, *op. cit.*,
157-158.

[103] *Art. cit., RQ* 5 (1965-66), 533-34.

[104] "Apocalypticism," *IDB* 1, 160. He continues: "The belief in a heavenly city,
misnamed the New Jerusalem, which is the perfect heavenly pattern of its earthly
counterpart, goes back, again, to astral thinking."

CHAPTER SIX

MESSIANISM AND PNEUMATOLOGY

The Person and Work of Christ

It is especially difficult to penetrate the polemic in this area and uncover the teachings opposed by the New Testament writers. Detecting what the opponents did not hold is easier. Analogy from church history throughout the centuries suggests that even in the beginning each side was apt to suspect each other's loyalty to Jesus.

In Romans 16:18 Paul states plainly that "such persons do not serve our Lord Jesus Christ." Their teaching was contrary to what the readers had learned from Paul (16:17). There may be some contrast between the enemies' food laws (see pp. 98-99) and the grace of Christ (16:21). That the opponents emphasized the righteousness of Christ may also be implicit in the fact that it is "the God of peace" who is to crush Satan (16:20), whereas Paul had taught in 1 Cor. 15:24-28 (cf. Phil. 3:21b) that it is Christ who is to vanquish all evil powers. The divisions in the church which false teachers caused stand in marked contrast to Paul's concept of fellowship in "the churches of Christ" (16:16). Early converts were "firstfruits εἰς χριστόν (16:5); others are characterized as being ἐν χριστῷ (16:7) or "ἐν κυρίω" (16:11). Individual members are described as "chosen ἐν κυρίω (16:13), "approved ἐν Χριστῷ" (16:10) and "beloved ἐν χυρίω" (16:8). The saints were to receive Phoebe ἐν κυρίω" (16:2). Church leaders were "workers ἐν χριστῷ 'Ιησοῦ" (16:3, 9) who "labor ἐν—κυρίω" (16:12). Those whom Paul stigmatized as non-servants of our Lord Christ were not apt to envision church membership as such an incorporation into Him. The emphasis on the close relation to Christ of the persons who were greeted serves to differentiate them, in Paul's mind, from the disturbers of the peace.

In Philippians 3 Paul terms the proponents of food laws, "enemies of the cross of Christ" (3:18-19). They gloried in earthly things and trusted in the flesh, rather than in Jesus Christ (3:3-4, 18-19). Their concern was righteousness according to the law (3:3, 5-7, 9), rather than the righteousness based on faith in Christ (3:7-10). Paul saw this as a matter of misplaced loyalty and confidence; their thinking was not Christocentric, or at least the cross (3:18) was not central in their thinking because of their attachment to the law. They denied that the cross decreased the need of the law. Γνῶσις of Jesus Christ for Paul meant gaining him, being found in him, knowing the power of his resurrection and the fellowship of his sufferings, being conformed to his death (3:8-10), and being laid hold of by him (3:12). Such excellence superceded all other religious values. But for the Apostle's opponents, knowledge of Christ was an aid, like legal obedience, on the path to perfection (3:12-13, 15). Possibly they claimed to imitate Christ successfully (3:16-18), who was born under the law (Gal. 4:4). Their relationship with Him was less mystical and personal than Paul's, at least in regard to sharing His sufferings. The destruction which awaits as an end the enemies of the cross (3:18-19) is not attributed to Christ, although earlier (1 Thess. 5:2-5; 2 Thess. 1:7-9; 2:8) Paul had not hesitated to promise vengeance and inescapable, sudden and eternal destruction at the hand of the Lord Jesus on his return.

Though the intruders at Corinth claimed to be apostles and ministers of Christ (2 Cor. 11:13, 15, 23) and to belong to Him (10:7), Paul charged that they were proclaiming another Jesus and a different gospel (2 Cor. 11:4). Paul insisted that he preached God's gospel (2 Cor. 10:14; 11:7) and that only the truth of Christ was in him (11:10; cf. 13:8; 6:7). As preacher of the Gospel of Christ, Paul boasted only of the Lord (10:15, 17). His every thought was captive to the obedience of Christ (10:5), and the power of Christ rested on him in his labors on behalf of Christ (12:9-10;13:3; cf. 5:20a). Christ spoke in him (13:3). Implicitly the teaching, service and power of his opponents were not so centered in Christ (cf. 11:3). They did not realize the significance of the crucifixion in weakness (2 Cor. 13:4; cf. 1 Cor. 1:18). The life and death of Jesus (ζωὴ τοῦ 'Ιησοῦ) were manifested in Paul's mortal flesh and body (4:10-11) through the resurrection of Jesus and of the Apostle σὺν 'Ιησοῦ (4:14). To suffer, die and rise with Christ in union with him (Rom. 6:3-12; Gal. 5:24; 6:14, 17; 2 Cor. 1:5; 4:10-14; 5:14, 17; 13:4; Phil. 3:10; Col. 1:24; 2:11-13, 20; 3:1, 3, 5, 9-10; Eph. 4:22, 24; 2 Tim. 2:11-12) was not a part of their teaching. Not holding to this faith, they did not pass the test of the presence of Christ in them (13:5; cf. 10:7; 12:2, 19). The evangelical mystery of "Christ in you" was also set before the Galatians (2:19-20) and Colossians (1:27). Paul obtained power, life and hope from associating himself in the suffering, death and resurrection of Christ (1:5,7; 4:7, 10-14; cf. 6:3-10; 11:23-31). Union with Christ (ἐν Χριστῷ, ἐν αὐτῷ) uncovers the meaning of the old covenant and makes believers become the righteousness of God (3:14; 5:21). "If anyone is in Christ, he is a new creation" (5:17). Such righteousness stems from transformation into the image of Christ (3:18) and from the fact that "far our sake he made him to be sin who knew no sin" (5:21).[1] For the Apostle the humanity of Jesus is the vehicle of his reconciling work (2 Cor. 5:18-20). Paul answers the charge that his gospel is veiled by calling it a manifestation (φανέρωσις) of the truth which "is veiled only to those who are perishing" (4:2-4), i.e. the ἄπιστοι (cf. Tit. 1:15). A subjective veil also hides the Christological meaning of the old covenant from those with hardened minds (3:13-16). Paul defines his "veiled" gospel in terms of "the glory of Christ, who is the likeness (εἰκών) of God," i.e. "the glory of God in the face of Christ" (4:4-6; cf. 3:18; 1 Tim. 1:11). His message of reconciliation and divinely inspired appeal was that "God was in Christ, reconciling the world to himself" through his death (5:14-15, 18-20). Through Christ came a new life-giving covenant, the glory of which passes not away, unlike the splendor of Moses when he received the law (3:6-16). Apparently the Judaizers considered the glory of Jesus to be like that of Moses; as a Hebrew and Israelite of the seed of Abraham (cf. 11:22) Christ renewed the Mosaic law. Paul's opponents largely based their Christology on the old testament, which was still veiled for them (2 Cor. 3:13-17), according to the Apostle. The "different Jesus" which they proclaimed (11:4) was not the same Jesus according to the flesh as preached by Paul. For him the meekness and gentleness of Christ were foremost (2 Cor. 10:1), rather than power: a quality which Paul's opponents must have esteemed in Jesus (cf. 13:4) as well as in themselves. But Jesus revealed to the Apostle: "My power is made perfect in weakness" (2 Cor. 12:9). Perhaps the Jewish nationalist concept of the Messiah as world-ruling king of Israel was being upheld[2]. The opponents gloried in appearance (5:12) and must have attributed to the visible Jesus the same glory they emphasized in the face of Moses (2 Cor. 3:7, 12). But Paul preferred to speak of the glory concealed in earthen vessels (2 Cor. 4:6-7). He admitted that "even though we once

---

[1] This concept of the Atonement is to be understood in terms of the suffering servant (Isa. 53:6, 9, 12), the scapegoat (Levit. 16), the sin offering (Levit. 4:2 ff.; Rom. 8:3), the assumption of sinful flesh (Rom. 8:3), propitiation by his blood (Rom. 3:25; cf. 5:8-9) and/or the cross (Gal. 3:3).

[2] As D. Ostendorp (op. cit., 54-56) argues in another context.

regarded Christ from a human point of view, we regard him thus no longer" in this light (2 Cor. 5:16b). He apparently was being criticized for emphasing the humanity of Jesus. This charge was grounded in fact (4:5b, 10-14); for, he compared the humanity of Jesus to the σαρξ of any man (5:16). Paul's opponents associated the glory of Christ with his lawgiving, transfiguation and ascension, rather than with his humiliation and crucifixion in the flesh. The transfiguration may have been of special interest; for in the vision of Peter, James and John (Mt. 17:1-9; Mk. 9:2-9; Lk. 9:28-36), Jesus, Elijah and Moses appeared in glory together and a voice from the cloud said, "This is my beloved Son; listen to him." Jesus then prophesied the resurrection of the Son of Man. "His face shone like the sun, and his garments became white as light" (Mt. 17:2; cf. 24:27; 28:2-3; Exod. 34:29-35; Ezek. 1:14; Dan. 10:6).[3] Several conclusions might be drawn by proponents of doctrines discussed in previous chapters. For example, at this time Jesus revealed or manifested his true angelic nature, which he holds following his resurrection, i.e. now at the Father's right hand and to be revealed at his Parousia. Moses and Elijah, as representatives of the law and prophecy, talked with Jesus about the law and approved his mission and revelatory interpretations. The event was an epiphany foreshadowed by the glory received by Moses when the law was given (Exod. 24:9-18). Some of the language of 2 Cor. suggests that Paul was alluding to Jesus' transfiguration: 3:18 (μεταμορφούμεθα into glory) and 4:18-5:4 (σκηνή).

From 1 Corinthians we may infer that the proponents of virginity were especially interested in the commandments of the Lord as a standard (7:10, 25; 14:37); they viewed him as a lawgiver (9:21), presumably like Moses. They were eager to "serve the Lord" (7:22, 34-35) and to please him (7:32) as his apostles (9:1-3). They claimed to belong to Christ (3:23). Yet they did not believe that he had bought their freedom with a price (7:22-23).

To the Galatians the Apostle expressed his astonishment that, under the influence of troublemakers, they were deserting "... the grace of Christ and turning to a different gospel," i.e. a perverted (μεταστρέψαι) gospel of Christ (1:6-7). Expressed in a controversial and historical context, this Pauline gospel concerns liberty in Christ (versus subjection to circumcision) (2:2-5; cf. 5:1-6) and justification

---

[3] According to the Melchizedek section of 2 Enoch manuscripts, "Methuselah's face shone like the sun as he went to the altar of sacrifice" (i, 10).

in Christ by faith in him (rather than by works of the law) (2:14-17a).
Paul had portrayed Jesus Christ as having been crucified, and the
Galatians heard the message with faith (3:1-2). "For in Christ Jesus
you are all sons of God through faith." With the coming of Christ
and faith in him, we have been justified and are no longer under the
law (3:23-26). At stake was the issue of how through Christ one
becomes a son of God. Paul insisted that "God sent forth his
Son,...to redeem those who were under the law, so that we might
receive adoption as sons" (Gal. 4:5). "For if justification were through
the law, then Christ died to no purpose" (2:21). Evidently Paul's
opponents denied that the Crucifixion and faith in Christ freed the
believer from the law or sufficed for justification and sonship. They
argued that Paul made Christ "an agent of sin" (2:17) rather than of
justification since he taught that Christ freed from the law those who
were still sinners. They would have strong reservations about the
Apostle's assertion: "If you are Christ's, then you are Abraham's
offspring, heirs according to promise" (3:29; cf. 3:16; 4:7). Again, a
relationship with Christ did not, in the opinion of the troublemakers,
obviate the requirement of legal obedience. But for Paul, the former
was the overriding consideration: "As many of you as were baptized
into Christ have put on Christ ... You are all one in Christ Jesus"
(3:27-28). While the Judaizers had their legal tests of membership in
Christ, Paul defined the relationship in terms of clothing oneself with
the garment of Christ (3:27), being crucified with him (in baptism),
living by faith in the indwelling Christ (2:20), and His being formed
in the believer (4:19). "Those who belong to Christ Jesus have
crucified the flesh with its passions and desires "(5:24). By the cross
"the world has been crucified to me, and I to the world," wrote Paul,
who gloried in the cross rather than in circumcision. Not the latter,
but a new creation through Christ, counts (6:14-15). The Apostle
associated his own sufferings with those of Jesus: "Henceforth let no
one trouble me; for I bear on my body the marks (στίγματα) of Jesus"
(6:17). The opponents' still germinal Soteriology was little influenced
by Christ mysticism. They could hardly grant that "For freedom
Christ has set us free" (5:1) and "redeemed us from the curse of the
law" by his crucifixion (3:13-14; cf. 3:1). Nor would they agree that
He ended bondage to the στοιχεῖα τοῦ κόσμου in so far as they gave
laws (4:3-10). They honored the role of "slave of Christ" (1:10)
without granting the title to Paul. The misled Galatians apparently
did not doubt the existence, or at least the possibility, of private

revelations of Christ (1:12, 16); but, again, Paul's claims were being questioned. Now, if Jesus were seen as a lawgiver, like the angels through Moses (3:19-20), and if an angel could preach "a gospel" (1:8-9), the Judaizers' Christology must have been related to their angelology. In this light we are to understand the curious recollection: "you received me as an angel of God, as Christ Jesus" (4:14). The Messiah at least functioned like an angel.[4]

Paul taught the Galatians that Christ "was born of a woman (γενόμενον ἐκ γυναικός) born under the law" (4:4). This condition as pertinent to the ordinary potential believer meant being a slave or infant enslaved to the στοιχεῖα τοῦ κόσμου (4:1-3); after being redeemed, he is adopted as son and heir and receives the Spirit (4:5-7). In 4:22-31 the one "born according to the flesh (κατὰ σάρκα)" from a slave (representing the old covenant) is contrasted with the heir born of the free woman (representing the new covenant) through promise and according to the Spirit. To be "born of a woman" is parallel to being "born according to the flesh"; both, in turn, are parallel to "γενόμενον ἐκ σπέρματος Δαυὶδ κατὰ σάρκα" (Rom. 1:3). The terms, γυναικός (rather than παρθένος), σπέρματος and κατὰ σάρκα, and the allegory of Ishmael son of Hagar, suggest a natural human birth. Was the Virgin Birth already under discussion?

Paul feared that the Colossians readers might be deluded by beguiling human wisdom "according to the στοιχεῖα τοῦ κόσμου, and not according to Christ" (2:4, 8). The Apostle expressed his wish that the Colossians and Laodiceans "have all the riches of assured understanding and the knowledge of God's mystery, of Christ, in whom are hid all the treasures of wisdom and knowledge (*gnosis*)" (2:2-3). This implies that Christ has revealed mysterious treasures which remain concealed to the false teachers or that they claimed to know mysteries not pertaining to Christ. Paul's office was "to make the word of God fully known, the mystery hidden ἀπὸ τῶν αἰώνων καὶ ἀπὸ τῶν γενεῶν," i.e. the mystery of "Christ in you, the hope of glory. Him we proclaim, warning every man and teaching every man in all wisdom, that we may present every man mature (τέλειος) in Christ" (1:25-28). Perfection is thus an aim of preaching the gospel, and Χριστὸσ ἐν ὑμῖν (cf. Rom. 8:10; 2 Cor. 13:5; Eph. 3:17) is emphasized as the content of Paul's preaching, in

---

[4] Richard N. Longenecker, *The Christology of Early Jewish Christianity*, Naperville, III. (Alec R. Allenson, 1970), 31.

apparent contradistinction from the Judaizers' teaching. "The word of truth, the gospel," which the Colossians had heard, concerned the grace of God and the hope laid up for them in heaven (1:5-6). This blessing includes transfer into the kingdom of the Son to be partakers of the inheritance (κλῆρος) of the saints in the light (1:12-13); servants of the Lord Christ will receive the reward of the κληρονομία (3:24; cf. 1 Pet. 1:4). Elsewhere the subject of evangelical teaching is termed, "the word (λόγος) of Christ" indwelling believers (3:16) and "the mystery of Christ" (4:3). Its definition is given in 1:22-23: Christ "has now reconciled (you) in his body of flesh by his death, in order to present you holy (ἅγιος) and blameless (ἄμωμος) and irreproachable (ἀνέγκλητος) before him, provided that you continue in the faith, stable and steadfast, not shifting from the hope of the gospel which you have heard." Aspects of the gospel and mystery of Christ which Paul was upholding ostensibly concerned his reconciling death, his presence in believers, and maturity or holiness in him. Paul upholds each of these principles elsewhere in the Epistle. Having been fulfilled (πεπληρωμένοι) in Christ (2:10) and having received him as Lord, believers are to "live in him, rooted and built up in him and established in the faith just as" they had been taught (2:6-7). The unusual order, ὁ Χριστός Ἰεσοῦς ὁ κύριος (2:6), emphasizes that this Christ has been received and that Jesus is the Lord. Through baptism they have undergone death, burial, resurrection and quickening with Christ (2:11-13, 20; 3:1-3).[5] Believers so identifying themselves with Christ are incorporated in him. Paul's association with the afflictions of Christ is even deeper (1:24). The permanence of believers' union with him is expressed in these terms: "your life is hid with Christ in God. When Christ who is our life appears, then you also will appear with him in glory" (3:3-4). He is the vital principle in the life of the believers (3:3; Gal. 2:20). It was fitting, therefore, that they should put off and put to death the old man and his practices, and put on the new man with his virtues (3:5-14). Salvation through the blood of the cross was not adequately understood by the opponents, in spite of their claim of wisdom. By the death of Christ have come reconciliation and peace (1:20-22), redemption and forgiveness of sins (1:14; 2:13-14; 3:13). Through the cross he has freed believers from

---

[5] Lewis Johnson, Jr., "The Complete Sufficiency of Union with Christ," *Bibliotheca Sacra* 120 (1963), 13-23.

bondage both to the law (2:14, 17, 20-21) and to the ἀρχαί, ἐξουσίαι and στοιχεῖα (2:15, 20). The change in status is aptly described as delivery from the ἐξουσία of darkness and transferral into the kingdom of the Son (1:13); such is the lot of those having a "share (μερίς) in the inheritance of the sons in light" (1:12). The relation of Jesus to the angels now came into discussion. Whereas the Galatian Judaizers recognized similarity in their functions, and the Corinthian "apostles" speculated on the manifestation of Jesus' glory (at the Transfiguration-?), the Colossian "philosophers" sought to understand his ranking in the celestial hierarchy. They differed with Paul on the questions whether "worship" of angels detracted from worship of Christ (2:18-19) and and whether or not the advent of Christ ended the saving role of angels. Lewis B. Radford [6] believed that the Colossian heresy "minimized His supremacy in the world-order" and denied "His sufficiency for all human need as the fount of spiritual life and the food of spiritual growth." The Apostle would allow no rivalry to him who is the head of the church (1:18), "the head (κεφαλή) of all rule (ἀρχή) and authority (ἐξουσία)" (2:10) and is πάντα καὶ ἐν πᾶσιν (3:11). "Consequently," remarked W. L. Knox,[7] "they were inferior to Him, and any power which they might possess was derived from Him." After warning against deceit "according to the στοιχεῖα τοῦ κόσμου and not according to Christ," he explains: For in him the πλήρωμα τῆς θεότητος permanently dwells (κατοικεῖ) σωματικός (2:9). For the same reason he holds first place (ἀρχή, πρωτεύων) in all things (1:18-19). The use of the term, πλήρωμα, may have been suggested by speculations on angelology, or more specifically, by a speculative division of the πλήρωμα τῆς θεότητος between (the archangel) Christ and the angels who are "worshipped," i.e. the cosmic στοιχεῖα. As Radford observed,[8] Paul's emphasis on the πλήρωμα in Christ "seems to be the answer to the idea that the divine power was distributed among a hierarchy of celestial beings." For Paul the divine attributes and functions were not distributed among angelic powers and Jesus, but wholly belong to Christ. His absolute

---

[6] The Epistle to the Colossians and the Epistle to Philemon (Westminster), London (Methuen, 1931), 60.

[7] Op. cit., 168. On Christ's lordship over angels, see the bibliography in Vanhoye, op. cit., 99, n. 49.

[8] Op. cit., 62; cf. Lightfoot, St. Paul's Epistles to the Colossians and to Philemon, 100, 110.

primacy and supremacy are asserted as the firstborn (πρωτότοκος; cf. Hebr. 1:6) of all created things (κτίσις: without the article) in whom, through whom and for whom (cf. Rom. 11:36; 1 Cor. 8.6) all visible things and all the angelic orders were created. He is the lord over the creation. Also as "image (εἰκών) of the invisible God" (1:15-17), his uniqueness is asserted. The twelve occurences of καὶ οὐτός in 1:14-20 underline Christ's superiority. All works and words of believers are to be dedicated to the Lord Jesus; God the Father is to be thanked through him (3:17) The opposing Christology granted uniqueness and exclusiveness neither of worship nor of nature to Jesus. However, the casual reference to his session at the right hand of God (3:1) indicates that the highest rank was still granted to Jesus by the angelologists. However, they de-emphasized his humanity because the angels aided human salvation without having a fleshly body. Paul emphasized that the πλήρωμα indwelled Jesus with a bodily manifestation (σωματικός) (2:9). He suffered for his church ἐν τῇ σαρκί (1:24) and brought reconciliation in his body of flesh (σάρξ) (1:22; cf. 2:11). In Eph. 6:12 flesh and blood are contrasted with the various angelic beings.

Ephesians 4:13-15 contrasts children tossed about by every wind of διδασκαλία and πανουργία (cf. 2 Cor. 4:2; 11:3) πρὸς τὴν μεθοδείαν τῆς πλάνης, on the one hand, and, on the other, mature manhood, which is characterized by unity of the faith, knowledge of the Son of God and the stature of the fullness of Christ in all respects. The error (πλάνη) ostensibly concerns knowledge of the Son and his fullness. This unity and growth into Christ, the head, is defineable as "one body, one Spirit, one Lord, one faith, one baptism..." (4:4-5). To unite in Christ all things in heaven and on earth is the divine purpose, plan and mystery (1:9-10). In Christ we have been chosen as God's lot (εκληρώθημεν) (1:11; cf. Deut. 32:9-10). The revealed mystery of Christ means that "the Gentiles are fellow heirs (συγκληρονόμα), members of the same body, and partakers of the promise in Christ Jesus through the gospel" (3:3-6). This process is described in 2:11-22. Through the blood and σάρξ of Christ on the cross (2:13, 15, 16) the law had been abolished, so that Gentiles might enter the covenanted commonwealth of Israel and be made one body with the Jews in Christ. The plan of the mystery, i.e. the eternal purpose which God has realized in Christ Jesus, has been made known through the church, whose members have "boldness and confidence of access" through faith in Christ. This mystery was

hidden from the heavenly powers, but made known through Paul
(3:5, 7-12). The παρρησία and πεποίθησις of access to God in Christ
through faith represents the new and ultimate stage in the unfolding
of the divine plan which was unknown to men in other generations
(3:5) and to heavenly rulers and authorities (3:10). By implication
previous access to God had been in fear or uncertainty, even in the
case of older mediators, i.e. Moses, prophets and angels. In 2:16-19
access by one Spirit unto the Father through the crucified Christ is
contrasted with being aliens to the commonwealth of Israel and the
covenants of promise (cf. 3:12). The growth into Christ, whereby the
divine plan is fulfilled, is made possible by being ἐν χριστῷ at every
stage. God "has blessed us in Christ with every spiritual blessing in
the heavenly places (cf. 2:5-6) even as he chose us in him before the
foundation of the world, that we should be holy and blameless before
him. He destined us in love to be his sons through Jesus Christ" (1:3-
5). "In him we have redemption through his blood, the forgiveness of
our trespasses" (1:7). We are "created in Christ Jesus (cf. 2 Cor. 5:17;
Gal. 6:15) for good works, which God prepared beforehand" (2:10).
"As the truth is in Jesus," those who have been taught ἐν αὐτῷ are
expected to put off their old nature and put on the new holy nature
(4:20-25). It was Paul's prayer that God might grant them strength
"through his Spirit in the inner man, that Christ might dwell in
(their) hearts through faith" and they might "know the love of Christ
which surpasses knowledge, that (they) may be filled with all the
fullness of God" (3:16-19). This love (cf. 5:25; Gal. 2:20) is described
in 5:2: "Walk in love, as Christ loved us and gave himself up for us, a
fragrant offering and sacrifice to God." The motive of imitation
appears in 4:32 as well: "forgiving one another, as God in Christ
forgave you" (cf. Col. 3:13). The casual nature of this appeal suggests
that imitation was not a debated question. But the repeated theme,
that all grace and blessings and unsearchable riches come through
Christ, is an aspect of the Gospel which belongs to the wisdom,
insight and knowledge hidden from the heavenly powers (1:7-9, 17-
18; 3:8-10) This knowledge of the Son belongs to a believer's
maturity and is the basis of the unity of the faith (4:13). The
suggestion is that those who hold a different doctrine are νήπιοι and
are less perceptive than the ἀρχαί and ἐξουσίαι.

The vision of unity in Christ, as found in Ephesians, may be
formulated as follows. To the church (the body of Christ: 1:22-23),
God has given all spiritual blessings through Christ (1:3, 17-20; 4:7,

11-12). God has done this by raising Jesus from the dead (1:20) and us from our sins and by making him and us to ascend to heavenly places (1:3; 2:5-6), far above all things (including the angels: 1:21). Christ fills (πληρουμένου) all things (1:23; 4:10), and all things in heaven and on earth are united in him (1:9-10; cf. Col. 1:20), by virtue of (1) his ascension and session (1:20; 4:8, 10), (2) his filling the church with all his gifts (including his living presence) as the head of his body (1:23; 4:12, 15-16; 5:23, 30), (3) his indwelling its members' hearts through faith (3:17-19a), (4) the attainment of all of us to the measure of the stature of the πλήρωμα of Christ (4:13; cf. 1:23), i.e. growing into him τὰ πάντα (4:15), (5) our being filled with the πλήρωμα of God (3:19), and (6) knowledge of the divine mystery among all the angels (3:9-11). This fullness of the work which Christ is to fulfill and the implicit omnipresence of Christ, are the doctrines which far exceeded the immature Christology and Soteriology known to the readers.

The Christology of the Epistle to the Hebrews is summarized in two emphatic, well-argued passages:

> But in these last days he has spoken to us by a Son, whom he appointed the heir of all things, through whom also he created the world. He reflects the glory of God and bears the very stamp of his nature, upholding the universe by the word of power. When he had made purification for sins, he sat down at the right hand of Majesty on high, having become as much superior to angels as the name he has obtained is more excellent than theirs. For to what angel did God ever say,
> 'Thou art my Son,
> today I have begotten thee'? (1:2-5)

> Since therefore the children share in flesh and blood, he himself likewise partook of the same nature, that through death he might destroy him who has the power of death, that is, the devil, and deliver all those who through fear of death were subject to lifelong bondage. For surely it is not with angels that he is concerned but with the descendents of Abraham. Therefore he had to be made like his brethren in every respect, so that he might become a merciful and faithful high priest in the service of God, to make expiation for the sins of the people. For because he himself has suffered and been tempted, he is able to help those who are tempted (2:14-18).

"He is able for all time to save those who draw near to God through him, since he always lives to make intercession for them" (7:25). As High Priest he offered up himself for the annulment of, and

redemption from, sins (5:1-3; 7:27; 8:3; 9:12, 24-28; 10:4, 10-12); he
bore the sins of many (9:28) and sanctified the people (10:10, 14;
13:12). He cleansed them of sins (1:3) and brought forgiveness (9:22;
10:16-19). He tasted death for everyone (2:9) in order to destroy the
devil and deliver those who were enslaved through fear of death
(2:14-15). His blood cleansed and perfected consciences (9:9, 14;
10:2, 22). By his blood he entered the heavenly sanctuary (9:12),
where he appears in God's presence on our behalf (9:24) and gives us
confidence to enter it by a new and living way (10:19-20). He brought
a perfection impossible under the old covenant (7:11, 19; 10:1, 14;
11:39). He is the mediator (μεσίτης) of a new covenant (12:24). "Christ
has obtained a ministry which is as much more excellent than the
old (priestly one) as the covenant he mediates is better, since it is
enacted on better promises" (8:6). He is as superior in honor to Moses
as a son is to a servant (3:1-6; cf. 2 Cor. 3:5-11). Evidently the readers
were disposed to understand the work and person of Christ in Old
Testament terms and they had to be convinced of his uniqueness.
Their inclination to understand him in angelic categories was stoutly
resisted. On the one hand, argued our author, the Son is closer to
God than angels (1:1-2, 4); on the other hand, the Son was a real man
(2:5-18).[9] He and his brethren whom he sanctified "have all one
origin (ἐξ ἑνός)" (2:11), i.e. as children of God sharing in flesh and
blood (2:13-14). The rhetorical questions, "For to what angel did God
ever say,. . ." (1:5) and "But to what angel has he ever said. . ." (1:13),
would not impress the readers unless they were finding such
resemblances of Jesus to angels that they compared him to one. After
demonstrating the Son's absolute superiority, the author argues that
Jesus was for a little while lower than the angels (2:7-9), i.e. he
partook of flesh and blood in order that by his suffering and death
"he might taste death for every one" (2:9, 14; cf. 10:19-20). Moreover,
"because he himself has suffered and been tempted, he is able to help
those who are tempted" (2:18), i.e. he is a high priest who is able to
sympathize with our weakness (4:15). "He had to be made like his
brethren in every respect, so that he might become a merciful and
faithful high priest in service of God" (2:17). While "it is fitting that
we should have a high priest, holy, blameless, unstained, separated
from sinners, exalted above the heavens" (7:26), he learned obedience

---

[9] Erich Grässer, "Der historische Jesus in Hebräerbrief," *ZNTW* 56 (1965), 63-91.

and was perfected (τελειῶσαι) through sufferings (2:10-11; 5:7-9; 7:28; cf. 12:2-3). His kinship with his brethren, the children given to him by God (2:11-14), results from his common origin (ἐξ ἑνὸς). For these reasons, Jesus, the high priest, could not have been an angel. The emphasis on the need that he be human is most noticeable in 2:5 ("For it was not to angels that God subjected the world to come"; cf. 2:8-9) and 2:16 ("For surely it is not with angels that he is concerned but with the descendants of Abraham"); in this context (2:5-18) the humanity of Jesus is underlined. As Hugh Montefiore comments on the latter passage:[10] "Our author has a final fling at the notion that Jesus was an angel. If he had been an angel, he argues, then Jesus might have helped angels; but since it is men whom he helps, therefore he could not have been an angel." R. Williamson [11] interprets 2:16 to mean that because "Christ really had come to save men, not πνεύματα only, . . . a real and full *Incarnation* was required . . . Angels are not the objects of Christ's saving intervention." A point of possible comparison between Christ and the angels is their common role of intercession before God, which belongs to Jesus (7:25; cf. 9:24). He is the only mediator of and under the new covenant (8:6; 9:15; 12:24).[12]

The fact that Melchizedek as both priest and king was taught by the Epistle to the Hebrews to be the prototype of Christ, has prompted many scholars [13] to find its background in the expectation of both a priestly and royal Messiah; Jesus was the fulfillment of all Messianic hopes and therefore was the only Anointed One. Yigael Yadin [14] notes that nearly half of the Epistle (4:14-10:23) is devoted to the subject of "Jesus the Priestly Messiah- a priest of an order superior to that of Aaron." "Consider Jesus, the apostle and high priest of our confession"(3:1). "Since then we have a great high priest who has passed through the heavens, Jesus, the Son of God, let us hold fast our confession" (4:14). He was "designated by God a high priest after the order of Melchizedek" (5:10; cf. 5-6; 7:17). "Into the inner shrine behind the curtain . . . Jesus has gone as a forerunner on

---

[10] *Op. cit.*, 66.
[11] *Op. cit.*, 191-92.
[12] *Ibid.*, 196-97.
[13] Bibliographies in Cross, *op. cit.*, 221, n. 48; Ringgren, *op. cit.*, 248, n. 13; Braun, *op. cit.*, ii, 181.
[14] *Art. cit., Scripta Hierosolymitana* 4 (1958), 41, cf. "A Note on Melchizedek and Qumran," *Israel Exploration Journal* 15 (1965), 154.

our behalf, having become a high priest for ever after the order of
Melchizedek" (6:19-20). "Now the point in what we are saying is this:
we have such a high priest, one who is seated at the right hand of the
throne of Majesty in heaven, a minister in the sanctuary and the true
tent which is set up not by the Lord" (8:1-2).

> For it was fitting that we should have such a high priest, holy,
> blameless, unstained, separated from sinners, exalted above the heavens.
> He has no need, like those high priests, to offer sacrifices daily, first for
> his own sins and then for those of the people; he did this once for all
> when he offered up himself. Indeed the law appoints men in their
> weakness as high priest, but the word of the oath, which came later than
> the law, appoints a Son who has been made perfect for ever (7:26-28)

Yadin rightly deduces:[15]

> It is quite clear that by repeating and stressing the onetime sacrifice of
> Jesus in offering up himself, the writer is aiming -inter alia- at the
> addressees' firm belief that even at the era of the End of Days the full
> and continuous ritual of the sacrifices—as prescribed by the Mosaic
> Law- would have to be resumed and continued for ever under the
> direction of the Aaronid high priest.

The author of Hebrews, in denying that Jesus was the eschatological
high priest who was to carry out the pure sacrificial cultus, reasoned
that Jesus belonged to a priestly order higher than that of Aaron.[16]

> See how great he [Melchizedek] is! Abraham the patriarch gave him a
> tithe of spoils. And those descendants of Levi who receive a priestly
> office have a commandment in the law to take tithes from the people
> ... But this man who has not their genealogy received tithes from
> Abraham and blessed him who had the promises. It is beyond dispute
> that the inferior is blessed by the superior... One might even say that
> Levi himself, who receives tithes, paid tithes through Abraham; for he
> was still in the loins of his ancestor when Melchizedek met him. Now if
> perfection had been attainable through the Levitical priesthood ...,
> what further need would there have been for another priest to arise after
> the order of Melchizedek, rather than one named after the order of
> Aaron? (7:4-11).

Evidently the readers were looking forward to an eschatological high
priest who belonged to the House of Aaron and whose Levitical

---

[15] *Art. cit., Scripta Hierosolymitana* 4 (1958), 45; cf. 48.
[16] Cf. Fitzmyer, "Further Light on Melchizedek from Qumran Cave 11," *JBL* 86
(1967), 41.

sacrifices would bring perfection. But the author of Hebrews not only downgrades this priesthood but also states that Jesus could not have belonged to it: the priest after the order of Melchizedek who was to arise "belonged to another tribe, from which no one has ever served at the altar. For it is evident that our Lord was descended from Judah, and in connection with that tribe Moses said nothing about priests" (7:13-14). Therefore the readers' understanding of the Messianic prophecies was in error; they, too, believed, that Jesus was the high priest, yet did not understand scriptural teaching concerning the priesthoods of Aaron and Melchizedek. The readers would have liked to trace our Lord's ancestry to a priestly family. But, as R. Williamson observes [17], "The Priesthood of Jesus does not ... depend on physical descent, birth or genealogy." Accordingly, our author, in the words of Yadin,[18] "tried to present to his readers Jesus the Messiah -king and priest- in such a manner and terminology as must have been intended to coincide both with their ideas of the Messiah priest and the Messianic king and at the same time to repudiate other beliefs which they might have held and which did not suit his concept." In Hebrews Jesus is presented as a royal priest; he was a combination of the priestly and royal dignities. "For this Melchizedek, king of Salem, priest of the most high God, ... is first, by translation of his name, king of righteousness, and then he is also king of Salem, that is, king of peace. He is without father or mother or genealogy, and has neither beginning of days nor end of life, but resembling the Son of God he continues a priest forever" (7:1-3). Van der Woude and de Jonge infer from this origin that the author "regarded Melchizedek as an (arch-) angel who appeared to Abraham long ago." [19] Samuel Sandmel [20] rhetorically asks: "Can this passage in Hebrews (7:3) be any less than a rejection of the entire process of genealogical tracing?" Death prevents Levitical priests from continuing forever in their office of intercession (7:23-25).

How futile it is for the readers to be concerned about Messianic genealogies! It could be generally agreed only that Jesus was of the

---

[17] Op. cit., 442.

[18] Art. cit., Scripta Hierosolymitana 4 (1958), 44.

[19] De Jonge and van der Woude, art. cit., NTS 12 (1965-66), 321-22; cf. Gerd Theissen, Untersuchungen zum Hebräerbrief, Gütersloh (Gerd Mohn, 1969), 28-29.

[20] The First Christian Century in Judaism and Christianity. Certainties and Uncertainties, New York (Oxford University, 1969), 175-76. He believes, further, that the genealogies of 1 Tim. 1:4; Tit. 3:9 were of Christ (p. 206).

tribe of Judah, like David (7:14; cf. Mt. 1:2, 6; Lk. 3:31, 33). As the king of righteousness Christ brings peace, not a sword of vengeance and retribution upon the wicked. His royalty did not imply a military role. Not to him, but to "the living God," is attributed fearful vengeance and "prospect of judgment and of a fury of fire which will consume" those who reject the Son (10:27-31; 12:25-29). Dreaded eschatological punishment is taken for granted by the readers. But, taught the author of Hebrews (9:28), Christ "will appear a second time, not to deal with sin but to save those who are eagerly waiting for him."

For what purpose did Christ shed his blood? Hebr. 2:10 teaches that it was fitting that God, "in bringing many sons to glory, should make the pioneer of their salvation perfect through suffering" (cf. 5:7-9); the salvation of the sons of God has resulted from Christ's suffering unto death. According to Heb. 9:11-12, as High Priest he entered once for all into the heavenly sanctuary, "taking ... his own blood, thus securing an eternal redemption." This blood shall "purify your conscience from dead works to serve the living God. Therefore he is the mediator of a new covenant, so that those who are called may receive the promised eternal inheritance, since a death has occurred which redeems them from the transgressions under the first covenant" (9:14-15). His blood offered in sacrifice and effecting eternal forgiveness of sins under the new covenant is contrasted with the old covenant's dead works and temporary purification of the flesh (9:14). The readers were aware of the parallel between Moses' sprinkling of the law code and all the people with the blood of calves and goats, on one hand, and the shedding of Christ's blood on the other. The confirmation and ratification of both covenants with blood is presupposed: "Hence even the first covenant was not ratified without blood" (9:18). The point in question was whether Christ's blood sealed another legalistic covenant and thus served the same function as the Mosaic sprinkling of blood, or, alternatively, whether "he has appeared once for all at the end of the age to put away sin by the sacrifice of himself" (9:26). By the blood of the eternal covenant, taught the author of Hebrews (10:29; 13:20-21), believers are sanctified. All Christians had to interpret the Master's words, "This is my blood of the covenant, which is poured out for many" (Mk. 14:24); disagreements arose from different understandings of Christ's role in fulfilling the new covenant.

Jeremiah's prophecy (31:33-34) of a covenant of forgiveness of sins to be made with men on whose soul the law had been engraved, is quoted in Hebr. 10:16-17. The citation is intended to support the Epistle's teaching that Christ's single sacrifice has taken away sins and "has perfected for all time those who are sanctified" (10:11-14; cf. 8:6ff.). "Therefore, brethren, since we have confidence (παῤῥησία) to enter the sanctuary by the blood of Jesus, by the new and living way which he opened for us. . . , and since we have a great priest over the house of God, let us draw near with a true heart in full assurance of faith, with our hearts sprinkled clean from an evil conscience . . . Let us hold fast the confession of our hope without wavering. . ." (10:19-23). The wavering readers lacked the confidence in salvation which comes from a right understanding of the new covenant and way of perfection brought by Christ. The readers were also instructed to hold fast their confession and to draw near with confidence to the throne of grace since they have a sympathetic "high priest who has passed through the heavens" (4:14-16; cf. 3:6). Confidence in the grace and power of Jesus as compassionate high priest was a needed element in the faith of the readers if they were to "hold fast."

The course of Christological developments through controversy in Asia Minor can be partially traced in the Pastoral Epistles. Here are found several rhythmical liturgical furmulations which were taken from hymns, creeds or baptismal confessions. To the extent that these confessions took shape through, and were motivated by, controversy, they suggest what had been earlier under discussion. The first is 1 Tim. 2:5-6: "For there is one God, and there is one mediator between God and men, the man Jesus Christ, who gave himself as a ransom for all, the testimony to which was borne at the proper time." That this profession is intended to exclude angelic mediators is suggested by Gal. 3:19-20 (see p. 172) and the *Testament of the Twelve Patriarchs,* Dan. vi, 2, which speaks of Michael in the following terms: "Draw near unto God and unto the angel that intercedeth for you, for he is a mediator [of the new covenant] between God and man." Whoever based his Christology on this "prophecy" would be inclined to view Jesus as more angelic than human, and as foremost of many mediators. In the credal formulation the lack of an definite article before ἄνθρωπος suggests that the Incarnation or the full humanity of Jesus had been questioned. But it is affirmed that his mediatorial role (as a man) consists of his giving himself as a ransom; the emphasis is on his death for our sins rather than on his teaching role. Divine testimony to this mediation and ransoming takes place in its own times (καιροῖς ἰδίοις); that is, redemption is a validated historical event, rather than an angelic "myth." This divine testimony took place through the Resurrection and Ascension and Pentecost, and if καιροι are future as well, will occur at the Parousia. A similar confession is found in 1 Tim. 3:16: "Great, indeed, we confess, is the mystery of our religion:

> He was manifested in the flesh,
> vindicated in the Spirit,
> seen by angels,
> preached among the nations
> believed on in the world,
>   taken up in glory."

Christ was vindicated by his Resurrection (cf. Rom. 1:4; 8:11) and Ascension. In both events he was seen by angels (Mt. 28:2; Lk. 24:4, 23; Acts 1:10; Eph. 3:9-10; 1 Pet. 1:12; cf. Lk. 2:13; Jh. 1:51; Ascension of Isaiah 9:13-15, 11:23 ff.),[21] whose inferiority as mere witnesses is implied. Moreover, since he was seen by angels and was manifested ἐν σαρκί, he is above the angels. A parallel is found in 1 Pet. 3:18: Christ "died for sins ... that he might bring us to God, being put to death in the flesh (σαρκὶ) but made alive πνεύματι." The epiphany of Christ in the flesh in 1 Tim. 3:16, while ostensibly referring to his lifelong condition in the flesh, probably has special reference to the crucifixion (cf. Col. 1:20-22); for it was this which was justified by the Resurrection and Ascension. This interpretation is supported by 2 Tim. 1:10, according to which the epiphany of the Savior abrogated death and brought life and incorruption, and by Titus 2:11, 14, where the appearance of the saving grace of God includes Christ's giving himself in order to ransom us from sin (cf. Tit. 3:3-7). The liturgical character of Tit. 2:13-14 reinforces the propriety of interpreting 1 Tim. 3:16 in light of it. The awaited "ἐπιφάνεια of the glory of our great God and Savior Jesus Christ" is parallel to one of the καιποι of 1 Tim. 2:6. The future epiphany is mentioned in 1 Tim. 6:14; 2 Tim. 4:1, 8 as well; it had apparently entered the theological vocabulary of the community. The application of the title, "God and Savior" to Christ suggests that some of the other references to the Savior as God (1 Tim. 1:1; 2:3; 4:10; Tit. 2:10; 3:4; cf. 1 Tim. 1:11) are more Christological than is

---

[21] Joseph Barbel, *Christos Angelos*, Bonn (Peter Hanstein, 1941), 297-311.

generally recognized; that is, implying that God is Savior through Jesus. In this sense are to be understood the "epiphanies" of Christ (cf. Eph. 3:9-12). To use Paul's words, "God was in Christ reconciling the world to himself" (2 Cor. 5:19). As ἄνθροπος ἐν σαρκὶ, Jesus Christ was both the unique mediator between man and God, and an epiphany of the divine, or a theophany. These were the maximum concessions that could be made to an angelic Christology. In the Old Testament (Gen. 18; Josh. 5:13-14; Judg. 13:20-21) angels had appeared in human form only temporarily and in disguise.

A saying attributed to Jesus not inherently acceptable to the Judaizers is that the Son of Man came "to give his life as a ransom for many" (Mt. 20:28; Mk. 10:45; 1 Tim. 2:6). Or, "whatever goes into a man from outside cannot defile him" (Mk. 7:18). Denial of these sayings could have occasioned the Pastor's invective against "anyone who teaches otherwise and does not agree with the sound words of our Lord Jesus Christ..." (1 Tim. 6:3-5). The ἑτεροδιδασκαλεῖν of 1 Tim. 1:3 and 6:3 is reminiscent of the ἕτεπον Gospel and spirit of 2 Cor. 11:4 and Gal 1:6.

Ignatius encountered Judaizers whose Soteriology and Christology were limited to their understanding of Old Testament prophecies:

> I have faith in the grace of Christ... When I heard some saying, 'If I do not find it in the ancient records, I will not believe the gospel'; on my saying to them, 'It is written,' they answered me, 'That remains to be proved.' But to me Jesus Christ is in the place of all that is ancient: His cross, and death, and resurrection, and the faith which is by Him, are undefiled monuments of antiquity...

> The priests indeed are good, but the High Priest is better ... He is the door of the Father, by which enter in Abraham, Isaac and Jacob and the prophets ... But the gospel possesses something transcendent, namely, the appearnace (παρουσία) of our Lord Jesus Christ, His passion and resurrection. For the beloved prophets proclaimed Him, but the gospel is the perfection of immortality (Philad. 8-9, A-N).

The prophets proclaimed the gospel and placed their hope in Christ; by this faith they were saved, "through union to Jesus Christ." Whoever does not speak of Him is like "monuments and sepulchres of the dead" (Philad. 5-6). His suffering has no meaning or value for those who "walk in strange doctrine" (3:1, 3). In Magnesians appears the same line of thought. Jesus Christ who existed before the ages with the Father was made manifest at the end (ἐν τέλει ἐφάνη) (6:1). Unless we choose to die through him, his life is not in us (5:2).

> There is one Jesus Christ, than whom nothing is more excellent. Do ye
> therefore all run together as into one temple of God, as to one altar, as
> to one Jesus Christ, who came forth from one Father, and is with and
> has gone to one ... For the divinest prophets lived according to Christ
> Jesus, ... being inspired by His grace to convince fully the unbelieving
> that there is one God, who has manifested Himself (φανερώσας ἑαυτὸν)
> by Jesus Christ, who is His λόγος proceeding from silence, who in all
> things pleased Him that sent Him .... If ... our life has sprung up
> again by Him and by His death—which some deny, by which mystery
> we have obtained faith, and therefore endure, that we may be found the
> disciples of Jesus Christ, our only Master (διδάσκαλος),—how shall we be
> able to live apart from Him, whom the prophets themselves ... in the
> Spirit did wait for as their Teacher? ... Whoever is called by any other
> name besides ['Christian'], is not of God ... Be changed into the new
> leaven, which is Jesus Christ. Be salted in Him, lest any one among you
> should be corrupted ... It is absurd to profess Christ Jesus, and to
> Judaize (chh. 7-10, A-N)

Ignatius wished to warn the Magnesians "not to fall into the snare of
vain doctrine, but to be convinced of the birth and passion and
resurrection, which took place at the time of the procuratorship of
Pontius Pilate; for these were certainly done by Jesus Christ" (11:1,
Loeb). The birth, suffering and resurrection (ad Philad. 9:2) are the
content of the Gospel of grace and the basis of our salvation; the
relevance of these events was not appreciated. In judging the heretics
of Asia, Ignatius naturally applied his anti-Docetic principle used at
Antioch, namely, that an Incarnation theology is the necessary basis
of a true Soteriology; in fact, a deficiency in one implied an error in
the other. Finding the Asian's Soteriology defective, he presumed that
they ignored Jesus' life in the flesh. Ignatius was disposed by his
controversies at home to judge all dubious teachings in the light of
Christology and Soteriology he had formulated in Antioch.
Furthermore, had the proponents of "old fables" of Judaism (ad
Magn. 8:1) deemed Jesus an archangel who lacked true and full
human nature, Ignatius would have insisted that he alone manifested
God. Be that as it may, Christ was not being acknowledged as the
only teacher and mediator ("door"), the pre-existent Word; his cosmic
status was thought to be less unique and absolute than that.

   Though a non-controversial writing, 1 Peter teaches a unique
Christology with ambiguous relation to that of the Judaizers.
Exegetical disputes may have formed the background of the following
teaching:

> The prophets who prophesied of the grace that was to be yours searched
> and inquired about this salvation: they inquired what person or time was

indicated by the Spirit of Christ within them when predicting the sufferings of Christ and the subsequent glory. It was revealed to them that they were serving not themselves but you, in the things which have been announced to you . . . , things into which angels long to look (1:10-12).

Thus Christ was active in the prophets before the Incarnation; they thereby understood their predictions about the sufferings, glorification and saving work of Jesus, although the angels remained in ignorance. Such a teaching takes for granted the Old Testament as a major source of Christology. The descent into Hades continued his spiritual relation with ancient Israelites. In the spirit he went to preach the Gospel to the spirits of the dead in prison (3:19-20, 4:6). Possibly the ancient teaching by Christ through the prophets was also taken for granted. But the Messiah and Spirit are linked and internalized (ἐν αὐτοῖς) by 1 Peter even for Old Testament times. The language of Ignatius and the Pastoral Epistles is found in 1 Pet. 1:20: Christ "was destined before the foundation of the world but was made manifest (φανερωθέντος) at the end of the times." His Parousia is termed, "ἀποκάλυψις Ἰησοῦ χριστοῦ" (1:7, 13). Yet the fact and importance of his humanity are emphasized. Through his bloody sacrifice (1:2, 19) he suffered and bore our sins in his body (σῶμα) on the cross (2:21, 23-24). He suffered in the flesh (σάρξ) (4:1; cf. 13; 5:1) and was put to death σαρκὶ (3:18). "By his wounds you have been healed" (2:24). "We have been born anew to a living hope through the resurrection of Jesus Christ" (1:3). Salvation is through faith in him (1:8-9; cf. 4-5, 21). God "has called you to his eternal glory in Christ" (5:10). For He "raised him from the dead and gave him glory" (1:21). The doxology of 4:11 reveals the extent of Christological developments: "that in everything God may be glorified through Jesus Christ. To him belong glory and dominion for ever and ever. Amen."

Rev. 1:6 repeats the doxology addressed to Christ: "to him be glory and dominion for ever and ever. Amen." The letter to the church of Laodicea (3:14-22), which had been troubled by the Asian heresy (Col. 2:1; 4:16), contains teachings about Jesus which would have been relevant replies. He is the αρχή of the creation of God (3:14), i.e. the Alpha or the first (πρῶτος) (1:17; 22:13). Since the latter term is also applied to God (1:8; 21:6), the closest parallel is to be seen in Col. 1:15, where Christ is designated "εἰκών of the invisible God, πρωτότοκος of all creation." Also implicit is his being πρωτότοκος of the dead (1:5), as in Col. 1:18 (πρωτότοκοσ from the dead, that in everything he might be preëminent πρωτεύων"). His primacy extends to both the old and new creation. Just as he himself conquered death and sat down with his Father on his throne, Christ will grant to other martyrs who conquer, the privelege of reigning with him (3:21; cf. 2:7, 26-27; 5:10; 20:4; Col. 3:1). He reproves and chastens those whom he loves (3:19), as does God (Prov. 3:12; Hebr. 12:5-6). But the Messianic banquet begins now for those who hear his voice and open the door (3:20). Having been instructed to write to "the angel of the church in Philadelphia" (3:7), John sets forth an apocalyptic Christology reflecting a background similar to that of the Asian "heretics." Christ is "the holy one, the true one, who has the key of David,[22] who opens and no one shall shut, who shuts and no one opens . . . I have set before you an open door, which no one is able to shut . . . He who conquers, I will make him a pillar in the temple of my God; never shall he go out of it, and I will write on him the name of my God, and the name of the city of my God, the new Jerusalem. . . , and my own new name" (3:7, 8, 12). To Jesus is thus attributed the power of David to admit His people to the new Jerusalem; his decision on admission and exclusion is final. His role in eschatological warfare is clearly enunciated by John. The Word of God in righteousness "judges and makes war. His eyes are like a flame of fire . . . He is clad in a robe dipped in blood . . . And the armies of heaven . . . followed him on white horses. From his mouth issues a sharp sword with which to smite the nations, and he will rule them with a rod of iron; he will tread the wine press of the fury of the wrath of God the Almighty" (19:11-15 cf. 1:16; 2:12, 16, 18, 26-27, 12:5; 17:14). The armies of the beast and kings are to be "slain by the sword of him who sits upon the horse, the sword that issues from his mouth" (19:21). The language would be appealing to the "heretics."

John the Baptist revealed himself only as a voice crying in the wilderness . . . (Isa. 40:3; Mk. 1:3; Jn. 1:23). He was preparing the way of the Lord by preaching judgment against oppressors (Mal. 3:1, 5; Lk. 3:10-14). W. H. Brownlee [23] and John Robinson [24] attractively suggest that he was carrying out this mission because the Qumran

---

[22] The keys to heaven are possessed by Michael (3 Baruch 11:3, cf. 4 Baruch 9:5); the keys on amulets belong to Jesus or Michael (Bagatti, op. cit., 240-41).

[23] Art. cit., ap. Stendahl, op. cit., 47.

[24] Twelve N.T. Studies, 13-15.

community had neglected it (1QS 8.12-16). Though thinking himself to be a prophet (Mk. 11:32; Lk. 3:2) like Elijah (2 Kings 1:8 LXX; Zech. 13:4; cf. Jn. 1:21),[25] he announced the coming of the eschatological fire-baptizer (Mt. 3:11-12; Lk. 3:16-17),[26] who is apparently Elijah, the man of fire (1 Kings 18:38; 2 Kings 1:10, 12; 2:9-11; Ecclus. 48:3-10; Mal. 3:1-3; 4:5-6; Mt. 11:14; Lk. 9:54; 4 Ezra 13:10-11; cf. Lk. 12:49-50; Rev. 11:5). No other Messianic figure appears in Sirach. As Elijah is to fight and destroy the Antichrist (Apoc. Elijah, ed. Steindorff 169; Tertullian, *de anima* 50; cf. Rev. 11:7) in later literature,[27] John probably thought that the Coming One would vanquish an anti-messiah. If fire awaited fruit trees (Jews), the great adversary of God would not be spared. Had not Elijah overcome Baal?

John was later honored as the forerunner of the Lord God (ἐνώπιον αὐτοῦ) (Lk. 1:16-17, 76), prophet of the Most High (1:76; cf. Mt. 11:9), "in the spirit and power of Elijah" (though not Elijah in person) (1:17). He was "to give knowledge of salvation to his people in the forgiveness of sin, . . . to give light to those who sit in darkness. . . , to guide our feet into the way of peace" (1:77, 79). These verses are a midrash on Malachi 2:5-6; 3:1, 18; 4:5. Thus [28] he fulfilled the role of Levitic messenger who will purify the sons of Levi, who have corrupted the covenant of Levi (Mal. 1:6; 2:1-9; 3:1-5). Jesus, on the other hand, was a Davidic Messiah (Lk. 1:27, 32-33, 69; 2:4), though his genealogy contained many priestly names (Lk. 3) [29] and his mother was a kinswoman of Elizabeth (1:36), a daughter of Aaron (1:5). Through the co-deliverers Israel would be saved from its enemies (Romans and wicked priests) and would be able to serve God "without fear, in holiness and righteousness" (1:68-75). The good news begins with John (1:19). Jesus is both royal and priestly Messiah; John is his subordinate eschatological collaborator. Though John was "great before the Lord" (1:15), he was inferior to the great Virgin-born Son of the Most High who was to reign forever over the house of Jacob (1:32-35).[30] John's manifestation (ἀνάδειξις) unto Israel

---

[25] Kraeling, *op. cit.*, 92, 143; J. Jeremias, Ἠλίας, in Kittel (ed.), ii, 936-37.

[26] Kraeling, *op. cit.*, 61-63, 116-17; Scobie, *op. cit.*, 67-70.

[27] Jeremias, *ap.* Kittel (ed.), ii, 940-41; Howard C. Kee, "The Transfiguration in Mark: Epiphany or Apocalyptic Vision?," in *Understanding the Sacred Text* (Essays in honor of Morton S. Enslin), ed. John Reumann, Valley Forge, Pa. (Judson, 1972), 145-46.

[28] Wink, *op. cit.*, 75.

[29] *Ibid.*, 77.   [30] Laurentin, *op. cit.*, 30-38.

(1:80) fulfills the eschatological good news (1:16, 19). But the overshadowing of Mary by the glory of God (1:35; cf. Exod. 40:34-35; Rev. 15:8) was a theophany reminiscent of the transfiguration (Mk. 9:7). The well-known parallelism of the two birth-infancy accounts demonstrates the belief that John and Jesus acted as a pair of God's agents in eschatological salvation; but the differences reveal an inequality. This unity [31] reflects a a long-standing veneration for both among followers of the Prophet who found the royal, priestly Messiah.

That the twelve men whom Paul found at Ephesus (Acts 19:1-7) were Christians is evident from their unqualified designation as disciples (μαθηταί) and believers (πιστεύσωσιν). Only recognized believers could be meaningfully asked if they had received the Holy Spirit upon believing. Only later did he learn that they, like many other Christians (Acts 1:22; 18:25), had received John's baptism. Nevertheless, Paul considered their brand of Christianity to be so immature and defective that he deemed rebaptism to be necessary. Their Christology and the form of their baptism were imperfect. When Paul asked, "Unto what as the object of faith and confession (εἰς τί) were you baptized?" (v. 3), he had to instruct them that John had told the people to believe in Jesus as the Coming One (v. 4). Upon learning that John had identified him as the object of faith, they were baptized in the name of the Lord Jesus (vv. 4-5) "for the remission of sins" (Western text addition). They apparently had not believed in the forgiveness of sins in the name of Jesus. These semi-Christian "disciples", however undevelopped and uncertain was the attitude toward Jesus, did hold him in honor and were fully receptive to Paul's mature Christology. They had venerated him as at least an inspired teacher and prophet who had completed the work of John in preparing "the people" for the eschaton.

Hegesippus (ap. Eusebius, H.E. ii. 23) has James, brother of Jesus, preach that the Messiah is Savior, the Son of David, the Son of Man who "sits in heaven on the right hand of the Great Power, and is coming on the clouds of heaven", i.e. "coming to reward each according to his works." Hegesippus (ap. Eusebius, H.E. iii, 20.1)

---

[31] Wink, op. cit., 72, 74, 78, 81-82. Augustin George ("Le parallèle entre Jean-Baptiste et Jesus en Lc 1-2," in Mélanges Bibliques en hommage au R. P. Béda Rigaux, Gembloux [J. Duculot, 1970], 171. He points out the parallelism of Moses and Joshua, Moses and Elijah, and Elijah and Elisha (155-56) and suggests that the parallel of Paul and Peter in Acts (159-64) is Luke's reaction against a tendency to oppose Peter to Paul.

records the tradition that Judas' (grand)sons taught that Christ's kingdom was "heavenly and angelic, appearing at the end of the age, when he would come in glory to judge ... and to give to each according to his merits."

The Ascension of Isaiah 10:7-11:17 describes in detail "the coming forth of the Beloved from the seventh heaven, ..., and his transformation, his descent and the likeness into which he was to be transformed, namely, the likeness of a man" (3:13). The Father instructed "my Lord Christ who shall be called Jesus: 'Go and descend through all the heavens, ... even to the angel in the realm of the dead ... And thou shalt become like to the form of all who are in the five heavens; and with carefulness thou shalt resemble the form of the angels of the firmament and the angels who are in the realm of the dead. And none of the angels of this world will know that thou, along with me, art the Lord of the seven heavens and of their angels" (10:7-11). He was born of a holy virgin from the family of David, who uttered no cries of pain and whose "womb was found as it was before she was with child" (11:2, 5, 9, 14). "Mary straightway beheld with her eyes and saw a small child, and she was amazed" (11:8, cf. 10)." "In Nazareth he sucked the breast like a baby, as was customary, so that he would not be recognized" (11:17). In other words, he *acted like* a baby, just as he had "become like the angels of the air" (10:30), so that his identity might be hidden from the angels. Isaiah is told that after "the Lord, who will be called Christ, ... has descended and become like you in appearance," "all the righteous from Adam" "will think that he is flesh and a man" (9:7, 13). Thus "the Lord of all those heavens" was "transformed till he comes to your image and likeness" (8:10). The prophet is further told that the Lord Christ "will be called Jesus on earth, but his name thou canst hear till thou has ascended out of thy body" (9:5; cf. 10:7). After his crucifixion and burial and descent to the underworld (8:14; 9:16; 11:19-22), "the angel of the Holy Spirit and Michael, the chief of the holy angels, would open his grave on the third day, and the Beloved, sitting on their shoulders, will come forth and send out his twelve disciples" (3:16-17; cf. 7:23). After 545 days (9:16; 11:21), Isaiah "saw him ... in the firmament, but he had not changed to their form, and all the angels of the firmament and the Satan saw him, and they worshipped him" (11:23; cf. 10:14-15). Seated thereafter on the other hand of the Father was the angel of the Holy Spirit" (9:35-40; 11:32-33). "The Lord will come with his angels" and "drag Beliar with his hosts into Gehenna" (4:14) and will destroy him (7:12). "The Beloved will cause fire to go forth from himself, and it will consume all the impious" (4:18).

The Apocalypse of Peter (Ethiopic 15-17) presents an elaboration of the Transfiguration narrative in the setting of the Ascension from the holy mountain (cf. 2 Pet. 1:16-19; Pistis Sophia 4-10) or the Mount of Olives (Ethiopic 1, 15) following the eschatological discussions (1 ff.; cf. Mt. 24) and farewell instructions to Peter (14). At this time the glory, Sonship and heavenly tabernacle of Jesus were revealed (16-17). Jesus, Moses and Elijah were greeted by men in the first heaven (Hades-?) amidst amazed angels before they all proceeded to another, higher heaven (17).[32] Thereby he fulfilled his promise (Rainer Fragment), "I shall depart, I and my exulting chosen, with the patriarchs, into my eternal kingdom." He further promised, "with my cross going before my face, I will come in my glory, shining seven times as bright as the sun"(1). His promise to give to his elect a baptism unto salvation from the Acherusian lake (Rainer Fragment; cf. Ethiopic 14) corresponds to the baptism by Michael in the same lake (Apocalypse of Paul 22; Coptic Book of the Resurrection by Bartholomew, ed. Budge 208; James, *Apocr. N.T.*, 185; cf. Apoc. Moses 37). Erik Peterson [33] perceives that "Peter" christianized a Jewish apocalyptic teaching.

IV Baruch 9:14 describes Jesus Christ as "the light of all the ages (αἰώνων) (cf. 9:3, 25; Test. Levi 18:3-4, 8, 13), the unquenchable lamp (λύχνος; cf. Rev. 21:23; 22:5) and the life of the faith (cf. 6:4). Jeremiah beheld him "adorned (κεκοσμημένον) by His Father and coming into (ἐρχόμενον εἰς) the world on the Mount of Olives; and he shall fill the hungry souls" and "make them fruitful ἐν the word of the mouth of the Christ himself" (9:18-19). Presumably this was (to be) done through the Twelve's preaching of the Gospel (9:20), which includes his post-resurrection teaching. The adornment and the appearance on the Mount of Olives were seen as a fulfillment of Psalm 8:4-5 ("What is man that thou art mindful of him, and the son of man...?[34] Yet thou hast made him little less than God, and dost crown him with glory and honor"). He was glorified through his

---

[32] Ernst Kähler, *Studien zum Te Deum und zur Geschichte des 24. Psalms in der alten Kirche*, Göttingen (Vandenhoeck & Ruprecht, 1958), 53-55.

[33] *Art. cit., VC* 9 (1955), 9-12.

[34] "Baruch's" treatment of such parallel terms is revealed in 9:19, where the Ascension of Isaiah (3:9; 11:32) is quoted concerning the Son of God: "I beheld God and the Son of God" (cf. 9:13).

resurrection and ascension (Jn. 17:1; Acts 3:13). "Glorify (δοξάσατε) God, and the Son of God who awakened me from sleep" (4 Bar. 9:13), proclaims Jeremiah. The apocalyptic writer was apparently claiming a vision of the descent of the glorified Lord just before his final ascension. This is distinct from the prophecies, "Γίνεται ... καὶ ερξχεται εἰς τὴν γῆν" (9:14) and ἐλεύσεται, καὶ ἐξελεύσεται (9:18). His pre-existence is implied. His role as Judge is implicit in the prophecy that he will strike down the trees that exalt themselves to the clouds (9:14). Other negative, world-denying aspects of his eschatological career will include turning scarlet white, sweet water salty and white snow black "in the great light of the joy of God" (9:16). The eschatological rejoicing of believers is promised in 6:3-4 (cf. Apoc. Peter 14 [Ethiopic]).

The Christology of the Testament of our Lord Jesus Christ in Galilee is rather unique and developped. Quoting Lev. 17:14-15 and Isa. 22:12-14, respectively, Jesus says: "Through the prophets I have already told their fathers. . ." and "Through the prophet Isaiah have I spoken to them and said. . ."(8, 9). His authority to teach in God's name is manifest in ch. 2: "Listen and pay attention to the voice of your Father. And I will reveal to you. . ." He promises to impart to his people "the will of my Father" (7). "I will reveal what will happen in the world" (2) in the last day. His disciples ask him to explain and show to them what would happen to them before the end of the world, and Jesus promises to teach what would happen both to them and to believers taught by the disciples (4). Jesus thus revealed both the Law and the future through Moses, Isaiah and his own earthly teaching. In form the Testament itself is a record of the words which he "spoke after he rose from the dead" (2). His disciples were able to question him and converse with him during this post-resurrection period (4; cf. Acts 1:1-9). In what form was he then? In a setting which is either Eucharistic or vegetarian, or both, (8) Jesus warns: "But they who are carnal think carnal thoughts of me" (Schmidt), or, "consider me a corporeal being" (Guerrier). As this sentence follows the mention of corpses, it apparently represents a reaction against a corporeal view of Jesus, at least after the Crucifixion. He promises to welcome on the last day those who follow God's commandment to scorn wealth; "their countenance will gleam seven times brighter than the sun" (6).[35] Those who "have followed the way of righteousness

---

[35] Cf. Apoc. Peter 15 (Eth.); 7 (Akhmim). In the Epistle of the Apostles (16) and the Apocalypse of Peter (1, Eth.) Jesus promises that when he comes to judge, he will

will inherit the glory of God and his power" (11). Presumably Jesus
was to be viewed in this eschatological, rather than a corporeal, light.
He applies to himself the words spoken by God in Exod. 6:7 and 2
Sam. 7:14: "I will become God to them and they will be my people. I
will become a father (to them); they will be my sons and daughters. I
will become an altar for them, and they will become a temple for
me" (7). "My people" include those who are misled by their bishops
and pastors (9). Their becoming sons of Jesus (7) means they are to
hearken to his voice and revelations (1). In a covenantal sense we may
think of "children of Abraham" receiving the inherited promises, or
of the blessed descendants of Jonadab and Rechab who "drank no
wine and heeded the commands of their fathers" (9). But Jesus'
relation to "my heavenly Father" (4, 7) was obviously deemed closer
than that of Abraham or Rechab; he was to "become God to them"
(believers) and their altar. That is, their sacrifice of worship with a
pure heart (9) was to be offered through Christ; they would approach
God through him as mediator, and address their prayers to him. For
"the glory and power of God" was his (11). Faith in him is a corollary.
His disciples taught men who believe in him (4). The sinners are
"those who do not believe in me, who will not recognize my signs;
but my beloved will" (2). "The Lord will appear to those who have
trusted in him" (God -?) (7). They love his name more than their own
(7). "Then will the believers and also they who do not believe see a
trumpet in heaven which comes down to earth" (4). The disciples are
to preach "to Israel and to the Gentiles, that they may be saved and
flee from the coming wrath and flame of fire" (4). "Prepare your
throne for your King; prepare yourself for the day of destruction" (5).
His role at this time was manifold. "I will be witness of your deeds
and of all your error" (4). His judgment (punishment) will come upon
misleading bishops and pastors (9). The Lord (God-?) will cast
(sinners) in the fire which is not extinguished and where the worm
does not sleep" (11). But the righteous "will rejoice in my kingdom"
(11; cf. Test. Levi 18:14), teaches the risen Lord.

The Hebrew Christian utilization of the angelic category for the
Messiah was based on the Old Testament. Either the humanity or the
divinity of angels could be thereby stressed. Maurice Jones [36]
observed that "the Angelology of the Old Testament is marked by a

"come as the sun which bursts forth, ... shining seven times brighter than it in glory"
(cf. Asc. Isa. 4:15-16; 8:14-15; 9:9, 27).
[36] *Art. cit., Expositor* viii-15 (1918), 375.

strong anthropomorphic character. Angels, so far as they are delineated, appear in human form, and human terminology is invariably associated with them." In Rabbinic and other late Jewish literature, likewise, angels appear in human form.[37] On the other hand, M. Takahashi has astutely written:[38]

> The angel is, so to speak, a concrete manifestation of God,... an important form of theophany. Angelology in the Old Testament corresponds with Christology in the New Testament; at least it may be said that the former has become a starting point of the latter.

He cites[39] several epiphany stories wherein "God and angels take turns to reveal themselves," namely, Gen. 18:1-33; 19:15-22; 21:17-18; Judg. 6:7-24; 13:3-22. This "fluctuation between God and angels" illustrates the angelic epiphany. Accordingly it would not have been impossible for those Christians whose frame of reference was angelological, to say that God appeared on the earth in the form of a man, Jesus, who like an angel, could be invisible after his resurrection and communicate revelations to the apostles.

The Ebionites, according to Epiphanius (*Haer.* 30, 16.4), said that Christ was "created as one of the archangels, yet greater, and that he reigns over the angels and over all things made by the Almighty."[40] The Clementine Recognitions (ii, 42) and Homilies (xviii, 4) teach that God granted to every nation an angel ("prince" or "god" or star [ix, 27]), but the government of the Hebrews was committed to the greatest archangel, the god of "princes" or "gods, the prince of light" i.e. Christ. As Michael[41] is the angel of the Jewish people and generally considered to be the highest archangel, he is the one believed to be the Messiah (cf. Hermas, *Sim.* viii, 3. 3). The Pseudo-Cyprian treatise, *De Centesima sexagesima tricesima*,[42] contains a comparable teaching: "When the Lord created the angels from fire numbering seven, He constituted one of them his Son. And it is he whom Isaiah declares to be the Lord Sabaoth. We see that there were six angels who had been created together with the Son" (lines 216-20). Elsewhere (line 50) the treatise states that Christ is the Son of God created (*creatus*) by the divine mouth. According to the Clementine Recognitions (i, 68), James, the Lord's brother "showed

---

[37] Michl, *art. cit., Reallexicon f. Ant. u Chr.*, v(1962), 68, 88-89.

[38] *Art. cit., Zeitschr. Alttest. Wiss.* 78 (1966), 344.

[39] *Ibid.*, 346-48.

[40] Danielou, *Histoire des doctrines...*, 171-77; 121-27 (ET).

[41] On the identification of Christ as Michael, see Testa, *op. cit.*, 61-62.

[42] Ed. R. Reitzenstein, *ZNTW* 15 (1914), 82.

that the two advents of Him are foretold: one in humiliation, ... the other in glory."

In the Book of James (14:1) Joseph confesses the possibility that Mary's pregnancy "may have sprung from the angels." The Infancy Gospel of Thomas (7:4; 17:2) includes the acclamation of the Christ Child as a god or an angel of God. In the Gospel of Didymus Judas Thomas (Log. 13), Peter confesses that Jesus is "like a righteous angel."

Marcion, a native of Sinope in Pontus, taught that Jesus bore the nature of an angel (Tertullian, *de carne Christi* 14) and suddenly in the fifteenth year of Tiberius came down to Capernaum (Tertullian, *Adv. Marc.* I, 19; IV, 7).

Justin frequently spoke of appearances of the angel of the Lord or the angel of mighty counsel in the Old Testament as Christophanies (*Dialogue* 59-60, 76, 86, 126-29). Yet caution is necessary in interpreting the Martyr's terminology. For, in *Dial.* 56 he wrote that the Lord who appeared in human form to Abraham (and Moses: Apol. 63.4) is "called an ἄγγελος, because he announces to men whatsoever the Maker of all things ... wishes to announce to them." The angel who appeared to Jacob was the first begotten of all creation (*Dial.* 125) and the permanent Logos (*Dial.* 128). Because even Justin, Tertullian (*adv. Marc.* iii, 9), Irenaeus (*Demonstration of the Apostolic Preaching*, 44-46; cf. 50, 73), and later Cyprian (*Testimonies* ii, 5-6) thought that Christ appeared to the Patriarchs as an angel, and because Philo could equate λογος and ἄγγελος (Conf. 146-47), the natural inclination at an early date to use angelic categories to describe Christ should be recognized. D. Plooij [43] pointed out that the titles, "God" and "angel" are together applied to Jesus by Justin (*Dial.* 125) and Cyprian (*Testimonies* ii, 5).

> Justin speaks of ἄγγελος καὶ ἀπόστολος as the two titles given to Christ as well as to the Prophets ... The proof-texts quoted by Cyprian are Gen. 31:13, Ex. 13:21 (*deus praeibat*), Ex 14:19, Ex. 23:20f; the last being the testimony also quoted by Justin. In none of these passages is there any other word used by either the Massorah, or the Targum or the LXX except *malak* ἄγγελος. But if we look up the Samaritan Targum, we shall find that in Ex. 23:20, 23 it has instead of *malak* ... the reading *shalach* my Apostle ... And it would seem that Hebrews, or theTestimony Book used by Hebrews, had avoided the title *angelos* on purpose, using the alternative reading ἀπόστολος in its stead [3:1].

---

[43] "Studies in the Testimony Book," *Verhandelingen der Koninklijke Akad. van Wetensch. te Amsterdam. Afd. Letterkunde*, 1932, 46, 47.

J. Rendel Harris [44] and Adolphine Bakker [45] believed that this mid-first century Palestinian Aramaic Christian Testimony Book was being attacked by Josephus when he described Jesus in his *War* ii.9 (between 174 and 175), Slavonic text:

> At that time a certain man appeared, if indeed it is proper to call him a man. His nature and form were human, but ... his deeds were divine ... Therefore it is impossible for me to call him a human. But again, ... I will not call him an angel...

While it is most improbable that the Testimony Book or Josephus' *War* rejected the title "angel" for Jesus, the authors of Hebrews and of this Slavonic text [46] did know and reject the title. The Shepherd of Hermas, however, was willing to ascribe angelic titles to Christ. [47]

The Elkesaites taught the gigantic nature of the angel Jesus (Hippolytus, *Ref.* ix, 13.1-3; Epiphanius, *Haer.* 19, 4; 30, 17.7; 53, 1; cf. 5 Esra 42-48; Gospel of Peter 10, 40). As giants were born from the union of the sons of God and women (Gen. 6:1-4), the Elkesaites probably taught the angelic paternity of Jesus.

A number of ossuaries and archaeological monuments [48] associate the letters *aleph* and alpha with Christ as if he were "The Firstborn" (cf. Rev. 21:6; 22:13). Other inscriptions (e.g. the ancient Semitic letters *hé, heth* and *kaph* and the Greek *psi*) represent Jesus with Michael and Gabriel; he is associated with the six angels of creation by a six- or eight-ray star. His designation on ossuaries as *Gheburoth* ("power") was symbolized by the initial *ghimmel* or *gamma*.

Luke 1-2 unites the Aaronic and Davidic types of Messianism (see above, p. 160, n. 58). Hippolytus, who had access to Jewish

---

[44] *Josephus and His Testimony*, 8, 10.

[45] "Christ an Angel?", *ZNTW* 32 (1933), 254-61, 263-64.

[46] See Eisler, *op. cit.*, 384, 389-91, 429, 456 (cf. 149, 152). He makes a strong case for the original inclusion and later repression of a physical caricature of Jesus (393-456); such was also the case in the Slavonic text's description of John as an unlearned, hairy wild man (224, 225, 239-40). Both John (224-25) and Jesus are accused of arousing anti-Roman hopes for freedom. We would concur with Goguel (*The Life of Jesus*, New York [Macmillan, 1954], 89) that Jesus is viewed as a timid imposter, and with Eisler that John was also treated as an imposter. Though Jesus was a wonder-worker, he was unlike Moses and one "sent by God" (i.e. an angel) in regard to lawgiving and freeing his people. For a bibliography on the Slavonic version, see Louis Feldman, *Studies in Judaica. Scholarship on Philo and Josephus* (1937-1962), New York (Yeshiva Univ., n.d.), 28-30. Felix Scheidweiler ("Sind die Interpolationen im altrussischen Josephus wertlos?", *ZNTW* 43 [1950-51], 176) thinks that the additions came from a contemporary Jewish history with a standpoint differing from Josephus'.

[47] Danielou, *Hist. des doctrines*, 169-72; Longenecker, *op. cit.*, 27, n. 6.

[48] Bagatti, *op. cit.*, 147-60; cf. 211, 237.

Christian traditions, traced the genealogy of Jesus as priest and king to the tribes of Levi and Judah (*On the Blessings of Isaac, Jacob and Moses, PO* 27[1954], 72, 144-45). Hegesippus related that Simeon and the (grand) sons of Judas belonged to the family of the Lord and the family of David (*ap*. Eusebius, *H.E.* iii, 20.1; 32.3). On the other hand, it was lawful for James to enter the Holy of Holies and to wear linen (ii, 23.6). Epiphanius (*Haer*. 29.4; 78.14) concurs in making him a priest, as he wore the πέταλον. The successor of James was his cousin Simeon, son of Clopas (Hegesippus, *ap*. Eusebius, *H.E.* iv, 22), and was identified as the Rechabite priest who tried to stop the stoning of James (ii, 23.15-17; Epiphanius, *Haer*. 78.14). As Simeon was considered to be a son of David and of Rechab (see above p. 161), as well as a son of Clopas, the brother of Joseph (Epiphanius 78.7),[49] it appears that the family of Clopas and Joseph was both Davidic and Rechabite. A Davidic origin was attributed to Mary's family (Ascension of Isa. 11:2; Book of James 10.1; Justin, *Dial*. 43.1; 45.4; 100.3; 120.2). A scribe of Tiberius drew up a genealogy showing her Davidic descent (*P.O.* 8, 722 & 778). Thus in some circles, a royal and a poor priestly origin was deemed appropriate for *both* Joseph and Mary. Thereby Jesus would have both lineages, irrespective of the divisive issue of the Virgin Birth.

According to Sokolov's chief Slavonic manuscript of the Book of the Secrets of Enoch, Melchizedek was conceived and born miraculously (iii.2, 7-21) and was taken by Michael up (cf. Rev. 12:4-6) to the paradise of Eden for forty days during the Flood (iii. 28-29; iv. 1-9). He was "the great high priest, the Word of God, and the power to work great and glorious marvels above all that have been" (iii. 34). The seal of the priesthood on his breast was "glorious in countenance" (iii.19). After him another Melchizedek was to arise (iv. 6; cf. iii.37).[50]

Melchizedek was considered by the Asian Theodotus the Banker to be a great unbegotten power who is mediator and intercessor for angels and heavenly powers (Hippolytus, *Philos*. 7.36; Epiphanius, *Haer*. 55.1; Philaster, *Haer*. 52; Pseudo-Tertullian, *Adv. Omn. Haer*. 8). The teaching that Melchizedek was an angel was known to Origen and Didymus (according to Jerome: *Epist*. 73.2 *ad Evangelium*), Cyril of Alexandria (*Glaphyr. in Genes*. ii, 3; Migne, *P.G.* 59, 84C & 101C)

---

[49] See my forthcoming article, "The Family of Jesus," in *Evangelical Quarterly*.

[50] David Flusser, "Jesus in the Context of History", in Arnold Toynbee (ed.), *The Crucible of Christianity*, London (Thames & Hudson, 1969), 229.

and Pseudo-Augustine (*Quaest. in Pentateuch.* lxxii; Migne, *P.L.* 34, iii, 567).[51] As Hebrews compared Melchizedek to Christ, the development of Christology in the first centuries brought with it a potential reassessment of the earlier angelic identity of the priest-king of Salem. As the angelic category for Christ fell into disuse, so it might for Melchizedek as well. It was supplanted by the related Logos category, possibly under Montanist influence.

Mark the Hermit reported the following teachings of the Melchizedekians. They denied that "Melchizedek was a man and not Christ himself" (*P.G.* 65, 1121A). They argued: "Suppose Melchizedek were a man, likened (ἀφομοιωμίνος) to Christ. Explain to us how he is 'without father and mother, having no beginning of days or end of life', likened in everything to the Son of God. Show us the comparison (ἀφομοιωσιν), so we may recognize that Melchizedek is a man and not Christ himself" (1120-1121A). They asked, "If Melchizedek is a man, how does he remain a priest forever?" (1120C; 1125A). They said further, "How was he a priest before (*prò*) the Law if he were not God?" (1133B). They asserted that "Melchizedek is God by nature (φυσει θεὸς)" (1128D; cf. 1136 A & B). "If he is not God, how did he by his own blood drive away the destroyer of angels" and ". . . how did he heal those injuries received from the serpents?" (1128A). They said, "Unless he were God, how could he be without father and mother?. . . Melchizedek would no longer be Son but Father . . . He was not the Father but the God Word (ὁ θεὸς Λογος) before he put on flesh (σαρκωθῆναι) and was born from Mary. . . And how was Christ, being born from the tribe of Judah, without father and mother, according to the order of Melchizedek?" (1120B). They taught: "Say of Christ what you say of Melchizedek, that he had neither beginning of days nor end of life . . . The Word changed Himself (τραπεὶς) into a man" (1121 C & D). "The Lord assumed our body. . . The God Word was born a bare (ψιλος) man" (1124A). "Because Melchizedek is likened to the Son of God, he is not Son by nature, and he is the King of Righteousness by interpretation (ἐρμηνευόμενός), not by nature" (1133D). "If he was the King of Righteousness and King of Peace, he was not so by nature, but by interpretation" (1128B). "If he were not the Son of God, how could he be called the King of Peace and King of Righteousness? . . . The Apostle does not call him King of Peace by nature (φυσει), but by

[51] Bardy, *art. cit., RB* 35 (1926), 500; 36 (1927), 28-29; de Jong and van der Woude, *art. cit., NTS* 12 (1965-66), 323-26.

interpretation" (1120A). In sum, the Melchizedekians considered
Melchizedek to be, not a human, but Christ the Word, who by nature
was God rather than Son. The Melchizedekians known to Timothy of
Constantinople also extolled (αὐχοῦσιν) Melchizedek (P.G. 86, 33B).
This glorification, as it did not meet with Timothy's approval,
ostensibly was the attribution of a higher status to Melchizedek than
he merited, i.e. assigning him a status too much like Christ's and a
nature too divine. The Paris. graec. 364 manuscript may contain a
false, but easily made, inference where reading, "They declare that
Melchizedek is the God and Father of our Lord Jesus Christ; that is
why, they say, he is said to be without father, mother or genealogy."

In spite of its uncertain, if not late, sources, the Gospel of
Bartholomew has an illuminating Christology. "We praise thee as
God," proclaimed Bartholomew (IV, 69). "Abba, Father, who . . . were
pleased to be contained easily and without pain in the body of the
Virgin. . . ,[52] you who wore a crown of thorns, in order to prepare for
us repentant sinners the precious heavenly crown, who hung upon
the cross in order to give us to drink the wine of contrition. . ." (IV,
61-62; cf. 17). Jesus said his role was to "heal every sin of the
ignorant and give to men the truth of God" (IV, 65). When he rose
again, he had "put off this body of flesh"; "his appearance was not as
it was before, but revealed the fulness of his godhead" (I, 2 3). He
reveals: "I went to the underworld to bring up Adam and all the
patriarchs, Abraham, Isaac and Jacob. The archangel Michael had
asked me to do this" (I, 9). When he descended to the underworld. . ."
Hades said to Beliar: I perceive that God has come down here" (I, 10
H; cf. 19), but Beliar said, "God does not come down upon the earth"
(I, 18 H).

The Council of Laodicea's decree that "on the sabbath the Gospels
are to be read with the other Scriptures" (Can. 16) suggests that
Christology in some circles was being based on the Old Testament to
the virtual exclusion of canonical Gospels.

Because Paul, in formulating his Christology, ignored the Son of
Man motif as found in the words of Jesus and Jewish apocryphal
literature, there is reason to suspect that his opponents were using the
concept for their Christology. Daniel (7:13-14) had beheld the
coming, "with the clouds of heaven", of "one like a son of man," to
whom everlasting dominion was given. The pre-existence of the Son
of Man is taught in 1 Enoch 48:2-3, 6, and his epiphany in 38:2;

[52] Cf. Asc. Isa. 11:14; Acts of Peter, ch. 24.

69:29. Sigmund Mowinckel [53] points out that "it is the epiphany or revelation of the Son of Man which absorbs the interest of the apocalyptists, which they behold in vision after vision." The word, epiphany, conveys the thought that "from his hidden state of pre-existence he will suddenly appear, and reveal himself to the longing righteous ones in his celestial splendour and glory." Leaving aside the question of the original text and interpolations, we can find several references to the Messianic appearance in the Testaments of the Twelve Patriarchs: ". . . until the salvation of Israel shall come, [until the appearing (παρουσία) of the God of righteousness], that Jacob [and all the Gentiles] may rest in peace" (T. Jud. 22:2). The Most High said to Levi, "I have given thee the blessings of the priesthood until I come and sojourn (ἐλθὼν κατοικήσω) in the midst of Israel "(T. Levi 5:2; cf. 8:10-11, Ms. A: πορουσία of the Lord). Through the tribes of Levi and Judah "shall God appear (ὀφθήσεται) [dwelling among men] on earth, to save the face of Israel, and to gather together the righteous men from amongst the Gentiles" (T. Napht. 8:3). By Levi "and Judah shall the Lord appear (ophthésetai) among men "(T. Levi 2:11). "God will dwell with men on earth [in visible form]," according to the (interpolated) Vita Adae 29:7. The Syriac Testament of Adam (iii) [54] prophesies that "God will descend to earth from heaven at the end of time; he will be born of a virgin; he[55] will be clothed in a body; . . . he will grow as a child." According to the Testament of Solomon (xxii. 20 [121-22 Conybeare]), "The only ruling God . . ., whom the archangels worship,. . . is to be born of a virgin and crucified by the Jews upon a cross" (cf. T. Levi 4:1, where the crucifixion is the passion [πάθει] of the Most High). The Lives of the Prophets prophesy the arrival in Egypt of "a virgin bearing a child of divine appearance" who would be placed in a manger and bowed down to (Jeremiah). The Lord will come down upon the earth from heaven (Hosea; the Armenian, D¹EF add: "and will walk with men").[56] "God shall appear upon the earth in the form of a man and shall take upon himself all the iniquities of the world" (Daniel; the Armenian adds: "and shall be crucified," and B adds: his "ἀνασκολοπίζεσθαι by the priests of the law"). "Then shall a sign be

[53] Op. cit., 388 ff.
[54] Renan, art. cit., Journal Asiatique v-2 (1853), 455; cf. 456, 457; Kmosko, Patrologia Syriaca i-2, 1340-41, 1345, 1348.
[55] The T. of Isaac (Arabic 143; Coptic 63) prophesies: "Jesus the Messiah shall come of thy seed of a virgin whose name is Miriam".
[56] This reading (κύριος . . . τοῖς ἀνθρώποις συναναστρεφόμενος) recurs in T. Dan 5:13.

glorified greatly unto Israel, for the Lord God appearing (φαινόμενος) on earth shall come [as man], and saving through him man" (T. Sim. 6:5). The latter passage continues, "God hath taken a body (σῶμα) and eaten with men and saved men," though this passage is bracketed by Charles. The case is similar for T. Ash. 7:3 ("Until the Most High shall visit the earth, coming Himself [as man, with men eating and drinking] ... He shall save Israel and all the Gentiles [God ὑποκρινόμενος of man]") and for T. Benj. 10:7-8 (Greek, not Armenian texts) ("... worshipping the King of heaven, who, appeared [φανέντα or φαινόμενον] upon earth in the form of a man of humility [ταπείνωσις] ... When he appeared [παραγενόμενον] as God in the flesh to deliver them, they believed Him not"). Zebulon tells his sons that they shall see the Lord Himself, the light of righteousness, in Jerusalem [ἐν σχήματι ἀνθρώπου] (T. Zeb. 9:8). Although these "incarnation" passages are to be used cautiously, the undisputed texts do allow for the personal appearance of God on earth to save Israel and the Gentiles. Whether or not his were a truly human form, it could be as an angel. I Enoch 46:1-2 describes the Son of Man as a "being whose countenance had the appearance of a man, and his face was full of graciousness, like one of the holy angels." Likewise, Noah at his birth resembled "sons of the God of heaven," as if he had "sprung from the angels" (1 Enoch 106:5-6). "One having the appearance of a man" signified an angel in Dan. 8:15; 10:16, 18 (cf. Gen. 18:1-2, 8; 32:24-32; Judges 6:11 ff.; 13; Apoc. Abr. 10). Hence, having the appearance of the Son of Man is analagous to resembling an angel. The Messianic "eating with men" (T. Sim. 6:7; T. Asher 7:3) is reminiscent of angels' eating with Abraham (Gen. 18:8;19:3). This apocryphal Hebrew Christian Christology becomes more intelligible in light of some of Robert North's conclusions in his article, "Separated Spiritual Substances in the Old Testament":[57]

> The *malak* who seems to speak as God himself either really is God or is a being distinct from God ... The earlier OT focuses *malak* as bearer of God's word, representing him but not 'sent' by him ... The basic sense of *malak*, the Hebrew word rendered *angelos*, is 'Presence.' As applied to God himself appearing to men, this presence may be called 'manifestation.'... The theophanic angel is either God himself or it is not. If or when it is God, this fact is known only because it speaks as God, not from any description of its external appearance or activities, or of its nature: it is a superhuman being, but not ... messenger ... If or when the *malak yhwh* is not God, it is ... an apparently human person

---

[57] *CBQ* 29 (1967), 142, 118, 132; cf. 119.

... There is no evidence that this quasi-messenger, if not God, is a pure spirit ... It is a heavenly being, but in its activities rather than its nature.

The apocryphal affirmation that God appeared on earth in human form did not go beyond Scriptural categories.

One of the roles of archangels is to overcome the devil. In the Apocalypse of Abraham (ch. 10) the angel Jaoel boasts: "Unto me are subject the attack and menace of every single reptile" (cf. ch. 23, where Azazel is identified as a serpent). In ch. 29 Azazel and the heathen worship the man who is insulted and beaten in the last days. In the Assumption of Moses 10:1-2 the chief of the angels leads in the ultimate defeat of Satan. That he is probably to be identified with Michael may be deduced from the latter's role in resisting the angels of other nations (Dan. 10:13, 21; 12:1) and in fighting against the dragon and his angels (Rev. 12:7-9). In the Testament of Solomon, Christ is the "angel of great counsel (βουλῆς) who has bound certain demons (11:5-6; 12:3; 22:20); he whose name is 644, which is Emmanuel, has ἐξουσία over spirits (15:10). The Testament of Judah promises that after the Messianic star from Jacob judges and saves and the patriarchs are resurrected, then "there shall be no more spirit of deceit of [Beliar], for he shall be cast into the fire forever" (25:3). Levi tells his children about the new priest to be raised up by the Lord: "Beliar shall be bound by him, and he shall give power to His children to tread upon the evil spirits" (T. Levi 18:12). It is natural to associate this passage with T. Sim. 6:5-6: when the Lord God appears on earth and saves man, "then shall all the spirits of deceit be given to be trodden under foot, and men shall rule over wicked spirits." When the Most High visits (ἐπισκέψηται)the earth, he shall "break the head of the dragon in (διά) the water" (T. Ash. 7:3; cf. Ps. 74:13). The reference in T. Dan 5:10-11 is probably Messianic:[58] And there shall arise unto you from the tribe of [Judah and of] Levi the salvation of the Lord; and he shall make war against Beliar, and execute an everlasting vengeance on our enemies; and the captivity shall he take from Beliar the [souls of the saints (ἅγιοι)]. After the crucifixion, "Belial and his impure spirit shall be crushed and immediately the spirit of grace shall be poured upon all the heathen" (Lives of the Prophets, Daniel, Armenian). After the resurrection "the Lord shall judge Israel first ... And then shall He judge all the Gentiles." The

[58] Beasley-Murray (*JTS* 48 [1947], 4-5) considers the passage non-Messianic.

intervening passages bracketed by Charles tell of His appearance on earth in human flesh (T. Benj. 10:8-10). Levi promises that the Lord would "raise up a new priest ... And he shall execute a righteous judgment upon the earth for a multitude of days" (T. Levi 18:2). I Enoch attributes to the Son of Man, the Elect One, [59] all judgment: over angels and earth-dwellers (41:9; 61:8; 62:2ff.; 69:27; cf. 48:9). The Apocalypse of Abraham divides judgment thus: "I will send mine Elect One, having in him all my power ... and this one shall summon my despised people from the nations, and I will burn with fire those who have insulted them" (ch. 31). The Hebrew Apocalypse of Elijah (ed. Buttenweiser, 18-19, 63-65) predicts the Messiah's descent with angels of death in order to vanquish in battle first the warring armies and then all the remaining heathen. Eldad and Medad prophesied that during Messianic times in warfare with the Jews the heathen of Magog will be slain by the Lord or the Messiah (Targ. Yer. to Num. xi, 26).[60]

The positive aspect of the work of the new priest is set forth by the Messianic hymn of T. Levi 18:

> And his star shall arise in heaven as of a king,
> Lighting up the light of knowledge as the sun the day...
> And there shall be peace in all the earth...
> [And the knowledge of the Lord shall be poured forth upon the earth,
>   as the water of the seas;]...
> And in his priesthood the Gentiles shall be multiplied in knowledge
>   upon the earth,
> And enlightened through the grace of the Lord:...
> [And the just shall rest in him.]
> And he shall open the gates of paradise,
> And shall remove the threatening sword against Adam.
> And he shall give to the saints to eat from the tree of life,
> And the spirit of holiness shall be on them...
> And the Lord shall rejoice in His children,
> And be well-pleased in His beloved ones for ever...
> And all the saints shall clothe themselves with joy.

The First Book of Enoch has a similar vision:

> (The Son of Man) shall be a staff to the righteous whereon to stay
>   themselves and not fall,
> And he shall be the light of the Gentiles,
> And the hope of those who are troubled of heart (48:4).

---

[59] J. A. Fitzmyer (art. cit., CBQ 27 [1965], 366) points out that the Messianic title, the "Elect One", is found only in that part of 1 Enoch which is as yet unattested at Qumran.

[60] K. Kohler, "Eldad and Medad," Jewish Encyclopedia 5 (1903), 92.

> For wisdom is poured out like water,
> And glory faileth not before him for evermore.
> For he is mighty in all the secrets of righteousness,
> And unrighteousness shall disappear as a shadow,
> And have no more continuance;
> Because the Elect One standeth before the Lord of Spirits,
> And his glory is for ever and ever,
> And his might unto all generations (49:1-2)

His role in saving the righteous is taught in the same writings.

> He proclaims unto thee peace in the name of the world to come;. . . .
> And all shall walk in (his) ways since righteousness never forsakes him:
> With (him) will be their dwelling-places, and with (him) their
> heritage. . .
> And the righteous shall have peace and an upright way,
> In the name of the Lord of Spirits for ever and ever (1 Enoch 71:15-17).

Simeon foretold: "For the Lord shall raise up from Levi as it were a High-priest, and from Judah as it were a King [God and man], He shall save all [the Gentiles and] the race of Israel" (T. Sim. 7:2). The star arising from Jacob "shall pour out the spirit of grace upon you; and ye shall be unto Him sons in truth, and ye shall walk in His commandments first and last. [This Branch of God Most High, and this Fountain giving life unto all.] . . . And from your root shall arise a stem; and from it shall grow a rod of righteousness to the Gentiles, to judge and to save all that call upon the Lord" (T. Jud. 24:3-6). Dan foresees the salvation of the Lord arising from the tribe of [Judah and of] Levi; and he shall "turn disobedient hearts unto the Lord, and give to them that call upon him eternal peace" (T. Dan 5:10-11). Naphtali charged his descendants to "be united to Levi and to Judah; for through them shall salvation arise unto Israel, and in them shall Jacob be blessed. For through their tribes shall God appear [dwelling among men] on earth, to save the race of Israel, and to gather together the righteous from amongst the Gentiles" (T. Napht. 8:2-3). Joseph likewise exhorted: "My children, honour Levi and Judah, for among them shall arise the salvation of Israel" (T. Jos. 19:11). Charles bracketed T. Benj. 10:8, where the Greek, though not the Armenian, text state that the unrighteous did not believe the Lord "when He appeared as God in the flesh to deliver them."

Mowinckel [61] observes that the wisdom of the Messiah is emphasized. "Wisdom and counsel imply the ability both to see what

---

[61] Op. cit., 309.

is right and to bring it about." He shall be able to judge men's secret ways (1 Enoch 61:9; cf. 49:4).

> And the Elect One shall in those days sit on My throne,
> And his mouth shall (pour) forth all the secrets of wisdom and counsel:
> For the Lord of Spirits hath given (them) to him . . . (1 Enoch 51:3).

> This is the Son of Man who hath righteousness,
> With whom dwelleth righteousness,
> And who revealeth all the treasures of that which is hidden (46:3).

"[And there shall arise in the latter days] one beloved of the Lord, [of the tribe of Judah and Levi], a doer of His good pleasure in his mouth, [with new knowledge enlightening the Gentiles] "(T. Benj. 11:2). T. Levi 18 is a hymn to the Messianic priest:

> Then shall the Lord raise up a new priest,
> And to him all the words of the Lord shall be revealed (v. 2)

And in his priesthood the Gentiles shall be multiplied in knowledge upon the earth,
> And enlightened through the grace of the Lord:
> In his priesthood shall sin come to an end (v.9).

"Benjamin" prophesied that the twelve tribes and all the Gentiles shall be gathered together in the glorious last temple "until the Most High shall send forth His salvation in the visitation of an only-begotten prophet" (T. Benj. 9:2; cf. T. Levi 8:15: "his presence is beloved, as a prophet of the Most High"). According to the Lives of the Prophets, Joel prophesied the "sacrifice and passion of the prophet, the just one" (Armenian, F), and Habakkuk foresaw that "a prophet, the Son of God, should teach in the temple" (Armenian).

In the Lives of the Prophets the relation between the law, the temple and the Messiah is clarified. Jeremiah "before the destruction of the temple, took possession of the ark of the law and the things within it, and caused them to be swallowed up in a rocky cliff . . . in the wilderness where the ark was at first, between the two mountains on which Moses and Aaron were buried, and by night there is a cloud as it were of fire, according to the primal ordinance that the glory of God should never cease from his law . . . No one shall bring forth this ark but Aaron, and the tables within it no one of the priests or prophets shall unfold but Moses." Habbakuk prophesied that when a western nation ends the temple, the angels will secretly carry the inner sanctuary veil and the capitals of the two pillars "into the wilderness where in the beginning the Tabernacle of Witness was

pitched." Jeremiah saw that "in the resurrection the ark will rise first
... from the rock, and will be placed on Mount Sinai; and all the
saints will be assembled to it there, awaiting the Lord and fleeing
from the enemy." The Lord (The Lawgiver of Zion: Armenian) "will
come again with might; and this shall be for you the sign of his
appearance, when the Gentiles worship a piece of wood." Habakkuk
foretold that through the angels (who hid the temple veil and pillars)
the presence of the Lord shall be revealed and those who are fleeing
from the serpent shall be enlightened. Moreover, according to the
Armenian Ezekiel, the temple shall be rebuilt as well as the closed
door "through which the Lord shall enter, in whom all the heathen
shall put their trust." "They that should believe in Him should see
the light and contemplate the glory ...; and they who should not
listen to Him, should remain in darkness" (Habakkuk, Armenian).
Thus the law and the sanctuary are eternal institutions and the
Messiah is to illumine the faithful; "he shall shelter them in the
eternal righteousness" (Habakkuk, Armenian).

It has been much disputed [62] whether the Testaments of the
Twelve Patriarchs tell of two Messiahs: from Levi and from Judah.
The evidence suggests to the present writer but one Messiah
descending from both tribes and exercising both the royal and
priestly roles. Thereby both tribes were glorified. The starting point
was Balaam's prophecy that "a star shall come forth out of Jacob, and
a scepter shall rise out of Israel" (Num. 24:17). The new priest's "star
shall arise in heaven as of a king, lighting up the light of knowledge
as the sun the day ... He shall shine forth as the sun on the earth"
(T. Levi 18:3-4; cf. T. Napht. 5:1-4). Jean Danielou comments [63] on
the passage that "the star becomes a symbol of the Messiah himself,
as a sign of the light he is to shed upon the world." Judah foretold to
his children that "after these things shall a star arise to you from
Jacob in peace, and a man shall arise [from my seed], like the sun of
righteousness ... Then shall the sceptre of my kingdom shine forth"
(T. Jud. 24:1, 5). In spite of Judah's authority in the earthly kingdom
(T. Reub. 6:11; T. Jud. 12:4; 15:2-3; 17:3, 5-6; 21:2-3; 22:3; T. Iss.
5:7) and the superiority of the priestly [64] to the royal leadership in

---

[62] De Jonge, op. cit., 86-89, 124; Mowinckel, op. cit., 287, n. 1; Kuhn, in Stendahl
(ed) op. cit., 257, n. 18; Ringgren, op. cit., 172, n. 20; Grelot, in Massaux (ed.), op. cit.,
33, n. 5; Robert B. Laurin, "The Problem of two Messiahs in the Qumran Scrolls," RQ
4 (1963-64), 44-45.

[63] Danielou, Histoire des doctrines ..., 240-41; 218 (ET).

[64] Beasley Murray (art. cit., JTS 48 [1947], 9) observed: "The priesthood was more

ancient Israel (T. Jud. 21:2-5; 25:1-2; T. Napht. 5:3-5), these functions become blurred in a Messianic context. Thus in T. Levi 8:14-15 we find a vision that "a king shall arise in Judah, and shall establish a new priesthood . . . And his presence is beloved, as a prophet of the Most High." Levi "shall wage the war of the Lord" (T. Sim. 5:5). T. Reub. 6:7-12 has Levi's descendants carrying "both swords":

> To Levi God gave the sovereignty [and to Judah with him. . .] Hearken to Levi, because he shall know the law of the Lord and shall give ordinances for judgment and shall sacrifice for all Israel until the consumation of the times, as the anointed High Priest . . . He shall bless Israel and Judah, because him the Lord hath chosen to be king over all the nation. And bow down before his seed, for on our behalf it will die in wars visible and invisible, and will be among you an eternal king.

From both tribes arises salvation (T. Sim. 7:1-2; T. Levi 2:11; T. Dan 5:10; T. Napht. 8:2-3; T. Gad 8:1; T. Jos. 19:11). The new priest "shall execute a righteous judgment upon the earth" and bind Beliar (T. Levi 18:2, 12; cf. T. Dan 5:10-11), whereas the star and stem arising to Judah is meek and sinless (T. Jud. 24:1 Greek; T. Dan 5:13; cf. 6:9; T. Benj. 10:7 Greek). Only one figure is presupposed in T. Dan 5:10-11; T. Jos. 19:8-9; T. Benj. 11:2. A similar union of functions appears in Jubilees. Isaac prophesies that the seed of the sons of Levi "shall be judges and princes, and the chiefs of all the seed of the sons of Jacob; they shall speak the word of the Lord in righteousness, and they shall judge all His judgments in righteousness . . . and will declare My ways to Jacob and My paths to Israel. The blessing of the Lord will be given in their mouths to bless all the seed of the beloved" (31:14-15). Then to Judah, Isaac said: "A prince shalt thou be, thou and one of thy sons, over the sons of Jacob . . . In thee shall be the help of Jacob, and in thee be found the salvation of Israel. And when thou sittest on the throne of honor of thy righteousness there shall be great peace for all the seed of the sons of the beloved" (31:18-20). In the Messianic Kingdom "the children will begin to study the laws . . . and to return to the path of righteousness . . . And there will be no Satan nor any evil destroyer" (23:26, 29; cf. 23).

---

important than the sovereignty because in the Messianic age the Temple would be the focal point of all the world's life." Yet, "the Messianic King is more beloved than the righteous priests" (Abot de Rabbi Nathan, version A, 50a-b) (Gerald J. Blidstein, "A Rabbinic Reaction to the Messianic Doctrine of the Scrolls", *JBL* 90 (1971), 330-32.

Messianic views of the priest-king par excellence, Melchzedek, were known among Palestinian rabbis.[65] R. H. Charles [66] detected a possible reference to Melchizedek in T. Levi 8:14. He further believed [67] that following Jub. 13:25 there is a lacuna telling of Abraham's meeting with Melchizedek. "Our author would naturally be interested in the first man who bore the title assumed by his heroes, the Maccabees," i.e. "a priest of the most high God" (Gen. 14:18). While the detection of specific historical references is open to question, there is no need to doubt that the warlike character and achievements of the Maccabees influenced Messianic doctrine.[68] Charles [69] noted that the offices of prophet, priest and king were united in the reign of John Hyrcanus.

The originality of other elements of the Christology of the Testaments of the Twelve Patriarchs is variously assessed. Charles,[70] Philonenko,[71] Klaus Koch [72] and B. Murmelstein [73] have upheld the pre-Christian Jewish origin of the text telling of Joseph's vision: "I saw in the midst of the horns a virgin ($\pi\alpha\rho\theta\acute{\epsilon}\nu\circ\varsigma$) [... and from her] went forth a lamb; and on his right ... all the beasts and all the reptiles rushed (against him), and the lamb overcame them and destroyed them" (T. Jos. 19:8). The militant lamb appears also in Rev. 6:16; 17:14; 1 Enoch 90:38; cf. 6-16; 89:16, 21-22, 36-38, 42-44, 49, 72. According to the textually corrupt T. Benj. 3:8, the Lamb of God shall destroy Beliar and his servants after the Lamb dies for the ungodly. The Lamb in the Testaments is obviously a victorious

---

[65] Bardy, art. cit., RB 35 (1926), 497-98.

[66] The Testaments of the Twelve Patriarchs Translated from the Editor's Greek Text, 45n.; cf. Delcor, art. cit., RQ (1967-68), 421-22; R. A. Stewart, "The Sinless High-Priest," NTS 14 (1967-68), 128-29.

[67] The Book of Jubilees or the Little Genesis, lxxxviii; 100-01, n. 25; 191, n. 1; The Apocrypha and Pseudepigrapha of the O.T., ii, 33.

[68] Beasley Murray, art. cit., JTS 48 (1947), 9; A. J. B. Higgins, "Priest and Messiah," Vetus Testamentum 3 (1953), 326-27, 329-31.

[69] The Testaments of the Twelve Patriarchs Translated from the Editor's Greek Text, 45-46. Bo Reicke ("Official and Pietistic Elements of Jewish Apocalypticism," JBL 79 [1960], 137-50) detects an early pro-Hasmonean stratum in 1 Enoch 90; T. Levi 8:2-3, but 'later "pietistic', sectarian parts of apocalypses (e.g. 1 Enoch 91-108) are critical of Hasmonean high priests.

[70] The Testaments..., 194.

[71] Les interpolations chretiennes des Testament des douze Patriarches et les Manuscrits de Qumran, Paris (Presses Universitaires de France, 1960), 19.

[72] "Das Lamm, das Ägypten vernichtet. Ein Fragment aus Jannes und Jambres und sein geschictlicher Hintergrund," ZNTW 57 (1966), 79-93.

[73] "Das Lamm in Test. Jos. 19:8," ZNTW 58 (1967), 273-79. He and Koch note the influence of ancient Egyptian thought.

horned ram overcoming the hostile powers. But was a sacrificial significance also attached to the concept? The Lamb's victory over Beliar and his servants is associated with "the blood of the covenant, for the salvation of the Gentiles and of Israel" in Greek, though not Armenian, texts of T. Benj. 3:8. The same textual problem afflicts T. Jos. 19:11, according to which the Lamb of God "saveth all the Gentiles and Israel" from sin. Yet the term, "Savior (σωτηρ)" of the world occurs both where textual witnesses are united (T. Levi 10:2; 14:2; T. Dan 14:9) and divided (T. Dan. 6:7, 9; T. Gad 8:1; T. Jos. 1:6; T. Benj. 3:8). His saving his followers from the powers of Beliar is a definite teaching of either the Jewish or original Christian text, but uncertainty of origin surrounds the doctrine that he was the slain Lamb whose blood sealed a new covenant. However, the text of T. Levi 16:3 is adequate where foretelling the slaying of "a man who reneweth the law in the power of the Most High." The Armenian text of T. Benj. 9:3 ("The Lord shall be treated with outrage and set at naught") is theologically neutral and perhaps more primitive than the Greek. The Christianized text, at least, of the Testaments attached a sacrificial significance to the blood (i.e. the life: Lev. 17:11) of the Lamb: it expiated sin (like a sin offering: Isa. 53:10-12) and inaugurated a new covenant (cf. Lk. 22:20; 1 Cor. 11:25). The Crucifixion, which is eschatologically foretold in the textually uncertain T. Levi 10:2-3; 14:1-2; T. Benj. 9:3-4, renewed the law and overcame Beliar. Liberation was effected from sins and Beliar and his spirits, rather than from the law and its effects.[74] The Lamb was also the oppressed, afflicted one led silently to slaughter (Isa. 53:7-8, 10; Acts 8:32). Soteriological import is attached also to the victorious descent into Hades (T. Levi 4:1; T. Dan. 5:10-11; some Greek, not Armenian, texts of T. Benj. 9:5).[75] Inspiration may have been drawn from Zech. 9:9-11 where, following a triumphant Messianic prophecy, we read: "By the blood of thy covenant I have sent forth thy prisoners out of the pit. . ." The new priest "shall open the gates of Paradise" (T.Levi 18:10).

The need to believe in the Messiah is affirmed in T. Dan 5:13 and Greek (not Armenian) texts of T. Benj. 10:7, 9. Christians seem to be

---

[74] But there is no suggestion of the Pascal Lamb to be eaten (1 Cor. 5:7; cf. Jn. 19:14, 36) nor of Pauline mysticism of suffering with Christ.

[75] Danielou, *Histoire des doctrines...*, 263-68; 239-42 (ET). Justin (*Dial.* 72.4) and Irenaeus transmitted a teaching of "Jeremiah" that "the Lord God the holy one of Israel" preached to the dead (Denis, *op. cit.*, 76, 292).

called his sons in truth, though possibly "his" refers to God. "He shall give the majesty of the Lord to his sons in truth for evermore" (T. Levi 18:8). "Ye shall be his true children by adoption" (T. Jud. 24:3). The prophecy of Isa. 53:10 ("when he makes himself an offering for sin, he shall see his offspring") was fulfilled in him.

Whether the Damascus Document mentions one or two Messiahs has long been a controversial question.[76] The eschatological arising of "the Annointed one of Aaron and Israel" (12.23-13.1; 14.19; 19.10-11; 20.1), who will "expiate iniquities" of some errant Covenant members (14.19) and deliver others to destruction (14.10-14), ostensibly pertains to one figure. But, in spite of the singular used in the Hebrew text, the construction does not exclude the possibility of two Anointed ones. The plural is explicitly found in 1QS 9.10-11: "And they shall be governed by the first ordinances in which members of the Community began their instruction, until the coming of the Prophet and the Anointed (ones) of Aaron and Israel." Two Messianic figures are found also in the Cave 4 Florilegium (i. 10-13), where Nathan's prophecy of Yahweh's son established on a royal throne (2 Sam. 7.11-14) is commented on:

> This is the Branch of David who will arise with the Seeker of the Law and who will sit on the throne of Zion at the end of days; as it is written, 'I will raise up the tabernacle of David which is fallen.' This tabernacle of David which is fallen (is) he who will arise to save Israel.

This Searcher of the Law is most readily identified with the Teacher of Righteousness who will come at the end of time (CD 6.7-11). Whether this Seeker of the Law (cf. CD 7.18) is the priestly founder of the sect *redivivus* (like Elijah) is a most question;[77] but it is clear that the royal Messiah would be accompanied by an authoritative interpreter of the Torah who could be further identified with the Prophet or, more likely, with the Anointed of Aaron. Uncertainties likewise beset interpretations of 1QM 12.7-15, where the "holy one of Adonai" and the "King of glory" might have Messianic meanings.[78] Balaam's prophecy of the Star from Jacob and the Scepter out of Israel (Num. 24:15-17) is quoted in 4Q Test. 5-13 together with Deut. 18:18-19, which refers to God's raising up a prophet like

---

[76] Bibliographies in Black, *op. cit.*, 145; Gartner, *op. cit.*, 36, nn. 1 & 4; Laurin, *art. cit.*, RQ 4(1963-64), 39-52; E. A. Wcela, "The Messiah(s) of Qumrân," *CBQ* 26 (1964), 340-49; Fitzmyer, *art. cit.*, *CBQ* 27 (1965), 349-50, n. 7; R. E. Brown, "J. Starcky's Theory of Qumran Messianic Development," *CBQ* 28 (1966), 54-55.

[77] Ringgren, *op. cit.*, 184, n. 36.

[78] Black, *op. cit.*, 155-56.

Moses. In the War Scroll (11.6) the Star and Scepter prophecy is quoted again in the context of praising God for His power in battle. Likewise in a martial context (1QSb 5.24 ff.) the Prince of the Congregation (5.20) is blessed with these words: "Thou shalt devastate the earth by thy scepter, and by the breath of thy lips shalt thou slay the ungodly." Fortunately the citation of Balaam's prophecy in CD 7.18-21 is accompanied by the explanation that "the scepter is the Prince of all the Congregation, and at his coming 'he will break down all the sons of Seth' " (cf. 4Q Test. 12-13). The Star is identified as the Searcher of the Law who will come to Damascus (CD 7.18-19), i.e. to the sectarian Community.

The simplest way to reconcile these Messianic views is to adopt the suggestion of Dupont-Sommer:[79] "It may very well be that the sect's doctrine on the question of messianism was not rigorously uniform, and that two tendencies showed themselves-one attributing the sacerdotal (or spiritual) and kingly (or temporal) functions to two different Messiahs, and the other tranferring both these roles to one and the same Messiah." Those who made a distinction awaited the Anointed of Aaron, the Star, the Seeker of the Law, the Teacher of Righteousness, on one hand, and the Anointed of Israel, the Scepter, the Prince of the Congregation, the Davidic military leader, on the other hand. The Prophet like Moses in some circles was still another eschatological, though not strictly Messianic, figure.

The High Priest, it was believed, would play an important eschatological role. He was to command all the priests who "shall be in perpetual service before God" (1QH 2. 1-2). In the camp before the battle with the forces of the Kittim and Belial

> the chief priest shall stand, together with his brethren [the priests] and Levites and all the officers with him, and he shall read into their ears the prayer in time of walr and all the bolok of the rule of that time, together with all the words of their hymns of thanksgiving. Then he shall form all the lines there according to alll the words of this rulle (1QM 15.4-6).

During the battle "the chief priest shall draw near and shall stand before the line and strengthen their heart. "He shall exhort them about the Mysteries of God relating to His trials of His people in

---

[79] *Op. cit.*, 134, n. 5. Wayne A Meeks (*The Prophet-King*, Leiden E. J. Brill, 1967, 171) thinks: "with the passage of time the eschatological High Priest may have absorbed *all* the functions of the eschatological Prophet-just as he took on many of the functions of the eschatological Prince."

history (16.13-16). At sunset he shall bless the God of Israel and pray for light to pursue the enemy (18.5ff.). The next morning he shall praise the God of Israel for the victory (19.11-13). He functions like an intermediary between God and the armies of His people. In the fragmentary Book of Blessings allusion is made to the crown(?) upon his head, his sovereignty, fighting at the head of thousands, and subjugating many peoples unto God (1QSb 3.3, 5, 7, 18). On the other hand, the High Priest should be divinely favored with the Spirit of holiness, the everlasting covenant and truth, divine delight in his sacrifices, and presence in the company of the holy angels (2.24, 25, 28; 3.1-2, 6). Thus we have a Messianic figure who is both priestly and military. If 1QSb 4.22-28 is referrable to the High Priest, further Messianic features are noteworthy: his likeness to an angel of the Presence in the dwelling-place of holiness, his presence in the company of God while ministering in the royal palace, and his being made holy among His people and a light to illumine the world with knowledge Raymond E. Brown [80] points out that priests interpreted the Law at Qumran and that "4QTest cites Deut. 33:8-11, where Levi is told, 'Let your Law shine before Israel'."

The military Messiah is described in Fourth Cave Commentary on Isaiah (4Q 161.17). Isa. 11.1-5 is interpreted as a reference to the Branch "of David who will arise at the e[nd of days. . .] and God will uphold him by [the Spirit of po]wer [. . . a thr]one of glory, a crown of ho[liness]. . . [a scepter-?] in his hand, and he will rule over all the n[ation]s, and Magog[. . .and al]l the peoples his sword will judge. . ." The surviving portion of the War Scroll mentions only once the Prince of all the Congregations; it is in the context of the standards of the congregation and the formations of the fighting battalions. A more helpful description of the Prince of the Congregation appears in 1QSb 5.20-29. For him God

> will renew the Covenant of the Community, that he may restore the kingdom of His people for ev[er and. . .] that he may rule with e[quity the hum]ble of the land and walk before Him perfectly in all the ways [of truth. . .] and that he may restore [His holy] Coven[ant at the time] of the distress of those who seek [Him] . . . And [thou shalt strike the peoples] by the might of thy [mouth]; thou shalt devastate the earth by thy scepter, and by the breath of thy lips shalt thou slay the ungodly. [The Spirit of couns]el and eternal might [shall be upon thee], the Spirit of Knowledge and of the fear of God. And righteousness shall be the girdle [of thy loins, and faith] the girdle of thy haunches. May he make

⁸⁰ Art. cit., CBQ 28 (1966), 56, n. 15.

thy horns of iron and thy shoes of bronze! May thou toss like a [young]
bull [. . .and trample the peopl]es like the mud of the streets! For God
has established thee as a scepter over the rulers [. . .and all the peo]ples
shall serve thee. . . And thou shalt be as a l[ion. . .]

Matthew Black [81] has called attention to the avoidance here of the
title "king" and the preference of *nasi* (prince)" on the basis of its use
in the eschatological passage of Ezekiel 45-47. Here the Prince is
responsible for a sacrificial cultus. The fact that in 1QSb 5 he is
endowed with the knowledge and perfect righteousness appropriate
for the New Covenant suggests that he was conceived of as a teacher
as well as a warrior Lion of Judah (Gen. 49:9). Covenant and kingship
are united in the Messianic passage of the fragmentary Patriarchal
Blessings, which comments on Gen. 49:10:

> A monarch will [not] be wanting to the tribe of Judah when Israel rules,
> [and] a (descendant) seated on the throne will [not] be wanting to David.
> For' the (commander's) staff' is the Covenant of kingship, [and] the' feet'
> are [the Thou]sands of Israel. 'Until' the Messiah of Righteousness
> comes, the Branch of David; for to him and his seed has been given the
> Covenant of the kingship of his people for everlasting generations,
> because he has kept [. . .] the Law with the members of the Community.

It is a fair deduction that characteristics of the royal Messiah were
being transferred to the priestly Messiah and vice versa. This process
could represent a stage in the development of Messianic doctrine.

Nevertheless, the (High) Priest and the "Messiah of Israel" remain
two distinct personalities in 1QSa 2.11-22. In assembilies of the
Council of the Community the Priest "shall enter [at] the head of all
the Congregation of Israel, then all [the chiefs of the sons] of Aaron
the priests called to the assembly, men of renown; and they shall sit
[before him], each according to his rank. And afterwards, [the
Mess]iah of Israel [shall enter]; and the chiefs of [the tribes of Israel]
shall sit before him, each according to his rank." Likewise at the
Community table no man was to touch the first fruits of bread and
wine before the Priest. After he blesses it, "the Messiah of Israel shall
(str]etch out his hands over the bread," and then "all the
Congregation of the Community shall [bl]ess, ea[ch according to] his
rank." The basis of the Priest's superiority in rank may have been
hierocratic, as Matthew Black holds.[82]

The saving work of atonement for sins belongs less to a Messianic

---

[81] *Op. cit.*, 152.
[82] *Ibid.*, 104-05, 146.

figure than to the Community itself.[83] For, the Community constitutes the temple for the Spirit of God.

The potentiality of a saving faith in the Messiah came from the sectarian faith in their historical Teacher of Righteousness.[84] God will deliver the righteous observers of the Law "from the House of Judgment because of their affliction and their faith in the Teacher of Righteousness" (1Q p Hab. 8.2-3). This teaching is readily understood in terms of that in the Damascus Document (20.27-34):

> All who have clung of those ordinances [i.e. of the Covenant], going and coming in accordance with the Law, and have heeded the voice of the Teacher ... and who have lent their ear to the voice of the Teacher of Righteousness, and have not disputed the precepts of righteousness when hearing them, they will rejoice ... And God will forgive them, and they will see His salvation because they sought refuge in His holy Name.

If an analogy is permissible for faith in the eschatological Teacher of Righteousness, the faith leading to forgiveness would be in his authority so to interpret the Law that those who observed his precepts would be saved. Faith in the founder of the sect was faith in him as the authoritative expositor of the laws of the Covenant. Faith means to listen to, heed and not dispute; it is almost the equivalent of obedience. Concerning the prophet like Moses God said: "I will put my words into his mouth and he shall say all that I command him. Whoever will not listen to my words which this prophet shall utter in my name, I myself will call him to account" (4 Q Test. 5-8).

The publication of 11Q Melch has opened up a new dimension to the Qumran Messianic doctrine of the first half of the first century A.D.[85] In the end of days those who have been taken captive and imprisoned(4) will be the recipients of blessings from Melchizedek, "who will restore them to them, and he will proclaim release to them, to set them(?) free [and to atone] for their iniquities and. . ." (5-6). As in the Jubilee year all possessions are to be returned and debts paid(1-3), the restoration of possessions (especially the Zadokite priesthood) seems to be envisioned. Fr. Joseph A. Fitzmyer[86]

---

[83] Gärtner, op. cit., 123-42.

[84] Brown, "The Messianism of Qumran," CBQ 19 (1957), 72-77.

[85] A. S. van der Woude, "Melchisedek als himmlische Erlösergestalt in den neugefunden eschatologischen Midraschim aus Qumran Höhle XI," Oudtestamentliche Studien 14 (1965), 357.

[86] Art. cit., JBL 86 (1967), 34. Robert J. Poveromo and Paul E. Dinter ("Melchizedek at Qumran," Dunwoodie Review 11 (1971), 42-44) likewise hold that the

plausibly suggests that the Qumran priests are those who are to receive the priestly "heritage of Melchizedek"(5). At the last day the prophecy of Isa. 52:7 will be fulfilled, concerning the herald proclaiming peace and salvation (15-16). This Messianic herald [87] is explicitly identified with the Anointed One (18), probably as described in Dan. 9:24-27.[88] The prophecy of Isa. 61:1-2 is envisioned (4, 6, 9, 19-20) as being fulfilled by the Messianic Melchizedek, just as Mt. 11:5; Lk. 4:18-19; 7:22 relate the fulfillment in Jesus. "And Melchizedek shall exact the ven[ge]ance of the jud[g]ments of God ('E1)" (13). Jean Carmignac [89] notes that 11Q refers to his royal military rather than his priestly function. The role of Melchizedek in the execution of divine judgment during the eschatological Jubilee year is further described in line 9: "He has decreed a year of good favor for Melchize[dek. . .] and the holy ones of God for a re[ig]n of judgment." God's judgment in the heavenly court is the subject matter of Pss. 7:8-9; 82:1-2, which are partially quoted in lines 10 and 11. Melchizedek is to judge especially Belial and the spirits of his lot; this interpretation is explicitly given to Ps. 82:2 in lines 11-12. Belial and his lot will no longer be allowed to judge unjustly (11); judgment will be taken "[from the hand of Be]lial and from the hand(s) of all [the spirits of] his [lot]" (13). Those of Zion (24) who have "turned from Belial" (23; cf. 26) and away from the "[p]ath of the people" (25) are "the establishers of the covenant" (25) (i.e. at Qumran) who understand "the judgment[s of] God" (24). Corresponding to the evil spiritual host of Belial are "the holy ones of God (qedōše 'E1)" (9), "the as[sembly of 'E1], in the midst of heavenly ones ('Iwhym)" (10), or "all the . . . heavenly ones ('elim)", who are for the help of Melchizedek (14) in the divine judgment. Above this angelic court Melchizedek is exalted, as Ps. 7:8-9 is applied to him (10-11). However, as Ps. 82:1, when applied to him, would include him amidst the assembly of God (10), it may be deduced that Melchizedek was viewed as chief of the heavenly court. Such an interpretation would fit A.S. van der Woude's hypothesis [90] that

---

Qumran dwellers saw themselves as the "men of the lot of Melchizedek" (8); they were to be released and their inherited priestly rights were to be restored.

[87] Fitzmyer, art. cit., JBL 86 (1967), 30.

[88] Ibid., 30, 40.

[89] "Le document de Qumrân sur Melkisédeq, RQ 7 (1970), 368-69, 377.

[90] Art. cit., Oudtest, Studien 14 (1965), 369-72; de Jonge and van der Woude, art. cit., NTS 12 (1965-66), 305; cf. Fitzmyer, art. cit., JBL 86 (1957), 32. This view is supported by the possibility of esoteric word-play on the names of Michael,

Melchizedek was identified with the archangel Michael. "But," as Fitzmyer notes, [91] "it is complicated by the fact that the author of the text seems to refer to Melchizedek as 'Elohim (see lines 10 and possibly 25). This is the suggestion of van der Woude and it seems correct."

Militant Messianic apocalypticism among the Essenes (see p. 57, nn. 265-66; 297) was not fully disguised by Josephus.

THE SPIRIT

The differences in Christology between the Judaizers and the mainstream of the church can be partially described in terms of teaching on the relation between Christ and the Holy Spirit. In general it can be said that, whereas the work and spiritual nature of Christ was described in angelic terms by the Judaizers, the early Pauline church tended to assimilate Christ and the Spirit, at least more than has the later church.

As the descent of the Spirit at the time of Christ's baptism was accepted even by the Judaizing Ebionites (Epiphanius, *Haer.*, 30, 13.2 & 7-8), there is no need to question its general acceptance in Asia Minor as well. Its O.T. foundation (Isa 11:1-5; 42:1-4; 61:1), if interpreted Messianically, states that he shall receive the spirit of wisdom, knowledge and might which shall enable him to judge the world. The bestowal of certain powers at this time of divine testimony would not be counter to his angelic nature. Indeed, "son of God" is an angelic title (Gen. 6:2, 4; Job 38:7; Pss. 29:1; 82:6; 89:6) to which Jesus' baptismal account could have been witnessing, in the view of the Judaizers. The divine proclamation, "This is my beloved Son, with whom I am well pleased," occurs in the narratives of both the baptism (Mt. 3:17; cf. Mk. 1:11; Lk. 3:22) and the Transfiguration (Mt. 17:5; Lk. 9:34; Mk. 9:7), an epiphany of special interest to Paul's opponents (see p. 212) Both events, as Gerhard Münderlein [92] has

---

Melchizedek, *malak* (angel) and *melek, malka* (king). According to the Armenian and Greek Lives of the Prophets, because he was honored for his chastity, meekness and blameless piety, the prophet "was called Malachi, which means angel; for he was of a beautiful countenance" (Armenian). But see the criticisms by Carmignac (*art. cit., RQ* 7[1970], 364-67). On identity of the heavenly high priest as Michael in the Babylonian Talmud, and of Michael and Melchizedek in Kabbala, see Lueken, *op. cit.*, 30-31; H. Strack & P. Billerbeck, *Kommentar zum N.T. aus Talmud u. Midrasch.*, iii, 701.

[91] Fitzmyer, *art. cit* JBL 86 (1967), 32; cf. 37, 41.

[92] "Die Erwählung durch das Pleroma. Bemerkungen zu Kol. i. 19," *NTS* 8 (1962), 267, 271-73.

argued persuasively, are alluded to in Col. 1:19, in the term, "εὐδόκησεν." The πλήρωμα, which was pleased to dwell in the Chosen One, is in Paul's mind related, if not identical, to both the Holy Spirit descending into Jesus and the Old Testament Shekinah, Wisdom and glory. Münderlein points out, further, that while the ingressive aorist, εὐδόκησεν (1:19), pertains to Christ's being elected as the recipient of the Holy Spirit, the present indicative (κατοικεῖ) (2:9) implies that the Spirit of God inhabited his body. For Paul, then, the πλήρωμα was the Holy Spirit, while his opponents believed it includes angels and spirits. Bornkamm [93] thinks that 2:9 is polemically directed against the teaching that in the στοῖχεῖα the "πλήρωμα *der Gottheit*" dwells. P. Testa thinks Paul's opponents "reduced the concept of the pleroma of divinity which bodily indwelled Christ into fantasy on the [sacred] letters of the alphabet, στοιχεῖα, and on sacred numbers." [94] The Ascension of Isaiah (3:15; 7:23; 9:36, 39-40; 10:4; 11:4, 33) frequently mentioned "the angel of the Holy Spirit."

In Hebr. 9:14 only casual reference is made to "eternal πνευμα" through which Christ offered up himself in a bloody sacrifice. The resurrection state of Jesus is characterized as being "in the spirit" by 1 Tim. 3:16 and 1 Pet. 3:18 (cf. Rom. 1:3-4), as contrasted with his being manifested and put to death "in the flesh." While his σάρξ and πνεῦμα are paired, the relation of the πνεῦμα of the vindicated, quickened Jesus to the Spirit of God (cf. Rom. 8:9-11) is not clearly indicated. It is natural to suppose that the angel (or one of the two) in human form seen at the empty tomb was believed in some quarters to be Jesus (Mt. 28:2-5; Mk. 16:5 ff.; Lk. 24:4-10, 23; Jn. 20:12-18; cf. Acts 12:13-16). The work of the πνεῦμα of Christ following has ascension to the Father's right hand was disputed. The Pauline church insisted that Christ now worked through *his* Spirit dwelling in believers. Because you are sons, "God has sent the Spirit of his Son into your hearts crying 'Abba! Father!'" (Gal. 4:6) in prayer (Rom. 8:15-16); the Son had been born of woman in order that we might receive adoption as sons (Gal. 4:4-5). The work of the incarnate Son bears fruit through the work of his indwelling Spirit (cf. Gal. 2:20). In this sense is to be understood the benediction: "the grace of our Lord Jesus Christ be with your spirit, brethren" (6:18). The work of Jesus and the Spirit is united in the liberation from the law. While the

[93] *Op. cit.*, i, 140; cf. 146.
[94] *Op. cit.*, 194-96, 570.

Apostle could contrast the Spirit and the law, the Judaizers could not. According to 3:13-14, by his crucifixion "Christ redeemed us from the curse of the law ... that in Christ Jesus the blessing of Abraham might come upon the Gentiles, that we might receive the promise of the Spirit through faith." The Spirit is received through faith in Christ crucified (3:1-5), as both a promise to believing Jews and Gentiles (cf. Acts 1:4; 2:33, 38-39) and the beginning of the new life in Christ (3:3). "Freedom in Christ Jesus" (2:4; 5:1, 13) is the correlate of being led by the Spirit (5:16-18); likewise for belonging to Christ and living in the Spirit (5:24-25). The fruits of the Spirit (love, joy, peace, patience, kindness, goodness, faithfulness, meekness and self-control) (5:22-23), in which Paul and his opponents were equally interested, come, in the Apostle's view, from being led by the Spirit of Christ, rather than by the Spirit's activity in fostering adherence to the law.

In 2 Cor. 11:4 the false apostles are accused of preaching another Jesus than the Jesus preached by Paul, so that the Corinthians receive a different Spirit. Since Paul's gospel is "Christ crucified" (1 Cor. 1:23; 2:2; Gal. 3:1; 6:14) and the Spirit received is the Spirit of Christ (e.g. Rom. 8:9; 2 Cor. 3:17), it appears that the opponents de-emphasized his crucifixion and his closest possible relation with the Spirit given to believers. The mystery of Christ's indwelling, which had been questioned, is explained by the fact that "he was crucified in weakness, but lives by the power of God" (2 Cor. 13:3-5). Those who are established in Christ have been given the pledge (ἀρραβών) of the Spirit in their hearts (1:21-22). But the opponents alternated between "Yes" and "No" in their teachings about Christ's fulfillment of all the Old Testament promises of God; they did not believe that He firmly establishes the believers in Christ in baptism by sealing them and giving them his Spirit as a guarantee (1:17-22). God has given us the Spirit as the ἀρραβών of eternal life (5:4-5), Paul taught. In 2 Cor. 3:3, 6-9 Paul contrasts the written Mosaic code, which kills, with the church, which is "a letter from Christ ... written ... with the Spirit of the living God"; for, "the Spirit gives life." In 1 Cor. 15:45 Paul wrote that the new Adam became a life-giving Spirit. The dispensation of the Spirit is attended by a far greater splendor than the old dispensation. Paul's opponents are charged with lacking this life-giving Spirit because they do not live decisively under the new covenant centered in Christ; they tied the gift of the Spirit to conformity to their traditional interpretations of the Mosaic covenant.[95] As Oostendorp noted,[96] it was agreed "that the new covenant is characterized by the Spirit, righteousness and permanence." But, claimed Paul, we all are being transformed into the likeness of the Lord by the Lord Spirit (2 Cor. 3:18). Altogether foreign to the false apostles' way of thinking is 3:17: "The Lord is the Spirit, and where the Spirit of the Lord is, there is freedom," i.e. from the condemnation and death under the old covenant (3:6, 7, 9).

Against the circumcizers Paul claimed that we worship God by the Spirit and boast in Christ Jesus (Phil. 3:3). The former phrase suggests the role of the Spirit in making intercession (Rom. 8:26-27) and impelling the cry, Abba, Father (Rom. 8:15; Gal 4:6). Another parallel is Rom. 7:4, 6 ("you have died to the law through the body of Christ, so that you may belong ... to him who has been raised from the dead, ... so that we serve not under the old written code but in the new life of the Spirit (ἐν καινότητι πνεύματος). Life under the law is contrasted with life under the Spirit. The accompanying confidence in Jesus implies gaining him and being found in him through union with his sufferings, death and resurrection (3:7-12). As Vincent [97] commented on 3:9: "To be in Christ is to have the Spirit of Christ and to be one Spirit with him (Rom. 8:9; 1 Cor. 6:17)."

Eph. 1:13-14 (cf. 4:30) teaches that believers in the Gospel of salvation have been sealed with the promised Holy Spirit, who is "the guarantee of our inheritance (ἀρραβών τῆς κληρονομίας)." Why should such power be attributed to the Spirit? The inheritance is certain because through the Spirit Christ and God indwell the believer and the church. In 3:16-19 is found the interesting Trinitarian prayer to the Father that "he may grant you to be strengthened with might through his Spirit in the inner man, and that Christ may dwell in your hearts through faith; that you ... may ... know the love of Christ which surpasses knowledge, that you may be filled with all the fullness of God." If the πλήρωμα indwelling Christ (Col. 1:19; 2:9) is rightly understood as the Spirit, the prayer of asking to be filled with the Spirit of God corresponds with the blessing of simultaneous inner strengthening by the Spirit and the indwelling of Christ. This interpretation fits 2:22 (in the Lord you are being built into a dwelling place of God in the Spirit) and 2:18 (through Christ, we have access in one Spirit to the Father). The ecclesiastical significance

[95] Oostendorp, op. cit., 35-38, 45-46.
[96] Ibid., 38.
[97] Op. cit., 102.

of πλήρωμα has been emphasized by P.-A. Harlé.[98] There is but one Spirit in the body of Christ (4:3-4; cf. 2 Cor. 11:4). The mystery of Christ, moreover, was revealed by the Spirit to the prophets and apostles (Eph. 3:5), upon whom the church is built (2:20). None of this teaching would be compatible with an angelological understanding of the πλήρωμα, or with limitations on the deity of the Spirit (because of preoccupation with spirits).

1 Peter 1:12 contrasts the ignorance of the angels with the evangelization of the readers by those who announce the Gospel through the Holy Spirit sent from heaven. The work of the Spirit in the church is placed in parallel to the revelation by the Spirit of Christ to the prophets about the sufferings and glorification of Christ. The Holy Spirit and the Spirit of Christ are equated, and the identification is made clear by the reversal of the expected order, which would have been: the Holy Spirit inspiring the prophets and the Spirit of Christ inspiring the apostles. The good news, i.e. "the grace that was to be yours" through Christ, is the object of the angels' curiosity, but of the readers' perfect hope (1:13; cf. 8-9). Implicitly, the Old Testament prophecies are rightly understood, not by angels, but by the Church through the Spirit.

The letters written by the prophet John to the seven churches were dictated by the heavenly Son of Man (Rev. 1:13), the Alpha and Omega (1:17) who died and lives for evermore (1:18). John was in the Spirit (ἐν πνεύματι) when he heard the command to write (1:10). In each of the letters (2:7, 11, 17, 29; 3:6, 13, 22) is included the admonition, "He who has an ear, let him hear what the Spirit says to the churches." The vital messages to the churches from the glorified Christ and from the Spirit are identical. The authority of Christ is not distinguished from that of the Spirit; the teachings are in both their names. If the expression used by Jesus, "He who has ears, let him hear" (Mk. 4:9, 23; Mt. 11:15; 13:9, 43; Lk. 8:8; 14:35), were a model for Christ's words in Revelation, then it could be inferred that the Spirit was speaking through Jesus. But any distinction is only a formal one.

Ignatius of Antioch taught that the prophets, who were in union with (ἐν ἑνότητι. . .ὄντες) Jesus Christ through their faith and hope (ad. Philad. 5:2), were in the Spirit (ὄντες τῷ πνεύματι) as they waited for him as their διδάσκαλος (ad Magnes. (9:2). Ignatius also emphasized

---

[98] "Le Saint-Esprit et l'Église chez saint Paul," *Verbum Caro* 19 (1965), 13-29.

the role of the Spirit of Christ in preserving ecclesiastical unity. Jesus Christ has established bishops and deacons by "his Holy Spirit" (*ad Philad., Introd.*). To the Spirit is attributed the prayer,". . . Love unity. Flee divisions. . ." For God does not dwell where there is division. Ignatius goes on to warn against Judaizing (*ad Philad.* 7:2 ff.). He closes his letter to the Magnesians "in the peace of God, possessing the indivisible (ἀδιάκριτος) Spirit who is Jesus Christ" (15:1). This farewell reminder refers back to his call "to do everything ἐν ὁμονοίᾳ θεοῦ" under the leadership of the bishop and deacons (6:1), and to run to the unity of the one temple of God and of the one Jesus Christ (7:2). He proceeds to warn against being deceived by the Judaizers (chh. 8-9). Before pleading for unity among the Philadelphians, Ignatius observed that some wished to deceive according to the flesh, but the Spirit is not led astray (7:1).

John expected a Holy Spirit baptism by the Coming One (Mk. 1:7-8). Thereby God would raise up children, though they would not necessarily be descendants of Abraham (Mt. 3:9; Lk. 3:8). In so far his preaching was "good news" (Lk. 3:18), God's people would be purified (the counterpart of the fire of punishment) (cf. Mal. 3:2-3: refiner's fire. . . purify the sons of Levi and refine them. . .) and share in the blessings promised to Abraham. John saw his own work as one of water purification and the Messiah's as one of Spirit purification. As to "bear fruit that befits repentance" (Mt. 3:8; Lk. 3:8) was deemed a sign of the soul's purification by righteousness (Josephus, *Antiq.* xviii, 5.2), the coming Spirit purification must have involved legal righteousness. John's Spirit possession and abstinence from wine were related (Lk. 1:15). By the spirit of Elijah he turned the disobedient to righteousness (1:17.). In the messianic age light would be given "to those who sit in darkness. . ." (1:78-79).

The twelve disciples at Ephesus were not ignorant of such spiritual gifts as prophecy, inspiration and ecstatic trances; rather they had not heard "whether any are receiving the Holy Spirit" (Acts 19:2, Western text). They did not know about the outpouring of the Spirit of the Lord, as prophecied by Joel 2:28-32 (cf. Zech. 12:10-13:1) and John, according to nearly all commentators. But is it not more likely that they had heard about Christian prophesying and speaking with tongues (19:6; cf. 2:38; 8:16) and had failed to understand it to be the fulfillment of the prophecies they had heard? That is, they had been looking for a different sort of eschatological Spirit baptism, namely the counterpart of Johannine water baptism: a Messianic spiritual purification. They did not know that Pentecostal phenomena were what John had prophesied and were normal accompaniments of baptism in the name of Christ. They had focused upon ancient and recent prophecies of the terrible Day of the Lord as described by Joel, Zechariah and John in the context of their mention of a Spirit outpouring. When Paul learned of their preoccupation with apocalyptic prophecies and purification as the eschatological work of the Spirit, he saw in them no sign of the freedom and ecstasy given by the Spirit of Christ. Their concept of the Spirit vastly differed from Paul's and Luke's.

Baptismal doctrine and practice inevitably separated the Pauline church and the Judaizers. The latter did not suffer, die, undergo burial and rise with Christ in baptism; there was no mystical union with the indwelling Spirit of Christ. Nor did they view the church as the body of Christ which was animated by his Spirit. The Dominical logion, "Where two or three are gathered together, there am I in the midst of them" (Mt. 18:20), must have been among those which they rejected (see p. 227). Whereas the Pauline church experienced a union with Deity through the individual and corporate indwelling of Christ's Spirit, the Judaizers sought to approach God through the intercession of Christ and other angels. On what terms did the Judaizers accept converts? They were not initiated into the new covenant and dispensation of the life-giving Spirit, as if the new were attended by greater glory than the Mosaic one; they knew no contrast of the Spirit and written code (2 Cor. 3:6, 8). In addition to the Spirit, angels were probably associated with the Judaizers' baptism. That is, they were cleansed of sins in the water by the action of an angel (cf. Tertullian, On Baptism 6). According to the Cappadocian Gregory of Nazianzus, "the angels give glory to the baptism because of its relation with their own sparkling purity" (Oratio 40, 4). Not only were angels thought to preside over baptism, but the newly baptized were entrusted to the care of angels whose purity guided the converts into doing good.[99] However, Pope Damasus (Epistle 4.25; Migne, P.L. 13, 363-64) noted: "We are not baptised in the names of archangels, as heretics do".

Elkesai, who taught a baptism of forgiveness for "anyone who is defiled by any licentiousness and pollution and lawlessness" (Hippolytus, Ref. 9, 13.3-4) if he be converted and believe in the Book of Elkesai, taught therein:

---

[99] Danielou, The Angels and their Mission, 59-61, 71-72.

Let him purify himself and sanctify himself, and call to witness the seven witnesses written in this book, heaven and water and the holy spirits, and the angels of prayer, and the oil and the salt and the earth" (*ibid.* 9, 15.2; cf. 15.4-16.1) (see above, p. 189).

A spirit of God was speaking in Isaac as he gave his instructions of life (T. Isaac).[100] The Son of Man, the Elect One, is described in 1 Enoch 49:3 in these words:

And in him dwells the spirit of wisdom,
And the spirit which gives insight,
And the spirit of understanding and of might,
And the spirit of those who have fallen asleep in righteousness.

The star from Jacob is foretold by Judah (T. Jud. 24:2-3) thus: "And the heavens shall be opened unto him, to pour out the spirit, (even) the blessing of the Holy Father; and He shall pour out the spirit of grace upon you; and ye shall be unto Him sons in truth, and ye shall walk in His commandments first and last." With this view coincides Levi's prophecy (Test. Levi 18:5-8) concerning the new priest:

And the angels of the glory of the presence of the Lord shall be glad in him.
The heavens shall be opened.
And from the temple of glory shall come upon him sanctification,
With the Father's voice as from Abraham to Isaac.
And the glory of the Most High shall be uttered over him,
And the spirit of understanding and sanctification shall rest upon him [in the water].
For he shall give the majesty of the Lord to His sons in truth for evermore. . .

That is, the Messiah shall be empowered and sanctified by the outpouring of the spirit. The work of the Spirit is illustrated by the cases of Joseph and Levi. "Now Joseph was a good man, and he had the Spirit of God within him: being compassionate and merciful," he loved Simeon (Test. Sim. 4:4). "The spirit of understanding of the Lord came upon" Levi and he "saw all men corrupting their way" (T. Levi 2:3). On Judgment Day all the angels shall praise the Lord of Spirits "in the spirit of faith, and in the spirit of wisdom, and in the spirit of patience, and in the spirit of mercy, and in the spirit of judgment and peace, and in the spirit of goodness" (1 Enoch 61:11).

"Two spirits wait upon man — the spirit of truth and the spirit of deceit. And in the midst is the spirit of the understanding of the

---

[100] Coptic, 63.

mind, to which it belongeth to turn whithersoever it will. And the works of truth and the works of deceit are written upon the hearts of men" (T. Judah 20:1-3; cf. T. Asher 1:3-5). The spirits in this passage are to be understood psychologically, as are numerous other references to spirits in the Testaments of the Twelve Patriarchs: the spirits of desire, of envy, of fighting, of filth, of fornication, of hatred, of injustice, of insatiableness, of jealousy, of lucre, of lust, of lying, of obsequiousness, of pride, of profligacy, of riot (ἀσωτία), of sleep, of vainglory and of wickedness.[101] It is tempting to find counterparts of these spirits of various sins in the spirits of various virtues (wisdom, understanding, might, truth, faith, patience, mercy, peace and righteousness). Such was the case in the Shepherd of Hermas. The women clothed in black garments (unbelief, incontinence, sorrow, anger, disobedience, etc.) had their counterpart in virgins (spirits) in white garments (faith, purity, continence, truth, love, patience, etc.) (Simil. ix, 15.1-4; cf. Vis. iii, 8.2-5, where the list includes self-restraint, chastity, guilelessness, simplicity, etc.). "Self-will and empty confidence is a great demon" (Simil. ix, 22.3); doubt is an earthly spirit coming from the devil (Mand. ix, 11). Grief, doubt and anger are spirits which crush out the Holy Spirit (Mand. x, 1.2). "When all these spirits [anger, bitterness, frenzy] dwell in one vessel in which the Holy Spirit also dwells, the vessel cannot contain them, but overflows ... Then, when He withdraws from the man in whom He dwelt, the man is emptied of the righteous Spirit, and (is) henceforth filled with evil spirits" (Mand. v, 2).

An obvious reference to Pentecost appears in T. Benj. 9:3-5: "He shall be lifted up on a tree. And the veil of the temple shall be rent, and the Spirit of God shall pass to the Gentiles as fire poured forth. And He shall ascend from Hades. . ."

The Qumran Community's pneumatology is summarized in 1QS 3.18-4.6:

> He allotted unto man ... the Spirits of truth and perversity. The origin of Truth is in a fountain of light ... Domininion over all the sons of righteousness is in the hands of the Prince of light ... The God of Israel and His Angel of truth succour all the sons of light ... It is [of the Spirit of truth] to enlighten the heart of man, and to level before him the ways of true righteousness and to set fear in his heart of the judgment of God. And (to it belong) the spirit of humility and forbearance, of abundant mercy and eternal goodness, of understanding and intelligence, and

---

[101] Charles, The Testaments of the Twelve Patriarchs, 246.

almighty wisdom with faith in all the works of God and trust in His abundant grace, and the spirit of knowledge in every design and zeal for just ordinances, and holy resolution with firm inclination and abundant affection towards all the sons of truth, and glorious purification from hatred of all the idols of defilement, and modesty with universal prudence, and discretion concerning the truth of the Mysteries of Knowledge. Such are the counsels of the Spirit to the sons of truth in the world.

The role of the Spirit in giving knowledge is clarified in Hymn 12.11-13:

And I, gifted with understanding, I have known Thee, O my God, because of the Spirit that Thou hast put in me; and I have heard what is certain according to Thy marvellous secret because of Thy holy Spirit. Thou hast [o]pened Knowledge in the midst of me concerning the Mystery of Thine understanding. . .

Elsewhere the Hymnist praises God:

And I, Thy servant, I know by the Spirit which Thou hast put in me [that Thou art truth] and that all Thy works are righteousness and that [Thy]wo[rd] shall not turn back, [and that all] Thy seasons are desti[ned. . . (1QH 13.18-20).

Thou hast appeared unto me from my youth (giving) understanding of Thy judgment (to me) and hast upheld me by certain truth, and in Thy holy Spirit Thou hast set my delight (1 QH 9.31-32).

And Thou hast favoured me, Thy servant, with the Spirit of Knowledge, [to love tr]uth [and righteousness] and to loathe all the ways of perversity (1 QH 14.25-26).

Thy Hymnist thanks God also for purifying him from sin: "Thou hast poured forth [Thy] holy Spirit upon Thy servant [and hast clea]nsed my heart from [all the rebellions of] my [sin]s!" (1 QH 17.26). God had graciously put the Spirit in him to cleanse him by His holy Spirit and causing him to go forward in the divine will (1 QH 16.11-12). The underlying principle is stated in 1 QS 3.6-8:

For by the Spirit of true counsel concerning the ways of men shall all his sins be atoned when he beholds the light of life. By the Holy Spirit of the Community, in His truth, shall he be cleansed of all sins; and by the Spirit of uprightness and humility shall his iniquity be atoned.

"The way of man is not firm unless it be by the Spirit which God has created for him to make perfect a way for the sons of men" (1 QH 4.31-32; cf. 1 QH 7.6-7; 16.1-3).

The goal of the Hymnist was "searching [Thy] Spirit [of Knowledge] and clinging fast to [Thy] ho[lly] Spirit, and adhering to the truth of Thy Covenant and serving Thee in truth and with a perfect heart..." (1 QH 16.6-7). The association of the Spirit and the Covenant is found again in 10 QSb 2.24-25: "May He favour thee with the Spirit of holiness ... and may He favour thee with the everlasting Covenant." The Hymnist may have attributed both gifts to God, if the text of 1 QH 14.13 reads: "It is by Thy will that [I have] entered [Thy Covenant] and [received] they holy [Spi]rit." At the Final Judgment:

> God will cleanse by His truth all the works of every man,[102] and will purify for Himself the (bodily) fabric of every man, to ... purify him of all wicked deeds by the Spirit of holiness; and He will cause the Spirit of Truth to gush forth upon him like lustral water ... The just will comprehend the Knowledge of the Most High ... For God has chosen them for an everlasting Covenant... (1 QS 4.20-22).

These various texts cumulatively imply that it was through the Holy Spirit that men clung to the truth of the (New) Covenant and thus abode in it.

The members of the Community sought to act "according to all that is revealed," i.e. the Law of Moses and "that which the Prophets have revealed by the Holy Spirit" (1 QS 8.15-16). Though the Israelites rebelled "against the commandments of God (revealed) by the hand of Moses and also by [the hands of the] Anointed of holiness,... God remembered the Covenant of the Patriarchs" and sent the Teacher of Righteousness (CD 5.20 ff.; cf. 1 QM 11.7-8). The association of the Holy Spirit with the anointed prophets appears in CD 2:12-13: to the elect God "made known His Holy Spirit by the hand of His Anointed and He showed the truth." However, in spite of the role of the Spirit in the revealing and reception of truth which leads men to righteousness, no passage in the published Qumran documents connects the Spirit with the Messiah.[103]

The Slavonic edition of Josephus' description of the Essene oath (War ii, 8.7.139) states that the living God and his omnipotent Law and the ineffible Divine Spirit are invoked. The only other possible source of information on the Essene teaching on the Spirit is the

---

[102] Joel (2:28) had prophesied the outpouring of the Spirit on all flesh in the new age.

[103] Braun, op. cit., ii, 255.

saying of the second century rabbi, Phinehas ben Jair, whom
Kohler [104] called "the last Essene of note":

> Our Rabbis taught: The words, 'Thou shalt keep thee from every evil
> thing' [Deut. 23:9], meant that one should not indulge in such thoughts
> by day as might lead to uncleanness by night. Hence R. Phineas b. Jair
> said: Study leads to precision, precision leads to zeal, zeal leads to
> cleanliness, cleanliness leads to restraint [perishut],[105] restraint leads to
> purity, purity leads to holiness, holiness leads to meekness [humility],
> meekness leads to fear of sin, fear of sin leads to saintliness [piety],
> saintliness leads to the (possession of the) holy spirit, the holy spirit
> leads to the resurrection of the dead, and saintliness [chasidut] is greater
> than any of these, for Scripture says, 'Then thou didst speak in vision to
> thy saintly one'.[106]

Whether or not these be specifically Essene stages of piety, they
certainly were influenced by Hasidic ideals. Most significant in light
of Paul's teaching is the association of the Spirit and perfectionism
according to the law. If this be an Essene description of growth in
holiness, then it would not be difficult for some Essenes to perceive
that Jesus had recapitulated these virtues in his growth to perfection
(Lk. 2:52; Hebr. 2:10).

---

[104] *Art. cit., Jewish Encyclopedia* v (1903), 231b. Jellinek and Ginsburg (*art. cit.,*
DCB ii, 204b) had declared this teaching to be Essene.

[105] Literally, separation, abstinence, i.e. in the sexual area; see Büchler, *op. cit.*, 48-
53.

[106] Abodah Zarah 20b; transl. I. Epstein in Soncino Press edition. See also
Ginsburg's translation (*art. cit., DCB* ii, 204b) based on a comparison of all recensions
(listed by Büchler, *op. cit.*, 42, n. 1). The addition in some, "and the resurrection of the
dead shall come through Elijah", might witness to the late development in Essene
circles of an eschatological role for him.

CHAPTER SEVEN

APOCALYPTIC, MYSTIC GNOSTICISM

In Galatians Paul notes a local readiness to receive angels and their teachings (1:8; 4:14) and insists that his gospel was received from a revelation of Jesus Christ, rather than from man (1:1, 11-12, 16; 2:2; cf. 3:23). Since Paul was trying to establish his credentials, his references to private and angelic revelations indicate that they were esteemed among his readers. Many of them were pneumatics (3:2-5; 5:25-6:1). Before the Galatians knew (εἰδότες) God, they served στοιχεῖα τοῦ κόσμου, who were not gods by nature (4:8; cf. 3); νῦν δὲ γνόντες θεόν, they should not turn again to them (4:9). Their earlier state of ignorance is contrasted to the attainment of the knowledge of God [1] Frederic C. Crownfield [2] may be right in detecting an astrological γνῶσις in Galatians, i.e. concerning the cosmic spirits who govern the stars.

In Colossians 2:18 the Apostle warns against the angel worshipper who humbles himself by fasting (see pp. 95-96) in order to obtain visions (ἃ ἑόρακεν), being "puffed up without reason by his sensuous mind." Evidently the claim to have a spiritual mind which received visions and their interpretation from angels underlay the practice of judging members of the church. Angelic "appearances to them in a vision would mark the stages of their progress to higher things," as W. L. Knox [3] has observed. Whether ἐμβατεύειν means "stand on", or "examine (contemplate, explore, investigate, inquire into, search) thoroughly [4] or, more probably, "enter into" (i.e. heaven by the visionary's ascent with the angels; cf. Greek Apoc. Baruch 2:2; 3:1 ff.; 11:1-4), [5] it is clear that heavenly visions, when their meaning was penetrated, were a source of the pride supporting censorious judgment of those who did not accept the special revealed laws. That certain claims of γνῶσις were being made may be decuced from

---

[1] *Lightfoot, St. Paul's Epistle to the Galatians*, New York (Macmillan, 1892), 171.
[2] "The Singular Problem of the Dual Galatians," *JBL* 64 (1945), 494-95.
[3] *Op. cit.*, 170.
[4] Williams, *op. cit.*, 109 ("searching the meaning of visions"); bibliography on interpretations in Stanislas Lyonnet, "L'épitre aux Colossiens [Col. 2, 18) et les mystères d'Apollon Clarien," *Biblica* 43 (1962), 417 ff.
[5] Francis, *art. cit., Studia Theologica* 16 (1962), 119-26.

φυσιούμενος (2:18; cf. 1 Cor. 8:1; 13:2; 2 Cor. 12:7: (ὑπεραίρωμαι) and from the Apostle's charge of empty deceit (2:8). The warning in the Shepherd of Hermas (Vis. iii, 10) that desiring too many revelatory visions would harm his flesh implies that fasting occasioned revelations. He is told that "all inquiries require humility (ταπεινοφροσύνη); fast, therefore, and you will receive what you ask of the Lord" (iii, 6.10; cf. 2.3; Col. 2:18, 23). Similar methods may have been used by the false teachers in Colossae. This line of thinking, according to Paul, devalues the work of Christ (2:17, 20). Similarly, in 2:2-8 he contrasts faith in Christ, "in whom are hid all the treasures of wisdom and γνῶσις," with the beguiling speech, the (τῆς) philosophy and empty deceit apart from Christ, i.e. of men following traditions and the στοιχεῖα τοῦ κόσμου. These perjorative terms as applied to the opponents have their counterpart in σύνεσις ἐπίγνωσις τοῦ μυστηρίου τοῦ θεοῦ, γνῶσις, σοφία and ἀπόκρυφοι. The controversial context suggests that Paul was claiming for Christ knowledge of the mystery of God; this was what the opponents were claiming for their angelic revelations which, though obscure, they claimed to interpret wisely. The classification of angels, since it is not ostensibly scriptural, appears to be among the revealed traditions. Ἀπόκρυφος is a presupposition of ἃ ἑόρακεν. The textual problem of τοῦ μυστηρίου τοῦ θεοῦ χριστοῦ (2:2) would be partially resolved if "the God of Christ" is a counterpart of "the God of angels and στοιχεῖα," whom the opponents worshipped. Such a reading (2:2) is adequately paralleled in ὁ θεὸς πατηρ τοῦ κυνίου ἡμῶν Ἰησοῦ Χριστού (Col. 1:3) and ὁ θεὸς τοῦ κυρίου ἡμῶν Ἰησοῦ χριστοῦ (Eph. 1:17). The relation between God, Christ and the angels is discussed in 1:15-20 and 2:9. The issue at stake, according to this reading (2:2), is whether the divine mystery has been revealed through Christ or by angels. This very thought had already been expressed in 1:25-28. Paul's sufferings had foreshortened the expected eschatological tribulations (1:24) [6]. His divine office was to make fully known "the word of God," i.e. "the mystery hidden ἀπὸ τῶν αἰώνων καὶ ἀπὸ τῶν γενεῶν, (cf. 1 Cor. 2:7 ff.; Eph. 3:9-10), but now made manifest to his saints." This glorious mystery is defined as "Christ in you, the hope of glory." He ἐν ὑμῖν is proclaimed by Paul and Timothy to "every man," so that "every man" may be mature in Christ. The threefold mention of

---

[6] Eduard Lohse, *Colossians and Philemon*, transl. W. R. Poelmann and R. J. Karris, Phuladelphia (Fortress, 1971), 69-71.

πάντα ἄνθρωπον (1:28; cf. 1:23: κηρυχθέντος ἐν πάσῃ κτίσει τῇ ὑπὸ τὸν οὐρανόν) combats the opponents' assertion that their esoteric wisdom was only for the τέλειοι. To all the saints, countered Paul, "God chose to make known how great among the Gentiles are the riches of the glory of this mystery" (1:27). Against the opponents' claim to fullness of truth, Paul wrote that he was praying that the readers "may be filled with the knowledge of his [God's] will in all spiritual wisdom and understanding" (1:9). They had heard and fully known (ἐπέγνωτε) the grace of God in truth (1:6). The "pneumatic" σοφία and σύνεσις may well be an expression borrowed from the proto-gnostics, since Paul derides their laws and thinking as carnal (2:18, 20-3:2). Their reputation (λόγον) of wisdom (2:23) was undeserved.

Much of the same language recurs in Ephesians. It was the Apostle's prayer that the God of Christ might "give you a spirit of wisdom and of revelation in the knowledge of him, having the eyes of your heart enlightened, that you may know what is the hope to which he has clalled you, what are the riches of his glorious inheritance in the saints, and what is the immeasurable greatness of his power in us who believe" Ϝ-1/). was the phrase, πνεῦμα σοφίας καὶ ἀποκαλύψεως, borrowed from those who defined enlightenment by a different content? The divine power at work in uniting all things in Christ for the church (1:19-23) is akin to the human power (for which Paul also prayed) "to comprehend with all the saints what is the breadth and length and height and depth, and to know the love of Christ which surpasses knowledge, that you may be filled with all the fullness of God" (3:17-19). The essence of the γνῶσις, according to Ephesians, is the theme of unity in Christ. Thus in 1:9-10 we read that God "has made known to us in all wisdom and insight the mystery of his will, according to his purpose which he set forth in Christ as a plan for the fullness of time, to unite all things in him, things in heaven and things on earth." This "mystery of the Gospel" "of peace" made known by Paul (6:15, 19) pertains to "how the Gentiles are fellow heirs, members of the same body, and partakers of the promise in Christ Jesus" (3:6; cf. 1-5; 2:13-22). The unity through the church (2:19-22; 3:10) was previously unknown to "the sons of men in other generations" (3:5) and to "the principalities and powers in the heavenly places" (3:10). We all will come, nevertheless, to the unity of the faith and ἐπίγνωσις of the Son of God, rather than being misled by erroneous teaching (4:13-14), which, by contrast, may have been made known by angels to men in the past. Ἐπίγνωσις is an aspect of human perfection (4:13). The presentation of the Gospel in terms of a hidden (3:9), but now revealed, mystery concerning the unsearchable riches of Christ (3:8) and as the wisdom of God which is apprehended by σοφία and φρόνησις (1:9, 17), suggests that the readers had previously looked for their γνῶσις from human tradition and angels, who knew only the simple (i.e. not πολυποίχιλος) wisdom of God (3:10). But now the readers had been quickened (συνεζωοποίησεν) with Christ and raised up and seated with him in the heavenly places (ἐν τοῖς ἐπουρανίοις) (2:5-6).

According to the Robertson and Plummer [7] commentary on 1 Cor. 7:40,

> Other people may believe that their views are inspired, but the Apostle ventures also to believe that he is guided in his judgment by God's Spirit. It seems to be clear from this that some of those who differed from him appealed to their spiritual illumination.

Their contradictory opinion concerned widows at least, and quite possibly virgins as well; it was alleged that they were not free to be married (7:39). These pneumatics were moved to asceticism by the desire to be holy in body and spirit (τῷ πνεύματι) (7:34). By virtue of their advanced spiritual state they claimed wisdom and γνῶσις (chh. 1, 2), though they were not alone in this claim (cf. ch. 8). Spiritual gifts (ch. 12) were distributed among those who "belonged to Peter, Apollos or Paul" and Paul's counsels and warnings on this topic were not restricted to one group. The most spectacular of the spiritual gifts was speaking in tongues, i.e. the language of angels (13:1); not all in the church had the gift (12:28-30), though in self-defense Paul could write: "I thank God that I speak in tongues more than you all" (14:18; cf. vv. 6, 14, 19). Tongues should be a sign, not for believers, but for unbelievers (14:22-25), though in 2 Cor. 12:12 in self-defense he points to his signs and wonders as an apostle. T. W. Manson [8] made this illuminating suggestion concerning γλωσσαλαλιά

> He deals elaborately with it as though it were a new thing about which the Corinthians needed detailed instruction and guidance ... The thing is something of a novelty in the Corinthian Church ... The Apostle is dealing with ... a demand which was being made on the Church to produce this particular fruit of the Spirit. I suggest that the demand came from the leaders of the Cephas party, and was part of the concerted move to instil Palestinian piety. [cf. Acts 2:4; 10:46-47].

---

[7] *Op. cit.*, 161
[8] *Op. cit.*, 204-05.

Be that as it may, in 14:37-39 we learn that to speak with tongues was a practice of those who thought themselves to be a πνευματικός. The associated claim to be a prophet came from those who edified the church (14:3) through their γνῶσις and revelations (13:2; 14:6, 24-26). The mysteries were primarily eschatological (15:51); prophecies will be fulfilled and abolished (13:8). There is a hint of excessive claims when Paul writes of "knowing all mysteries and all knowledge" (13:2) and insists that we presently know in part and prophesy in part (13:9-12). His polemic in chapters 13 and 14 was not directed against a simple teaching ("milk for babes": 3:1-2), but a γνῶσις allegedly for the mature.

At Corinth the "false apostles" claimed to be wise, but called Paul a "fool" (2 Cor. 11:19). His unskilled speech was despised (10:10; 11:6). He spoke foolishness (11:1, 16-17, 21; 12:6, 11), they charged. Yet Paul claimed to overthrow the reasonings (λογισμός) of his opponents and every high thing rising up against the knowledge of God (10:4-5). Lofty obstacles to the Gospel were being erected because all thoughts were not being subjected to Christ. But the Apostle intended to make Christ central(2 Cor. 10:4-5). Paul would not admit to being unskilled in γνῶσις, as he preached the true Gospel of God (11:4, 6-7). He commended Titus for his γνῶσις, i.e. knowing the grace of our Lord Jesus (2 Cor. 8:7, 9). Evidently the opponents were claiming an exalted knowledge of God; had the "false apostles" apprehended the true Gospel, they would not have called Paul a fool, according to their standards of σοφία. Paul's Gospel of the glory of Christ is hidden to the unbelieving who are blinded and perishing; enlightenment (φωτισμός) is from "knowledge of the glory of God in the face of Christ" (2 Cor. 4:3-6). The Apostle's boasting was not in "fleshy wisdom, but in the grace of God" (1:12). The opposing teachers, however, boasted about what Paul saw as carnal matters: their Jewishness (2 Cor. 11:18, 21-22) and their strength and wisdom (10:10-13; 11:16-21, 30) and possibly a knowledge of cosmic secrets (1:12; cf. 1 Cor. 2:12).[9] They claimed to be more sufficient or worthy (ἱκανός) for the ministry than Paul was (2:16; 3:5).[10] Paul also polemically characterized their boasting as ἐν προσώπω καὶ μὴ ἐν καρδία (5:12), i.e. in matters of external appearance and privelege. The claim of possessing "human traditions" and rightly interpreting and obeying the Mosaic law would also give grounds for such boasting.

---

[9] Georgi, op. cit., 137.
[10] Ibid., 220 ff.

Their appeal to their Jewish heritage supported "their claim of access to reliable (esoteric) ancient traditions of the Torah which their spiritual interpretation could explain" (3:16-17), as Robert Jewett points out.[11] But these advantages and outward displays did not pertain to the heart. It is on the heart that has shone "the light of the knowledge of the glory of God in the face of Christ" (4:6). Moreover, it is ἐν ταῖς καρδίαις ἡμῶν that we have been given the Spirit as a guarantee of establishment εἰς χριστὸν (1:21-22).Paul's opponents took pride in neither of these matters of the heart. For they had a different wisdom and gnosis: a different Christ and another Spirit and Gospel (11:4). Moreover, on human hearts the Spirit of the living God has written a letter from Christ (3:3). The veiling of the heart of the Jews reading Moses (3:14-16) and the contrast of these hearts with the Mosaic tablets of stone (3:3) presuppose that Paul granted to his Judaizing opponents no right to boast about matters of the heart, anyway. Rather, they took pride in their Jewish wisdom as it pertained to carnal, external legal matters. Schmithals[12] points out that for Jews, γνῶσις of God is knowledge of the will of God. They also boasted of "knowledge of the glory of God" (4:6), which Paul called πᾶν ὕψωμα ἐπαιρόμενον κατὰ τῆς γνώσεως τοῦ θεοῦ (10:5) because such γνῶσις was not centered in Christ. Its source, about which the opponents also boasted, was a lifting of the veil of the letters (or literal sense) of the Mosaic old covenant through a spiritual interpretation which was made possible by turning to a spirit not identifiable with Christ the Lord (3:12-17). Their ecstatic spirit-possession resulted in visions and revelations (12:1-7).[13] The charge that Paul was weak while they were strong (see pp. 100-101) may connote a comparison of their ability and his to see visions through angels. For, in order to give his own comparable credentials without impugning those of his opponents, Paul found it necessary (δεῖ) to boast of his own experience of being caught up into the third heaven and paradise and hearing unspeakable words. The Apostle's opponents may have been dismissing his ecstasies (ἐξέστημεν) to God as madness (5:13; cf. Mk. 3:21). But the Apostle claimed to be ἐν χριστῷ when, during his heavenly ascent, he received revelations "of the Lord" (12:1-2). In manifesting the truth (4:2), he was manifesting himself in γνῶσις (11:6); that is, his words of wisdom and knowledge

---

[11] Op. cit., 31; cf. 30.
[12] Schmithals, Die Gnosis in Korinth, 137.
[13] Georgi, op. cit., 296, n. 5; Oostendorp, op. cit. 14.

were a φανέρωσις of the Spirit (1 Cor. 12:7-8). Paul was opposing his enlightenment to the claims of his critics, who held that to be an apostle like themselves, it was necessary to be a πνευματικός.

Knowledge and revelation are points at issue in Philippians 3. Paul's γνῶσις Χριστοῦ Ἰησοῦ τοῦ κυρίου μου (3:8, 10), which involves a personal relation between the knower and Christ and leads to righteousness based on faith (3:9), is contrasted with what leads to righteousness according to the law (3:6, 9). The excellency (ὑπερέχω) of γνῶσις (3:8) which the opponents claimed, resembles the Jewish claims for their Law (cf. Rom. 2:18-20).[14] Boasting in Christ is contrasted with trusting in the flesh and in circumcision (3:2-4). The opposing γνῶσις pertained to such carnal laws. While his opponents claimed that their program led to perfection (i.e. a maturity contrasted with juvenile ignorance [cf. 1 Cor. 13:11; 14:20; Eph. 4:14; Hebr. 5:13-14]), Paul more modestly considered perfection not as a present attainment, but as the goal of God's upward call in Christ Jesus (3:12-14; cf. 1 Cor. 13:12; 2 Cor. 5:7). Those who are really τέλειοι should think of perfection as Paul did (3:15a). To those who disagree with the Apostle God will reveal the hidden truth (ἀποκαλύπτειν) (3:15b). That they have already received other revelations, presumably of a γνῶσις concerning "maturity," is indicated by καὶ τοῦτα. D. W. B. Robinson[15] argues that τελειοι is employed in the mystery-initiate sense (cf. 1 Cor. 2:6; Col. 1:28); Hebrew believers were "the first initiates into God's hidden mystery."

According to the doxology of Romans 16:25-27,[16] with the proclamation of Jesus Christ according to Paul's Gospel there has come "the disclosing of the secret purpose (κατὰ ἀποκάλυψιν μυστηρίου) which, after long ages of silence, has now been made known (in full agreement with the writings of the prophets long ago), by the command of the everlasting God to all the gentiles, that they might turn to him in the obedience of faith" (Phillips). The only wise God through Jesus Christ (16:27a) has strengthened and established the readers through this Gospel (16:25) in the face of false teachers (16:17-20). The fair and flattering speech (χρηστολογία, εὐλογία) which deceived the innocent, simple hearts was attractive because it was smooth and easy, plausible and specious. This rhetorical skill presupposes a display of wisdom and clever reasonings. The

---

[14] Klijn, art. cit., NT 7 (1964-65), 281.
[15] Art. cit., Australian Biblical Review 15 (1967), 33.
[16] On its Pauline origin see Gunther, op. cit., 80-86.

opponents may have been distinguishing between the wise and the simple (v. 19). Paul's speech, by contrast, would seem contemptible (2 Cor. 10:10), unskilled (2 Cor. 11:6). The venom of the Apostle's reaction presupposes such a personal attack on him. Admittedly, his preaching was not distinguished by excellence of speech or wisdom or by persuasive words of wisdom (1 Cor. 2:1, 4). If it is reasonable to deduce that Paul countered a deceptively reasoned wisdom with his teaching of the revealed mystery of the wise God's hidden purpose, we have a close parallel to Col. 2:2-4. Commenting on Daniel 12:10 Arthur Jeffrey writes:[17] "Wise in the sense of understanding the ways of God occurs in II Chr. 30:22; Prov. 15:24; Amos 5:13." The Apostle's reference to "my Gospel" (16:25) may indicate a distinction from another alleged revelation of the divine mystery.

Timothy was warned to guard the deposit of the faith and to avoid the profane, empty sounds (κενοφωνιαι) and the contrary casuistic objections or tenets (ἀντίθεσις) of falsely called γνῶσις (1 Tim. 6:20-21). The "knowledge" which was opposite to the Pauline faith led some to miss the mark (ἀστοχέω). Apparently it was held that some persons were unable to understand, or at least accept the γνῶσις, because "Paul" affirmed that God our Savior "desires all men to be saved and to come to the knowledge (ἐπίγνωσις) of the truth (1 Tim. 2:4; cf. 2:6; 4:10; Tit. 2:11). The emphatic prefix, ἐπὶ- suggests that the teachers who claimed saving γνῶσις held that it could not be fully, clearly and with certainty known and followed by all Christians. But the Pastor charged that whoever teaches in disagreement with pious doctrine and the wholesome words of Christ "is puffed up with conceit. . . , knows nothing (μηδὲν ἐπιστάμενος)" and morbidly battles over words (λογομαχιαι (1 Tim. 6:3-4). Evidently the opponents were very proud of their casuistry and γνῶσις. Its content is alluded to in Titus 1:15-16. Those who were preoccupied with purity and defilement professed to know (εἰδὲναι) God, but they denied him through (1) their ascetic non-recognition that everything created by God is good and to be received with thanksgiving (1 Tim. 4:3-5), and by (2) being abominable or disgusting (βδελυκτός) to God because of their defiled (μεμίανται) mind and conscience (Tit. 1:15), and by (3) being disobedient in matters of the faith and the truth (Tit. 1:13-14; cf. 3:9-11), of which the church of the living God is the pillar and bulwark (1 Tim. 3:15). Their works did not meet with divine approval

---

[17] "Daniel," IB 6 (1956), 547.

(ἀδόκιμοι) (Tit. 1:16). Those who have fully known the truth (ἐπεγνωκόσι) (cf. 1 Tim. 2:4) gratefully partake of the foods created by God (1 Tim. 4:3). But the vain-talking pseudo-teachers of the law do not understand (μὴ νοοῦντες) "either what they are saying or the things about which they make assertions" (1 Tim. 1:6-7; cf. Lk. 11:52; Rom. 2:20). They do not understand that the τέλος of the law "is love that issues from a pure heart and a good conscience and sincere faith" (1 Tim. 1:5). The source of the false γνῶσις is deceptive spirits and demons; to their teaching some persons pay such attention that they abandon the faith. These seductive ascetic laws of angels stand in contrast to the warning words of the Spirit (1 Tim. 4:1). These teachings have been imposed on apostates by speakers of lies who hypocritically display their abstinence from marriage and foods (4:2-3). Their myths and pious bodily exercise are contrasted with the nourishing words of the faith and good teaching (4:6-8). The latter are set forth in 1 Tim. 3:16. "Great is τὸ τῆς εὐσεβείας μυστήριον: He was manifested in the flesh, vindicated in the Spirit, seen by angels...." This confession (ὁμολογουμένως) of the truth (ἀλήθεια) (3:15; cf. 3:9: μυστήριον τῆς πίστεως) not accidentally precedes the warning about the ascetic teachings of spirits. The content of the mystery was at stake. As Père Spicq [18] has written, "*non une vérité, mais une personne vivante qui s'est manifestée.*"

Ignatius, in the context of teaching (a) the observance of the Lord's Day rather than the Sabbath and (b) the need to live according to Him whom the prophets as His disciples awaited, insisted that His death, "ὃ τινες ἀρνοῦνται," is the mystery by which we have received faith and endurance (ad Magnes. 9:2). Apparently the Judaizers found insufficient significance in the crucifixion to consider it part of their μυστήριον. Likewise, while favorably comparing the High Priest to the priests and to patriarchs and prophets, Ignatius wrote that to Him alone have been entrusted the secrets (τὰ κρυπτα) of God (ad Philad. 9:1). As this passage immediately follows the Antiochene martyr's account of his dispute with those who refused to accept what is in the Gospel concerning the Crucifixion and Resurrection unless it can be proven from the Old Testament (8:2: γέγραπται as in ad *Magn.* 12; ad *Eph.* 5:3; ἀρχεῖα or prophets, as in *ad Philad.* 5:2; 9:2), the superiority of Christ is to be seen as part of Ignatius' argument that the Gospel is superior to the Old Testament. The Gospel, which pertains to the

---

[18] *Saint Paul: les Épitres Pastorales*, 106-07.

coming, suffering and resurrection of the Savior (9:2) is a better transmitter of the divine secrets. But the Judaizers found in the Old Testament no new κρυπτά concerning the Passion and Resurrection.

In his Revelation the prophet John, who in the Spirit had ascended to heaven (4:1-2), saw in God's right hand "a scroll written within and on the back, sealed with seven seals" (5:1). "And no one in heaven or on earth or under the earth was able to open the scroll or to look upon it" (5:3). Only the Lamb, the Lion of Judah, the Root of David, was worthy to take the scroll "from the right hand of him who was seated on the throne" and to open its seals (5:5, 7, 9). One by one the Lamb opened the seals (6:1, 3, 5, 7, 9, 12; 8:1), revealing eschatological mysteries which were hidden from the angels. John also saw the mighty angel of Yahweh descend from heaven with "a little scroll open in his hands" (10:1-2). The visionary "heard a voice from heaven saying, 'Seal up what the seven thunders have said, and do not write it down'" (10:4-5). The angel then swore that "in the days of the trumpet call to be sounded by the seventh angel, the mystery of God, as he announced to his servants the prophets, should be fulfilled" (10:6-7). Another mystery revealed to John concerned evil. An angel carried him "away in the Spirit into a wilderness," where he saw a woman sitting on a scarlet beast (17:3). "And on her forehead was written a name of mystery: 'Babylon the great...'" (17:3.5). The angel said to the prophet: "Why marvel? I will tell you the mystery of the woman and of the beast ... that carries her" (17:6-7). "And the dwellers on the earth whose names have not been written in the book of life [of the Lamb: 13:8] from the foundation of the world, will marvel to behold the beast" (17:8; cf. 20:12, 15; 21:27; Asc. Isa. 9:21-23). The Lamb will conquer the imperial beast (17:14). As Danielou observes,[19] "In the *Revelation* then, the slain Christ appears as the one who reveals and accomplishes the design of God contained in 'the sealed book'". Also among the mysteries of the future which John saw and wrote is that of the seven stars or angels of the seven churches (1:19-20).

The apocalyptic exposition of the Law and the prophets by John the Baptist rested on his own prophetic authority. On what other basis could he have been so certain of the imminent eschaton and

---

[19] *Histoire des doctrines* ..., 159 (200 ET); cf. W. C. van Unnik, "Worthy is the Lamb. The Background of Apoc. 5," in *Melanges Bibliques en hommage au R. P. Béda Rigaux*, 449 f.

the necessary human response? His father, too, had been filled with the Holy Spirit and prophesied (Lk. 1:67) concerning final things (1:68-79). When an angel appeared to Zachariah (1:11-12), he saw a vision (1:22) and learned the Messianic role of his future son (1:13-20). John would give γνῶσις of salvation to his people through divine mercy (1:77) and would turn the disobedient to the φρόνησις of the righteous (1:17). Thus it was believed that God's mysteries were revealed through angels and Spirit-filled prophets.

When Peter was attacked in the Jerusalem church for having eaten with the uncircumcised, he silenced his opposition by describing his hunger-occasioned trance-vision (Acts 10:10-17, 19; 11:4-5).

The twelve disciples at Ephesus must have had aroused eschatological hopes if they knew John's baptism of repentance and if they accepted Paul's identification of "the one coming after" (Acts 19:3-4). They were looking for a different type of eschatological outpouring of the Spirit than was Paul (see pp. 264-265). Having apocalyptic expectations, they had no realized eschatology.

Elkesai wrote in his book: "Do not read this word to all men, and keep these commandments carefully, because not all men are faithful, nor all women upright" (Hippolytus, *Ref.* 9, 17.1). He left behind an Aramaic prayer to be repeated verbatim, though none was to seek after its interpretation (Epiphanius, *Haer.* 19, 4.3). The "ineffable and great mysteries which he delivered to worthy disciples" (Hippolytus, *Ref.* 9, 15) had allegedly been revealed by an angel (9, 13.1). The disciples of Dositheus possessed his βίβλός (Origen, *Comm. in Jn.* xiii, 27); his books were secret (Chronicle of Abu-al-Fath).

The Clementine Epistle of Peter to James is a model of esotericism:

> Peter has strictly ... charged us concerning the establishment of truth, that we should not communicate the books of his preachings ... to any one at random, but to one who is good and religious, and who wishes to teach, and who is circumcised, and faithful. And these are not all to be committed to him at once;. . . let him be proved not less than six years (iv. 1).

The recipient is to call to witness heaven, earth, water and air that he will be obedient to him who gives the books and that he will not communicate their contents in writing or keep them carelessly or let anyone see them (iv. 2 & 4), lest he himself incur eternal punishment (v).

The Jewish Christian symbols studied by E. Testa [20] were mystical and esoteric. The setting of the Revelation of Peter is a gathering of the disciples on the Mount of Olives before they see Jesus ascend. He explains to Peter the parable of the fig tree (Ethiopic 2). He drew near to Jesus and asked the identity of the two radiant men and Jesus answered him (16). Christ showed Peter in His right hand the souls of all men and their separation on the last day. "I will show thee" the works of sinners (3). After the revelations, he says, "Behold, I have manifested all unto thee, Peter, and expounded it" (Rainer Fragment, cf. Ethiopic 14). He corrected Cephas' misunderstanding of the heavenly tabernacle (16). Thus he is the mediator of this eschatological gnosis to the fellow disciples.

The Ascension of Isaiah contrasts wisdom and lawlessness (2:3-4; 3:23-24). The trance and ascension of the prophet to the seventh heaven are described (6:10-15). An angel whose name he could not find out (7:5) raised him on high and answered his questions. A still more glorious angel let Isaiah read the books on which "the deeds of the children of Israel were recorded" (9:21-23; cf. 7:27). "The vision which he had seen Isaiah narrated to Hezekiah, his son Jasub, Micaiah and the rest of the prophets" (7:1; cf. 6:16). "But the leaders, the eunuchs and the people did not hear, with the exception of Sebna the scribe, Joachim and Asaph the chronicler" (6:17). Isaiah told Hezekiah: " 'All this vision will be consumated in the last generation'. And Isaiah made him swear that he would not tell this to the people of Israel, nor permit any man to write down the words" (11:38-39). A secret tradition is implied also by the reference in 4:21 to "the words of Korah and Ethan, . . . the words of Asaph, . . . the remaining Psalms which the angel of the spirit caused to be written by those name is not recorded . . . and the words of Joseph the Just."

The Testament of our Lord Jesus Christ in Galilee is an apocalypse in which after the Resurrection he promises to "reveal what will happen in the world" on the last day (2). Earthly and heavenly signs and wonders preceding the end are taught (4). The Antichrist is described (6). Some of the themes are the fewness of days (2), and the nearness of Judgment (3) and the Antichrist's harvest (6). "Hell has opened its jaws and wishes to fill its belly" (2). "Flee the approaching wrath and flames of fire" (4). "Your woe is coming" (5). For Scripture and prophecy must be fulfilled (3, 4). The eschatological mystery

---

[20] *Op. cit.*, 34-40, 444-46.

concerning the righteous, however, is that God will give them "what eye has not seen and ear not heard" (cf. 1 Cor. 2:9; Isa. 64:4; Apocalypse of Elijah [Origen, *In Matth*. 27:9]; Gospel of Thomas, Log. 17; Acts of Peter 39; Asc. Isa. 11:34; *Apost. Consts*. vii, 22).[21]

The Montanists claimed "the power of . . . the prophetic spirit," i.e. the "prophetical gift of the Holy Spirit" ("Anonymous" *ap*. Eusebius, *H. E.* v, 16.8 & 20). Montanus and the prophetesses claimed to belong to a succession of Asian prophets (*ibid*. 16.14; 17.3-4). Their prophets, according to Tertullian (*adv. Marc*. v, 8), "predicted things to come and made manifest the secrets of the heart"; in ecstasy or rapture they interpreted tongues and produced psalms, visions and prayers. In iv, 22 he describes the ecstasy or rapture accompanying the new prophecy: "When a man is rapt in the Spirit, especially when he beholds the glory of God, or when God speaks through him, he loses his sensation, because he is overshadowed with the power of God." Tertullian defines this ecstasy as "*excessus sensūs et amentiae instar*" (*On the Soul* 45). Opponents ("Anonymous" *ap*. Eusebius, *H.E.* v, 16.4, 7-8, 9, 12; 17.1-3) accused them of false prophecy, noise, frenzy, babble, strange sounds, spurious utterances, possession by a demon or spirit of error, an unbridled tongue, abnormal ecstasy and involuntary madness of soul. Tertullian (*On the Veiling of Virgins* 17) relates that an angel beat the neck of a Montanist sister, as if to applaud, and told her it was well that she unveiled herself. "We have now amongst us a sister . . . favored with sundry gifts of revelation, which she experiences in the Spirit by exstatic vision amidst the sacred rites of the Lord's day . . . ; she converses with angels, and sometimes even with the Lord; she both sees and hears mysterious communications" (*On the Soul* 9). Prisca claimed, "Christ came to me in the likeness of a woman, clad in a bright robe, and He planted wisdom in me and revealed that this place (Pepuza) is holy, and that here Jerusalem comes down from heaven" (Epiphanius, *Haer*. 49.1; cf. 48.14; Philaster, *Haer*. 49; Augustine, *Haer*. 27). That Montanus named the Phrygian towns Pepuza and Tymion "Jerusalem" is confirmed by Apollonius of Ephesus (*ap*. Eusebius, *H.E.* v, 18.2). According to Tertullian (*adv. Marc*. iii, 24), Ezekiel

---

[21] These words are quoted in the Acts of Thomas (36) with the explanation: "We speak about the world above, about God and angels, about watchers and saints, about the ambrosial food and the drink of the true vine, about clothing that endures and does not grow old." Bibliographies in James, *The Apocryphal N. T.*, 485; Hennecke-Schneemelcher, *op. cit.*, i (1963), 300; ii (1965), 144, n. 2; 752 (ET).

knew and John beheld the heavenly Jerusalem which would come down and become a thousand year earthly kingdom after the resurrection. "The new prophecy ... foretold that there would be for a sign a picture of this very city exhibited for view previous to its manifestation." Maximilla prophesied wars and uprisings (Anonymous, *ap.* Eusebius v, 16. 18-19) and that "After me there shall be no more προφῆτις, but the συντέλεια (Epiphanius, 48.2). The "martyr Perpetua on the day of her passion saw only her fellow-martyrs there, in the revelation she received of Paradise" (Tertullian, *On the Soul* 55).

In the Gospel of Bartholomew all the apostles asked: "Lord, show us the secret of the heaven. But Jesus answered: I can reveal nothing to you before I have put off this body of flesh" (I, 1-2). In a rather Gnostic fashion Bartholomew is permitted to see certain "mysteries" which occur during the Crucifixion (I, 8, 26). After lengthy disclosures by Beliar,

> Bartholomew said to him: Lord, may I reveal these mysteries to every man? Jesus answered him: Bartholomew, my beloved, entrust them to all who are faithful and can keep themselves. For there are some who are worthy of them; but there are also others to whom they ought not to be entrusted, for they are boasters, drunkards, proud, ... seducers to fornication, slanderers, teachers of falsehood, and doers of all the works of the devil ... These things are also to be kept secret because of those who cannot contain them (IV, 66-68).

Jesus allows his disciples a brief look at "the abyss" with the help of angels (III, 4-9).

The role of angels in revealing wisdom and mysteries, which had been given impetus by Zech. 1-8, is well illustrated in Jewish apocryphal literature. Raphael secretly taught Tobit (12:6 ff.) and his son counsels of piety and the truth about his own intercession. The angel of the Lord taught Reuben (T. Reub. 5:3) about the wiles of women. Angelic revelations can also be specific: to Jacob concerning Reuben's incest (T. Reub. 3:15), and to Joseph concerning the Egyptian woman's wicked scheme of drugging food with enchantments (T. Jos. 6:2, 6), and to Job concerning the evils which Satan would bring on him if he destroyed an idol of Satan (T. Job I, 11-28; IV, 23).Following the command of the angel, Levi "destroyed at that time the sons of Hamor, as it is written in the heavenly tablets" (T. Levi 5:1, 3-4). Levi relates to his children: "There fell upon me a sleep, and I beheld a high mountain, and I was upon it.

And behold the heavens were opened, and an angel of God said to me, Levi, enter. And I entered from the first heaven" (T. Levi 2:2-7). Afterwards the patriarch tells: "the angel opened to me the gates of heaven, and I saw the holy temple and upon a throne of glory the Most High ... Then the angel brought me down to the earth." According to the T. of Isaac [22] "the angel of God took him to the heavens and showed him things in fear." An angel of the Lord took and led Baruch to the first five heavens (3 Baruch 2:2; 3:1; 10:1; 11:1-4). The T. of Jacob [23] is more vague about the role of the angel in the heavenly ascent: "I was taken up ... And he showed me all the places of repose and all the good things made ready for the just, and the things which eye hath not seen nor ear heard..." The case is similar in the *Vita Adae*: "When we were at prayer, there came to me Michael the archangel, a messenger of God... I was caught up into the Paradise of righteousness and I saw the Lord sitting on the right and left of that chariot" (25:2-3). According to Jubilees 32:20-22, the Lord spoke to Jacob,

> and He went up from him, and Jacob looked till He had ascended into heaven. And he saw a vision of the night, and behold an angel descended from heaven with seven tablets in his hands, and he gave them to Jacob, and he read them and knew all that was written therein which would befall him and his sons throughout all the ages. And he showed him all that was written on the tablets (cf. T. Levi 9:3; T. Jud. 3:10).

According to the Ladder of Jacob (cf. 3),[24] Sarekl, who is over visions, made Jacob understand the interpretations of the dream which he saw (cf. Dan. 8:15-26), and showed him all the things which he saw. Just as Jacob's dream at Bethel provided the basis for speculation concerning angelic revelations, so 1 Enoch opened the door to legends about the visionary's heavenly journeys with angels as the "tour guides."

> Enoch a righteous man, whose eyes were opened by God, saw the vision of the Holy One in the heavens, [which] the angels showed me, and from them I heard everything, and from them I understood as I saw, but not for this generation, but for a remote one which is for to come (1:2).
>
> ...My spirit was translated
> And it ascended into the heavens:

---

[22] Coptic, 67, 70; Arabic, 146-47, 148.
[23] Coptic, 83; cf. 82 and Arabic, 153.
[24] James, *Lost Apocrypha of the O.T.*, 98.

And I saw the (holy sons of God)...
And the angel Michael ... seized me by my right hand,
And lifted me up and led me forth into all the secrets,
And he showed me all the secrets of righteousness.
And he showed me all the secrets of the ends of the heaven,
And all the chambers of the stars, and all the luminaries,
Whence they proceed before the face of the holy ones.
And he translated my spirit into the heaven of heavens... (71:1-5).

"Elijah" wrote of his vision: "The angel of the Lord showed me ...
Gehenna," where "the souls of many sinners dwell and are tormented
in different ways..." (Epistle of Titus).[25] Michael took Abraham up to
heaven, where he beheld judgment, rewards and punishments and
answered the Patriarch's questions (T. Abr. 10 ff., longer; 8 ff.,
shorter). In the Apocalypse of Abraham the angel Jaoel promises the
patriarch:

> I will ascend upon the wings of the bird, in order to show thee in
> heaven, and on earth, and in the sea, and in the abyss, and in the
> underworld, and in the Garden of Eden, and in its rivers and in the
> fullness of the whole world and its circle — thou shalt gaze in (them) all
> (ch. 12).

> I will show thee the ages which have been created and established, made
> and renewed by my word, and I will make known to thee what shall
> come to pass (ch. 9).

The archangel also taught to Abraham the mystery of the glorious
Name in the form of the celestial hymn (ch. 17; cf. 1 Enoch 69:14).
To Enoch the angel of peace, who went with him, made known the
names of the "four presences" or angels of the Lord of Spirits.
Moreover, claims the visionary, he "showed me everything that is
hidden" (1 Enoch 40:2-10; cf. 60:11). God sent to Baruch (3 Bar. 1:3-
4, 6, 8; 2:4-5) an angel to make known and to show all the mysteries
of God. The same angel is "the interpreter of the revelations to those
who pass through life virtuously" (3 Bar. 11:7). Michael interpreted
Isaac's dream foreshadowing Abraham's death; a radiant man of great
size removed the sun and moon from Isaac's head (T. Abr. 7). From
the opening verses of Sefer Raziel, or Book of Raziel (Zohar I, 55b),
we learn the angel's answer to a prayer:

> I have received the charge to teach thee pure words and deep
> understanding, to make thee wise through the contents of the sacred
> book in my hand, to know what will happen to generations, if they will

---

[25] Hennecke-Schneemelcher, op. cit., ii, 158.

but read this book in purity, with a devout heart and a humbled mind
... Thou wilt also teach its contents to all those who shall be found
worthy of knowing what it contains ... It is the book out of which all
things worth knowing can be learnt, and all mysteries, and it teaches
also how to call upon the angels and make them appear before men,
and answer their questions. But not all alike can use the book, only he
who is wise and God-fearing, and resorts to it in holiness.[26]

References to the seven heavens are not uncommon in Jewish
apocrypha (e.g. Apoc. of Abraham 19; Apoc. Moses 37:3-5; 40:1-2; cf.
35:2; 2 Enoch 20 ff.).[27] The same is true of the mystic ascent and
heavenly voyage, even without the aid of angels (1 Enoch 70; Apoc.
Abr. 15, 30; Apoc. Sophonias, *ap.* Clement of Alexandria, *Strom.* v,
11.77; Apoc. Elijah; Apoc. Zephaniah 14 [ed. Steindorff]).[28]
Sometimes visions attributed to heroes of the past were symbolic (e.g.
T. Jos. 19). Levi at Bethel saw in a dream a vision of seven men in
white raiment who ordained him to the priesthood (T. Levi 8).
Reuben saw things concerning the seven spirits of deceit (T. Reub.
2:1). Naphtali supposedly (T. Napht. 5-7) saw in a dream on the
Mount of Olives a vision in which Isaac and Jacob gave directions to
the twelve patriarchs and in which holy writings appeared telling of
future Israelite captivities. Joseph seized a bull and "ascended up with
him on high" (T. Napht. 5:7). Nightly visions in which the Lord God
appeared were frequent in the Melchizedek section of 2 Enoch
manuscripts (i.5; ii.3, 11; iii.26-27, 30). Visions of writing on heavenly
tablets reveal knowledge of the future deeds of men (e.g. Daniel 7:10;
T. Levi 5:4; 1 Enoch 81:1-2; 89:61-64; 107:1; 108:6-7; Prayer of
Joseph;[29] Jub. 32:21; cf. 4:19; T. Judah 21:5). De Jonge[30] observes
that the apocalyptic tradition "derived its secret knowledge from
God's decrees written on the heavenly tablets." Enoch promised to
declare concerning the righteous and the wicked, "according to that
which appeared to me in the heavenly vision, and which I have
known through the word of the holy angels, and have learnt from the
heavenly tablets" (1 Enoch 93:2). The seer also proclaimed: "I know a
mystery and have read the heavenly tablets, and have seen the holy
books, and have found written therein and inscribed regarding

---

[26] Ginzberg, *op. cit.*, i (1912), 91-92.
[27] Charles, *The Book of the Slavonic Secrets of Enoch*, xxx-xxxix; *The Apocrypha and Pseudepigrapha of the O.T.* ii, 530-31.
[28] *TU* 17, 3a, 154.
[29] James, *Lost Apocrypha of the O.T.*., 23-24.
[30] *Op. cit.*, 84.

them. . ." (103:2); and, "I know the mysteries of the holy ones; for He, the Lord, has showed me and informed me, and I have read (them) in the heavenly tablets" (106:19). Enoch was credited with writing down in books "all the secrets" (1 Enoch 68:1; cf. 52:5; 63:3) and "the complete doctrine of wisdom" (92:1; cf. 82:1-3). He saw a "vision of wisdom"; "Till the present day such wisdom has never been given (by) the Lord of Spirits as I have received according to my insight, according to the good pleasure of the Lord of Spirits" (1 Enoch 37:1, 4). In the apocalypses "delivered to the wise among the people. . . is the spring of understanding, the fountain of wisdom, and the stream of knowledge" (4 Esdras 14:47).

Sigmund Mowinckel has aptly described the centrality of the divine secrets in apocalyptic.[31] He has characterized its background as follows:

> The latest phase of prophecy was, in large measure, an inspired revision, amplification, and interpretation of the earlier prophecy. It was spiritual learning, or 'wisdom.' Out of this wisdom (combined with elements of all kinds of ancient oriental learning on cosmography, astrology, angelology, and medical magic) there finally arose apocalyptic, which may be described as inspired learning or revealed theology, with eschatology as its centre.[32]

Eschatological secrets include judgment of angels (1 Enoch 68:2, 5; cf. 69:14) and "and the sins of the earth" leading to its destruction by the heavens' collapse (83:3-7). Jubilees 4:17 describes Enoch as "the first among men that are born on earth who learnt writing and knowledge and wisdom and who wrote down the signs of heaven according to the order of their months in a book" (cf. 21:10).[33] This writing is apparently preserved in "The Book of the Courses of the Courses of the Heavenly Luminaries" (1 Enoch 72-82; cf. 18; 34-36; 41:1-9; 43-44; 60:11-21; 3 Baruch 7-9 concerning the secrets of the lightning, thunder, winds, clouds, dew, stars and the orbits of the sun and moon), as shown by the angel Uriel (18:1-19:1), whom the Lord

---

[31] Op. cit., 386, 438.

[32] Ibid., 266; cf. 295, 376. On the relation of apocalyptic and gnosticism see G. van Groningen, First Century Gnosticism: Its Origins and Motifs, Leiden (E. J. Brill, 1967), 53.

[33] In the middle of the 2nd century B.C. Eupolemos in his book, Concerning the Kings of the Jews (ap. Eusebius, Praep. Evang. ix, 17 ff.), related that "Enoch had first invented astrology" and that his son Methuselah learned all about astrology through the angels. This clue suggests an early date for the Enoch legends and for the origin of this aspect of apocalypticism.

set over the host of heaven (82:7). Job, in defending God's wisdom before Bildad, said: "Why shall I betray (babble forth) the mighty mysteries of God..., revealing things belonging to the Master?" (T. Job VIII, 16, 19; cf. 20: "pry into matters concerning the upper world" and 23: "understand the celestial circuits").

Enoch's role as the "scribe of righteousness" (1 Enoch 12:4; 15:1) is explained in 104:12-13: "I know another mystery, that books shall be given to the righteous and the wise to become a cause of joy and uprightness and much wisdom. And to them shall the books be given... Then shall all the righteous who have learnt therefrom all the paths of uprightness be recompensed" (cf. 99:10). The Book of Daniel was an early record of the teaching that dream visions of the future were granted to the wise (1:17, 20; 2:18-30; 4:9,; 5:11, 14; 9:21-23), i.e. the pure and the righteous (12:3, 10; cf. 11:33, 35). Naphtali told his children: "Be ye therefore wise in God, and prudent, understanding the order of his commandments, and the laws of every word, that the Lord may love you" (T. Napht. 8:10; cf. T. Levi 13:7-8). What is the source of such understanding? "True repentance after a godly sort [destroyeth ignorance and] driveth away darkness and enlighteneth the eyes and giveth knowledge to the soul, and leadeth the mind to salvation. And those things which it hath not learned from man, it knoweth through repentance "T. Gad 5:7).[34]

To light up the light of γνῶσις is the role of Levi (T. Levi 4:3) and the Messiah (T. Levi 18:3, 9; T. Benj. 11:2). Σύνεσις belongs to Levi in his didactic role (T. Levi 4:5; 8:2; 13:2) and to the Messiah (T. Levi 18:7). It is associated with godliness (ενσέβεια) (T. Reub. 6:4). When the spirit of understanding of the Lord came upon Levi, he saw the unrighteousness of all men and he prayed for his salvation; his vision and heavenly ascent followed (T. Levi 2:3 ff.). He was then commissioned to declare the Lord's mysteries to men (T. Levi 2:10). However, he hid in his heart his dream vision of the seven men in white raiment (T. Levi 8:19). The mysteries of God include His commandments (T. Judah 16:4; cf. 12:6). In his Vita Adae the first man says that he "knew and perceived what will come to pass in this age" when he "had eaten of the tree of knowledge" (29:2). In the related Apocalypse of Moses Eve relates that she "beheld two great and fearful μυστήρια standing in the presence of God" (34:1).

In the Qumran writings there are many references to the mysteries

---

[34] On the rabbinic views of the need of humility for prophecy, see Büchler, *op. cit.*, 57, n. 1.

or secrets (raz) which have been revealed.[35] Some are recorded on heavenly tablets (Cave 4 fragments).[36] The basic raz concerns the wonders of God: His grace, mercy, wisdom and truth. These attributes are expressed through the mysteries of the divine plan of history. "From the God of Knowledge comes all that is and shall be, and before (beings) were, He established all their design" (1QS 3.15). One of God's marvelous mysterious was His raising up men of dust unto Himself while striking down the gods (angels) (1QM 14:14-15; cf. 2: 14-15, 18). To the Teacher of Righteousness "God made known all the mysteries of the words of His servants the Prophets" (1Q p Hab 7.4-5); i.e. he was "to explain all the words of His servants the Prophets by [whose hand] God has told all that will befall His people and [the nations]" in the last generation (1 Q p Hab 2.7-10). "The final time will last long and will exceed everything spoken of by the Prophets; for the mysteries of God are marvelous" (1Q p Hab. 7.7-8). In spite of delay of the final time, "all the seasons of God come to pass at their appointed time according to His decree concerning them in the Mysteries of His Prudence" (1Q p Hab 7.13-14). "The Book of Mysteries" from Caves 1 and 4 [37] concerns "the Mystery to come" (1Q 27 I.3-4, 7; cf. 1QS 11.3-4), i.e. when righteousness triumphs (cf. 1QM 17.7-9). This eschatological mystery is associated with "the mysteries of sin" (1Q 27 I. 2), for ultimately the unjust will be punished:

> When the children of Perversity are shut up, then Wickedness shall retire before Righteousness as [da]rkness retires before the light, and as smoke vanishes and [is] no more, so shall Wickedness vanish for ever and Righteousness appear like the sun ... and Knowledge shall fill the world, and then Foolishness shall be no mo [re] (1Q 27 I. 5-7).

"In His Mysteries of understanding and in His glorious Wisdom God has set an end for the existence of Perversity" (1QS 4.18). The destruction of ungodliness and overthrow of the sons of darkness are promised by the Mysteries of God (1QM 3.9). "The Mysteries of sin" (1QH 5.36; 1QH fr. 50.5) pertain to the transgressions of the wicked "during the dominion of Belial and amid the Mysteries of his hostility" (1QM 14.9).

---

[35] Starcky, art. cit., RB 63 (1956), 66.

[36] Rigaux, art. cit., NTS 4 (1957-58), 242; Ringgren, op. cit., 61.

[37] Starcky, art. cit., RB 63 (1956), 66; cf. Baillet, p. 55, who mentions an apocryphal prophecy from Cave 6. The Qumran gnosis was chiefly apocalyptic (Menahem Mansoor, "The Nature of Gnosticism in Qumran,"in Le Origini dello Gnosticismo. Colloquio di Messina 13-18 Aprille 1966. 395, n. 2, 398.

And because of the Angel of darkness all the sons of righteousness go astray; and all their sin and iniquities and faults, and all the rebellion of their deeds, are because of his dominion, according to the Mysteries of God until the end appointed by Him. And all the blows that smite them, (and) all the times of their distress, are because of the dominion of his malevolence (1QS 3.21-23).

The chastisement of the righteous with afflictions is another aspect of the problem of evil which belongs to the Mysteries to be understood at the end of time:

For at the ti [me of Judgment] Thou, O my God [. . .] wilt plead my cause. For thou hast chastised me in the Mystery of Thy wisdom and hast hidden the truth unto the ti [me of Judgment, but] then [Thou wilt reveal it]. And my chastisement has become for me a joy and a gladness, and the blows that have smitten me (have become) an ev [erlasting] healing [and bliss] without end, and the scorn of my enemies has become for me a glorious crown, and my stumbling, everlasting might (1QH 9.23-26; cf. 6-10).

Mysteries of the sect's interpretation of the Law have been well described by Raymond E. Brown.[38] The basic text is CD 3.12-16:

Because of those who clung to the commandments of God (and) survived them as a remnant, God established His Covenant with Israel for ever, revealing to them the hidden things in which all Israel had strayed: His holy Sabbaths and His glorious feasts, His testimony of righteousness, and His ways of truth, and the desires of His will which man must fulfill that he may live because of them. He opened (this) before them, and they dug a well of abundant waters.

"The well is the Law, and those who dug it are the converts of Israel who went out from the land of Judah and were exiled in the land of Damascus" (CD 6.4-5). But though the Israelites still continued to defile themselves, "God in His marvelous mysteries forgave their iniquity ... and He built for them a sure House in Israel," namely the Community of the Covenant (CD 3.17-19). On the other hand, "all perverse men who walk in the way of wickedness ... are not counted in His Covenant: for they have not inquired nor sought Him concerning His precepts in order to know the hidden matters in which they have guiltily strayed; and they have treated with insolence matters revealed. . ." (1QS 5.10-12). Within the Community the man of understanding is to guide in knowledge each man who has chosen the Way. "He shall instruct them in the marvelous and true

---

[38] "The Pre-Christian Semitic Concept of 'Mystery'" CBQ 20 (1958), 438-40; cf. Black, op. cit., 121.

Mysteries. . . , that they may walk with one another in perfection in all that has been revealed to them" (1QS 9.18-19). By analogy the Hymnist (the Teacher of Righteousness-?) says: "Thou hast made of me a banner for the elect of righteousness and an interpreter of Knowledge concerning the marvelous Mysteries, to test [the men] of truth and to try them that love instruction" (1QH 2.13-14). "And through me Thou hast illumined the face of many. . .; for Thou hast given me to know Thy marvelous Mysteries . . ." (1QH 4.27-28; cf. 1QH 7.26-27).

The mysteries of creation,[39] especially of the heavenly bodies, were also lauded in the Hymns. The paths of the heavenly lights and the functions of weather phenomena were providentially appointed "according to their mysterious (laws)" (1QH 1.9-13). These things and the role of man, sings the Hymnist, "I have known because of Thine understanding; for Thou hast uncovered my ear to marvelous Mysteries" (1QH 1.21). The secrets of the sectarians' calendar were doubtless among the revealed mysteries. In the context of praising God at the times of the day and year which were astronomically fixed by God, the Hymnist boasts:

> And I, gifted with understanding, I have known Thee, O my God, because of the Spirit that Thou hast put in me; and I have heard what is certain according to Thy marvelous secret . . . Thou hast [o] pened Knowledge in the midst of me concerning the Mystery of Thine understanding, and the source of [Thy] powe [r and the fountain of] Thy [goodness] (1QH 12.11-13).

He goes on to prophecy the eschatological triumph of light over darkness (vv. 14-18). Likewise in Hymn 13 God is praised for His marvelous Mysteries in the Creation (vv. 1-10) and in the new and abiding re-creation under a new covenant (vv. 11-13). Cave 4 has yielded texts describing cosmological visions resembling those of the Enoch literature.[40] The wisdom of the Elect of God encompasses knowing "the secrets of all living things" (4Q Mess ar 1.8; cf. 1 Kings 4:33).

Mysteries and knowledge are correlated (1QS 9.17-19; 11. 3-6).[41] Knowledge pertains to the Law (1QS 1.12; 3.1; 8.8-10; 9.17; 10.25) and to God's plan of history (1QS 4.2-4, 18-22; 11.3-4; 1Q p Hab.

---

[39] Brown, art. cit., CBQ 20 (1958), 441.

[40] J. Starcky, art. cit., RB 63 (1956), 66.

[41] Davies, art. cit., HTR 46(1953), 120-25; de Caevel, art. cit., Eph. Theol. Lov. 38 (1962), 442-46.

7.6-14). To the sons of God's lovingkindness He has made known His "secret of truth and given them understanding of all (His) marvelous Mysteries" (1QH 11.9-10; cf. 15-17, 28). "The counsels of the Spirit to the sons of truth in the world" concern "the truth of the Mysteries of Knowledge" (1QS 4.6). "When all His [God's] angels had witnessed it [the Creation], they sang aloud, for He showed them what they had not Known" (11Q Psa Creat. 5). Yet some mysteries cannot be understood by even the angels (1QH Fr. 1.2-3). Hymn 13.13-14 asks, what is man, who is born of flesh, to understand all the divine Mysteries "and to comprehend (the) great secret of truth?" Thus the unconverted sinner has no right to know the Mysteries. "From His wondrous Mysteries is the light of my heart, in the everlasting Being has my eye beheld Wisdom: because Knowledge is hidden from man and the counsel of Prudence from the sons of men" (1QS 11.5-6). Due to unrighteousness, man does not understand God's Mysteries (1QH 12.19-20) except through the Spirit (12.11-13). Man's knowledge comes by the Spirit of truth put in Him (1QH 13.18-19). Understanding grows through purification (1QH 6.8 ff.; 11:30-31; 1QS 3.7-9). The counsels of the Spirit concerning the Mysteries are to be kept secret (1QS 4.6). The man of understanding should "conceal the maxims of the Law from the midst of men of perversity" (1QS 9.17; cf. 22; 10.24-25). Even one entering the Covenant must be examined by the overseer before he is instructed in the regulations as derived from the Law of Moses (1QS 6.13-16; CD 15.8-12). At the end of one year his understanding and deeds with regard to the Law are examined (1QS 6.18). However,

> When they have established them in the Institution of the Community, in perfection of way, for two years ... they shall be set apart (as) holy (persons) within the Council of the members of the Community; and let nothing of that which was hidden from Israel, but found by the Man who sought [i.e. the Teacher of Righteousness], be hidden from them out of the fear of the spirit of apostasy (1QS 8.10-12; cf. 9.17-19).

An historical example of such apostasy was recalled by the Hymnist who wrote of his enemies who had entered the Covenant and joined the assembly: "they went among the sons of misfortune slandering the Mystery which Thou hast sealed within me; but it is in order that my wa[y] might be exal [ted], and it is because of their sin that Thou hast hidden the fount of understanding and the secret of truth" (1QH 5.25-26). At the end of time "all those who hold the marvelous Mysteries (unjustly) shall be no more" (1Q 27 I.7). It is uncertain whether such knowledge was acquired through indiscretions of Community members or through fallen angels.

What are the sources of knowledge of the Qumran mysteries? There is a fragmentary work from Cave 4 entitled, "Words which Michael Spoke to the Angels." [42] Angelic knowledge of mysteries is indicated by the so-called Angelic Liturgy: "The fifth among the chief princes will bless in the name of His wonders all who know the mysteries of the luminous ones of heaven with seven words of his exalted faithfulness" (lines 19-20). In the allegory of Hymn 8 the branch of holiness is said to have been kept hidden and its mystery sealed. God has fenced in the fruit of the branch by the mystery of the mighty angels and the spirits of holiness and the flaming sword (1QH 8.10-12; cf. Gen. 3:24; 1QH 5.11-12). Apparently only the archangels guarding the Garden of Eden knew about the mystery of the Teacher of Righteousness, but they did not reveal it immediately. Moreover, the Community felt itself to be in contact with angels knowing such mysteries. The description of the New Jerusalem (5Q15) was derived from a visionary accompanied by a guide who measured the city and Temple. An apocryphal Vision of Amran (father of Moses and Aaron) has also been discovered at Qumran. [43]

The Qumran Community believed in progressive revelation, in which the Teacher of Righteousness played an important role. To him "God made known all the Mysteries of the words of His servants the Prophets ... The final time will last long and exceed everything spoken of by the Prophets; for the Mysteries of God are marvelous" (1Q p Hab. 7.4-8). As the latter words are a commentary on Hab. 2:3a ("there is yet another vision...") the Teacher of Righteousness has had a vision concerning eschatological mysteries which were not understood by the prophets. The Teacher received the New Covenant "from the mouth of God" (1Q p Hab. 2.2-3). But betrayers at the end of days "will not believe when they hear all the things which will be[fall] the last generation from the mouth of the Priest whom God place in [the House of Jud] ah to explain all the words of His servants the Prophets, by [whose hand] God has told all that will befall His people and [the nations]" (1Q p Hab. 2.6-10). But for those who repented and sought God with a perfect heart, He raised up "a Teacher of Righteousness to lead them in the way of His heart and to make known to the last generations what He < would do > to the

---

[42] Starcky, art. cit., RB 63 (1956), 66.
[43] Milik, op. cit., 42.

last generation, the congregregation of traitors" (CD 1.10-12). This way of the Community "is the study of the Law which He has promulgated by the hand of Moses, that they may act according to all that is revealed, season by season, and according to that which the Prophets have revealed by His Holy Spirit" (1QS 8.15-16; cf. 9.12-13).[44] The writer of the Hymns received his knowledge of mysteries through revelation [45] by the Spirit (1QH 1.21; 2.13, 18; 4.27-29; 5.11-12, 25; 7.26-27; 12.11-14; cf. 4.5; 10.5-7; 11.3-4, 16-17). The line of revelation runs from Moses to the prophets to the Teacher of Righteousness to the Community itself (1QH 6.8 ff.) under Zadokite leadership. For, those entering the Covenant "undertake by oath of obligation to be converted to the Law of Moses according to all His commands, ... following all that is revealed of it to the sons of Zadok the priests who keep the Covenant and seek His will, and to the majority of the members of their Covenant" (1QS 5.8-9; cf. 1.7-9; 9.12-19; 1QH 2.17-18; 6.10-12; 12.22-24). Just as there was to be a priest wherever there were "ten persons of the Council of the Community", so it was a rule that "in the place where the ten are, let there not lack a man who studies the Law night and day, continually, concerning the duties of each towards the other" (1QS 6.3-4, 6-7). In the Council of the Community were to be "twelve men and three priests, perfect in all that is revealed of all the Law" (1QS 8.1). From the Community's Scriptural studies came the *pesher* commentaries, i.e. revealed explanations of the mysterious words of the canonical prophets and Psalms in light of contemporary and future history. [46] Knowledge could come from symbolic interpretations of dreams such as Abraham's (1Q Gen Apocr. xix. 14-21).[47] Whoever was the "Elect of God" in the 4Q Mess ar Text, "he shall become skilled in three books. [Th]en will he become wise and will be endued with disc-[retion] ... visions to come to him upon [his] knees" (1.5-6).[48] Wisdom obtained from esoteric (apocalyptic-?) books precedes visions.

The cumulative exegesis and angelic revelations of the Community constituted their esoteric traditions. The Community was to be guided by all these precepts (1QS 9.10-13). The esoteric nature of

[44] Black, *op. cit.*, 120-21
[45] Rigaux, *art. cit.*, NTS 4 (1957-58), 244.
[46] On the use and interpretation of Scripture, see Braun, *op. cit.*, ii, 301-25.
[47] Asher Finkel, "The Pesher of Dreams and Scriptures," RQ 4 (1963-64), 358.
[48] Text in Fitzmyer, *art. cit.*, CBQ 27 (1965), 359.

their writings is underlined by the reference to "the sealed book of the Law which was in the ark" of the Covenant; "it was not opened in Israel from the day that Eleazer and Joshua ... and the Elders died, ... and it remained hidden ... until the coming of Zadok" (CD 5.2-5). The scribe copying the Hebrew horoscope (4Q 186) employed cryptographic methods in order to conceal the contents of the secret manuscript.[49] Several other texts from Caves 2 and 4, including one with astronomical observations, are in cryptographic writing.[50]

The Essenes claimed great antiquity for their heritage. Pliny (Nat. Hist. v, 17.4) stated that the Essenes had existed for thousands saeculorum. According to Philo (ap. Eusebius, Praep. Evang. viii, 11.1), "Our lawgiver encouraged the multitude of his disciples to live in community: these are called Essenes." Kohler[51] pointed out that "the claim of antiquity for Essene tradition is ... essential to the Essene traditional lore." Its secrecy was also essential. "To those who wish to become disciples of the heresy, they do not straightway impart the traditions (παράδοσις), until they have first made trial of them" (Hippolytus ix, 23). The initiate swears to "tell nothing [of their secrets] to others even if he shall suffer violence unto death. Besides this, he swears to them to impart none of the doctrines (δογματα) [of the sect] otherwise than as he himself received them" (Hippolytus ix, 23; cf. Josephus, War ii, 8.7.141-42: "and to preserve the books of their sect likewise, as also the names of the angels").

"They apply themselves with extraordinary zeal to the study of the works of the ancients" (Josephus, War ii, 8.6.136; cf. Hippolytus ix, 22: "concerning the ἀνάγνωσις of the Law and the Prophets" and of any available σύνταγμα of the faithful [πιστον], i.e. treatises written by faithful teachers and exegetes of the sect). Presumably these edifying scrolls included expositions of their ancient traditions, such as mysteries of the law and of the celestial hierarchy. The method of instruction on the Sabbath yields a clue to the manner in which the Essenes transmitted and developped their δογματα: "One of them takes up the books and reads, and another from among the more learned steps forward and explains whatever is not easy to understand in these books. Most of the time, and in accordance with an ancient

---

[49] Carmignac, art. cit., RQ 5(1965-66), 199-200. Testa, op. cit., 432. On pp. 426-32 he discusses the Essene and Qumranian mystic symbolism, zodiac and cosmic scale.

[50] Baillet and Milik, art. cit., RB 63 (1956), 54, 61.

[51] Art. cit., Jewish Encyclopedia v (1903), 231a. Black (op. cit., 15-17, 58) finds the origin of Essenism in ancient tribal asceticism.

method of inquiry, instruction is given them by means of symbols",
i.e. allegorically (Philo, *Quod omnis probus* 82). Josephus (*War* ii,
8.12.159) wrote: "There are some among them who, trained as they
are in the study of the holy books and the < sacred > writings, and
the sayings of the prophets, become expert in foreseeing the future;
they are rarely deceived in their predictions." A. Dupont-Sommer [52]
comments that this passage "informs us that the Essenes preferred to
base their gift of divination and prophecy on the sacred texts
themselves. They searched out by means of subtle exegesis the
hidden meaning which would reveal the future to them ... Josephus
himself tells of many predictions, supposed to have been made by
the Essenes in various circumstances, which came true (*Jewish
Antiquities* xiii, 11.2; xv, 10.5; xvii, 13.3" [53]; cf. *War* i, 3.5). Josephus
also reported a symbolic dream interpretation by Simon the Essene
(*War* ii, 7.3.112-13), as if dreams were a vehicle of prophecy. That
Essene prophecies were sometimes apocalyptic is indicated by the
association of ideas in Hippolytus ix, 27:

> The doctrine of the Resurrection is also strong among them ... (They)
> say also that there will be a judgment and a conflagration of the All, and
> that the unjust will be punished everlastingly. And prophecy and the
> foretelling of things to come are practiced among them.

Josephus (*War* ii, 8.11) relates that bad souls, they thought, were
allotted a dark, tempestuous den, full of never-ending punishments.

The Therapeutae prayed for keenness of spiritual vision (ὀχυρία
λογισμός) (Philo, *de vita contempl.* 89). Even in their dreams they
allegedly uttered τὰ τῆς ἱερας φιλοσοφίας δόγματα (*ibid.*, 26). Studying
the law and the prophets was carried out both privately (*ibid.*, 25) and
publicly(*ibid.*, 75). Their interpretation was allegorical (*ibid.*, 28, 78).
Laws of fasting were part of the knowledge thereby derived, and those
who followed them were "performing the mysteries of the holy life
(τὰ τοῦ σεμνοῦ βίου μυστήρια τελοῦνται) (*ibid.*, 25).

Porphyry (*ap.* Cyril of Alexandria, Migne, *P.G.* 76, 776) gave this
account of the Essenes:

> From their way of life and by their ἄσκησις πρός truth and εὐσέβεια, there
> are among them many who foreknow the future; for, they are learned in
> the sacred writings and the utterances of the prophets and the various
> (ways) of ἁγνεία.

---

[52] *Op. cit.*, 34, n. 3.
[53] *Ibid.*, 35, n. 1. On Essene prophets see Constantin Daniel, "'Faux prophètes':
surnom des Esseniens dans le sermon sur la montagne," *RQ* 7 (1970), 51-55; cf. 65-67.

CHAPTER EIGHT

APOSTOLIC AUTHORITY

The identity of Paul's opponents is more concealed than revealed in Galatians. "The ones unsettling" (5:12) or "troubling" the readers and "wishing to pervert the Gospel of Christ (1:7) are not named. The Apostle indicated little knowledge of these intruders: "Who has bewitched you ...?" (3:1); "who hindered you from obeying the truth?" (5:7); "whoever he [the one troubling you] may be..." (5:10). Had their distorted gospel been indigenous, Paul would have attacked it when present in person and would have referred in his epistle to his earlier counterthrusts. However, his earlier personal warning against a different gospel was general (1:9), rather than specific and descriptive. Moreover, he would not have been astonished at the apostasy of some Galatians (1:6) and their submission to circumcision (5:2-3; 6:12-13) if the substance of the false teaching were already present in Galatia not long before (1:6: ταχέως). Accordingly, instead of a local aberration propagated by settled preachers,[1] we must find missionary apostles from the outside.

Whence came the intruders? Acts 15:1-2 and Gal. 2:12-13 provide some analogy, though there is insufficient information to support a direct connection of the Galatian missionaries and those who came to Antioch from Judea and from James, preaching circumcision and separation from Gentiles at meals. Whatever be the relationship between these Judaizing emissaries, it is clear that support from the Jerusalem church for Judaizing preachers was both available and effective. There are some indications that the intruders in Galatia availed themselves of it. Paul in self-defense had to explain his relations with Peter in order to show that he was not dependent on him or any other human for his Gospel (1:1, 11-12, 16-19; 2:2), and, therefore was not subject to Cephas (2:6-14)[2]; in other words, Paul had been accused of being a rebellious (2:11 ff.) disciple of Cephas who perverted his master's teachings. James, Peter and John had passed judgment on Paul as a charismatic (1:18-20; 2:2, 7-9) and, after instruction, permitted him to be an apostle; but his deviation from

---

[1] Zahn, *Intoduction to the N.T.*, i, 166.
[2] David M. Hay, "Paul's Indifference to Authority," *JBL* 88 (1969), 36.

their teaching was not due to divine revelation. Allegedly, after his conversion, he went to Jerusalem to confer with the original apostles (1:16-17). The readers had been led to believe that deference was owed to the pillars of the Jersalem church (2:6, 9); their reputation had been pitted against Paul's by his opponents. The latter appealed to Peter's authority as apostle to the circumcised (2:2, 7-8) and held that Paul owed obedience to the Jerusalem leaders who "ordained" him (2:9-10; cf. 1:19-20). He countered that it was due only to fear and hypocrisy that Jerusalem representatives achieved success in Antioch (2:12-14). Robert Jewett [3] rightly notes that "Paul's explanation of his relations with Jerusalem indicates that he is dealing with persons who had access to detailed information" unknown to the Galatians; moreover, his opponents' dwelling on "Paul's alleged dependency on Jerusalem indicates that they themselves had a Jerusalem-oriented viewpoint."

If it is legitimate to conclude that the intruders in Galatia claimed that Paul, unlike themselves, had become unduly independent of the "pillars", then we might look for some historical connection between their missionary journey into Galatia and Paul's itinerary. And if the personal attacks on the Apostle signify that there was a deliberate intent to interfere with his missionary work, then his opponents must have had some knowledge of the situation in Paul's churches. Such information was given by Paul to the Jerusalem Church after he left Corinth and Ephesus and before returning to Antioch (Acts 18:18-22; cf. 15:3-5; 21:17 ff.). If Paul's opponents emanated from Judea, they would have learned at this time of his absence from his churches. The stage was then set for an ongoing theological dispute concerning the Way.

II Corinthians 10-13 provides further information. Paul's antagonists claimed to be apostles (11:5, 13; 12:11-12); these travelling preachers gained a foothold by bearing letters of commendation (2 Cor. 3:1). Their outside origin is confirmed by their designation as διάκονοι of Christ (11:23; cf. 6:4; 1 Cor. 3:5; Eph. 3:7; 6:21; Col. 1:7, 23, 25; 4:7; Phil. 1:1; 1 Thess. 2:2), ὁ ἐρχόμενος (11:4) and ἐργάται (11:13; cf. Mt. 10:10; 1 Cor. 9:6 ff.; 2 Tim. 2:15). These letters doubtless gained them welcome into more churches than the Corinthian. As in Gal. 1:1, 11-12, Paul insists to the Corinthians (2 Cor. 2:14, 17; 3:5-6; 4:1; 6:1; 10:8; 12:12; 13:10; cf. 1

---

[3] "The Agitators and the Galatian Congregation," *NTS* 17 (1971), 204.

Cor. 9:1; 15:8-11) that his authority is directly from the Lord. His failure to exercise it (1 Cor. 9:15-19) was used against him.[4] Against the spiritual authority of proponents of celibacy he insisted that he also (κἀγώ) had the Spirit of God (7:40).[5] In his defence (ἀπολογία) against critics (ἀνακρίνουσίν) and against "others" not regarding him as an apostle (9:1-4), he pointed to his privelege to eat and drink. He had at least as much right to be supported by the Corinthians as did others (9:12; cf. 2 Cor. 11:20), who apparently baptized them (1 Cor. 1:13-17) and thereby claimed to be their "fathers in Christ" (4:15). The maintenance of Cephas, the Lord's brothers and the rest of the apostles (9:4-6), together with their wives, was a known and accepted fact. Paul insisted on submission to his own fellow workers (16:16). "Peter is mentioned separately because there were some at Corinth who at this early date venerated him." [6] "Perhaps it was those who belonged to Cephas who had questioned Paul's apostleship."[7] As Judaizers they had questioned his "freedom" and did not deem it appropriate for a true apostle (9:1, 19-22; 10:29-31). The existence of a Petrine party at Corinth (1:12; 3:22) cannot be convincingly explained by Peter's personal labors, since only Apollos is mentioned as the one who had watered what Paul had planted (3:6; cf. 4:15). Clement of Rome in his letter to Corinth referred to no Petrine visit. The absence of Peter's name in 1 Cor. 3:4 ("I am of Paul. . . I am of Apollos") can be explained by the fact Paul and Apollos were fellow workers at Corinth (3:5; 4:6) and Ephesus (16:12); together they faced common problems, including the careless (3:10) erection of the Cephas party on the foundation of the work of Paul and Apollos (3:10-15). It is likely that the authority of Peter was appealed to as the head of the church by those who chose not to join the parties of Paul or Apollos. T. W. Manson [8] sagaciously observed that the "other

---

[4] Plummer & Robertson, op. cit., 180-81. Perhaps it was claimed that his reason was: so that he could be free to eat anything.

[5] Allo, St. Paul. Première Épitre aux Corinthiens, 83.

[6] Grosheide, op. cit., 204; cf. Manson, op. cit., 201, n. 1.

[7] Barrett, op. cit., 204.

[8] "The Corinthian Correspondence (1) in Studies in the Gospels and Epistles, ed. Matthew Black, Manchester (University, 1962), 194. Oscar Cullmann (Peter: Disciple-Apostle-Martyr, transl. Floyd V. Filson, Philadelphia [Westminster, 1953], 47) and C. K. Barrett ("Cephas and Corinth," in Abraham unser Vater: Juden und Christen im Gespräch über die Bibel [Festschrift für Otto Michell, ed. O. Betz, M. Hengel, P. Schmidt, Leiden & Cologne [E. J. Brill, 1963], 6-7; see also his Commentary, pp. 87-88; cf. Craig's exegesis in IB 10, 47; A Feuillet, "Chercher à persuader Dieu' (Ga I 10a), NT 12 (1970), 358-59; Jewett, op. cit., 33.

foundation" which no one can lay beside the foundation of Christ (3:11; cf. 2:2; 2 Cor. 11:4; Gal. 1:7; Eph. 2:20) represents an early form of the claim, already advanced, that Peter was the rock upon which the church was being built (Mt. 16:18). Paul approved of neither the basis nor the work of this Petrine faction. The pertinent statement that the builders' works will be manifested and tested by the fire of Judgment Day (1 Cor. 3:12-15) is approximated by the thought in the more severe 2 Cor. (11:15) that the end of the so called "servants of righteousness" will be according to their works. Those who build with wood and straw are faulty teachers at Corinth who will be poorly rewarded; their work will perish. The affiliation of Peter, the chief apostle, and Paul's opponents gains further support from the ironic allusion of 2 Cor. 11:5 and 12:11 to the "super-apostles (ὑπερπλίαν ἀποστόλων), which is reminiscent of οἱ δοκοῦντες (Gal. 2:6). When Paul insisted (2 Cor. 12:11-13) that he was not inferior to the super-apostles because he, too, had performed among them "the signs of a true apostle," [9] i.e. "signs and wonders and mighty works." The Apostle to the Gentiles was being accused of being a lesser wonder-worker than the foremost among the Twelve. In order to show the parity of the miraculous powers of Peter and Paul, the author of Acts sets forth parallel accounts of 5:15; 9:32-42; 19:11 ff.; 20:8-12. The intruding Judaizers at Corinth hardly would fail to describe Peter's mighty works in Judea (Acts 2:43; 3:1-10; 5:15-16; 9:32-42).

Seemingly Paul was resisting at Corinth, as in Galatia, emissaries claiming Petrine authority,[10] which had been exalted above the Pauline. These intruders created a local Corinthian party which specially honored the Apostle to the circumcized (Gal. 2:7-8).[11] Paul's mention of Peter and James (1 Cor. 9:1-6; 15:4-10) in defense of his apostolic prerogatives may indicate that a Palestinian party existed at Corinth.[12] The Lord's brothers (9:5) were Palestinian church leaders who received support. It would be natural to expect that ἐργάται of the Judaizers would labor at Corinth, too, if they taught in Galatia, Colossae, Ephesus (1 Tim. 1:3; Rom. 16: 17 ff.), Philippi (Phil. 3) and Crete (Titus 1:10-14). According to 2 Cor. 10:12-16, Paul's opponents

---

[9] Oostendorp, op. cit., 15, 80.

[10] Maurice Goguel, The Birth of Christianity, New York (Macmillan, 1954), 311-12, 314. Schlatter and Reitzenstein thought that the superapostles were the original Jerusalem apostles.

[11] Barrett, art. cit., BJRL 46(1963-64), 296; art. cit. in Abraham unser Vater, 5.

[12] Oostendorp, op. cit. 82.

"boasting of work already done in another's field," measured themselves by one another and compared themselves with each other. In other words, the intruders boasted among themselves about the number of sheep they stole from Paul's flock. They worked only where others had already pioneered, but they took the credit. They did not keep to the limits God had apportioned to them, but overreached and overextended them. Their claim to his territory must have stemmed from their claim to a more legitimate apostolic rank. Paul had a right to complain if he thought their evangelization should have been limited, even more than Peter's, to Hebrews (11:22-23) or new territory or areas nearer their homeland. That they had previously invaded other Pauline churches in indicated by 2 Cor. 10:10: they said of Paul, "His letters are weighty and strong, but his bodily presence is weak, and his speech of no account." His opponents had access to his letters and knew the impressions which he made upon those who heard him preach. Besides his earlier correspondence with the Corinthians, his letter to the Galatians was probably included in the reference of 10:10; for in 10:8-9, 12 he indicates that his opponents knew that in his correspondence he had defended his divinely given authority. Their claim to apostleship probably implies that they belonged to the five hundred brethren (1 Cor. 15:6) who had seen the risen Lord (1 Cor. 9:1; 15:8; Acts 1:22).

E. Käsemann has pointed out that Paul is not dealing with obscure opponents; "only very important authority in the enemy camp explains the bitter harshness of the Apostle." [13] This would also explain their influence and ability to gain the support and obedience of the Corinthian community. "Only the authority of the original community could shake that of Paul in his very own community." [14] J. Schoeps [15] agrees that "these Corinthian intruders would never have been able to undermine Paul's prestige had they not been able to appeal to a real authority, indisputable in Christian eyes, namely, that of the mother church." Diaspora Hebrew Christianity was not strong enough. Schoeps goes on to quote Käsemann: [16]

> The original apostles are only indirectly concerned in the conflict, in so far as their authority is exploited against Paul ... He cannot deny a

---

[13] *Die Legitimität des Apostels, eine Untersuchung zu 2 Kor. 10-13*, Darmstadt (Wissenschaftliche Buchgesellschaft, 1956), 23

[14] *Ibid.*, 26.

[15] *Paul. The Theology of the Apostle in the Light of Jewish Religious History*, transl. Harold Knight, London (Lutterworth, 1961), 76.

[16] *Die Legitimät...*, 29-30.

certain preeminence of the στυλοι ... Neither can Paul dispute the
authority of the original church which is completely expressed in the
letters of commendation ... He must unsparingly deal with the
intruders in Corinth, while at the same time not coming into conflict
with Jerusalem and the original apostles. He must as far as possible
keep the latter out of the conflict, and in fact he brushes them very
lightly with his emphasis on his equality of status (11:5; 12:11).

Many of the same remarks are just as applicable to the Galatian
conflict. Leonhard Goppelt [17] deduced that "by means of a
documented commission and succession" they "would prove that the
tradition they represented was genuine; this was a Jewish principle."
However, no trustworthy conclusions should be drawn concerning
the precise relationship between the Corinthian intruders, on the one
hand, and the Twelve, parties within the Jerusalem church and
James, on the other. It may be safely conjectured, nevertheless, that
Paul's opponents made the most of, and perhaps overstated, their
connections with the mother church and its leaders. If so, a setting
could be suggested for the Western text of Acts 19:1, according to
which Paul wished to return to Jerusalem when passing through the
upper country on his way back to Ephesus. Might he have just
encountered Judaizers claiming to be emissaries of the Jerusalem
church?

The Palestinian origin of the Judaizing missionaries is confirmed
by their claiming to be Hebrews (2 Cor. 11:22; Phil. 3:5). In these
two passages, observed Walter Gutbrod,[18] is found a progressive
argument. Paul claimed to be "not merely circumcised (as a convert
could be), nor a member of the race of Israel (who could lack
traceable genealogy), nor a Benjaminite (who could be hellenized),
but a Ἐβραῖος ἐξ Ἐβραίων" (i.e., of Palestinian descent and speaking
Aramaic as his mother tongue [cf. Acts 21:40] like his opponents).[19]
The Hebrews of Acts 6:1 are native Palestinians who were possibly
Aramaic-speaking, as this is a secondary meaning of the term.
Various inscriptions suggest that a "Hebrew" was an Aramaic-
speaking Jew from Palestine, or one of Palestinian nationality or
language.[20]

Paul's lengthy self-defense (vv. 4-17) and the bitterness of his

---

[17] Jesus, Paul and Judaism, transl. E. Schroeder, New York (Thomas Nelson &
Sons, 1964), 169.
[18] Theological Dict. of N.T., ed Kittel, iii (1965), 390.
[19] Ibid., 389-91.
[20] Ibid., 373-75.

denunciations (vv. 2,18-19) in Philippians 3 indicate that he had been subjected to personal attack for being imperfect in the flesh (vv. 3-4, 9, 12-13, 17, 19). The Apostle had experienced long-standing and painful difficulties with the many enemies (v. 18), and the readers were to be on the lookout (βλέπετε) for the evil missionaries (ἐργάται) (v. 2). They were still dangerous (v. 1b), though apparently not yet a menace in Phillippi as elsewhere. Phil. 1, 2 and 4 are free of references to further local troubles.

At Ephesus Paul's troubles with his opponents were greater. The readers of Romans 16 were warned to watch and avoid those who create divisions by teaching doctrine opposed to that which had already been learned (v. 17). Again, this presupposes "sheep-stealing"; alleged "servants of Christ" (v. 18) enter a church seeking converts to their own doctrine. Satan was already at work (v. 20) and the Apostle was concerned that the obedience of his readers would be shaken (v. 19). After his departure "fierce wolves" entered his flock (Acts 20:29-31). The Pastoral Epistles document the inroads of these "teachers" (1 Tim. 1:3, 6-7; 4:2; 6:3-4; Tit. 1:10-11, 16; 2:1) who denied that Paul was appointed a κῆρυξ and apostle (1 Tim. 2:7; 2 Tim. 1:11). Alexander the (copper)smith greatly opposed the λόγοι of Paul and was worthy of divine retribution for his evil deeds to the Apostle (2 Tim. 4:14-15). He warned Timothy to avoid him on his trip to Asia (4:13, 19; cf. 1:15-18; Rom. 16:3-4; 1 Cor. 16:19). Ἀνθίστημι for Paul meant a religious opposition (Rom. 13:2; Gal. 2:11); his words were his gospel of the cross (1 Cor. 1:17-18). According to 1 Tim. 1:19-20 an Alexander (subsequently?) was excommunicated ("delivered to Satan") for having made shipwreck of his faith "by rejecting conscience". His error in dogma was associated with his harmful behavior. He spoke injuriously (βλασφημεῖν) (cf. Rom. 14:16; 1 Cor. 10:30; Tit. 3:2). According to Acts 19:33-34 the Ephesian Jews put forth a fellow Jew named Alexander during a riot by smiths. G. H. C. Macgregor [21] prudently deduces that "Alexander was put up to try to avert [an attack on the Jews] by drawing the crowd's attention back to Paul, and making it clear that the Jews repudiated all responsibility for him and his teaching." Alexander would have been an ideal spokesman had he been a smith (making tools and utensils, though not idols) and had he been able to state with authority that Paul's gospel was beyond the pale of Judaism, i.e. that he was a renegade in

[21] Exegesis of Acts in *IB* 9, 259.

the eyes of Jews and a false apostle according to true Hebrew Christians. According to E.F. Scott,[22] Alexander (Acts 19:33) "seems to figure in the account of the riot as a Jew who attached himself to Paul and had then joined with his countrymen in opposing him."

The situation in Colossae, Laodicea and Hierapolis was different. The saintly and faithful (πιστοι) brethren (1:2) had learned "the word of the truth, the gospel" through Epaphras, the "beloved fellow servant" of Paul and "a faithful minister and δοῦλος of Christ" on behalf of Paul (1:4-8, 23; 4:12-13). By implication not all local Christians were faithful converts of Epaphras and thus recipients of the apostolic gospel. Most had not seen Paul's face (1:4; 2:1), though he was prepared to exercise a loving authority over them (1:3, 9; 4:8, 10, 16-17). The readers were primarily Gentiles (1:21; 2:13; 3:7). They were in danger of straying from the faith and the hope of the Gospel (1:23; 2:7) of which Paul became minister (1:23-25, 28). He felt it necessary to define this mystery and his ministry in terms of Christ (1:26-28; 2:2-3) lest someone delude them with beguiling speech (2:4), or make a prey of them (2:8), or pass judgments upon them in legal matters (2:16) or disqualify them (2:18). Μηδείς and τις suggest that an effort was being made to persuade them to follow a different gospel. Some success had been attained; the readers were already submitting to ascetic regulations (2:20-22). As Paul does not react as defensively as elsewhere, there is less likelihood here of recently intruding anti-Pauline missionaries than of influence from local established rivals, who had been converted earlier.

"Jeremiah" prophesied (4 Baruch 9:20) that the Son of God would "choose twelve apostles that they may preach the Gospel among the Gentiles."

The Ascension of Isaiah rests teaching authority in the twelve apostles (disciples) sent out by Jesus before his acension (3:17-18; 11:22) and whose teaching will be forsaken in later days (3:21 ff.). Beliar-Nero "will persecute the plant which the Twelve Apostles of the Beloved have planted; and one of the twelve will be delivered into his hand" (4:3). Although the tradition of a 545-day post-resurrection stay (9:16; 11:21) presupposes that Paul saw the risen Lord,[23] -an appearance whose reality Paul did not have to defend even in his controversial letters,—evidently his teaching authority is

---

[22] *The Pastoral Epistles* (Moffat N.T. Comm.), London (Hodder & Stoughton, 1936), 17.

[23] Gunther, *op. cit.*, 26.

subordinated to that of the Twelve. Erik Peterson [24] has observed that "between the Christian apocalypse in the Ascension of Isaiah and the Apocalypse of Peter stood some kind of literary connection," Both works speak of Peter's martyrdom in Rome by the devilish Nero as part of "the eschatological picture of history of Christians" (Rainer Fragment; Ethiopic 14). The Ethiopic Testament of our Lord Jesus in Galilee purports to relate what he spoke there to his disciples after the Resurrection (cf. Mt. 28:16 ff.). "Tell it to Israel and to the Gentiles that they may hear and believe, that they may be saved" (4). It is the Eleven who are entrusted to transmit the eschatological tradition. The Ascension of Isaiah (3:21, 27-28, 31; cf. 2:5, 10-11; 11:5) treats wandering ascetic prophets as those who still "speak reliable words."

Why was an epistle with a semi-Pauline theology written in the name of Peter to churches in the Pauline sphere of influence? Possibly because Cephas himself had passed through the area before proceeding to Rome. Possibly because the readers in Asia Minor were being deceived by a teaching alleged to be Petrine. The Galatian intruders sought to avoid being "persecuted for the cross of Christ" (6:12; cf. 5:11). I Peter not only contains advice on martyrdom, but also offers a less Judaic interpretation of Petrine teaching than the Asian Judaizers presented.

Accordingly, our search for the origin of Paul's opponents leads us to Palestine, where Aramaic- and Greek-speaking Hebrew Christians had come into contact with Peter and James the Lord's brother, and had obtained the support of a part of the Jerusalem church.

Hegesippus (ap. Eusebius, H. E. ii, 23) portrayed James as "holy from his mother's womb." He was called "the Righteous" (or "the Just") from the Lord's times, because of the greatness of his righteousness. The prophets foretold of him. He was permitted to enter the Holy of Holies. The Jews who believed did so on James' account. Epiphanius (Haer. 29.4; 78.14) adds that he wore the petalon (see p. 104, n. 17), and that he "received the first episcopal cathedra when the Lord entrusted His throne on earth to him first" (78.7); cf. Clement Alex., ap. Eusebius, H.E. ii, 1.4-5. He apparently functioned

---

[24] "Das Martyrium des H1. Petrus nach der Petrus-Apokalypse," in *Miscellanea Giulio Belvederi*, Citta del Vaticano, 1954, 183; more recently, M. Erbetta, "Ascensione di Isaia IV, 3 è la testimonianza più antica del martirio di Pietro?, "*Euntes Docete* 19 (1966), 427-36. Similarities between the Apocalypse of Peter and the Ascension of Isaiah were listed by H. Stocks ("Quellen zur Rekonstruction des Petrusevangeliums," *Zeitschrift für Kirchengeschichte* 34 [1913], 26).

as the chief Nazirite and high priest and holy man in the church, which was made up of priests, Nazirites and the righteous. Thus in the Clementine literature [25] he is called, "the chief of the bishops" (Rec. i, 68), "the lord (cf. Rec. iii, 74) and bishop of the holy Church" (Epistle of Peter to James 1), "the bishop of bishops, who rules Jerusalem, the holy church of the Hebrews, and the churches everywhere..." (Epistle of Clement to James 1). He was ordained bishop in the Jerusalem church by the Lord (Rec. i, 43; Ep. Peter to James 5). "Believe no teacher, unless he bring from Jerusalem the testimonial of James the Lord's brother..." (*Rec.* iv, 35). Yet in the Clementines Peter is the missionary par excellence. In the Gospel of Didymus Judas Thomas (12), in response to the question, "Who is he who shall be great over us?", Jesus says, "...you shall go to James the Just, for whose sake heaven and earth came into being."

Opposition to Paul existed at a later date in Palestine and parts of Syria from the Ebionites (Irenaeus, *Adv. Haer.* i, 26.2; Origen, *Contra Celsum* v, 65; *Hom in Jer.* xviii, 12; Eusebius, *H. E.* iii, 27.4; Epiphanius, *Haer.* 30, 16 & 25), the Elkesaites (Eusebius, *H. E.* vi, 38), Sampsaeans (Epiphanius, *Haer.* 53.1) and readers of the Clementine Preachings of Peter (*Clem. Hom.* ii, 17; xi, 34-35; xvii, 19; *Rec.* iv, 34.5-35.2; Ep. Peter to Jas. 2, 3-4).[26] In the Holy Land the widespread, if not general, early distrust of him is witnessed to by the Jerusalem party which caused dissension at Antioch (Acts 15:1-2; Gal. 2:12) and by Paul's need to show in Jerusalem his loyalty to the Law through Nazarite vows (Acts 18:18b, 21-22; 21:20-27).

---

[25] Cullmann, *Le Problème litteraire*..., 225, 230, n. 32.
[26] *Ibid.*, 243-52; Hennecke-Schneemelcher, *op. cit.*, ii, 71.

CHAPTER NINE

2 CORINTHIANS 6:14-7:1

This section has been widely considered an interpolated or even non-Pauline passage.[1] Its many points of resemblance to the language and thought of the Qumran documents and the Testaments of the Twelve Patriarchs evoke the question of its relation to the teachings of Paul's opponents. Could the compiler of 2 Corinthans have unknowingly included a short document emanating from a strange source? In order to answer that question we must raise another one: does the text of 2 Cor. 6:14-7:1 have more in common with the ideas and terminology of Paul or with those of his opponents? An examination now follows of as many of the pertinent points as possible.

Loyalty to the law is implicit in the contrast of righteousness and lawlessness (ἀνομια): a contrast comparable to that of light and darkness or of Christ and Beliar (6:14-15). Thus righteousness, νόμος, light and Christ are correlated. Similarly, Levi in his *Testament* (19:1) allegedly taught: "And now, my children, ye have heard all; choose, therefore, for yourselves either the light or the darkness, either the law of the Lord or the works of Beliar." Bertil Gärtner[2] reasons from the analogy of 1QS 4.5; 1QH 4.15-19; 4Q Flor. 1.16-17 (cf. Ezek. 14:4 ff; 37:23) that the "idols" of 2 Cor. 6:16 are the sin and uncleanness and evil impulses which cause a man to disobey the law. There shall be "no share in the House of Law" for those who despise the Covenant's precepts of righteousness and who have set idols upon their hearts" (CD 20.9-13).

A tendency toward perfectionism is revealed by the exhortation, "let us cleanse ourselves from every defilement of body and spirit, and make holiness (ἁγιωσύνη) perfect in the fear of God" (7:1). In his exegesis of this passage Alfred Plummer[3] called attention to the fact that in the Septuagint "ἁγιωσύνη is used generally of God" and that, according to T. Levi 18:11, the saints entering Paradise will eat from the tree of life, "καὶ πνεῦμα ἁγιωσύνη ἔσται ἐπ' αὐτοῖς." The holiness of

---

[1] See Gunther, *op. cit.*, 75-76.
[2] *Op cit.*, 51-52.
[3] *Op. cit.*, 212.

2 Cor. 7:1 is appropriate for the children of God (6:18) who walk in light and righteousness (6:14).

An ascetic tendency, or at least lofty sexual standards, may be implicit in the reference to "every pollution of the flesh (σάρξ)" (7:1). This carnal pollution is associated with ἀνομία, darkness, Beliar and idols. Such an association is found in the T. of Reuben (6:4), where fornication is said to separate the soul from God, "bringing it near to idols." Likewise, lust brings one near to Beliar (T. Sim. 5:3).

The dualistic contrasts of 6:14-15 underlie the call to cleansing from all pollution of flesh and spirit (7:1). Requisite for this purification are: not becoming yoked with unbelievers (6:14) but rather coming out from them, being separate from them and touching nothing unclean (6:17). Only then are the divine kinship (6:8) and perfect holiness possible (7:1). As contact leads to contamination, so separation is a necessary condition for purification. As the Temple of God, His people (6:16, 18), who fear Him (7:1), can have no agreement with opposite principles. Mixed marriages are forbidden in Tobit 4:12; Jub. 20:4; 22:20; 25:1-10; 30:7; T. Levi 9:10; T. Job. 45:3; Jos. & Aseneth 7:64. Two apocryphal texts in addition to those already cited reveal the same spirit or wording as the Corinthian text. "Hold aloof from all pollution (ἀπὸ πάντως μολυσμου)" (Test. Sim. 2:13). "And let ... no uncleanness be found in Israel throughout all the days of the generations of the earth; for Israel is holy unto the Lord, and every man who has defiled (it) shall surely die "(Jub. 30:8). "Defiling the Holy Spirit" appears in T. Napht. 10:8-9 (Hebrew) and CD 5.11; 7.3-4, cf. T. Issach. 4:4; Hermas, *Sim.* v. 6. 5-6; 7.2 & 4; *Clem. Rec.* iv, 36.

II Cor. 6:16, 18 teaches:

> We are the temple of the living God; as God said,
> 'I will live in them and move among them,
> and I will be their God,
> and they shall be my people. . .
> and I will be a father to you,
> and you shall be my sons and daughters. . .

The Christian people has become the people of God and is regarded as the equivalent of Israel, to whom God originally had addressed the passages. The Christian community is the ναός, the inner sanctuary or Holy of holies where God dwells. Gärtner [5] perceives that this "image

---

[4] References from Philonenko, "Le Testament de Job," *Semitica* 18 (1968), 21.

[5] *Op. cit.*, 50.

appears to have been used here as it was in Qumran, to show that the 'presence', *Shekinah*, of God had removed from the official Jerusalem temple to the 'new' people of God..." Two passages in Jubilees closely parallel that of 2 Cor. 6:

> And I will build my sanctuary in their midst, and I will dwell with them, and I will be their God and they shall be my people in truth and righteousness (1:17).

> They will fulfill my commandments, and I shall be their Father and they will be my children (1:24).

The Qumran community deemed itself the holy temple of God whose members had separated themselves from all the defilements of the Jerusalem Temple (see pp. 164-167).

Although our 2 Cor. passage makes no reference to angels, analagous passages in the Qumran documents suggest that their presence in the church was expected. There is an interest in fellowship and partnership (6:14). From it are excluded unclean believers (6:14-15, 17). For the living ναός in which God dwells should consist of the perfectly holy children of God (6:16,18; 7:1). From this perfect communion are we to exclude "the holy ones," "the sons of God"? The Qumran community was "the house where there shall not enter [anyone whose flesh has a] permanent [blemish] or an Ammonite or a Moabite or a bastard or an alien or a stranger for ever, for his holy ones one there [forever]" (1Q Flor. 3-5; see p. 203). Gärtner [6] comments that

> It was formerly believed in Israel that the temple was a meeting place for God and his angels, and that the man who entered the temple came 'before the face of God'; this belief was now transferred to the holy congregation. Just because these holy beings dwelt in the midst of the community, it was essential to preserve its absolute purity, otherwise there was a risk that they might abandon the 'new' temple.

The lot (μερίς) [7] of believers, in which unbelievers do not share (2 Cor. 6:15), may be the lot of the holy ones, in which God has granted a share to the elect of the Community (1QS 11.7). The μερὶς πιστῷ is parallel to a partnership of righteousness, fellowship (κοινωνία) of light, agreement of Christ, and union of a shrine of God (which we

---

[6] *Ibid.*, 32-33.

[7] J. A. Fitzmyer, "Qumran and the Interpolated Paragraph in 2 Cor. 6, 14-7, 1," *CBQ* 23 (1961), 274-75; *Lohse, op. cit.*, 35-36.

are). The context suggests that the believer enjoys some privelege of divine communion. Paul thanked God for qualifying "us to share in the inheritance (εἰς τὴν μερίδα τοῦ κλήρου) of the saints in light" (Col. 1:12) in heaven (Col. 1:5). The enlightened have been called to "the riches of his glorious inheritance in the saints" (Eph. 1:18). Francis W. Beare [8] believes that this phrase "probably means 'the inheritance to which he admits us, among the host of holy beings who surround his throne'; the resemblance to the phrasing of Col. 1:12, which is certainly in the writer's mind, makes it almost certain that this is the true interpretation." That angels aid those who receive a lot or portion is taught by Hebr. 1:14 and 1QM 17.7. The "lot (goral) of God" (1QM 1.15; 13.5; 15.1) for those "who walk perfectly in all His ways" (1QS 2.2) "is for [eternal] light" (1QM 13.5-6; cf. CD 13.12). The Lord's portion (μερίς) (T. Levi 2:12; cf. T. Iss. 5:5) is for those who fear Him (T. Benj. 10:10) and delight not in pleasure (T. Benj. 6:3). "I must have my portion with the inheritance of the Beloved," said Isaiah (Asc. Isa. 1:13).

Belial is associated with ἀνομία, darkness, idols, unbelievers and defilement (2 Cor. 6:14-17); he is directly contrasted with Christ. Likewise in the Testaments he is opposed to the commandments or law of the Lord (T. Levi 19:1; T. Iss. 6:1; T. Napht. 2:6-7) and to God Himself (T. Sim. 5:3; T. Dan 4:7; 5:1) and the Messiah (T. Levi 18:12; T. Dan 5:10; cf. T. Zeb. 9:8). He is associated with impurity (T. Reub. 4:11; 6:3; cf. 4:6: idols) and darkness (T. Levi 19:1; T. Napht. 2:6-7; T. Jos. 20:2). The fear of God is a shield against the blows of Beliar (T. Benj. 3:4). In Jubilees (1:20; an upright spirit is contrasted with the spirit of Beliar. The Qumran texts often mention Beliar. Christ is the enemy of Beliar and will overcome him—if we are to assume a parallel eschatological struggle between light and darkness.

The Christology of our fragment is vague. If Christ stands in relation to Beliar as members of the other dualistic pairs with each other, then it appears that he is the supremely perfect angel or heavenly being just as Beliar is the supreme fallen angel. His holy perfection(7:1) is describable in terms of righteousness and light (6:14), i.e. Νόμος; the Law and the prophets were fulfilled in him. H.L. Goudge [9] noted that "in verse 18 the old promise of divine adoption made to Solomon (2 Sam. 7:14) and applied to the expected

[8] Exegesis of Ephesians, IB 10, 631.
[9] The Second Epistle to the Corinthians (Westminster Comm.), London (Methuen, 1922), 72.

Messiah (Ps. 2:7), is extended in Christ to all His members." His coming has made it possible for believers to obtain the promises to Israel (6:16-18). The necessity of faith in Christ is underlined not only by the term, πιστός (6:15; cf. 14; Eph. 1:1; 1 Tim. 4:3, 10, 12; 5:16) but also by the parallelism of believer-unbeliever with all the other contasting pairs. But faith heightens the need for purity through separation (6:17; 7:1); faith itself apparently does not cleanse. Faith and legal obedience, moreover, are co-ordinates.

The exegetical method shown in 2 Cor. 6:17 (cf. Isa. 52:11-12) has been aptly described by Crawford H. Toy [10] in these words:

> The prophet's exhortation to the captives in Babylonia, to guard themselves against (ceremonial) defilement in that idolatrous land, is transferred by the apostle to the Christians of his day, according to the principle of interpretation that whatever is addressed to Israel is at the same time a prediction respecting the times and people of the Messiah.

Another exegetical method common at Qumran and displayed in 2 Cor. 6:16-18 is the free quotation and interweaving of several Old Testament texts. The formula, "as God said," which is unique in the New Testament, appears in CD 6.13; 8.9 ('sr 'mr 'l) [11] The author of the 2 Cor. passage would hardly be expected to share with unbelievers his *Testimonia* and their interpretation.

The ideal of "making holiness perfect (ἐπιτελοῦντες ἁγιωσύνεν) in fear of God" (7:1) is embodied in the term, *hasid*. Simon J. de Vries, in his "Note concerning the Fear of God in the Qumran Scrolls," [12] observed that "*yr'* tends toward becoming a technical and purely formal expression equivalent to 'piety' or simply 'religion'" in the Psalms, Proverbs, Job and Sirach: a tendency reaching its full development in rabbinic Judaism.

One can imagine that the author of 2 Cor. 6:14-7:1 had very high standards of admission to the Lord's Supper and to church membership.

In conclusion the spirit and language of the passage is so thoroughly in accord with those of the Qumran texts, the Testaments of the Twelve Patriarchs and Jubilees that we must conclude that it was written by a Christian who had been steeped in these traditions.

---

[10] *Quotations in the New Testament*, New York (Charles Scribner's Sons, 1884), 186.

[11] Fitzmyer, *art. cit., CBQ* 23 (1961), 276-79; cf. "The Use of Explicit O. T. Quotations in Qumran Literature and in the N. T.," *NTS* 7 (1960-61), 301-03; *art. cit.,* JBL 86 (1967), 32.

[12] *RQ* 5 (1964-65), 236.

Moreover, if 2 Cor. 6:14-7:1 is interpreted in light of the Dead Sea Scrolls, Jubilees and the Testaments, nothing in it is incompatible with the teachings and language of Paul's opponents. If it was not written by them, at least its teachings provide illustrative contemporary parallels to the thought of the Apostle's antagonists.

CHAPTER TEN

CONCLUSIONS

The following chart shows at a glance our findings of probable and questionable references to selected topics in anti-heretical letters.

	Tim. & Tit.	Col.	Gal.	2 Cor.	Phil. 3	Hebr.	1 Cor.	Eph.	Igna-tius	Rom. 16
Law	/	/	/	/	/	/	/	?	?	?
Judaism	/	?	/	/	/	/		?	/	
Circumcision	/	/	/	?	/			?	?	/
Times		/	/						?	
Food & drink	/	/	?	?	/	/	?			/
Sex	/	/	?	?		?	/	?		
Holiness	/	?		?	?		/	?		
Washings	/	?			?	/	?	?		
Own meals	?		/			/	/		/	?
Priest & sanctuary	?	?	?	?		/		?	/	
Angelology	/	/	/	?	?	/	?	/		?
Christology	/	/	/	/	/	/	?	/	/	/
Spirit	?	/	?	/	/			/	/	
Gnosis	/	/	/	/	/			/	/	?
Apostles		/	/			/		?		

Giving a half-value to ?'s, we find the following numbers of topics which are mutually alluded to:

	Col.	Gal.	2 Cor.	Phil. 3	Hebr.	1 Cor.	Eph.	Igna-tius	Rom. 16
Tim.&Tit.	9¼	8	7¼	8	7½	7	6¾	5½	4¼
Col.		8¼	7	7½	6	5¾	6½	5½	4
Gol.			7¼	6½	6¼	6¼	6	6½	4
2 Cor.				6½	4¾	5¼	6¼	5	3¼
Phil. 3					5	4½	5½	5	3¾
Hebr.						4½	4¼	4½	3½
1 Cor.							4½	3	3¼
Eph.								4¼	2¾
Ignatius									2¼
Rom. 16									

Generally, high quantitative measurements correspond with the quality of the more striking resemblances (e.g. honor of cosmic στοιχεῖα who determine Jewish calendars).

How justified is our postulate of the basic unity of Paul's Judaizing opponents? Even if they are separated and multiplied, it is fitting to seek common threads and to explain some correlations. Though the historical relationship between his personal opponents in various cities is unknown, there is sufficient theological coherence of their teachings to affirm the existence of an anti-Pauline movement with a definite religious perspective. Some of its converts came from the different branches of Essenism and the Baptist movement, and others from the readers of various apocalypses. Many of them cooperated in resisting the "pseudo-apostle" to the Gentiles. There was some convergence or pooling of pre-Christian ideas, though each teacher had his own vision of the central mysteries. Perhaps the spread in thought was no greater than the range between Philip, Peter, Barnabas and Paul. The teachings opposed in Paul's letters show a variety and spectrum no broader than that which we can find among Qumranian and apocalyptic literature.

Paul's literary adversaries were believers whose background was a mystic-apocalyptic, ascetic, non-conformist, syncretistic Judaism more akin to Essenism than to any other well-known "school" or holiness sect [1] The new apocalyptic baptizing movement of Christianity was attractive to many who were deeply influenced by such post-Hasidic traditions. Readers of apocalypses and followers of John the Baptist constituted a significant segment of the early church. It is likely that many apocalypticists, Nazirites and Essenes (in the broad sense) were attracted first to John, and then to Jesus or the church led by James; they were usually repelled by Paul. They knew and cherished some first century haggadah and apocalyptic concepts not explicitly recorded in published works from Qumran. Apocalyptic literature not only fostered a certain type of Jewish piety, but also required interpretation, which Essene propagandists were ready to supply. In respect to a decreased emphasis on priestly purity and organization, Paul's opponents resembled Pharisees. How many of their traditions were derived from, or were known also among,

---

[1] We would concur with Thomas (*op. cit.*, 435) that the baptist movement began among the Essenes, and would further suggest that these sects should be classified according to their beliefs concerning methods of purification (asceticism, water, sacrificial blood, eschatological fire, legalistic obedience, etc.), individual prophets (historical and contemporary) and eschatological expectations.

A tightly organized, geographically widespread group such as Essenes was more able to provide effective opposition to Paul than would members of an obscure, isolated sect. Resemblances of Pauline adversaries to baptizing sects could be attributed to any common Essene (or at least Hasidic) elements in their background.

Pharisees is unknown. Gershom Scholem [2] thinks Paul knew esoteric
Pharisaic speculation about angels (cf. Acts 23:8-9) and possibly about
apocalypse. How significant were the differences between Essenism
and esoteric Pharisaism in light of their common Hasidic origin?
Likewise obscure is the extent to which Essene colonies outside
Qumran were subject to the influence of Pharisaism and the
apocryphal literature which was absent from the Qumran library.
Because the Apostle's antagonists did not fully share Qumran's
preoccupation with priestly purity and exclusiveness, esoteric
Scriptural exegesis and communal, monastic discipline and
possessions, we may deduce that they were largely town dwellers
(Philo, ap. Eusebius, Praep. Evang. viii, 11.1; Josephus, War ii,
8.4.124-25) who, like members of medieval third orders, did not
isolate themselves from the impure world. Thus they were more able
to welcome Christian evangelists and later to send out their own
workers to foreign nations. A Gentile mission was encouraged by
Tobit 14:6-7; T. Napht. 8:3; T. Asher 7:3; T. Jos. 19:11; T. Benj. 9:2;
10:4-5. Acceptance of Jesus, who internalized purity (Mt. 7:4-5;
23:25-26; Lk. 11:38-41) and who lived among the unclean, must have
separated these converts (Paul's future antagonists) further from the
severe Qumran standards. John the Baptist had preached to tax
collectors and soldiers (Lk. 3:12-14). The καθαροι, who were
segregationsts in principle, went forth into the world because their
faith, γνῶσις, angelic companionship, χάρισματα and advanced status
of attainment made them feel secure from corrupting influences. It
was their commission to teach and cleanse others, that their "light
might shine before men..." (Mt. 5:16; cf. 28:19-20). Thus their
Essenism was attenuated by this commission and confidence and by
the teachings of apocalyptic literature, esoteric Pharisees, John and
Jesus. All forms of Christian baptism were closer to John's than to
Qumran's rite of admission. If a body of apocalyptic literature had a
wide, popular circulation outside of Essene circles, then it may have
prepared the way for the acceptance of Essene teachings, whether in
Christian garb or not, and whether in Palestine or among Paul's
converts. We do not know the extent of the spread of mystic-
apocalyptic, ascetic Judaism in the Diaspora in pre-Christian times.

In Greek-speaking areas Paul's antagonists (especially the later local
teachers opposed in Colossians and the Pastoral Epistles) of necessity

---

[2] Major Trends in Jewish Mysticism, Jerusalem (Schocken, 1941), 41-42.

used some Hellenistic terminology, as we noted in the Foreward. But they should not be judged syncretists or Gnostics on this account, any more than apocalyptic writers and Philo (or Therapeutae?) should be. Paul's adversaries were syncretists, gnostics and pneumatics in the same sense that the terms are applicable to the Essenes and Qumranians; their pneumaticism, of course, was enriched as the result of their Christian conversion. Apocalyptic and Scripture were their sources in their quest in pre-Christian days for a pure and perfect life in accord with the best in ancient religion and science. Although they would be reluctant to admit syncretism, Babylonian ("Chaldean")-Iranian apocalyptic[3] had provided their spiritual forebears and the author of the popular book of Daniel with the principles of ethical dualism of light and darkness, cosmology and astrology, angelology[4] and demonology, eschatology and esotericism. The person and teachings of Christ were accomodated gradually to their system; but Paul made his gospel of Christ the standard for re-interpreting all other matters of concern. Moreover, his persistent loyalty to Pharisaism (Acts 23:6; 26:5; Phil. 3:5) may have fostered a hostile attitude toward the Essenes,[5] whose teaching influenced his opponents. Christian divisions mirrored earlier Jewish divisions. A further study of either the sectarian Jewish or the early Christian "family tree" could illumine understanding of the other.

---

[3] For the influence of Chaldean-Iranian thought on apocalyptic, see Herodotus, *History* i, 131; F. Cumont, *Textes et monuments figurés relatifs aux mystères de Mithra*, Brussels (H. Lamertin), i (1899), 103, 107 ff.; W. Bousset, *Hauptprobleme der Gnosis*, Göttingen (Vandenhoeck & Ruprecht, 1907), 224-29; Guignebert, *op. cit.*, 86, 95, 131-32, 141; Cross, *op. cit.*, 76-77, n. 35; 98, 215; Mowinckel, *op. cit.*, 264-66, 271, 276-77; Russell, *op. cit.*, 18-19, 258-62, 347-48, 385-87; Schmidt, *op. cit.*, 105, 166, 205-09. For its influence on the Essenes see Schürer, *op. cit.*, ii-ii, 216 (ET); Guignebert, *op. cit.*, 177; Kittel, *op. cit.*, i, 81. For influence on the Testaments of the Twelve Patriarchs, see Eppel, *op. cit.*, 75-76, 88-89. For its influence on the Dead Sea Scrolls, see Ringgren, *op. cit.*, 78-80, 157; Philonenko *et alia*, *Pseudépigraphes de l'Ancien Testament...*, 10, n. 13; H. Braun, *op. cit.*, ii (1966), 4; Mansoor, *art. cit.*, *Le Origini dello Gnosticismo. Colloquio di Messina 13-18 Aprille, 1966*, 399, n. 5; for influence on the Ascension of Isa. and Narrative of Zosimus, see Philonenko *et al.*, 10, 37-43.

[4] Menahem Mansoor, *The Thanksgiving Hymns*, Grand Rapids, Mich. (Wm. B. Eerdmans, 1961), 77, n. 3

[5] Hugh T. Morrison, *Mysterious Omissions*, Chicago (Divinity House of Univ. of Chicago, 1969), 40; cf. 31-33.

INDEX OF AUTHORS

(Chapter and footnote numbers)

INDEX OF REFERENCES